Michigan and its Resources ... (Fourth edition). [With plates including a map.]

Anonymous

Michigan and its Resources ... (Fourth edition). [With plates including a map.]
Anonymous
British Library, Historical Print Editions
British Library
1893
287 p. ; 8°.
10411.cc.39.

Michigan and

Its Resources

COMPILED BY AUTHORITY OF THE STATE, UNDER THE SUPERVISION OF
JOHN W. JOCHIM, SECRETARY OF STATE

✦ 1893 ✦

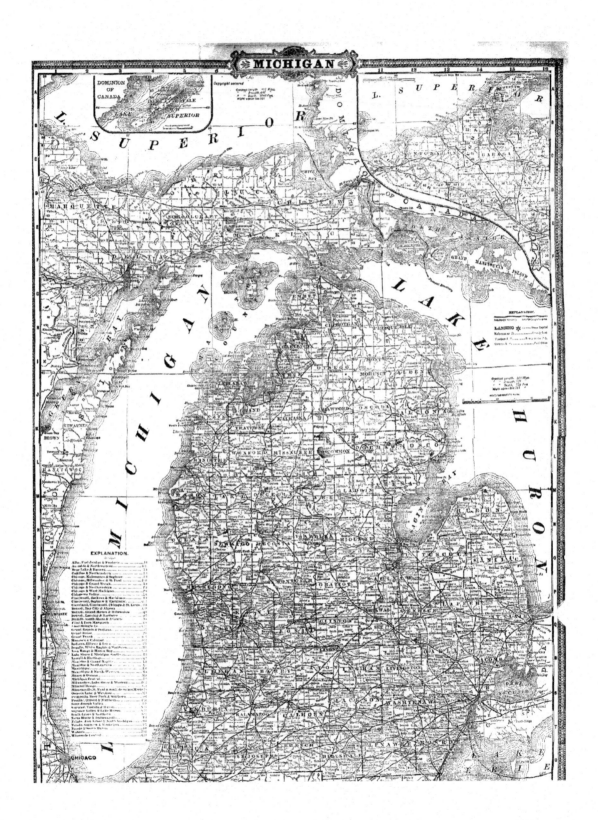

State Capitol at Lansing.

MICHIGAN

AND

ITS RESOURCES

SKETCHES OF THE GROWTH OF THE STATE, ITS INDUSTRIES, AGRICULTURAL
PRODUCTIONS, INSTITUTIONS, AND MEANS OF TRANSPORTATION;
DESCRIPTIONS OF ITS SOIL, CLIMATE, TIMBER, FINANCIAL
CONDITION, AND THE SITUATION OF ITS UNOCCU-
PIED LANDS; AND A REVIEW OF ITS
GENERAL CHARACTERISTICS
AS A HOME.

COMPILED BY AUTHORITY OF THE STATE, UNDER SUPERVISION OF JOHN W. JOCHIM,
SECRETARY OF STATE.

LANSING, MICH.
ROBERT SMITH & CO., STATE PRINTERS AND BINDERS.
1893

PREFACE TO FOURTH EDITION.

The first edition of this work was issued in 1881, consisting of 12,000 copies, and was exhausted early in 1882.

They were distributed upon application into every State and Canada. Soon after an edition of 5,000 copies was printed in the German language, also a similar edition in the Dutch language for Hollanders. Three thousand were issued in February following and the same number in April.

A little more than three months after the first edition was published a second edition of 20,000, enlarged and thoroughly revised, was issued. Much more valuable information was furnished in the second edition relative to finances, leading institutions and industries of the State, together with facts derived from the statistics of 1880, railroad development, etc. It was found later that this supply was insufficient and 10,000 additional copies were issued, making a total of 42,000 in the English language. Ten thousand more were ordered in February, which were soon exhausted.

The third edition was issued in 1883, giving a sketch of each county and general information about the State. This, too, was exhausted before 1885, and still applications were made for the book. The Legislature of 1891 authorized the reissue of the work, but the Governor failed to sign the act.

In 1893 the Legislature authorized its recompilation and the reissue of 12,000 volumes, 8,000 copies of which were to go to the World's Fair, at Chicago, for distribution.

The small appropriation and short time allowed to perform the work may largely interfere with its completeness, but such as it is we present it. There may be many errrors in it, that is the human part of it. To overlook errors would be the humane part, but a thorough investigation of the "Resources of Michigan" would cause you, in the honesty of your conviction, to exclaim, "The half was never told!"

TABLE OF CONTENTS.

———

ADMISSION INTO THE UNION.

A census of Michigan in 1834 showed a population 87,273, more than enough to entitle the territory to statehood.

In 1835 the legislative council authorized a convention to form a State constitution, which was done in May and adopted by the people. At the same election State officers were chosen.

The legislature met in the November following, and Stevens T. Mason, "the boy Govenor," entered upon the duties of his office.

At the same time John S. Horner claimed to be the Governor by virtue of an appointment by President Jackson. The history of the contest to settle this question forms a particularly interesting part of the history of Michigan, which want of space compels us to omit. It was at this time the historical "Toledo war" made an epoch of Michigan more ludicrous than serious.

Michigan claimed the boundary line established by the ordinance of 1787 must obtain. By this a considerable strip would be taken from northern Ohio, and even Toledo would be placed in Michigan. Ohio claimed the said ordinance had been set aside by the constitution.

Ohio was in possession. Michigan laid claim to the strip. Stevens T. Mason, with probably more spirit than mature judgment, determined at whatever cost to repossess the coveted strip, and Gov. Lucus, of Ohio, was equally determined to hold it.

In the spring of 1836 Gov. Mason called the State troops, formed an army of about 1,000 men, and marched to the scene of conflict. From the general history of the matter it was considered more boys' play than anything else by the authorities at Washington. No battle was fought, in fact it never assumed a very hostile or warlike appearance.

There was probably no intention on either side to spill either Wolverine or Buckeye blood. Not but the men on both sides of the conflict were brave and determined, but the whole affair wore the appearance of a snowball battle, and trickery took the place of military tactics. It has been said that there was an understanding among the troops on each side that blank cartridges only were to be used.

In order to conciliate both sides the general government made a proposition that Ohio should retain possession of the strip, and Michigan should have the entire upper peninsula. This was rejected by Michigan. A small strip of farm land and the village of Vistula or Toledo was considered worth more than the whole upper peninsula. But the State was organized and could be admitted to the coveted dignity of a real State by accepting the terms—washing off the war paint, and exchanging the implements of warfare for a state seal. Consequently on the 15th day of December, 1836, assented to the conditions, and on the 27th day of January, 1837, Michigan became a member of the great family.

There being no more serious results from the Toledo war than mere disappointment among a few ambitious persons, the whole matter has been looked upon as a joke.

There was no sectional hatred or animosities resulting from the Toledo war. It is likely the ambition of a few may have been chilled, but the whole matter has been looked upon as a joke, and now, when the great wealth of the upper peninsula is considered, the joke becomes richer. As stated, Michigan became a State in 1837 and took rank in population as 23d, having a population of 174,467. In 1890 it stood 9th, with a population of 2,093,889.

GEOGRAPHICAL.

In latitude it is the same as the State of New York and is located between 42 and 48° north latitude.

The most southern portion of England is 50° north. France is located between 42 and 50°, Norway entirely north of 58°, Sweden principally north of 56°. Marquette in Michigan is more than two degrees farther south than the city of Paris in France. Copper Harbor, in Keweenaw county, the most northern village of Michigan, is about the same latitude as the central part of France. The southern line of Michigan is in the same latitude as Rome in Italy and the northern line of Portugal, Oregon, Wisconsin, New York, Vermont, New Hampshire, Massachusetts and Maine are in the same latitude. The State is nearly surrounded by the grandest fresh water lakes in the world. On the north Lake Superior, the largest lake in the world, the navigation of which passes through one of the finest lock canals in the world, located at Sault Ste. Marie ("the Soo"). Lake Michigan, "the great unsalted sea," next in size, is the grandest and most beautiful body of fresh water in the world. Lakes Huron, St. Clair and Erie on the east are grand bodies of water. Michigan has a coast line of more than 1,600 miles. Vessels carrying 1,000.000 feet of lumber may be seen in her waters. It has 7,410 miles of railroad. There are 84 organized counties (not including Isle Royal), most of which have well built court houses. In the front line of products in the United States we find Michigan points to copper, lumber and salt, and in close proximity to the front, wheat, iron, fruit, potatoes, celery, etc. In manufactories, Michigan furniture, cars, carriages. engines, pianos, and in fact nearly all productions of soil, skill and labor are well up in the scale of excellence.

EARLY IMPRESSIONS.

For many years Michigan was handicapped by the impression becoming general that there was nothing in the State to induce settlers. In the early settlement of the State a commission was appointed to investigate and make report relative to the condition of the land, its value, etc. Their visit occurred at a time when the State, almost a wilderness, was very wet, and it is supposed they became disgusted. They reported that the State was a vast swamp. It was called the Great Black Swamp, the principal products being frogs and ague, and what timber there was on the land was entirely inaccessible. This, coming from the source it did, created a very unfavorable impression of Michigan and the tide of immigration was turned toward other States. This impression was strengthened by a letter written by a deputy United States surveyor when surveying Oakland county. It was probably very wet weather. The writer said in substance that the land was springy and indicated a submarine lake underlying the surface, rendering it very unsafe for horses or men, and finished his letter by saying that the balance of the State was a vast swamp, and inasmuch as this was about as far west as civilization was ever likely to extend, it would be useless expenditure of time and money to proceed any further with the survey.

Had a true representation of the vast resources of the State been made at the time instead of the erroneous impression that was not even worthy of investigation, the State today would occupy even a more exalted position in the galaxy of States.

The writer remembers an incident showing the impression of Michigan in Ohio. When the Illinois and Iowa fever struck Ohio thousands were going to the west to invest. A gentleman from Michigan visited my father's house in Ohio, and learing that the western fever had struck my father, asked him why not go to Michigan. "Michigan? Go to Michigan to shake with ague and starve to death, the frogs piping a requiem at my funeral? Why there is hardly an acre of farming land in the State. This we know, for we have it straight from the public statements. What do not starve or die with malarious diseases, will freeze to death." Such was believed of Michigan. School children were told of the "Great Desert of the west, and the Great Black Swamp of Michigan." Early geographers were at fault and the more pious wondered why the Creator had made such places as the Great Desert and Michigan.

Illinois, Iowa, Indiana, Kansas, Minnesota, and other States were benefited by these false statements and impressions. Thousands of enterprising persons from overcrowded eastern states went west.

Many who had never seen prairies were enchanted, nothing to do but begin farming. When crops were gathered the question arose, what will we do with them. When winter came the question of fuel became urgent. 'Tis true the Creator had spread out a beautiful panorama of his handiwork, but the great beauty of land was at the expense of timber for lumber to build and fuel to burn. The greatest school to teach appreciation of blessings is deprivation. Obstacles to perfect enjoyment are often rich blessings. The great unbroken forests of Michigan, "that dreadful country," was intended to supply the lumber for homes and comforts throughout the prairie and timberless regions of the west. It was also a storehouse with unlimited supply of iron, copper, and salt. Millions of people today enjoy the comforts of houses built of Michigan lumber. Stop and consider a moment. The State furnished say 4,000,000,000 feet of lumber per year; allow 20,000 feet to each house, this would be sufficient to build 200,000 houses for families of five each, 1,000,000 persons, and although this great drain on the timber supply has been going on for a quarter of a century or more, sufficient pine is left to supply the needs of the State, and it is safe to say that enough timber has been burned and otherwise destroyed to supply a good sized state with buildings.

The State is practically out of debt and can not get into debt very deeply, or more than $50,000. The public buildings, complete and elegant, are all paid for,

2

consisting of capitol, two penitentiaries, four asylums for the insane, one school. for the blind, and one asylum for the deaf and dumb, one of the largest universities in the world, the finest agricultural college in the United States, reformatory, industrial school for boys, same for girls, mining school, soldiers' home, and in fact about everything that could be called improvements. Michigan began where other older states stopped. She has not stopped and has seldom even called a halt in her steady march to the front ranks of civilization.

THE STATE CAPITOL.

The seat of government of the State was located at Lansing in 1847.

The old capitol was built and archives of the State removed. There was no city here, not even a village. It was almost an unbroken wilderness. To illustrate the wild condition of the land at that time an incident may be mentioned.

Arrangements were made to perform a wedding ceremony in the Governor's room. Guests were invited, among whom were a couple of ladies living near the present location of the Everett house, about five or six blocks from the capitol. Toward evening they left home to attend the wedding, lost their way, wandered around the country through the forest and thickets until dark and being unable to find the capitol took the back track, or in some way found home. They gave it up, disgusted with "city life," but glad they had escaped contact with bears and wolves.

Nearly opposite the capitol, or across the road, now Washington Ave., near the present location of the Hudson house, there stood a monster walnut tree. During a storm it fell across the road, completely blocking the road (probably the only road). It became necessary to get it out of the way. It was cut into logs, piled up and burned in a great log heap, no value being placed on the lumber it would have made.

The new capitol was begun in 1872. An appropriation of $1,430,000 was made, $1,427,743.78 expended and $2,256.22 turned back into the treasury. An act standing today as a living monument to the honesty of the building committee. An act having few if any parallels in the history of the country.

The building is 345x191.5 feet, or including porticoes and steps 420x274 feet. Extreme height, 267 feet. Covers one and one-sixth acres and has a walk around outside wall of 1,520 feet.

The superstructure is built of Amherst, Ohio, sandstone; 15,000,000 Lansing brick were used. English plate glass of best quality, in fact all materials were of the best. And although fifteen years have passed since it was built not a flaw is found in the work or design except, perhaps, the poor accoustic properties of the hall of representatives.

The two legislative halls are illuminated by electric lights. Through the building there are 271 chandeliers, 1,702 gas burners, one elevator, and about 20 elegant stairways. It is heated by steam throughout. The plumbing system is perfect. There is not the remotest danger from fire, wind or water.

In short it is the most elegant and complete capitol in the United States built for anything near the same amount of money.

POPULATION, VALUATION, ETC.

Population, valuation, total acreage, area in farms, public lands subject to sale or entry, chief products, compiled from statistics.

Counties.	Popu-lation, 1890.	Valuation. 1890.	Total acreage.	Acreage in farms.	Public lands subject to sale or entry.	Chief products.
Alcona	5,409	$1,500,000	435,257	31,586	27,147	Lumber and farm products.
Alger	1,238	2,500,000	588,862	3,380	28,409	Lumber, building stone, charcoal and fisheries.
Allegan........	38,961	16,000,000	529,951	364,798	984	Farm products, fruit, peppermint, lumber, paper and woolen mills.
Alpena	15,581	6,000,000	370,325	49,092	22,320	Lumber, farm products and fisheries.
Antrim	10,413	3,000,000	306,552	50,799	2,960	Lumber, bark, charcoal and farm products.
Arenac	5,683	1,250,000	234,993	46,825	1,035	Lumber, farm products, manufactories and fisheries.
Baraga........	3,036	2,000,000	582,601	1,423	34,346	Lumber, building stone, slate and farm products.
Barry.........	23,783	15,000,000	352,032	302,188	112	Farming products, fruits and manufactories.
Bay...........	56,412	27,000,000	285,820	123,735	....	Lumber, ship building, manufactories and fisheries.
Benzie........	5,237	2,000,000	204,133	34,509	5,630	Lumber and fruit.
Berrien........	41.285	18,000,000	363,414	278,661	....	Farm products, fruit, manufactories and fisheries.
Branch	26,791	20,000,000	320,443	282,488	....	Farm products, dairying and stock.
Calhoun	43,501	30,000,000	447,115	373,777	120	Farm products, fruit and manufactories.
Cass	20,953	16,000,000	312,927	260,440	....	Farm products, fruit and manufactories.
Charlevoix	9,686	3,500,000	247,099	55,020	8,070	Lumber, farm products, fisheries, etc.
Cheboygan	11,986	4,000,000	468,745	44,758	27,525	Lumber, farm products and fisheries.
Chippewa	12,019	5,000,060	995,225	48,000	121,009	*Lumber, grain, building stone.
Clair	7,558	2,500,000	364,020	29,366	6,497	Farm products.
Clinton	26,509	19,000,000	364,895	311,001	94	Farm products and stock.
Crawford......	2,962	2,000,000	359,459	14,065	31,124	Lumber, saw mills and farm products.
Delta	15,330	4,000,000	742,975	29,995	64,064	Lumber, iron ore, charcoal and farm products.
Dickinson	a	6,031,550	491,917	2,562	11,239	Iron ore, lumber and farm products.
Eaton	32,094	20,000,000	366,467	308,565	80	Farm products and manufactories.
Emmet	8,756	3,000,000	272,057	39,927	4,003	Farm products, fruit, lumber and manufactories.
Genesee	39,430	25,000,000	411,015	345,918	89	Farm products, fruit and manufactories.
Gladwin.......	4,208	2,000,000	330,018	22,090	28,030	Fruit and farm products.
Gogebic	13,166	15,000,000	687,145	1,277	11,798	Iron ore and lumbering.
Gd. Traverse...	13,355	4,500,000	297,002	30,189	3,120	Fruit, farm products, lumber, manufactories.

a Included in Marquette, Menominee and Iron.
* Eleven million tons having passed the "Soo" canal in 1892.

Population, Valuation, Etc.—*Continued.*

Counties.	Population, 1890.	Valuation, 1890.	Total acreage.	Acreage in farms.	Public lands subject to sale or entry.	Chief products.
Gratiot	28,668	$10,000,000	364,628	243,772	640	Fruit, farm products and mineral springs.
Hillsdale	30,660	22,000,000	384,950	329,585	....	Farm products, dairying and stock.
Houghton	35,389	40,000,000	646,470	26,098	48,670	Copper, limestone and slate.
Huron	28,545	8,000,000	535,953	273,972	70	Farm products, lumber, salt, lime, coal, building stone.
Ingham	37,666	21,000,000	354,227	287,483	80	Farm products, manufactories and stock.
Ionia	32,801	19,000,000	366,526	304,318	....	Building stone, silk mills, farm products and manufactories.
Iosco	15,224	5,000,000	354,128	26,861	51,800	Lumber, farm products, salt and plaster.
Iron	4,432	6,000,000	766,746	17,038	25,723	Lumber and farm products.
Isabella	18,784	6,000,000	368,740	142,894	240	Lumber and farm products.
Isle Royal	135	100,000	133,414	....	21,868	Stone, native copper and fisheries.
Jackson	45,031	31,000,000	453,874	355,721	400	Farm products, coal, sandstone and manufactories.
Kalamazoo	39,273	27,000,000	357,726	305,554	80	Farm products, celery, peppermint and manufactories.
Kalkaska	5,160	2,700,000	359,144	34,943	7,234	Farm products, charcoal and lumber.
Kent	109,922	50,000,000	545,658	402,256	....	Farm products, fruits, furniture and manufactories.
Keweenaw	2,894	3,000,000	213,754	4,518	2,934	Copper and lumber.
Lake	6,505	1,500,000	365,386	21,809	4,891	Timber, charcoal, farm products.
Lapeer	29,213	14,000,000	424,030	316,571	....	Farm products, lumber, charcoal and manufactories.
Leelanau	7,944	1,250,000	195,882	80,612	2,282	Charcoal, fruit and farm products.
Lenawee	48,448	30,500,000	484,211	382,071	....	Wool, farm products, fruits and cars.
Livingston	20,858	16,000,000	370,845	317,496	... .	Wool, stock, fruit and farm products.
Luce	2,455	2,000,000	581,437	....	39,041	Lumber, celery, charcoal and farm products.
Mackinac	7,830	2,000,000	641,329	29,088	30,792	Charcoal, ore, lumber and farm products.
Macomb	31,813	13,500,000	302,314	258,648	....	Stock, ships, mineral springs and fisheries.
Manistee	24,230	9,000,000	349,214	55,595	9,418	Lumber, salt, fruits and farm products.
Manitou	860	100,000	69,115	4,670	4,990	Fisheries and farm products.
Marquette.....	39,521	22,535,950	1,071,426	28,268	91,545	Iron, lumber, charcoal, pig iron, stone and fisheries.
Mason	16,385	4,500,000	315,326	54,070	2,780	Lumber, fruit and farm products.
Mecosta	19,697	5,000,000	361,875	113,925	160	Fruit, farm products and lumber.
Menominee	33,639	7,312,500	667,153	49,189	18,848	Iron, farm products and lumber.
Midland	10,657	2,000,000	335,867	71,112	1,028	Salt, lumber, farm products, bromine.
Missaukee	5,048	3,000,000	362,798	35,750	7,555	Farm products and lumber.
Monroe	32,237	16,500,000	359,444	266,994	....	Stock, farm products, manufactories and fisheries.
Montcalm	32,637	10,000,000	454,278	231,193	....	Farm products and lumber,
Montmorency..	1,487	1,000,000	355,540	16,966	37,759	Farm products and lumber.
Muskegon	40,013	13,000,000	321,476	96,995	1,699	Farm products, lumber, fisheries, fruit and manufactories.
Newaygo	20,476	4,500,000	542,222	430,427	1,779	Farm products, fruit and manufactories.
Oakland	41,245	29,600,000	575,394	478,898	40	Wool, stock, fruit and farm products.
Oceana	13,698	4,500,000	344,895	121,834	1,320	Lumber, fruit, furniture and farm products.

POPULATION, VALUATION, ETC.—*Continued.*

Counties.	Population, 1890.	Valuation, 1890.	Total acreage.	Acreage in farms.	Public lands subject to sale or entry.	Chief products.
Ogemaw	5,583	$2,000,000	365,962	38,242	5,204	Lumber, farm products and manufactories.
Ontonagon	3,756	2,000,000	858,880	7,967	118,974	Copper, fisheries, farm products, lumber.
Osceola	14,630	4,000,000	362,247	108,057	576	Timber and wood making factories.
Oscoda	1,904	1,000,000	365,299	25,146	61,397	Lumber and farm products.
Otsego	4,272	2,500,000	334,085	19,810	11,723	Logs and lumber.
Ottawa	35,358	15,000,000	354,185	209,079	440	Farm products, fruit, celery, stone, manufactories.
Presque Isle	4,687	1,500,000	428,309	....	36,958	Lumber, fisheries and farm products.
Roscommon	2,033	1,500,000	339,490	5,045	17,857	Lumber and farm products.
Saginaw	82,273	37,000,000	516,563	275,508	480	Lumber, salt, coal, building stone and lake commerce.
Sanilac	32,589	8,000,000	616,035	315,955	507	Lumber, farm products, manufactories and fisheries.
Schoolcraft	5,818	3,500,000	756,715	17,182	39,500	Pine, cedar, pig iron, fisheries and farm products.
Shiawassee	30,952	17,000,000	343,964	262,906	....	Farm products, coal and manufactories.
St. Clair	52,105	20,000,000	444,921	342,598	....	Farm products, salt, lumber, fisheries and mineral water.
St. Joseph	25,356	20,000,000	321,403	290,719	....	Fruit, peppermint oil, sand, brick and farm products.
Tuscola	32,508	10,500,000	519,098	284,426	400	Lumber products and farm products.
Van Buren	30,541	15,000,000	391,289	304,514	82	Fruit, stock, peppermint and farm products.
Washtenaw	42,210	31,000,000	454,638	376,300	....	Woolen and paper mills, fruit and farm products.
Wayne	2,571,141	90,000,000	385,033	286,868	....	Fruit, farm products, fisheries, shipbuilding, peppermint, furniture, etc.
Wexford	11,278	4,000,000	366,058	52,456	17,700	Lumber, fruit and farm products.

STATE GOVERNMENT.

Seat of government—Lansing.

Legislative power—Senate and House of Representatives.

Senate is composed of 32 members, presided over by Lieutenant Governor.

House of Representatives composed of 100 members; presiding officer, Speaker, who is chosen by the members from one of their number.

Convenes on first Wednesday of January in each uneven numbered year.

Executive power is vested in Governor who, with Lieutenant Governor, is elected each alternate year.

Judicial power is vested in Supreme Court and other courts below.

Supreme Court is composed of five members elected for term of ten years.

State Officers:—

Secretary of State.

Superintendent of Public Instruction.

State Treasurer.

Commissioner of State Land Office.

Auditor General.

Attorney General.

Regents of the University.

Appointive Officers:—

Commissioner of Banking.

Commissioner of Railroads.

Commissioner of Labor.

Commissioner of Insurance.

Commissioner Mineral Statistics.

Librarian.

Oil Inspector.

Salt Inspector.

Veterinarian.

Game and Fish Warden.

Adjutant General.

Quartermaster General.

The diversified interests of the State are managed by State boards, such as Board of State Auditors, State Swamp Land, Control, Equalization, State Canvassers, Claims for Relief, St. Mary's Falls Ship Canal, Fund Commissioners, Geological

Survey, Internal Improvement, Escheats of Property to State, Agricultural Land Grant, Review of Assessment of Telegraph and Telephone Lines, Railroad Crossings. Railroad Consolidation, Railroad Control, Labor Statistics, Fish Commissioners, Health, Correction and Charities, Pardons, Pharmacy, Dentistry, Sanitary Commissioners, Insurance Policy, Detroit Police, Jury Commissioners for Wayne Co., same for Saginaw Co., Soldiers' Home, Agricultural College, Forestry Commissioners, Normal School, Mining School, Public Schools, School for Deaf, Blind, Asylums for Insane (Michigan, Eastern, Northern), Industrial School for Boys, Home for Girls, State Prison (House of Correction, Upper Peninsula and Ionia), Insane Criminals. Detroit House of Correction.

Every institution in the State of a public character is managed by boards.

THE STATE—GROWTH, POPULATION AND WEALTH.

ITS VALUE DISCOVERED.

It is only within a very few years that the northern counties of the lower peninsula have been known and understood, except by a few enterprising men, even among Michigan people. The extension of the lumber interests, seeking fresh material for the mills, led to their first thorough exploration, and it was not until those interests had acquired enormous magnitude that the now undoubted fact was realized that, great as had been their profits, the discoveries they had made and the great wilderness they had partially cleared promised more to agriculture than it had yielded to the ax. Immense tracts of hard-wood timber were found containing no pine, and it was found, too, that large portions of our northern territory which produce the best pine produce also the best crops. There are pine barrens bearing an inferior and scraggy wood, which the fastidious lumberman utterly neglects. But these occupy only limited areas in what are known as the pine regions of the State, and cover only a comparatively small portion of its territory. Most of the great trees which constitute the pride of our lumber forests, and have made Michigan pine famous at home and abroad, grow largely among beeches and hard maple and other valuable wood, which only flourish on soils capable of yielding good crops. A few of these noble pines, standing among scores of hard timber, give character to the discoveries of the "land looker" for the saw-mills, while in no wise detracting from the value of the soil on which they grow. Of course there are different degrees of value in these lands, as in all others, and the settler will exercise the same discretion in his choice as he does in determining other accessories to a home. But there are thousands of acres in Michigan from which pine trees have been cut, as well as many other thousands which have never borne pine, into the soil of which no ploughshare has ever penetrated, which will well repay the labors of the husbandman, and the fee simple of which can be bought for less than a year's rental of many of the lands of Europe.

AN UNSTIMULATED GROWTH.

No organized effort has been made by the State to promote general immigration. Whatever means have been employed to invite population from abroad

3

have been isolated and fragmentary. The growth of the State has been entirely natural and unstimulated. The result has been to make its people peculiarly homogeneous in character. New elements have been assimilated with marked success and rapidity. The natural resources and attractions of the State, however, have continued to draw people hitherward from other States and from Europe, until the population of 57 years ago has increased nearly ten-fold. The territory which entered the Union in 1837, with 174,467 inhabitants of both sexes and all ages, sent to its defense less than thirty years later more than 90,000 soldiers. The State which stood twenty-third in rank in 1840 had advanced to the 9th in 1890. A table based upon the returns of the United States census in each succeeding decade tells the whole story:

Table showing the population of Michigan at each Federal Enumeration since the Admission of the State in 1837, with the Progressive Increase and Rank.

CENSUS YEAR.	Population.	Increase.
1837	174,467	
1840	212,267	37,800
1850	397,654	185,387
1860	749,113	351,459
1870	1,184,059	434,946
1880	1,636,937	452,878
1890	2,093,889	456,952

UNITED STATES LAND OFFICES.

UPPER PENINSULA.

BY GEO. A. ROYCE.

On the first day of July, 1892, we prepared a list of the vacant government lands for the annual report of the honorable Commissioner of General Land Office, showing that there were 523,411 acres of vacant government land in this district, divided among the several counties as follows:

Counties.	Acres.	Counties.	Acres.
Alger	12,118	Isle Royal	15,400
Baraga	26,480	Keweenaw	2,170
Chippewa	101,235	Luce	23,800
Delta	32,063	Mackinac	15,910
Dickinson	7,520	Marquette	77,530
Gogebic	2,460	Menominee	9,000
Houghton	40,630	Ontonagon	108,120
Iron	21,380	Schoolcraft	27,595

We do not know the character of these lands except in a general way, and are therefore unable to give definite information concerning any particular tract. There is a great deal of timber land in this district, pine, hemlock, birch, maple and poplar, predominating. Considerable farming is done in this peninsula and we have the reputation of growing the finest root crops in the State. Small fruits are also a certain crop. Wheat, oats, rye and barley are successfully raised and hay is generally an abundant crop. I do not know that stock raising has been followed to any extent in this country and it occurs to me that our geographical position would render such an enterprise unprofitable, owing to our long and severe winters. It is a well known fact, however, that the farmer of this locality is better rewarded for his labor than the farmer of almost any other locality. Our remoteness from the great markets of the country make it necessary for lumbermen and others doing business in the country, to purchase our farm crops at a much higher price than can be obtained for the same sort of produce in the more thickly settled districts.

LOWER PENINSULA.

BY OSCAR PALMER.

The vacant government lands in this district are subject to *Homestead Entry only* and are approximately as follows, by counties:

	Acres.		Acres.
Oscoda	43,763	Benzie	1,750
Crawford	19,402	Iosco	19,780
Presque Isle	16,117	Lake	1,380
Montmorency	22,020	Mason	2,180
Alpena	6,500	Newaygo	300
Ogemaw	1,600	Leelanaw	1,700
Alcona	1,700	Grand Traverse	1,560
Roscommon	7,685	Kalkaska	2,760
Manistee	3,400	Missaukee	3,180
Manitou	2,000	Wexford	380
Gladwin	26,864	Clare	4,380
Cheboygan	6,860	Arenac	160
Otsego	2,500	Oceana	720
Total			200,641

STATE LANDS FOR SALE.

The following is the latest circular issued by Michigan State Land office, showing amount of land for sale or entry on January 1, 1893, with general instructions and information relative thereto:

[Circular No. 1.]

MICHIGAN STATE LAND OFFICE, AT LANSING.

ALL LANDS OWNED BY THIS STATE ARE CONTROLLED BY THIS OFFICE. THERE ARE NO LOCAL AGENTS. BUSINESS CAN BE DONE BY LETTER. IT IS NOT NECESSARY TO COME HERE.

This office cannot give information about the soil and timber of any particular lots, but buyers and settlers are advised to examine for themselves before taking.

PLATS.

SECTION 1. To aid in looking up State lands we furnish plats at the legal prices, payable in advance, as follows:
Showing vacant lands, 25 cents per township.
Same, with streams drawn on, 50 cents per township.
Showing vacant lands, streams, and names of purchasers of State lands, $1.50 per

township. In ordering plats, always give the number of the town and range of the townships wanted.

A plat showing all the vacant State lands in any county will be furnished for the price named in our land table in section 10 of this circular.

Cash should be sent with orders by mail.

SWAMP LANDS.

SECTION 2. Prices range from $1.25 to $8.00 per acre, the main body being held at $1.25. Only a few townships in the northern part of the State are held at more than $1.25 per acre.

Eighty acres or less of these lands, in one body in the lower peninsula can be bought by any person on a first payment of one-quarter of the price down. The buyer must make affidavit that he will settle on the land within one year after the purchase. Blank affidavits furnished. Ten years' time allowed to pay the balance at seven per cent annual interest. Swamp land scrip cannot be used in purchase or payment of balance due.

These lands are subject to homestead entry; any citizen over 21 years old, and not already owning 40 acres of land, may homestead not to exceed 80 acres, but he may buy an adjoining 80 acres or less on quarter payment down, with ten years' time on the balance, with seven per cent annual interest. Blank applications furnished at this office.

In cases where swamp lands are paid for all down, payment will be received in money or in swamp land scrip, and there is no limit to the quantity purchased.

The State constructs wagon roads and ditches in the newly settled portions of its territory, making payment for the work in swamp lands, so-called. Thus a contractor having finished his road job receives a swamp land credit at this office, on which he may draw orders in favor of any person.

SCHOOL LANDS.

SECTION 3. Price $4.00 per acre.

Where these lands are valuable for pine, cedar or hemlock timber they must be paid for all down. But where they are valuable mainly for farming purposes they can be sold on time.

Persons desiring to buy on time are required to furnish this office with a timber affidavit, and by this affidavit the commissioner will decide whether the desired lots are subject to sale on time, and if so subject to sale on time, first payment of not less than one-half the price down will be received. Blank timber affidavits furnished.

On the balance due the time is not limited, and seven per cent yearly interest is charged.

COLLEGE LANDS.

SECTION 4. These lands have been recently examined by competent men, and appraised by the State Board of Agriculture at from $5.00 to $12.50 per acre. They may be sold on not less than one-quarter payment down, if they are not mainly valuable for the timber thereon.

Time on balance due not limited. Interest seven per cent. The balance due or any part of it may be paid at any time.

OTHER LANDS.

SECTION 5. University lands are held $12.00 per acre, asset lands at $10.00 per acre, asylum lands, salt spring lands, and State building lands at $4.00 per acre, the terms being the same as for school lands.

FORFEITED LANDS.

SECTION 6. The price of forfeited part-paid lands, now held by the State, is the original minimum price per acre, and all improvements and unpaid taxes added thereto.

APPLICATIONS.

SECTION 7. No lands can be withheld from market for the benefit of purchasers until the purchase price is received at this office, and all deposits to purchase on part payment must be accompanied with an acceptable affidavit as required by law.

When full payment down is made, no particular form of application is required but the applicant should be particular and give full name and address of person to whom patent is to issue.

SEC. 8. For information as to government or railroad land apply to United States land office at Marquette, upper peninsula, and Grayling, lower peninsula, as this office has no record of such lands entered or unentered.

SENDING MONEY.

SECTION 9. Money to make any kind of payments at this office can be sent by express or mail.

In sending by express always pay the express charges yourself.

In sending by mail get a postoffice or express order, or send in registered letter. National bank drafts on Detroit or New York will be received as money. Other bank drafts will not be received as payments until collected, nor will Canada money be received at this office.

Make all postoffice or express orders or bank drafts payable to "Commissioner of the State Land Office."

In your letter always tell plainly what you want, mention description of land, and number of certificate if any; give your name, postoffice address, and put in a postage stamp for our answer.

JOHN G. BERRY, *Commissioner*,
Postoffice, Lansing, Michigan.

NUMBER OF ACRES OF STATE LANDS OF ALL CLASSES SUBJECT TO ENTRY JAN. 1, 1893.

	Acres.		Acres.
Swamp Land, per acre $1.25	101,323.81	University Land	80.00
Swamp Land, per acre $2.00	9,769.16	Salt Spring Land	440.00
Primary School Land	222,519.78	Asylum Land	1,482.93
Agricultural College Land	103,068.46		
Total			438,684.19

The above totals are being changed by sales, entries and forfeitures, continually, consequently cannot remain correct any length of time.

Besides the above the following is a list of lands claimed and for sale by the railroads and other corporations mentioned below:

Name of corporation.	Com. or agent.	Acres.
Jackson, Lansing & Saginaw R. R.	O. M. Barnes, Lansing	270,504
Marquette, Houghton & Ontonagon R. R.	E. W. Allen, Marquette	82,343
Detroit, Mackinac & Marquette R. R.	E. W. Cottrell, Detroit	1,255,181
Chicago & Northwestern R. R.	Chas. E. Simmons, Chicago	312,363
Grand Rapids & Indiana R. R.	W. O. Hughart, Grand Rapids	269,976
Flint & Pere Marquette R. R.	A. W. Newton, { Saginaw, E. S. / Marquette. }	64,470
Mich. Land & Iron Co. (limited)	Horatio Seymour, { Boston. / Madison, / Wis. }	155,493
Lac LaBelle Harbor Grant	J. M. Longyear, Marquette	90,700

Name of corporation.	Com. or agent.	Acres.
Portage Lake & Lake Superior Ship Canal	J. M. Longyear, Marquette	438,110
St. Mary's Falls Mineral Land Co.	R. R. Goodell, Houghton	————
Ontonagon & Brulé River R. R.	E. Mariner, Milwaukee	————
Ft. Wilkins & Copper Harbor Mil. Road	W. W. Manning, Marquette	174,000

For price, terms, etc., of State lands, apply to Commissioner of State Land Office, Lansing, Mich.

For railroad and other lands apply to commissioner or agent of such corporation. For information relative to government land, apply to general land office, Washington, D. C., or U. S. receiver at Marquette, or Grayling land offices, Michigan.

MICHIGAN SOILS.

BY R. C. KEDZIE, AGRICULTURAL COLLEGE.

No State has suffered more in reputation by reason of ignorant misrepresentation than Michigan. At the time of its earliest settlement it was considered the fit home of the Indians, wild beasts and malaria. For the white man it was uninhabited and unhabitable. In a report made to a religious body regarding the feasibility of establishing missionary stations to christianize this heathen wild, it was stated that the project was impracticable "because only a narrow strip along the border of the territory was inhabitable, the interior being a vast and impenetrable swamp." The surveyor general of Ohio in 1815, after speaking of the "swamps alternating with barren sands which make up the great mass of the interior," says: "Taking the country altogether, so far as has been explored and to all appearances, together with the information received concerning the balance, it is so bad there would not be more than one acre out of a hundred, if there would be one out of a thousand, that would in any case admit of cultivation."

Such statements only awaken a smile now that the territory has been explored and settled; for here was found, not indeed the Eden of old guarded by flaming sword, but an earthly paradise clasped in the loving arms of "the vast unsalted seas." The nature of the soil and the climatic conditions were found to be admirably fitted for all the agricultural products of the temperate zone and unsurpassed for most fruits. Soil and climate, after all is said, are the enduring conditions of the prosperity of a people. Mines will finally be exhausted, forests will disappear, commerce may find new channels, but soil and climate are the physical basis of the life of a people; they are a possession for all time.

THE DRAINAGE LAW.

One cause that led to a marked change in the condition of our State and the public estimate in which it was held was the drainage law, whereby each land owner was compelled to bear his just part of expense in draining a district, and no churl could block the drainage of a neighborhood because he chanced to control the outlet. A large area of worthless swamp was thus reclaimed to useful purposes and malaria banished. No law since the giving of the ten commandments has produced more good and inflicted less evil.

AGRICULTURAL CAPABILITY OF THESE SOILS.

The capacity of the soil in the southern counties of the State for the production of grains is wide known. Wheat, corn, oats, and barley find here the fitting and enduring conditions for growth. The distinctive wheat belt embraces the four southern tiers of counties. Other counties will produce large crops of wheat, but the counties named are distinguished in this respect. Characteristic specimens of wheat soil are shown in the display of Michigan soils in the Michigan building, Nos. 1 to 90. The analyses of these soils is given by labels attached to each jar. The remarkable productiveness of some of these soils is shown in No. 1, from Lenawee county, a soil that had been in continuous cropping for forty years without manure, yet it produced 83 bushels of shelled corn to the acre in 1879. The production of 40 bushels of wheat to the acre has often been secured in these counties.

SOIL SPECIMENS ON EXHIBITION.

Thirty-eight different kinds of soils from widely reported localities are placed on exhibition with a statement of the chemical composition, the kind of timber naturally growing on them and a brief statement of their physical qualities. Attention is called to this collection of Michigan soils. They are not unusual and extraordinary specimens gathered to astonish and mislead, but the average soils of the county or locality. The are ordinary and not extraordinary, and hence more valuable for presenting the truth.

SOILS OF THE FRUIT BELT.

The whole State produces apples of the highest quality, and "Michigan apples" are quoted as the type of excellence in all the States east of the Rocky mountains. The special fitness of the southeastern part of the State to raise grapes is shown by the name River Raisin, so named because of the abundance of wild grapes that grow along its banks.

But the name "Fruit Belt" has been more particularly applied to the counties on our western border, under the lee of Lake Michigan, where the peach has found a home and where other fruits flourish. Nine specimens of soil—Nos. 10 to 18— are shown. The soils show wide range in physical appearance and chemical composition. The peach belt is produced by climatic conditions more than by the nature of the soil.

The counties forming "The thumb," south of Saginaw bay and bordering on Lake Huron, are distinguished for the excellent quality of their plums.

THE POTATO DISTRICT.

While potatoes of excellent quality are raised in all parts of the State, a district around Grand Traverse bay, consisting of the counties of Grand Traverse, Benzie, Leelanaw and Antrim, is distinguished for its superior quality of potatoes. The soil bore a very heavy growth of hardwood trees, the hard maple very abundant.

4

The soil is open and porous and the tubers are protected from frost when left in the ground all winter by reason of the heavy coating of snow which falls before the ground is frozen. They may thus be wintered in the hill, and when dug in the spring have the same crisp, mealy quality so prized in potatoes first dug from the ground in the fall in other localities. These spring dug potatoes may yet become an important element of market gardening. Specimens of these soils—Nos. 19, 20 and 21—are on exhibition.

THE JACK PINE PLAINS.

These are extensive tracts of light, sandy soil in the northern central part of the lower peninsula bearing a light forest growth of dwarf pines and scarlet oak, with a few trees of Norway pine. The *Pinus banksiana*, or Jack pine, is the leading forest growth, and the region is known as the Jack pine plains. The experiment station of the college has made some experiments on the Jack pine soil to see what could be done by the use of what the soil contains, what could be gathered from the atmosphere, and the mineral materials found in abundance in the small lakes of this region, to bring such soil into productive conditions. The raising and plowing under of green crops and the application of marl have been the principal means employed. Three specimens of such soil from Grayling, Crawford county, are exhibited. No. 22 is the soil in its natural condition; Nos. 23 and 24 contain soils which have raised crops of sperry, vetch and peas, the same plowed under for green manuring; No. 25 is the marl found so abundantly in small lakes and swamps. The change in physical properties will be evident on inspection, and the chemical changes will appear from the analysis showing how the insoluble materials may become soluble by the transforming influence of green manuring.

SOILS FOR EXCEPTIONAL CROPS.

While Michigan soils are good for the every-year use of the farmer and fruit grower, there are certain soils which are invaluable for the growth of special crops. These special productions have of late years come to the front in a way to challenge the attention of the whole country. Singularly enough these crops are raised on the kind of soil once held to be the opprobrium of our State, "the Michigan swamps." Passing by the enormous crops of timothy hay now raised on tamarack swamps, I need only mention celery, cranberries and peppermint, which are now grown on this mucky soil in perfection. Specimens of the soil suited to each of these crops and their analysis are exhibited for the information of the public. No. 26 is a sample of muck contributed by the Dunkley Celery Co., of Kalamazoo, on which is raised celery of such excellence that Kalamazoo celery has acquired a national reputation. No. 27 is muck from the celery plantation of Geo. Hancock, of Grand Haven, whose celery has a good reputation among the lovers of this delicious vegetable. No. 28 is muck sent by the Newberry Celery and Improvement Co., of Newberry, Luce county. The director of the Newberry company writes: "We ship you this day by express a sample of soil taken from our garden for the purpose of having it placed on exhibition at the World's Fair with other soils of this State. On this soil we have produced the finest celery grown in the State. The celery grown here has a fine nutty flavor unknown to the celery grown in the southern part of the State. We have also grown large crops of grain and hay on this land. Two years ago we seeded one and a half acres to spring rye, which yielded seventy bushels of fine plump grain. From this one and one-half acres we cut three and one-half tons of hay. The soil is from sixteen feet to unknown depth. There are thousands of acres of the same character of soil in our vicinity. We would also say that during the eight years we have been growing celery here we have not had a failure of a crop."

PEPPERMINT LANDS.

I wrote to a gentleman in the peppermint district asking for a specimen of the soil for raising peppermint, and not receiving the specimen, I wrote again and received the following reply: "Your first communication was referred to Mr. ———, of this town, who is the largest mint raiser in the State, and who promised me he would forward the soil desired, but I saw him this morning and he said the ground was so frozen he could not get it without being to greater expense than he wished to incur. The facts are he does not want published to the world the benefits of reclaiming marsh lands, for that is all there is of it. Any marsh land that can be drained so it can be worked and still hold moisture enough to carry the crop through is good enough mint soil. Moisture is the great secret. It must have moisture enough to retain the leaves until it is in bloom, for all of the oil is in the leaves."

Evidently Mr. ——— has a good thing, and is willing to keep it.

CRANBERRY SOIL.

I also wrote to a successful grower of cranberries in St. Joseph for a specimen of cranberry soil, but he was in the south and failed to get my letter in time. Some time ago I made an analysis of his cranberry soil and also of some neighboring soil that would not raise the fruit. The most marked difference in these soils was that the barren soil was very acid, while the fruitful soil was neutral to litmus paper. This I find to be the most common distinction between fertile and barren muck. All these celery soils in the fresh state were entirely free from acid. All the muck lands in the State, when properly drained, and in a suitable physical condition, and free from acid, may produce large crops of cranberries, mint and celery. Muck is a mine for the skillful cultivator.

There is nothing in either the soil or the climate, or other natural advantages of Michigan, which exempts those who settle in the State from the common conditions of success in every part of the world. If a man without means chooses to lead an idle and thriftless life, he can starve to death here as soon as anywhere else. But there is no portion of the Union, either in the states or territories, which offers larger encouragement to industry and economy. The laborer, seeking employment with an honest desire to earn a living, and willing to render a fair day's work for a fair day's wages, can always, under ordinary business conditions, find something to do for which he will be well paid. A few years of labor and frugality, in which steadiness and growing experience will, as in every other pursuit, enhance from year to year the value and compensation of his services, will ensure savings enough to buy land. If he has chosen one of the newer sections of the State for his residence he may readily secure a farm in the neighborhood to which he has become accustomed, at low prices and on easy terms, and the same qualities which gave him a start will establish his prosperity and independence on a sure and enduring basis.

It is not alone the work of the farm that affords openings to labor. The mines, furnaces, lumber camps, mills, manufactories, and mechanic arts of the State, continually increasing in number and variety, furnish a growing and diversified demand for every kind of employment that a man can pursue either with his head or his hands. And there is no region on earth where brains and muscle can work more advantageously together.

DIVERSITY OF LABOR.

The range of labor in Michigan is great. Some branches of industry are not found such as the raising of oranges and bananas, the manufacture of whisky (excepting possibly moonshiners) or digging for diamonds. But there is a great diversity of labor and nearly every kind of industry is carried on. One peculiarity is noticeable. Labor is performed on the most approved plans. The best of machinery and appliances are used. This is accounted for by the fact that Michigan's population is drawn from the most enterprising element of other states. Drones stay in the old states, enterprising young men seek new fields. Michigan as a manufacturing state employs the best skill and enterprise to be found and the results very clearly establish the wisdom of this plan. The cost of power is more in Michigan than in the coal regions of Ohio and Pennsylvania, but much less than in the western states. There is plenty of coal in Michigan, but water transportation makes the cost of fuel reasonable. Taken with the fact that the State has an abundant supply of wood for fuel for family purposes, there is but little anxiety about the question of supply. Lumber is cheap, land is cheap, and there is no reason why labor in Michigan cannot result in comfortable homes. An order for any manufactured article excepting glass can be filled in Michigan by Michigan products.

In farming success follows intelligent labor as surely as in any state. There are vast tracts of land in the State patiently awaiting the manipulation of intelligent labor. Land easily accessible and close to good markets. Unlike the description of a part of the wilds of West Virginia by a fourth of July orator, who said "there were places in West Virginia that the foot of man had never trod and the eye of God had never seen," Michigan is peculiarly favored in location, as are nearly all peninsulas. The labor of the farmer has paid above the average. Extremes of wet and dry weather, heat, cold and wind, are not common. Taking all things into consideration labor is fairly remunerated. Years to come, with transportation for all production, there can be no doubt of employment in Michigan.

FARMING.

Farming is a much abused industry. There are a very large number of people styled farmers and who claim to be farmers, but few real farmers. A real farmer, possessing the requisite qualificaions, always succeeds.

What is a farmer? "One who cultivates land" (Webster). The act of cultivating land in this connection would imply, of course, proper, full, correct cultivation; one who understands the soil; how, when, where, and what to plant; how to cultivate and take care of, to cure and harvest crops; to do all things pertaining to the business in the proper way at the proper time.

This involves a liberal stock of knowledge and adaptability to the work. A man who never saw a farm buys some land, a team, some tools, seed, etc., moves to a farm and is immediately rated as a farmer. Should he trade his farm for a blacksmith shop and take charge would that act make him a blacksmith? He opens a select school, would that act make him competent to teach? Should he buy a physician's practice would that act make him competent to practice medicine?

There is much to learn in connection with farming. Many follow the business through life and never learn. Farmers may be classed under three heads: First, those who know nothing of the business; second, habitual and instinctive farmers; third, scientific farmers. The first fail, and generally become politicians, and next calamity howlers. Everything goes wrong. It is too dry, or too wet, too hot or too cold, frost always kills his fruit, he cannot get a price for anything and has to pay too much for everything he buys. The second class hold their own, and the rise of the price of land sometimes makes them wealthy. The third class are the successful ones. Their farms wear a look of prosperity and comfort. Crops are good, stock well fed and well bred, buildings are good and homes comfortable, fences in good order, no run down land, no mortgages. He makes a compost heap and does not allow the alkalies to eat up the acids. He knows what kind of fertilizer his weak land needs. While number one is talking politics and complaining he is analyzing his soil and fertilizers. He succeeds, and ought to.

One great mistake made by farmers is undertaking to farm on 40 acres. It is too little land for general farming. The woodland must be kept, the garden is necessary. The cows and horses necessary for farming 40 acres would do for 80; fencing for 40 is nearly as much as for 80, if properly divided. If 40 acres will support a family the products of the surplus over 40 is clear. One hundred and sixty acres is not too much for a small farm. At $10 per acre (and thousands of acres can be bought for less) 160 acres will cost $1,600, 40 acres will cost $400, $1,200 difference. If the farm is workable the $1,600 will be paid with more ease than $400 on 40 acres. (The same proportions will not hold good indefinitely.) It does not pay to hold unproductive land except timber land. Very many think the vacant lands are all State lands. This is not correct. There are more vacant lands owned by individuals and corporations than by the State, which can be bought cheap, and even improved land can be bought at reasonable rates. It is said the average Michigan man will sell anything but his family.

HORTICULTURAL RESOURCES OF MICHIGAN.

BY L. R. TAFT, AGRICULTURAL COLLEGE.

Ten years ago when the name of our State was mentioned to the people of some of her sister states, it was generally associated in the mind of the listener with some of the crops for the raising of which her fame is world wide. Desirable as may have been her reputation for the raising of corn, oats, wheat, wool and other agricultural products, with which the people not only of this but of foreign countries have been fed and clothed, the renown obtained from her Michigan apples was far greater. Today, although no other state can equal her in the size, color and quality of this the most important of all fruits, the increased attention given to the growing of peaches, plums and grapes has forced the apple to give up some of its glory in the race for fame.

Moreover, proud as Michigan horticulturists are of the reputation so nobly won and so richly deserved for the production of luscious fruits, they are not content with this, but have pushed forward in other lines, and today the renown of Kalamazoo celery and Grand Rapids lettuce has extended until it has reached the Atlantic shore on the east and has surmounted the summits of the Rockies on the west.

The State owes its success in these lines to three things: First, skill and industry of her horticulturists; second, the advantageous location with large bodies of water upon three sides; third, the possession of a variety of soils most of which are particularly adapted to horticulture and which are arranged in a gentle undulating manner that is favorable to both water and air drainage.

Another thing that has been of inestimable benefit in stimulating the people in horticultural work is the excellent market facilities enjoyed.

Not only do the railroads radiate to all parts of the country, but being surrounded upon three sides by the great lakes, very cheap water rates can be secured. Not only do Detroit, Grand Rapids, Saginaw, and hundreds of other thriving cities stretch out their hands to be fed, but Michigan grapes, peaches, plums, strawberries, etc., find a ready market in all of the adjoining states. From at least a dozen harbors upon the lake shores large steamers laden to their gunwales with fruit and vegetables make daily trips to Chicago and Milwaukee, from which points the surplus is distributed through the northwest. While the tempering influence of Lake Michigan upon the cold southwest and westerly winds makes a narrow strip along its shore particularly adapted to the growing of some of the more tender fruits, a large part of the land in the counties that make up the six southern tiers can be used to advantage for fruit growing. Nearly, if not all, the counties in the southern peninsula have land that will grow all of the hardier fruits. The northern peninsula seems well adapted to growing currants, gooseberries, raspberries, strawberries, and other small fruits. The large fruits also seem to thrive in properly selected locations.

THE STRAWBERRY.

Although the demand for this fruit has repeatedly doubled it has never outstripped the supply. A few years ago a single crate would perhaps cause a glut of the market, in a small town, where now a wagon load can be disposed of readily. There are a few localities in the State where this fruit, if given a well drained soil and proper care, will not thrive. While it seems to do best upon a rich sandy soil, almost any soil from a light sand to a heavy clay can be used for growing it. As usually grown the plants are set about eighteen inches apart, in rows from three and one-half to four feet wide. The plants are thoroughly cultivated the first season and are allowed to form matted rows covering about one-half of the ground and leaving rows for the pickers to work in.

If large and fine fruit will bring an extra price it will often pay to layer a few of the plants and remove all runners that form later in the season. As soon as the runners begin to form the stronger ones are selected and are layered over a strip so that they will stand eight or ten inches apart. If the others are nipped off as soon as they appear the entire vigor of the plant will be used in forming strong crowns. In this way, the stronger runners can be selected and as they will have all of the food and moisture, instead of sharing it with hundreds of other plants, the growth secured will be able to develop a large number of plants and fruit. Particularly if the season is a dry one the crop will equal that secured from a thick matted row, and the price obtained for the fruit will be much more than could be secured for fruit grown in any other way.

Frequently, too, it might happen that in case there is a glut in the market the choice fruit can be sold at a satisfactory price while the others will be wasted.

Although most varieties do best in matted rows, others give good returns when grown in hills. For field culture these are generally planted about one by two and one-half feet, and all runners are cut off that start during the season. In the home garden, if placed in beds with five rows one foot apart each way and a narrow walk between the beds, a large quantity of fruit can be grown upon a very small area. Particularly when grown upon heavy soils a good mulch of marsh hay, straw or similar material is applied in the fall as soon as the ground has frozen. While the depth over the plants should not be much more than an inch, a considerable greater depth may be applied between the rows. This will prevent the alternate freezing and thawing and the consequent breaking of the roots and heaving of the plants. As spring opens the mulch should be removed from over the plants. It may be left to cover the ground between the rows with a cultivator. Whether mulched in the winter or not, something of the kind is desirable during the fruiting season as it serves to keep the sand from washing upon the plants and to hold

5

the moisture and thus prevent the drying of the plants in time of drouth. The spring set plants bear a full crop the following summer. As a rule the plantation is then freed from grass and weeds and retained for another year.

As a rule girls and women are preferred as pickers to boys as better work is done by them. Various methods of managing the pickers and keeping account of the amount picked are in use.

Perhaps the most common method is to furnish each picker with a light carrier holding four one quart boxes. He is then started upon a row and gathers the berries, cutting each of the stems off close to the hulls with the thumb nail. When the boxes are full, the pickers generally carry them to the packing shed where they receive a ticket for the four quarts.

A better way, however, and one that is in use by several large growers, is to have one or more reliable pickers whose business it is to gather up the boxes as they are filled and deliver them to the packer.

In this way much of the confusion and loss of place by the pickers, that is so common when the other plan is used, is prevented.

When sold in a fastidious market the berries are generally assorted into two or three grades, only the large and perfect berries being placed in the first class. If the boxes are nicely packed, with the upper layer faced, they will bring considerably more than berries put up in a careless manner.

While the supply for all of the villages and small cities is generally grown in the immediate vicinity, some localities have large areas devoted to the raising of strawberries for shipment to other states.

The most extensive plantations are in the vicinity of St. Joseph and Benton Harbor, although many are grown in Van Buren, Allegan, Ottawa, Kent and Muskegon counties.

RASPBERRIES AND BLACKBERRIES.

Closely following the strawberry in season come the raspberry, red and black, and the blackberry. Not only is there a large local demand in the larger villages and cities, but they are shipped by rail and boat to Chicago and Milwaukee in large quantities.

In several sections of the State, where these fruits thrive exceptionally well, there are large evaporators, and plantations of from 30 to 50 acres are grown to supply them.

When placed upon well drained and moderately rich soil the crop is almost a sure one. For evaporating purposes the Ohio blackberry is generally grown, while the Gregg is the favorite for market purposes. The early varieties of blackberry are most profitable, and the Early Harvest, with slight winter protection, is preferred to all other kinds by growers in the vicinity of Benton Harbor where from 20 to 40 acres are devoted to this one variety by several planters.

CURRANTS AND GOOSEBERRIES.

These fruits seem at home and consequently thrive in all sections of Michigan, particularly in the southern and western portions. Large areas are grown for market purposes and they prove very remunerative crops. The Chicago market in particular takes immense quantities of both fruits, and as they only thrive in the cooler portions of the country there is little or no opposition from the south.

While the Downing is the variety of gooseberry most commonly grown, the Industry and other large sorts of European origin can be grown with good success in many parts of the State where the soil is deep, cool and moist.

In some localities the currant borer has been so destructive to the cherry and similar varieties that they are little planted for market purposes, the principal reliance being upon the Victoria and Red Dutch.

The demand for white currant is comparatively small and the black varieties are but little grown.

CRANBERRIES.

Within the past ten years the interest in this fruit has rapidly increased, and it is likely that within a short time the home grown berries will supply the demand. There are thousands of acres of marsh land in the State that are well adapted to this crop and at the present prices it will be a profitable one. The largest plantation is the Comings marsh, in Berrien county, near St. Joseph.

THE NURSERY INDUSTRY.

The propagation of fruit trees in Michigan dates back to the time of the early French settlements, and although many of the old apple and pear trees that are still growing near several of the old French towns and Indian villages were brought from Montreal, others were grown from seed.

The extent to which fruit, both large and small, is grown, requires annually many thousand trees for the planting of new orchards, and many of these are the product of Michigan nurseries.

Nearly every county in the southern half of the State has several nurseries and many of the firms are doing an extensive business. Along the lake shore counties in the peach district are a large number of nurseries which are principally devoted to the growing of peach trees for local planting. From 150 to 200 acres are used in these sections.

MARKET GARDENING.

While the truck farmer grows but two or three kinds of vegetables and these on a large scale, the market gardener cultivates a full variety of and endeavors, by careful selection of varieties, to prolong the season. His products are sold to market men, or retailed from the wagon. Our large manufacturing towns and cities consume immense quantities of fresh vegetables, and good prices can generally be obtained. Not only is the climate adapted to the growing of a great variety of vegetables, but light sandy loam soil suitable for the purpose can be found in most localities. In addition to the sale of the vegetables, most gardeners are able to add to their income by the sale of vegetable plants. The canning and pickling factories of the State use immense quantities of tomatoes, and the growing of sweet corn, tomatoes and seeds, particularly of beans, give employment to thousands of men. Cabbages have been produced in Muskegon county weighing 67 pounds per head and of first quality.

THE POTATO,

while grown successfully and to a considerable extent in all parts of the State, is to the northern half of the lower peninsula the leading money crop of the farmer. Upon soil that will not produce remunerative grain crops and where the late springs and early fall frosts render the corn an uncertain crop, the potato thrives. Not only is the yield as a rule satisfactory but the tubers are large, smooth and of exceedingly fine quality. There has been little or no loss from potato rot and blight and the Colorado beetle is each year becoming less troublesome. The acreage is each year increasing and from several small railroad stations 50,000 to 150,000 bushels are shipped annually. In the loose sandy loam soil, machinery can be used for planting, cultivating and harvesting, and the cost of production thus reduced to the minimum while their superior flavor and keeping qualities place them at the top of the market.

CELERY.

Few crops have done more to keep our State in the minds of the people of the distant, as well as the neighboring states, than the celery from Kalamazoo and other sections.

It is now some fifteen years since the first celery was shipped, but it is only within the last ten years that the business began to take on its present mammoth proportions. Kalamazoo has within a radius of four miles 3,000 acres of marsh land adapted to this crop. The land is first drained by means of open ditches, after which it is plowed and subdued.

Manures are used in large quantities as even upon this rich soil they cannot be dispensed with. Seed for the first crop is sown either in hot beds or greenhouses early in March, the plants are set out in May and the crop harvested in July. A second crop is set out in June to be harvested in August, while plants for winter use are set the last of July or the first of August. The crops for summer use are bleached with boards or with paper, while that for winter use is hilled up with earth.

In Kalamazoo alone there are some thirty firms engaged in shipping celery, and the industry of growing the crop gives employment to 2,000 men. The daily shipments amount to forty or fifty tons in the heighth of the season. Land equally suited to the crop is found in hundreds of other places in the State and the marshes at Kalamazoo, Tecumseh and Durand will undoubtedly find strong competition.

WINTER FORCING OF LETTUCE.

Until recently lettuce has been known as a spring and summer salad crop, and was but sparingly grown for winter use, and then only in hot beds or in some spare greenhouse as a catch crop by the florists. Some six or eight years ago the growing of winter lettuce as a commercial greenhouse crop was begun. By careful selection a variety well adapted to the purpose was obtained, which is now used exclusively by the growers of Grand Rapids and has become known all over the country as the "Grand Rapids variety of lettuce." This lettuce was so attractive in appearance that a demand at once sprang up for it, and as it was easily grown it produced a very profitable crop. The business soon became quite extensive. Many erected houses and went into the business of lettuce growing. The Grand Rapids lettuce soon obtained a reputation all through the neighboring states, and regular shipments were made to Detroit, Chicago, Indianapolis, Cleveland, Columbus, Cincinnati and other large cities, and although the prices secured were considerably higher than lettuce from local growers could be obtained for, the demand could not be supplied. While some of the houses are three-quarters span, the common even span has for the most part been used in the greenhouses erected for lettuce growing. The houses are sometimes heated by steam and hot water, but the use of the hot air flue is more common. The furnaces are placed at the end of each house, or if they are long a furnace is constructed at both ends. Flues built of brick or of vitrified pipe lead from these furnaces through the house and back, passing up as a chimney over the furnace. Three crops are taken off during the winter and as the variety grown can be planted quite closely the profits are very satisfactory. The prospects for this industry are very flattering.

TRUCK FARMING.

In certain localities of the State where climatic and soil conditions are favorable and whence there is ready communication with large cities, this new industry is a favorite.

The term applies to the growing of one or more vegetable crops upon a large scale and their shipment to market or wholesale dealers. If the crops are properly handled it can at once be seen that the large trucker can grow larger and better crops and can place them on the market at a lower price than the average small grower. Aside from the celery and potatoes which have been mentioned above the principal truck crops grown in Michigan are onions, tomatoes and melons.

The onion is now grown in large quantities on swamp land in various parts of the State. Upon this soil large yields are obtained with little expense for labor and nothing at all for fertilizers, while there is little danger of injury from drouth. It is also largely grown upon the uplands, and the crops thus obtained, on account of their superior flavor and keeping qualities, bring a much higher price than those grown upon the low land.

In localities within easy reach of market the tomato is generally found to be profitable by trucksters, and immense quantities are grown, particularly in Berrien county. They require a rich, but warm and early soil, and with good selection of varieties and well grown plants, but little skill is required to grow them.

In a general way the same can be said of melon growing. The water-melon is not very largely grown, but the musk-melon is a profitable crop and is quite largely grown by trucksters, especially in the vicinity of Benton Harbor.

COMMERCIAL FLORICULTURE.

Where ten years ago one would seldom see flower beds in the yards or plants in the windows the reverse is now the rule, and this gives to the florist a large sale of bedding and house plants. The principal increase in the business of the florist has been in the sale of cut flowers for the adornment of the person, the table or the parlor.

Nearly every large town has its florist, and in the cities particularly the business is an excellent one. In addition to supplying the local demand for plants and flowers, several firms have a large shipping trade in both, the flowers being for the most part sent to commission merchants in Chicago and the plants to florists in all parts of the country.

MICHIGAN AS A FRUIT GROWING STATE.

BY J. G. RAMSDELL.

The soil, topography and climate of the lower peninsula of Michigan is well adapted to the growing of every variety of orchard and garden fruit that can be grown north of the thirty-seventh parallel, and its marketing facilities are unequaled. Every variety of apples, pears, plums and cherries can be successfully grown upon nearly every farm, and the peach is a safe and profitable crop on all of the high rolling lands lying within thirty miles of the eastern shore of Lake Michigan. Grapes do well on the hillsides everywhere, and all varieties of berries yield large annual crops. Successful and profitable fruit growing depends principally upon four conditions: First, a soil naturally adapted to a strong and healthful growth of trees and plants, for the manuring of orchards is generally difficult and always expensive. Second, topography that will admit of free and rapid atmospheric drainage in clear cold weather, and thus aid the general climate in protecting trees and fruit from extreme freezing in winter and from damaging vernal and autumnal frosts during the blossoming and fruiting season. Third, a climate by which the extreme heat and blasting winds of summer, and the extreme cold and violent storms of winter are tempered to harmless conditions, for it is not the general average of heat in summer, or the general average of cold in winter that the orchardists have to consider, but the extremes of heat that blast and the extremes of cold that destroy, that he has to fear. Fourth, a ready and convenient market with cheap and rapid transportation. All these conditions are more completely fulfilled in the soil, topography, climate and market facilities of lower Michigan than in any other territory of equal extent in the union of states.

COMPOSITION OF SOIL.

The inorganic substances which must exist in a soil to make it naturally fertile —that is fertile without manuring—are silica, alumina, lime, magnesia, oxide of iron, oxide of magnesia, potash, soda, chlorine, sulphuric acid and carbonic acid, either free or combined with one another, or with other substances. A soil containing these ingredients with from six to ten per cent of organic matter will remain permanently fertile until exhausting crops require the replacement of some of these ingredients. The rocks from which the soil of the lower peninsula of

Michigan is derived furnish all these inorganic substances in great abundance, and the decomposition of ages of forest growth has furnished the needed supply of organic matter.

At some period in the geological history of this continent there was a great uplifting in the Lake Superior region. The trap and granite underlying the azoic formation was forced up through all the superincumbent strata of rocks, upturning the broken edges to the surface. During the subsequent glacial period these strata were broken, ground and pulverized into drift material and spread over lower Michigan to a great depth, varying from six hundred feet in the northern to fifty feet or more in the southern part.

The rock strata thus ground up and commingled are composed of the following geological formations: Trap and granite in every variety of composition, the azoic formation; the Lake Superior or Potsdam sandstone, highly impregnated with peroxide of iron; the Trenton group, a siliceous limestone; the Hudson river group, an argillaceous limestone abounding in fossils; the Clinton group, an argillaceous calcareous limestone; the Niagara group, a crystalline magnesian limestone, rich in fossils; the Onondaga salt group, rich in chloride of sodium (salt) and sulphate of lime (gypsum); the Helderberg group, a limestone composed largely of fossil coral; the Hamilton group, a bituminous limestone; and the Huron group, a dark bituminous clayey shale.

Those familiar with the mineral composition of the several rock formations above named will readily see the extraordinary richness in plant-feeding elements of a soil composed of the mingled constituents of these rocks. The feldspar and mica of the trap and granite furnish an abundance of potash; the fossil remains of the limestone rocks, an abundance of phosphates; the salt and gypsum of the Onondaga salt group, an abundance of these materials. The ferrugineous sandstone of the Potsdam group furnishes the iron oxide necessary to healthy growth and high color of fruit and foliage; the mica, feldspar and argillaceous limestones and shales furnish sufficient alumina to give the proper adhesiveness to the soil, and the limestone siliceous rocks, amply supply those materials. The dense forests of deciduous timber that originally covered the most of the State, the magnificent growth of oak, ash, maple and elm which composed those forests, give abundant evidence of the fertility of the soil in the elements of vegetable growth and confirm the conclusions which science maintains.

TOPOGRAPHY.

The lower peninsula is bordered on the west, north, and east by lakes Michigan, Huron, St. Clair and Erie. The watershed that divides the streams flowing into these lakes rises to the height of 600 feet above the lakes in Hillsdale county in the southern part, falling gradually northward to less than 100 feet between the tributaries of the Saginaw river and the Grand in Gratiot county, then gradually rising northward until it reaches an elevation of over 1,000 feet in Otsego county. The largest streams, such as the St. Joseph, Kalamazoo, Grand, Muskegon and Manistee, on the west, and the Saginaw, Huron and Raisin on the east, take their rise in the higher lands and form broad fertile valleys along their course. The divides between these rivers and their tributaries form gently rolling uplands, without either extended plains or precipitous hills. On the higher plateau which forms the watershed between the great lakes, numerous lakes abound varying from a few acres to many square miles in extent. The natural drainage of the whole is complete. The effect of the topography of lower Michigan upon the growing of fruit will be considered with the

CLIMATE.

Lake Michigan has an average depth of 1,000 feet, an average width of sixty miles, and contains an area of 23,150 square miles. This vast body of water lying along the west and northwest border forms a thermal regulator, absorbing the heat of summer and gradually yielding it up again to temper the cold of winter, thus avoiding the extremes of heat and cold that damage foliage in summer and injure buds and trees in winter.

The prevailing winds in winter are west and northwest. These winds, passing over the open water of Lake Michigan in winter are raised in temperature from ten to thirty degrees; so that storms that register from twenty to thirty degrees below zero on the western shore of the lake seldom fall to zero on its Michigan border.

The amount of heat which a gallon of water will absorb and then give off again when surrounded by a lower temperature is immense. Take a gallon of water, heat it to the boiling point, put it in a common jug, and place it under the robes in a sleigh, and it will keep the feet comfortably warm for a whole day's journey with the thermometer at zero. Such is precisely the effect of Lake Michigan, less in degree but infinitely greater in amount. Warmed up by the summer's heat of sun and wind, as the air over the water falls below it in temperature, the water yields up a portion of its heat in constantly ascending vapor which these westerly winds bring directly to the Michigan shore, softening almost past credibility its climate as far north as the forty-fifth parallel. In this respect the great lake seems almost endowed with consciousness; the colder the weather the greater its effort to temper the air. Go out in a still clear morning with the thermometer at zero and look out upon the lake; you will see a dense column of vapor rising from its surface, as though all the fires of Pluto were seething at its bottom. This vapor is wafted over the land and meeting with the colder upper air is condensed and falls in snowflakes so clean and pure and white that nature furnishes no object with which to compare them. This evaporation is going on constantly during the winter season, giving a great depth of snow, particularly in the northern portion, where the depth is so great that the ground is wholly protected from freezing.

The same causes that temper the winter, acting inversely, also temper the heat of summer. The water having cooled down to near the freezing point during the winter, absorbs the excessive heat of summer, so that those blighting winds which so often sear and destroy the foliage of trees and plants in other states are unfelt in this.

While the hydrographic advantages of Michigan regulate and temper its general climate, its favorable topography is a valuable element in successful orcharding. Along the whole eastern shore of Lake Michigan, for at least ten miles inland, and around Grand Traverse bay, for a distance varying from three to five miles, damaging frosts either in spring or fall seldom occur, and the same is true upon the hillsides and ridges of the rolling lands of the interior. The philosophy of this is

6

so simple and yet so little understood that an explanation here will not be out of place.

Every one has observed that ordinary frosts vary greatly in their severity in the same neighborhood, low places, level lands, and basins or depressions, suffering more injury than sidehills, knolls and ridges. On a clear, still night heat radiates from the surface of the earth into space. As this radiation goes on the surface grows colder and colder. If level the air remains stationary and falls in temperature with the surface of the earth.   At first the moisture of the air is condensed and forms dew; at 32° Fahrenheit it is crystalized into hoar frost; if it sinks still lower the sap of tender plants is frozen, and expanding bursts or injures the cells and kills the plants. Cold air is heavier than warm air, and the colder it gets the heavier it grows. On hillsides, knolls and ridges, as radiation cools the surface the air becomes heavier and runs down the hill to the valley or plain below and warmer air takes its place; this in its turn grows dense and passes down, forming a current of air down the hill, leaving none of it still long enough to reach the freezing point. If the valley is inclosed so as to form a basin, the cold air draining into it may fill it up so that the frost will reach up the hillside to the level of the dam which incloses it. But where the drainage reaches a body of water, heat escaping from the water reheats the air, causing it to rise and flow back again to take the place of that which is flowing down the hill. In the cold, still nights of winter the difference in temperature between hillsides and inclosed basins and level land is surprising.

On February 9, 1865, the coldest night ever known in the Grand Traverse region. Messrs. Avery and Marshall of Old Mission found a difference of twenty-two degrees in less than 100 feet elevation; and Messrs. Parmely & Brinkman eleven degrees in fourteen feet elevation. These tests were, however, in places where the drainage was obstructed by ridges across the line of drainage forming basins. Where the valley or hillside opens without obstruction to the bay or lakes, the difference is not so great. I found on my farm which descends rapidly towards Grand Traverse bay, a difference of ten degrees to one hundred feet elevation on the same night of the Old Mission test.

When we consider how close the margin is between absolute exemption from injury and the total destruction of the tender varieties of fruit trees by freezing, we can see how important is this matter of atmospheric drainage. With twelve degrees peach buds are comparatively safe; at fifteen degrees the buds are pretty sure to be killed, and the trees are in danger; and at twenty-two degrees destruction of the tree is almost certain. A hundred feet elevation, with open drainage to lower levels, may determine the difference between a crop of fruit and a ruined orchard; and in inclosed valleys or basins twenty feet may do the same.

This simple matter was not understood in the early planting of orchards in this State. For ease of cultivation and convenience in gathering the fruit, level lands were selected for orcharding, to the great disappointment and loss of the owners.

MARKETS.

A glance at the map of Michigan and the west is all that is necessary to show its great advantage in respect to markets. At the very gates of Chicago, the greatest distributing fruit point in the world, with both water and rail transportation to the vast fruitless region of the west and north with its unlimited demand, gives to Michigan fruit growers market advantages superior to the fruit growers of any other state.

CHARACTER OF FRUIT.

The fruits grown in Michigan, while less in size than the same varieties grown in the Mississippi valley and on the Pacific coast, are firmer in texture, more spirited and pronounced in flavor, higher colored, fairer, and of greater specific gravity, and their keeping qualities, especially apples, surpass all other districts. My peach orchard is on Grand Traverse bay, elevated 100 feet above its surface, in latitude 44° 41'. I had a heavy crop last summer, and today, March 21, 1893, notwithstanding the severity of the past winter, the buds are uninjured and the promise for a heavy crop again this year is certain.

PEPPERMINT AND OTHER ESSENTIAL OILS.

BY GEO. W. OSBORN, OF MENDON, PRESIDENT OF THE CENTRAL MINT GROWERS'
CO-OPERATIVE ASSOCIATION.

Michigan produces annually more peppermint oil than all the other states combined, and St. Joseph county, in which it was first successfully produced commercially in this State, still furnishes something more than half of Michigan's annual product. Next in order of their product come Kalamazoo, Wayne. Van Buren. Allegan and Cass, and peppermint is raised and stilled to a small extent in several other counties.

Peppermint was first cultivated and distilled in Michigan in about 1835, on White Pigeon Prairie, township of Florence, St. Joseph county, by a Mr. Sawyer, but for some reason the venture was unprofitable and was abandoned. Peppermint oil was first successfully produced commercially in 1842, by Messrs. John Smith and Harrison Ranney, who had had experience in the business in Wayne county, N. Y., on the farm of the late Norman Roys, in the same township of Florence. The sandy loam of the burr oak plains seemed particularly adapted to its growth. That farm and township were soon covered, the business extended to the townships of Lockport, Nottawa, Park and Mendon, so that by 1850 the yearly product of peppermint in St. Joseph county alone was estimated at 100,000 to 150,000 pounds—an amount exceeding the production of all the rest of the world at that time. These details for the early history of this industry I get from Mr. George Roys, who was born in Florence and is thoroughly familiar with it, and though, at this distance in time and in the absence of statistics, the estimate may seem wild, it must be remembered that at that time the land was new, injury by winter freezing or summer drouth practically unknown, and that the average yield was about twenty pounds per acre on uplands, whereas at present a very small proportion of the crop is grown on uplands. The big crop of 1850 also so overloaded the market that the price of oil dropped to less than one dollar a pound, driving many out of the business.

Although it was known that peppermint was a plant of an aquatic nature, it was not until 1880 that it was demonstrated that it could be successfully produced on reclaimed marsh land. This induced Messrs. Sidney Johnson and Henry Hall, of Three Rivers, to buy and reclaim 1,000 acres of the "Florence marsh" for this purpose, on which Mr. Hall still successfully operates the largest mint farm in the world.

Marsh mint, however, is not free from failures. Cut worms, spring frosts, summer floods and grasshoppers serve to keep the supply even with the demand. Though an average successful crop is fifteen to twenty pounds of oil per acre, yet owing to reasons given fields are often cut yielding only two to four or five pounds, and frequently as high as one-fifth of the acreage in the State reported to the Mint Growers' Association is an entire loss, so this keeps the average per acre for the State low as compared with the average per acre for a fairly good crop. As the mint is only cultivated the first year and requires afterward no expense of labor except cutting with a mower and distilling, fields are often harvested which yield little more than enough to pay for mowing and distilling.

WORMWOOD, SPEARMINT, ETC.

Wormwood was first cultivated and distilled in Michigan in 1860, by the late Alvin Calhoun, likewise of Florence, St. Joseph county, who was the only grower for several years. In 1871 he sold 150 pounds of oil at twelve dollars per pound, and the exorbitant price so stimulated over production that the price dropped to about two dollars; too near the cost to leave any profit to the grower.

The other essential oils grown and distilled by farmers are spearmint, tansy and erigeron. All these oils are produced in sufficient quantities to supply the demand, and their annual sales add several thousand dollars to the essential oil industry.

ACREAGE IN PEPPERMINT.

The number of acres of peppermint now raised in the State from a close estimate made by the Mint Growers' Association, is about 11,000. The average yield per acre is about 8 pounds, making a total of 88,000 pounds. The average price paid growers for the past four or five years has been $2 per pound. Total value to growers, $176,000. The oil is sold by the producers to local buyers, who sell it to exporters and speculators in New York and other markets, except what is handled by the Mint Growers' Association and sold direct to the large dealers in New York and elsewhere for the benefit of its members. Michigan's only considerable domestic competitor in peppermint oil is the State of New York, where the industry first started.

MODE OF DISTILLATION.

As a rule the farmers distill their own mint, except the small growers, who draw it to the nearest still to be manufactured. These stills are generally run night and day until the crop is secured. The oil is obtained by evaporation, the steam passing through a series of tin pipes, where it is condensed by using cold water upon them. The water and oil thus condensed runs into a receiver; the oil being the lighter rises to the top and is dipped off into cans and is ready for market.

EXPORTS OF ESSENTIAL OILS.

The exports of peppermint oil from the United States for a number of years past, so as to get an average cannot be obtained, for the reason that previous to the year ending June 30, 1891, this oil was classed in exports with other essential oils and drugs. In 1890 the association succeeded in getting peppermint in a separate list, and the annual statement of the exports of the United States for the year ending June 30, 1891, shows in pounds as follows:

To Germany	25,191
Great Britain and Ireland	15,326
France	4,513
All other countries	291
Total amount exports (pounds)	45,321
Total export value	$120,831
Average value exports, per pound	82 66

FOREIGN COMPETITION.

A small amount of peppermint oil is produced in England, Germany and France, but not enough to affect prices in the world's markets.

The most serious competition we have to meet is from an inferior oil produced in Japan. This oil has an unpleasant odor and taste, but is a heavy oil and rich in menthol. The following table of exports from Japan from 1884 to 1890, with the export value at the date of shipment will show the competition from that country:

Year.	Pounds.	Per pound.
1884	12,020	$1 60
1885	20,480	1 67
1886	81,330	50
1887	115,231	51
1888	25,586	60
1889	31,734	65
1890	39,149	85

This oil was sent to the following countries: Germany, Great Britain, China, France, United States, Italy, British India, and other countries in the order named.

It will be seen that Japanese oil enters largely into the world's consumption and is a strong competitor of American oils. Its cheapness, and the facility with which it can be mixed with our oil as an adulterant, makes it a dangerous rival.

MICHIGAN AT THE FAIR.

BY WORLD'S FAIR COMMISSIONER.

AT THE FORE IN THESE GREAT INDUSTRIES:

FIRST IN LUMBER, IRON ORE, CHARCOAL, IRON, SALT, GYPSUM, FURNITURE, FRUIT, PEPPERMINT OIL, INLAND FISHERIES, LAKE COMMERCE, SHIP BUILDING; SECOND IN COPPER AND VESSEL TONNAGE OF ALL KINDS. FIRST ALSO IN YIELD OF WHEAT PER ACRE AND VALUE. PRODUCT PER ACRE OF THE MAIN FARM CROPS.

A summary of statistics regarding Michigan's chief industries, compiled under direction of the State World's Fair Commissioners for bulletin in the Michigan building, makes a remarkable, and in some respects a showing as surprising as it is gratifying in respect to those industries in which the Peninsula State either leads all other states in the Union, or stands in the front rank in the extent and value of annual product.

By this exhibit, compiled in most cases from official sources, Michigan stands first in lumber and saw-mill products, hardwood forests, hardwood manufactures and furniture. First in iron ore, charcoal iron, salt and gypsum. Second in copper. Among the first in yield of wheat per acre and in the value product per acre of farm crops generally as compared with states west of New York. First in peppermint oil, and not second in apples, peaches, plums and fruit generally. Third in value of sheep and wool, only Ohio and California surpassing her. First in extent of coast line, with over 1,600 miles on Lakes Superior, Michigan, Huron, St. Clair and Erie. First in inland commerce; first in inland commercial fisheries; first in ship building, and second only to New York in vessel tonnage of all kinds. First in number and variety of its summer resorts, and in its wealth of brook trout, grayling, bass, pike, perch, and other stream and lake sport fishing. First in its State university, with 2,800 students (science, literature, law and medicine); and not second in its common, high, normal and mining schools and agricultural college; or in its State benevolent institutions, including school for the blind at Lansing; for deaf mutes at Flint, soldiers' home at Grand Rapids, State public school at Coldwater, industrial home for girls at Adrian, industrial school for boys at Lansing, asylums for insane at Kalamazoo, Pontiac, Traverse City and upper peninsula, asylum for insane criminals at Ionia, and home for the feeble-minded.

Some of these statements are almost startling. For instance, nearly half the total domestic product of iron ore and half its value come from Michigan's mines. Product for 1892, 7,543,544 tons; increase over 1890 census of 1,687,375 tons. (Report statistics geological survey for 1892.) Total value of product of United States for census year, $33,351,978; total tons, 14,518,041, of which Michigan produced 5,856,- 169, valued at $15,800,524; Alabama next in tonnage with 1,570,319 tons, valued at $1,511,621; New York second in value product, $3,100,216, with 1,247,537 tons; Pennsylvania third in value product, $3,063,514, with 1,560,234 tons. Average value per ton of ore, Michigan, $2.70; Alabama, $0.96; New York, $2.49; Pennsylvania, $1.96. (Census bulletin 113).

"The total production of iron ore in the United States in 1890," says State Commissioner of Mineral Statistics Lawton in his official report, "was about 17¼ million tons, to which Michigan contributed 7,185,175 tons, worth at the mines at least $26,000,000. The quality of Michigan ore is greatly in its favor. The average in 1890 was 62 per cent. in metallic iron some 68, while much of the ore produced elsewhere has but 50 per cent or less. About half of the product, too, was Bessemer, i. e., so free from phosphorus as to be suitable for making Bessemer steel.".

"Nearly 55 per cent of all the iron ore mined in the United States in 1892 was furnished by the Lake Superior region, and of this amount Michigan furnished 86 per cent."—Richard A. Parker.

The report of the mining division of statistics in the geological survey for 1892 puts the total iron ore product for the United States for 1892 at 16,296,666 long tons, or 1,778,625 tons increase over census year. Michigan produced in 1892, 7,543,544 tons, an increase over census year of 1,687,375, or 95 per cent of the increase for the whole country, and over 46 per cent of the total output. Alabama stands next to Michigan in output with 2,312,071 tons; Minnesota third, with 1,255,463; Pennsylvania fourth, 1,084,047; New York fifth, 891,099; Wisconsin sixth, 790,179 tons. Twenty-four states produced iron ore in commercial quantities. With only 43½ per cent of the total output in the census year Michigan's value product was 47½ per cent. With 46 per cent of the total output in 1892, as per report of geological survey, the value product of Michigan iron ores for '92 should be a trifle over 50 per cent of the total value product; and with 47.3 per cent of the total output, as per R. A. Parker's figures, 51.4 per cent of the total value product.

Michigan, Wisconsin and Minnesota produce, according to 1890 census, more than one-third of all the lumber in the United States. while Michigan's output just about equals that of Wisconsin and Minnesota combined, and was a fifth (to be exact, 19.75 per cent) of the total domestic product. The total Michigan product of lumber, shingles, staves, etc., for the census year aggregated $68,141,189, an increase over 1880 of $15,691,261. United States census bulletin No. 5, page 6,

MICHIGAN WORLD'S FAIR BUILDING.

puts the value of lumber and sawmill products and their manufactures for 1890 census year as follows:

States.	No. miles.	Capital.	No. hands.	Value product.
Michigan	1,957	$111,302,797	43,827	$68,141,189
Wisconsin	863	84,586,623	31,050	49,547,410
Minnesota	320	27,497,187	9,927	19,123,023
Total	2,140	223,386,607	84,814	$136,811,622

The acting superintendent of census under date of May 5, 1893, states that it was "not yet possible to publish final and complete totals, but that Michigan's product constituted nearly one-fifth (19.73 per cent) of the total value of lumber and sawmill products thus far obtained for the census of 1890." He, however, gives a summary, by groups of states, of the lumber and sawmill products (exclusive of manufactures) as follows:

White pine group (Michigan, Wisconsin, Minnesota)_____$115,699,014
Pacific coast (California, Washington, Oregon)_____ 24,192,367
Hard pine states (Maryland. Virginia, North Carolina, South Carolina, Georgia, Florida, Alabama, Mississippi, Louisiana, Texas, Arkansas, Missouri)_____ 54,747,266
Central (Ohio, Indiana, West Virginia, Kentucky, Tennessee)_____ 49,433,293
Eastern (Maine, New Hampshire, Vermont, Massachusetts, Rhode Island, Connecticut, New York, New Jersey, Pennsylvania, Delaware)_____ 62,087,984
All the other states and territories_____ 4,119,246

Total for United States_____$323,134,009

The total United States lumber and sawmill products (according to same authority) for 1880 were $233,600,043, or $89,474,052 less than in 1890, while Michigan, Wisconsin and Minnesota produced in 1880, $77,768,313, or $37,930,691 less than in 1890. In 1880 these three states furnished 33.34 per cent of the total United States lumber and sawmill product, while in 1890 they furnished 35.81 per cent. The Pacific group furnished 7.49 per cent; the southern, 16.94 per cent; the central, 15.29 per cent; the eastern, 19.21 per cent; all other states and territories, 5.26 per cent.

The United States produces half of the world's copper, and Michigan one-third that of the United States. Michigan's 1889 product, 43,728 tons; 1890, 50,303½ tons; 1891, 54,635 tons. "The total value of Michigan's 1890 copper output, at 15¾ cents per pound (average rate for year in New York) was 15,855,427." (Report of Michigan Commissioner of Mines and Minerals, 1891, page. 36.) Total United States product in 1889, 113,028 tons; Michigan, 43,728 tons; Montana, 49,111. Total for 1890, 136,704 tons; Michigan, 50,303½ tons; Montana, 61,475. Michigan 1891 product, 54,635 tons.

7

According to 1890 census Michigan produced one-third the charcoal iron made in the country, $3.932,278 out of the $11,985,103 total domestic product.

In salt Michigan's output is almost one-half in amount and value of the total domestic product; $2,302,570 in value in 1890; in 1891, 3,927,671 barrels; in 1892, 3,812,054 barrels.

Of gypsum Michigan produces almost half the total domestic product—131,767 tons in 1890; New York next with 52,206 tons.

For an average of ten years ending in 1890, as shown by report of United States Statistician Dodge, Michigan not only led Ohio, Indiana, Illinois, and all the great northwestern wheat states in the yield of wheat per acre (18½ bushels in 1891 as per Michigan "Farm Statistics"), but also in the value product per acre of wheat, corn, oats, barley, buckwheat and hay.

Michigan has 178 furniture factories in 60 cities and villages, with an invested capital of $9,855,000. Grand Rapids has 45 factories, with a capital of $5,000,000, employing 5,000 hands and is the recognized furniture center of the country.

More peppermint oil is produced in Michigan than in all the rest of the country together. The acreage for 1892 is put at 11,000; average yield per acre, eight pounds; value per pound at still, $2.00, or a total value in first hands of $176,000. In 1890–91 the United States exported 45,321 pounds of oil, valued at $2.06 per pound, while Japan, the only other country producing a surplus of peppermint, exported same year 30,149 pounds, valued at eighty-five cents. The Japan article is a heavy oil and rich in menthol, but in every other way inferior and is largely in use as an adulterant.

But probably the most surprising figures are those grouped under the heading, "First in inland commerce, first in ship building, and second only to New York in vessel tonnage of all kinds." According to the quoted report of United States Statistician Dodge, the total vessel tonnage on the Great Lakes in 1891 was 1,063,063 tons; number of vessels, 2,945; value, $75,590,950. The ton mileage on these lakes in same year was 25 per cent of the railway ton mileage of the United States. The freight tonnage passing the Sault canal in 1890 was 8,554,434, or 1,664,341 tons more than passed through Suez canal, and this although the Suez is open the whole year, while the Sault is closed several months. The freight tonnage passing through Detroit river in 1890 was 21,684,000 tons, about the same as that of Liverpool and London combined, or our entire Atlantic coast foreign trade tonnage. The character of the lake tonnage is given as follows: Steamers, 1,277; sail, 927; unrigged, 771; steel, 89; iron, 39; wood, 2,817. Statistician Dodge is quoted further on this point as follows: "About one-quarter the tonnage of our entire merchant marine is on the northern lakes, and the large steam tonnage (1,000 tons and upwards) on the Great Lakes exceeds the total similar tonnage of all the rest of the country by 131,093 tons." Michigan leads in this great lake commerce and her vessel tonnage for the year ending June 30, 1892, exceeded that of every other state in the Union, except New York, the great ocean carrier. The figures on which this statement is based are furnished by the United States statistician from the last report of the United States bureau of navigation. The table following shows the number of vessels and vessel tonnage of the sixteen leading states (totaling 4,373,040 tons in 1892) for the years ending June 30, 1892, 1891, 1888 and 1886 and includes all states having 50,000 tonnage:

States.	No. vessels '92.			Tonnage.			
	Sail.	Steam.	Total.	1892.	1891.	1888.	1886.
Michigan	522	628	1,150	390,920	388,021	276,750	226,391
Massachusetts	1,494	188	1,682	389,942	393,775	439,133	442,353
Pennsylvania	486	477	963	353,157	284,744	273,203	282,416
Maine	1,902	147	2,043	352,574	369,014	409,664	487,574
California	695	257	952	316,872	311,726	281,132	251,142
Ohio	151	397	548	315,849	267,795	276,540	164,684
Maryland	2,063	174	2,236	143,536	....	141,431	146,899
Connecticut	460	178	638	134,413	....	119,754	108,672
Wisconsin	251	196	447	111,267	....	91,043	83,025
New Jersey	965	125	1,090	101,088	....	91,996	89,412
Washington	150	172	322	59,074	....	64,724	49,776
Illinois	161	214	375	84,632	....	77,470	73,522
Louisiana	359	181	540	57,974	....	62,402	69,952
Oregon	51	158	209	56,499	....	53,317	59,192
New York	2,302	1,457	3,759	1,339,937	1,029,233	1,136,154	1,218,113

From the foregoing table it is seen that the growth of Michigan's tonnage has been continuous since 1886, and that its increase in six years has been 73 per cent. New York's tonnage for the same period shows a net increase of only 10 per cent; its tonnage showing a steady decrease amounting to 15½ per cent for the five years ending 1891, and then in a single year jumping up 310,704 tons. Massachusetts shows a net decrease since 1886 of 52,401 tons, or about 12 per cent; Maine a decrease of 135,000 tons, or 27⅔ per cent. The seven Atlantic seaboard states, New York, Massachusetts, Pennsylvania, Maine, Maryland, Connecticut and New Jersey, which in 1892 had considerably more than half the total tonnage of the country, showed in that year a net increase over 1886 of only 39,078 tons, or 1½ per cent, while the tonnage of the lake states, Michigan, Ohio, Wisconsin, Illinois, Indiana and Minnesota, increased during the same period 330,406 tons, or 60 per cent, 315,774 tons being credited to Michigan and Ohio. The lake tonnage of New York and Pennsylvania has not as yet been given separately from the ocean tonnage.

Not less surprising is the way Michigan has forged to the front in ship building. Of the total 294,123 vessel tonnage built in 1890 in the United States 169,091 tons were built on the seaboard, 16,560 tons on western rivers, and 108,526 tons on the northern lakes. Of this 108,526 lake tonnage Michigan yards at Bay City, Detroit and Grand Haven built 45,733 tons, 65 vessels, including two 4,000 ton steel steamers for the ocean trade, while Cleveland and other Ohio yards built 41,000 tons. United States Statistician Dodge, who is authority for the foregoing, further says: "The steam tonnage built on the Great Lakes in 1890 was 40 per cent greater than that of the entire seaboard. For the lakes, 86,023 tons; seaboard, 61,137." It may not be amiss, in this connection, to add that but for the treaty with Great Britain, which forbade it, some of the great war cruisers for the United States navy would have been constructed at the Bay City yards.

As indicative of Michigan's yet undeveloped, as compared with developed resources, farming and other, the following figures are also given: Population in 1890, 2,093,889; increase over 1880, 28 per cent. Tax value, State equalization,

1892, $1,130,000,000; square miles, per United States survey, 58,915. Acres of land in farms as per "Michigan Farm Statistics" of 1893, 12,720,610. Acres land not in farms, 24,254,741. Acres in farms improved, 8,328,189; not improved, including reserved woodlands, 4,392,430. Considering the large proportion of Michigan's yet undeveloped resources in connection with what she has already achieved, her inexhaustible mines and minerals, her wealth in hard wood forests lying convenient to consuming centers, her advantageous position as the center of the commerce of the Great Lakes, and the great amount of virgin agricultural land yet untouched by the settler, it must be conceded that no state in the Union offers brighter promise for the future.

Michigan is a great State. She is surpassed by no other state in the Union, if indeed equaled, in the extent, number and diverstiy of the great industries in which she either leads or stands in the front rank; and this fact will be made more and more prominent as the days roll by at the great World's Fair in Chicago.

THE UPPER PENINSULA.

BY HON. J. M. LONGYEAR.

The upper peninsula of Michigan, lying between Lake Superior on the north and Lakes Michigan and Huron on the south, and adjoining the state of Wisconsin on the southwest, is something over three hundred miles in length and nearly one hundred and fifty miles in extreme width. Its average width is perhaps fifty or sixty miles, its irregular outlines making it extremely difficult to give any comprehensive verbal description of it. In surface characteristics it presents more variety than is found in any other part of the State. The eastern half of the peninsula is comparatively level, being underlaid on the south by horizontally bedded limestones and on the north by sandstone. In this part of the peninsula occur very extensive swamps, some of which are heavily timbered with spruce, cedar, tamarack, etc., while others consist of extensive wet marshes or savannas. There are also large areas of land in this region with rolling and, in places, broken surface, particularly on the north or Lake Superior shore where sandstone often rises to heights of several hundred feet above the lake, notably at the Pictured Rocks, where the rugged scenery, the fantastic and beautiful forms into which the waters of the lake has worn the sandstone, create a coast whose beauties have been famous since the country was first known to the earliest explorers. The streams in this region generally flow southward into Lake Michigan, the watershed, or divide, being only a few miles south of Lake Superior. The Teh-qua-me-non river is the largest which enters Lake Superior from the eastern half of the peninsula, the other streams being generally small. The streams flowing into Lake Michigan are sluggish and of considerable volume, considering the area drained. Those entering Lake Superior are generally of rapid current and many of them form interesting and picturesque waterfalls in their rapid descent to the lake.

The surface of the western part of the peninsula is generally rolling and often broken with high, rocky hills rising to heights of from six hundred to one thousand five hundred feet above Lake Superior. The most rugged and mountainous regions are the Huron mountains, east of Keweenaw bay, and the Porcupine mountains, near the west end of the peninsula. The streams in this portion of the peninsula are generally full of rapids and contain numerous cataracts, some of which have already been utilized for water-power. Many others will be utilized in the future, as the natural power, aggregating many thousand horse power, will certainly be used as the region is developed. Most of the streams in this western portion of the peninsula are small, but a few carry a very considerable volume of water and the power they are able to furnish will be permanent and valuable.

Scattered about over the surface of the entire peninsula are hundreds of lakes of various sizes, from mere ponds to several thousand acres in area. Fish abound in nearly all of these lakes and many of them are visited every year by sportsmen, the number of visitors steadily increasing from year to year as better transportation facilities are afforded.

The region is an enticing one to the tourist, the sportsman, the artist and the man of business, all finding within its boundaries ample scope for the exercise of their respective talents and skill.

IRON ORE.

The great business of the upper peninsula is the production of iron ore, in which the western half abounds. It is safe to say, however, that great as the production now is, the capacity of the peninsula is many times greater than has yet been demonstrated. The greater part of the peninsula is still a wilderness and there are miles of iron ore indications yet untouched by miners or explorers. Many of these indications are fully as good as those first found on the older ranges. The iron ore business of the peninsula multiplied over seven times in the eighteen years between 1873 and 1890, both seasons inclusive, and it is safe to say that it may be still multiplied seven times more before the limit of its productive capacity has been reached. It is estimated by many experts that in the not very distant future the iron business of this country will have increased to such porportions that it will be impossible to supply the quality of ore now being furnished and that it will be necessary to mine and smelt the so called lean ores. When that time comes the upper peninsula of Michigan will be able to supply many billions of tons of such ores, which are at present ignored by the miner.

IRON MANUFACTURING.

Thus far the manufacture of iron in Michigan has been practically confined to furnaces using charcoal for fuel. It is, however, now confidently asserted by experts, who have carefully studied the subject, that it is perfectly feasible to manufacture iron, using coke as fuel, at Lake Superior points and this industry will probably be added to those of the upper peninsula in the near future. Charcoal iron for special purposes will undoubtedly continue to be made in the upper peninsula for many years to come and the thousands of miles of hardwood forests in this part of the State offer superb facilities for obtaining such fuel.

COPPER.

The enormous productions of native copper from Lake Superior mines are almost entirely the output of about half a dozen mines, the Calumet and Hecla producing more than half the entire output. The working mines are all situated on Keweenaw Point. The copper range, however, extends from the extremity of Keweenaw Point southwesterly, running nearly parallel to the shore of Lake Superior, to the State line, a distance of about one hundred and twenty-five miles, of varying width, but the copper bearing formation is usually several miles wide. Probably not more than forty miles of this territory have been prospected and much of that but imperfectly. The possibilities of copper production in Michigan are beyond calculation.

In addition to the formations carrying native copper on the Keweenaw Peninsula there are, in various parts of the iron and copper regions, known veins of copper ore (gray sulphurets, etc.). These veins, however, have had practically no attention, although some of them are doubtless well worth examination. and search would reveal many more.

LUMBER.

The pine lumbering industry of the upper peninsula has developed very rapidly within the past few years and is now of very considerable volume. At present this industry is confined almost entirely to the manufacture of pine, although some cedar is cut. The hardwoods are also receiving some attention, but practically the forest wealth of the upper peninsula, excepting pine, may be said to be untouched and undoubtedly the lumber business in this region has a great future before it.

GOLD.

The existence of deposits of gold-bearing veins have been known for years and one company has operated a mine and stamp mill for several years. Not enough work, however, has been done in the gold deposits to speak very positively, as yet, of their value, but considerable rock of fabulous richness has been discovered by the explorers. The gold-bearing region is generally a wilderness and but very little known. A few explorers have investigated it somewhat and report the existence of gold-bearing quartz veins, placer deposits, and also some tellurium. The future undoubtedly will have some interesting developments for the State in this direction.

SILVER.

More or less silver has always been found in the copper mines and some years ago considerable exploring was done in Ontonagon county on veins which carried more or less native silver. No thorough test of this region, however, was made and the experiments resulted in no practical demonstration either of the richness or poverty of the lodes. The formation in which this silver was found appears to be nearly as extensive as the trap range, on the northwesterly side of which it is found. Wherever it was found silver was present. The few openings made covered many miles on the length of the formation and it is not at all unlikely that veins of sufficient richness for profitable working will be found.

Veins carrying galena have been discovered in various parts of the peninsula, but thus far have had very little attention.

SLATES.

Ridges of slate are of rather frequent occurrence and many of them contain material suitable for roofing slates. Some attempts have been made to quarry these slates for the market, and although slate of magnificent quality was produced, the enterprises, for some reason, did not appear to be profitable. There has, however, been but one persistent attempt made at slate quarrying and it is likely that future efforts in this line may be more satisfactory to the operators. There are certainly many attractive looking deposits of slate and some of them will undoubtedly prove desirable for quarrying purposes.

Excellent pressed brick have been made from pulverized slate chips and this industry, added to the quarrying business, would likely make the waste product of the quarries profitable.

At many points and running with the slate have been found beds of graphite, but as yet no developments have been made in this direction and no thorough prospecting.

SANDSTONE.

About four hundred miles of the Lake Superior coast of the upper peninsula is composed of sandstone. It forms cliffs at many points on the lake from a few feet to several hundred feet in height. The formation generally extends inland for several miles. Several very profitable quarries of building sandstone have already been opened. There is a vast field for exploring and development of this industry. The stone produced from the quarries is of unsurpassed quality for building purposes. The colors are white, red, brown and variegated, the variegated being the least valuable and the most common.

GRANITE.

There are vast areas of so-called granite rocks in the upper peninsula, the greatest development of which are in the Huron Mountain region, although it is of frequent occurrence in all the counties in the west half of the peninsula. Practically no exploration for building stone has been done among the granites and, while it is supposed that granite exists of quality suitable for building material, it has not yet been demonstrated.

MICA.

Mica has been found in sufficiently large samples to lead to the expectation that workable deposits of this valuable mineral will be found in the upper peninsula.

MARBLE.

In Marquette county a range of serpentine exists from which specimens of various shades of green, veined with white and red in almost infinite variety, have been produced as samples, but no quarrying on a commercial scale has yet been done. The few specimens which have been polished are very beautiful and a brilliant future undoubtedly awaits this industry.

Dolomite is also known to exist in extensive beds. It is generally white, but in places indications of pink and light green shades have been noticed. This is a marble of which great quantities are used for building purposes, being put to both exterior and interior uses. The upper peninsula dolomite is entirely undeveloped. By burning it is said to produce a magnificent quick lime and has been used in plastering buildings near outcrops, giving great satisfaction.

LIMESTONE.

The extensive area in the upper peninsula underlaid with limestone is but little known, except on the coast where there are many ledges suitable for building purposes. In many places the action of the elements on these coast ledges has produced very picturesque scenic effects. Several thousand square miles of limestone will contribute greatly to the business prosperity of this region in the future. A few small lime kilns at various points are now manufacturing quick lime and near the Straits of Mackinaw several deposits of gypsum have been discovered.

TIMBER.

At least four-fifths of the entire area of the upper peninsula of Michigan is now timbered with pine, white cedar, hemlock, sugar maple, soft maple, black, yellow and white birch, basswood, spruce, tamarack, poplar, fir and other varieties of timber. Pine and white cedar are already extensively cut, much of it being manufactured in the district. Large quantities are also shipped out of the district in rough shape to be manufactured elsewhere. A limited quantity of maple, birch, etc., is also cut. Considerable spruce and white poplar are cut and used in the manufacture of paper. Hemlock is used somewhat for lumber, but more for mining timber. Michigan is now the greatest producer of merchantable wood of any State in the Union, but with the exception of pine the timber reserves of the upper peninsula are practically untouched; an immense and promising field for future business.

CLAYS.

In some parts of the peninsula extensive beds of clay are known, but they have as yet had little attention. There are a few small brick yards in various parts of the district, but the most promising clay beds have thus far been neglected. There are clays in the southwestern part of Houghton county from which samples have been burned, producing a very rich chocolate colored brick of superior texture. A bed of kaolinite is known in Ontonagon county, which has had a little attention. It is now owned by a pottery company in another State and is operated only to furnish a limited amount of material for special uses. Other beds of this material would undoubtedly be revealed by prospecting.

A bed of clay in Marquette county shows by analyses a composition somewhat similar to that of pozzualana, the famous Roman hydraulic cement. Clay from this bed has also been used for cheap paint, giving excellent satisfaction. This

8

bed is also unworked. Clays from the Chocolate river valley have been made into cheap pottery, producing a yellow ware of superior quality.

It is altogether likely that exploration would reveal beds of clay suitable for fine pottery and perhaps for porcelain. The decomposition of the laurentian rocks, of which immense areas are found in the upper peninsula, is likely to produce such material.

It is believed that there are materials in various parts of the peninsula suitable for the manufacture of hydraulic cement, but little or no attention has been paid to the discovery of such material.

FERTILIZERS.

Beds of marl, or diatomaceous earth, are known in several localities and exploration would undoubtedly reveal a great many such deposits. This is another undeveloped source of wealth in the upper peninsula, which will undoubtedly receive attention in the future.

PEAT.

Beds of peat are known to exist in various localities and, about 1870, a small iron furnace was constructed at Ishpeming, in which peat was used for fuel in smelting iron ore. The fuel was satisfactory, but the cost of labor at that time prevented the enterprise from becoming a commercial success.

Some of the other undeveloped resources of the upper peninsula are novaculite, of which several beds are known, and many years ago a partially successful attempt was made to work one of them, but the expense of doing the business under many disadvantageous conditions prevented its becoming a successful enterprise. The whetstones, or hones, produced were of very fine quality and commanded a high price in the market.

Beds of quartzite, suitable for use as ganister have been worked to a limited extent and these beds are capable of producing an almost unlimited quantity of this material.

Sand suitable for glass making appears, in extensive deposits, near Grand Island.

Asbestos is also known in various localities, but no attempt has yet been made to utilize it.

AGRICULTURE.

Perhaps in its soil the upper peninsula has the greatest, certainly the most enduring, of its undeveloped sources of wealth. Cultivation of the soil has had comparatively little attention in this district, but the number of farms and the cultivated area is steadily increasing. Fine crops are raised and an extensive home market with good prices is sure to produce an important development in this direction. All of the cereals, excepting Indian corn, are successfully raised, producing large crops, and the grain is of superior quality. Hay is quite extensively produced and is an easy and sure crop. All root crops, such as potatoes, beets, turnips, garden vegetables, etc., yield liberally and are of very superior quality. Many people from this and other states who are acquainted with the quality of upper peninsula potatoes annually provide themselves, if possible, with "Lake Superior potatoes." Sugar beets have been experimented with somewhat and the reports of the agricultural department show that upper peninsula beets are superior in yield, both as to quantity and quality, to any others raised in the State. Field peas have also proved a very satisfactory crop. Muck soils found in the upper peninsula have been found especially adapted to the growth of celery and this industry is rapidly becoming an extensive one in the vicinity of Newberry. This plant is successfully raised in all parts of the peninsula of a quality which has no superior.

Small fruits, such as strawberries, raspberries, whortleberries, cranberries, etc., grow in a wild state, yielding abundantly, and the tame varieties thrive unusually well under cultivation. Orchard fruits are also satisfactorily grown. Apples, pears, plums, cherries, crab-apples, etc., are successfully raised. Plums and cherries yield very abundantly.

Destructive insects, worms, etc., in other regions the pest of the farmer, are but little known here.

Stock raising has received little attention but the few experiments which have been made demonstrate that it is perfectly feasible, and it is claimed that cattle raised in this region for food, yield meat of superior quality and flavor. The use of silos will undoubtely enable the Lake Superior stock raiser of the future to compete successfully with the cattle dealers of more southern latitudes. It has long been the subject of comment that imported cattle, arriving here in poor condition, rapidly take on flesh by grazing upon the native grasses, no other food seeming to be required to produce almost marvelous results in this direction.

The most successful farmers in this region appear to be people from the north of Europe, where the same climatic conditions are found. Many of these people who arrived here only a few years ago, without means, have already achieved a competence. Their success brings others and the region is slowly becoming populated with a hardy, energetic, honest, thrifty people. The class of immigrants who engage in this industry are usually of the best and become good citizens and valuable acquisitions to the commonwealth.

The soils of the upper peninsula are almost infinite in variety, ranging from light sand through loam of various qualities to heavy, stiff clays. Much of the sandy soil has a clay sub-soil, rendering it very desirable for cultivation. Extensive tracts of muck are also found, being especially suited to the raising of celery, etc.

TRANSPORTATION.

In the matter of transportation the upper peninsula is exceptionally well situated. Nearly twenty harbors give access to the water transportation system of the great lakes, from which its products may be floated to the harbors of seven of the best states in the Union and the dominion of Canada. Four of the great railway systems of the country are represented in the peninsula and two others reach its borders. These facilities insure the best possible rates to the most desirable markets. .

The situation of the upper peninsula, lying between Lakes Michigan and Superior, and forming a great central highway through which the rapidly growing traffic between the great western states and the Atlantic seaboard must pass, make it certain that in the near future several trunk lines of railroad must traverse this region throughout its entire length. Two such systems have already been constructed and others are projected. A glance at a map of the United States will show that the natural course for the traffic between the east and the west of the northern part of the United States and the southern part of Canada is by way of the upper peninsula of Michigan. Its geographical position alone would insure a great development of all its resources. Its population has more than doubled during each of the past two decades and this increase is composed of active, energetic, pushing citizens. It is certain that a region so situated, so populated and abounding in great natural resources must have a glorious future.

Many wagon roads have already been built in this region, but many more and better roads are imperatively necessary to its best development, and, while this is perhaps not the best place to advocate the measure, it seems proper to suggest that the unemployed prisoners in the various state prisons might be employed with great profit to the commonwealth, and without interfering with the much discussed rights of honest labor, in constructing wagon roads in both peninsulas.

CLIMATE.

The climate of the upper peninsula is colder than that of regions further south, but the atmosphere is clear, bracing and invigorating. Malaria is practically unknown and its people are hardy, healthy and alert. The region has long been a Mecca for a steadily increasing number of invalids from less favored regions, who here find relief from hay fever, asthma, bronchial and pulmonary troubles. Lying within five hundred miles of the center of population of the United States, the upper peninsula of Michigan is bound to become a great summer resort, as, indeed, it already is. Inducements offered to the invalid, pleasure seeker, artist and the sportsman annually bring thousands of people from other states to enjoy its superb climate.

UPPER PENINSULA RESOURCES.

BY R. A. PARKER, C. E.

GEOGRAPHICAL.

When the classic city on the Tiber was at the zenith of her power she was the geographical center as well as the seat of government of a vast empire, the remotest parts of which were accessible by a magnificent system of highways. Though it was not strictly true that all roads led to Rome, yet the exaggeration was so little wide of the truth and at the same time so tersely descriptive of the method by which the regnant city kept in close touch with all her dependencies, that it passed unchallenged, and that "all roads led to Rome" was universally accepted as a fact. At any rate, the geographies of the day located all places with reference to the then mistress of the world, and the guide-boards or whatever served their purpose, told the traveler that in such a direction and in so many days' journey lay Rome.

The year 1893 affords a modern instance of a similar condition, so that the present moment it holds figuratively and literally true that all roads lead to the World's Fair. Chicago is the center of civilization for the time being; the Rome of a broader and nobler empire; a Rome which has achieved and maintained supremacy by the arts of peace; whose walls are the enterprise and patriotism of her people; whose conquering armies are the intellectual, industrial and commercial classes.

The mining districts of Michigan must necessarily attract many from among the hosts who visit this country and the World's Fair this year, and to them these pages modestly essay to serve as a guide. The meridian of Chicago traverses the very heart of the iron district of Michigan. The palace of mines and mining in Jackson park is on an exact north and south line with the iron mines of Ishpeming and Negaunee.

TRANSPORTATION.

Three great railway systems, the Chicago & Northwestern, Chicago, Milwaukee & St. Paul and the Wisconsin Central, reach northward from Chicago along the line of this meridian and bring all parts of the mining district within twelve to fifteen hours ride from the western metropolis. Hugging the same meridian a maritime route takes the tourist in one day from Chicago to the greatest iron port of the world, Escanaba, adding all the comforts of steamship accommodations to the delights of travel and without for a moment quitting sight of the shore panorama of undulating hills, verdant forests, smiling meadows and busy cities. A three days' prolongation of this voyage will culminate at the head of Lake Superior, after the voyager has passed through the wonderful St. Mary's canal and entered every port where can be heard the noisy rumble of the crude ores as they plunge from bins high in air through iron troughs and into the holds of great vessels for transportation to the furnaces of the east.

Another great trunk system, the Canadian Pacific, gives a direct connection with the Atlantic seaboard and the agricultural northwest. This line is also paralleled by a maritime route of unsurpassed beauty and grandeur, and traversing the entire chain of the great lakes except Lake Michigan.

Such is the peculiarly advantageous geographical situation of the upper peninsula of Michigan, a rough scalene triangle of about 20,000 square miles area, with the angles marked by Menominee, Sault Ste. Marie and the mouth of the Montreal river.

TIMBER.

Timber is almost the sole natural resource of the eastern half of the peninsula. The western half is equally rich in forests of pine and hardwoods, while in the central portion it possesses treasures in its mines of iron, copper and gold, and quarries of sandstone and marble. In time the great clay and kaoline beds will be immensely valuable. Slate is abundant and graphite is known to exist.

CLIMATE.

The climate knows neither extreme heat nor cold, thanks to the equalizing influence of the adjacent great lakes, though the district lies between the parallels of forty-five degrees and thirty minutes and forty-seven degrees and thirty minutes north latitude. The air is pure and invigorating. The water of Lake Superior is remarkable, not only for its purity, but its average temperature, being about forty-six degrees Fahrenheit. The streams afford ample power and supply for every purpose. The Dead river, near Marquette, being harnessed to a motor, furnishes electric light for municipal and household purposes.

The population of 150,000 souls is heterogeneous, owing to the comparative newness of the district and the vicissitudes of mining. But in no mining district in the world is there a population of better average intelligence and education.

HISTORICAL.

In the history of early exploration and discovery, there is a peculiar fascination, and it is especially so with regard to the famed Lake Superior regions of northern Michigan, a territory which half a century ago was marked on the map as the "unexplored country lying north of the straits of Mackinaw," but which is now the greatest iron producing region in the world, and has within its borders the Calumet & Hecla copper mine, one of the largest copper producers in the world, and the only one in which that metal is found in a pure state.

It is the purpose of this article to review not so much the wonderful development of the northern peninsula of Michigan, a peninsula nearly encircled with the greatest lakes in the world (Lake Superior on the north, with its water clear as crystal, and pure as a living spring, fringed by some of the most magnificent scenery in nature, with Lake Michigan and Green bay delightfully situated on the south), as to narrate a few of the facts and incidents concerning the discovery of this mineral wealth, the efforts of its pioneers for its development, and the settlement of this unknown region.

In 1844 the lands in this northern peninsula of Michigan had been partly surveyed into townships, but not subdivided into sections. The government surveyors engaged in dividing this territory into townships during that year carried to the east reports that it contained evidence of valuable mineral deposits, and some of these reports were of a glowing character, as is usually the case where the rich minerals of mother earth are either known or supposed to exist.

This was about the time similar reports were sent from the gold fields of California, which carried flocks of people to the Pacific coast and caused many to leave their bones bleaching upon the plains in the unsuccessful effort to reach the goal of their hopes.

These reports with regard to the copper and iron region reached the early citizens and settlers of Jackson, Michigan, which was then a small inland town, in the then sparsely settled lower peninsula, and during the long winter of 1844 and 1845, when there was little for the inhabitants of that enterprising village to busy themselves about, they canvassed the probabilities of the future wealth of the northern peninsula, and the more they canvassed that subject and speculated upon the probabilities, the brighter the visions of easily and rapidly accumulated wealth appeared, and these visions became a settled conviction in their minds that a fortune of no small proportions awaited them in this unexplored region, if they would but "go out and possess it."

Guided by these convictions, eleven residents of Jackson and one of Detroit, including Col. A. V. Berry, Frederick W. Kirkland and Philo M. Everett, formed an association called the "Jackson Mining Company," for the purpose of conducting and prosecuting the business of mining, in the mineral district so called on the south shore of Lake Superior, and for the purpose of smelting the ore of copper and other minerals to be obtained from said lands.

These enterprising men sent out exploring parties to this new and undeveloped region during the year 1845. They journeyed north by a small steamboat, that made occasional trips as far as the rapids of Sault Ste. Marie and from there by Indian canoes coasted along the south shore of Lake Superior to the north of Dead river, a stream emptying into Marquette bay, and now in the limits of the present flourishing city of Marquette. At Sault Ste. Marie they met Marji Gesick, a subchief of the Chippewa tribe of Indians, a shrewd, bright king of the forest, who possessed none of the accomplishments of polite society, but was well acquainted with every river and stream flowing into Lake Superior, and every bay and inlet along its grand and beautiful shore. These pioneers from Jackson, while at Sault Ste. Marie, succeeded in inducing Marji Gesick to guide them to the iron regions now lying in Marquette county, in this northern peninsula; and landing at the mouth of Dead river, following this Indian guide through the woods, they were taken to a high hill sloping to the north, and at its base and along the side of the hill there was an outcrop of the finest quality of gray granular iron ore that stood out to view like a quarry of granite; and at the foot of this hill and near this iron was a large, massive pine tree, about four feet in diameter, standing in the midst of a forest of hard wood.

As the government had not surveyed these lands, and they were not in market, this territory could not be purchased by these pioneers, but Congress had passed an act that where mineral territory was discovered on the lands of the government, the discoverer might obtain a mining right by applying to the war department, describing the territory as best he could, and receive from the department a certificate known as a "permit to mine," with an agreement upon the part of the government that, under certain conditions, when the land should be surveyed, the government would lease the territory to the party holding such permit.

Under these provisions of congress a mile square might thus be selected, and in order to designate the territory including this wonderful deposit of iron ore, these explorers marked this stately pine on two sides, putting their specific marks of designation on the tree, and considered that tree the center of a mile square; and the year following, Col. Berry and F. W. Kirtland, both surveyors, taking that pine tree as the center of the section, marked out the boundary of the mile square thus designated by blazed lines, and thus was located what has been known during half a century as the "Jackson Mine of Lake Superior."

As a reward for his services, Marji Gesick received from the Jackson Mining Company the following certificate:

"River Du Mort, Lake Superior, May 30th, 1846.—This may certify, that in consideration of the services rendered by Marji Gesick, a Chippewa Indian, in hunting ores of location No. 593, of the Jackson Mining Company, that he is entitled to twelve undivided thirty-one hundredth parts of the interest of said mining company in said location No. 593. A. V. Berry, President; F. W. Kirtland, Secretary."

This paper Marji Gesick kept in a little box of birch bark in his wigwam, and when he went upon fishing excursions in his canoe, carried this little box with him in the bottom of his canoe. He died at an old age in his canoe, and in this canoe this box was found by his daughter Charlotte, the wife of Charles Kobogum, now chief of the remnants of the Chippewa tribe in this northern country, who has adopted the habits of civilization and lives in a beautiful park in the outskirts of the city of Marquette, on Presque Isle Point, where he is the overseer and protector of its natural growth of trees, consisting of pines, balsam, fir, cedar, white birch, maple, beech and native shrubbery.

Charles Kobogum is over eighty years of age and is as straight as an arrow, six feet in height, with massive head and a brain that would have made him a warrior of distinction in his tribe in its warlike days, or, if reared in civilization, a commanding figure in public life. His wife Charlotte, now totally blind, is also a specimen of the native intelligence and kindly disposition of the aborigines when not goaded to revenge by outrageous treatment. Charles and his wife are now largely supported by the proceeds of a judgment collected against the Jackson Iron Company, based upon the above certificate received from the predecessor of the present company.

The records of the Jackson Iron Company showed, upon the trial of the suit brought against the company for enforcement of the right of the heirs of Marji Gesick, that up to 1884 that company had realized in dividends and surplus about nine million dollars from this iron hill, thus discovered to the pioneers in question by Marji Gesick. It is just to say that these early pioneers who discovered this mine never questioned the justice of Marji Gesick's right and were not responsible for the necessity of a lawsuit to recover them. This rich property passed from their control at an early date. The struggle to develop it upon this northern shore involved such expense, and the difficulty of bringing the product to market at that time was such that the members of the pioneer association lost their stock largely by oppressive assessments and the property passed into the hands of eastern capitalists, who refused to recognize the rights of discovery due to Marji Gesick until the supreme court of Michigan pronounced favorably upon the justice of the claim.

The Jackson mine is located about thirteen miles from the shore of Lake Superior, by the traveled route from Marquette, and though the ore was discovered in 1845 no shipments for market were made until 1856, as there were no means of transportation until that time.

While the people of Jackson, Michigan, were being awakened to the mineral wealth of this northern country, the people in old Massachusetts were also canvassing. not only the wealth of the gold fields of California, but also the mineral resources of this northern region, and at Worcester, in that state, an association was also formed consisting of Amos R. Harlow, Waterman A. Fisher, Robert J. Graveraet and Edwin Clark, to make explorations and locations similar to those proposed and made by the Jackson parties, and Mr. Harlow, as the first agent of that association, landed at the mouth of Carp river on July 6, 1849, having coasted from Sault Ste. Marie in an Indian canoe, leaving his wife and family at Sault Ste. Marie, to follow him. The purpose of this association was not only to locate iron, but to smelt it, and certain government leases were procured by this company covering the territory now known as the mine of the Lake Superior Iron Company, then under the name of the "Briggs lease," and also the Cleveland mine, also held under what was known as the "Moody lease," all procured from the war department of the government. This association erected a forge on Marquette bay, on Lake Superior, upon the site of the now beautiful city of Marquette, located upon one of the most beautiful bays in the world, a bay often likened by European travelers to that of Naples. Marquette is a city of beauty as it rises from the water by undulating ground, with a landscape background of towering hills, well deserving the name of mountains.

The Jackson Iron Company also located a forge within two miles of its mining location about the same time the Marquette Iron Company (the association from Massachusetts) located its forge on the shores of Lake Superior. These smelting enterprises were neither of them financially successful, but served the purpose of testing the ores and pointing out to capital the great wealth of the region, and were therefore pioneer enterprises of the greatest importance to the country. In speaking of these forges and their early history the Hon. Peter White, of

9

Marquette, one of its earliest settlers and today one of the most prominent men in the State, described Marquette as follows: "A few houses, a stumpy road winding along the lake shore, a forge which burnt up after impoverishing its first owners, a trail westward just passable for wagons leading to another forge (still more unfortunate in that it did not burn up) and to the undeveloped iron hills beyond, a few hundred people uncertain of the future, they were all that was in Marquette in 1851-2."

For many years after the discovery of the Jackson, Lake Superior and Cleveland mines, they were the only ones operated, and together in 1861 shipped about one hundred tons of ore; whereas during the year last passed there has been shipped from these iron regions of the north over nine million tons, and the greater portion of it from that part of the territory known as the northern peninsula of Michigan, some of it from the new bordering fields of Wisconsin and Minnesota.

The early pioneers to whom we have referred struggled against privation, as is almost universally the case where man enters nature's sanctum and wrests from her her privacy. These men have lived to see the wonderful growth in the mineral industries which they had so much to do with bringing to the attention of the capital of the country, and to see the wilderness blossom into prosperous cities, and to behold the development of mighty industries, which is one of the rewards to the pioneer who has braved privations and hardships upon the frontier, a pleasure that those schooled and housed in luxury, and who know nothing of pioneer life, cannot realize.

THE COPPER COUNTRY.

"Let it not be thought that I am cracking up the country," wrote John R. St. John in 1849, prefatory to a book he published descriptive of the copper country of Lake Superior, its climate, resources and development to that date. If his modest little book was deemed incomplete then without an apology for its seeming exaggeration, what would the author say could he witness the achievements of this year, 1893, scarce half a century later! The "giant corporations" of his day were the Lake Superior Mining Co., and the Pittsburg and Boston Co., operating upon fissure veins in Keweenaw county. The Agate Harbor, Eagle Harbor, and other mines long ago abandoned as worthless were then considered rich mines. Nowhere was there a shaft exceeding eighty feet in depth. One company had a very crude and diminutive open air stamp-mill. It was spoken of as erected at a great expense and a failure as to its returns on the investment. But though almost utterly deserted now, Old Keweenaw can justly be said to be only hibernating. In the springtide of a new era she will awaken under the stimulus of railway extension and closer contact with the world, which will bring her resources into greater prominence; for, although thrown into the shade by her great rival, the Portage Lake district, her reservoirs of mineral wealth are by no means pumped dry.

The story of Michigan copper mining is old and very romantic. It extends back as far as the history of the country and throws a ray of light into the prehistoric darkness. A race of intelligent beings mined copper systematically long before the savage Indian possessed himself of the territory. Their traces were most distinct on Isle Royal and in the Ontonagon district. They consisted of pits in which were found detached masses of metal, some of great weight accompanied by crude implements whose form left no doubt of their use as mining tools. In one instance a mass was found lying upon a substructure consisting of layers of timbers placed crosswise, evidently for the purpose of lifting the mass to the surface. A shallow pit found on the outcrop of the Calumet and Hecla conglomerate in the earliest days of that mine was believed to have been made by those prehistoric miners. The museums and private collections of the country now contain all that was found of the implements, and the operations of modern miners have obliterated the excavations of the ancients.

The written history of the Lake Superior copper district may be said to begin with "Legardes Travels," a book published in Paris in 1636, and containing the first mention of copper on Lake Superior, the *Lac de Tracy*, and the only one for many subsequent generations. Speaking of the lake's south shore, he says: "There are mines of copper which might be made profitable if there were inhabitants and workmen who would labor faithfully." He speaks of having seen an ingot of copper procured from the Huron Indians, meaning by "ingot" doubtless a small mass of native copper. The Jesuit fathers who penetrated the region thirty years later were alive to the resources of the country as well as the state of the savage souls. They made careful note of the metals found in possession of the aborigines and their journals published in Paris contain frequent mention of large pieces of refined copper; not at all remarkable as the native copper of Lake Superior was as highly refined in nature's furnace as any that could be produced by the art of the metallurgist of 1660 to 1700. One writer in 1640 speaks "of a large island in Lake Superior fifty leagues in circuit upon which was found a beautiful mine of copper." The island was Isle Royale and the beautiful mine was the pit dug by the prehistoric miner, and within the present generation wrought as the Minong mine. Doctor Ben Franklin had read these old French manuscripts and books while resident in Paris, a fact which he turned to practical account when he became one of the commissioners to settle the northern boundary of the United States. With apparent unconcern he drew his pencil over the map of Lake Superior so as to leave Isle Royale on the United States side of the line, and so it was ratified.

In 1765 one Capt. Carver published a somewhat fanciful account of a journey from Mackinaw to the Mississippi, and upon the representations of his book the first company was organized in London to mine copper on Lake Superior. Alexander Henry, a gentlemen of adventurous spirit, became the agent and historian of this enterprise. He began operations in the side of a clay bank on the shore of the Ontonagon river in 1770. After digging through forty feet of clay he ran up sharp against sandstone, and left further operations to those who could guide their attempts to gain copper by the use of at least a little knowledge of geology.

To Dr. Douglas Houghton, the first State Geologist of Michigan, the State and the world owe the development of the copper mining industry. He it was who first intelligently explored the district and reduced the geologic data he obtained into such form and system that the miner knew approximately where and how to look for copper. He began his researches in 1830, and devoted to it all his energy until the melancholy tragedy of 1845 put a sudden and premature end to a life that was invaluable to civilization. He was drowned during a violent storm near Eagle river on the night of Oct. 13, 1845. He was almost ready to make his final report and with him were lost all his field notes.

It was Boston capital that first undertook the development of the copper region after Henry's failure, and it is Boston capital that today holds the predominant interest in the mines.

The organization of companies and location of permits were begun in 1842. Actual work was for some years confined to the extremety of Keweenaw point. Some good mines, notably the Cliff, Phœnix and Copper Falls, were opened on the fissure veins. The only mine now operating on a fissure vein is the Central, a mine which has yielded handsome dividends and is still profitable. The Copper Falls mine maintains a sporadic activity, but its operations are confined to the "ashbed" and amygdaloid lode lying along the formation. Some exploring had been done at Portage Lake near the site of the Quincey mine in 1846–47, but that district did not come into prominence until 1860. The Quincey then began the pace which took her to the front rank of amygdaloid mines, a position she still maintains without a rival.

Operations on the Ontonagon began in a very small way in 1843, but it was not until 1847, when the discovery of the Minnesota lode brought the district into prominence, that mining began to be conducted there on a large scale. The discovery of the Calumet and Hecla conglomerate lode in 1866 marked an epoch in copper mining, and another epoch was marked when in June, 1885, the bold conception of Captain John Daniell was brought to successful fruition. That was the cutting of the Calumet and Hecla lode at a verticle depth of 2,270 feet by the Tamarack shaft. The event provided the Calumet and Hecla a means of measuring its resources; but, better still, it demonstrated the possibility and profit of deep mining.

Such, in brief, is a ragged outline of the history of the Lake Superior copper region. Its details are fraught with the incidents of the most interesting character, but there is not space for them here.

COPPER PRODUCTION.

Up to January 1, 1892, the Lake Superior copper mines produced a grand total of 1,400,031,411 pounds of refined copper, and are now producing nearly twenty per cent of the world's supply. The vein matter as it comes from the mines now being wrought with profit, varies from seven-eighths of one per cent (the average at the Atlantic mine) to five per cent. After passing through the stamp mills the resulting product, in the local vernacular called "mineral," separated from its matrix by the action of ponderous steam hammers and water, is concentrated by jigs and Evans tables and goes to the smelters 85 per cent fine and there reduced to commercial copper in the form of bars, plates and ingots. In view of its remarkable purity and freedom from base metals, is it any wonder that Lake Superior copper is given the preference the world over for all purposes requiring a superior grade of the metal.

In 1891* the copper production of the Lake Superior districts was 109,370,000 pounds, furnished by the principal mines as follows:

Calumet & Hecla	65,000,000	Peninsula	1,609,689
Quincy	10,300,000	Copper Falls	1,450,000
Tamarack	10,199,415	Central	1,329,000
Osceola	6,425,740	Allouez	1,227,000
Franklin	4,253,575	Huron	1,215,734
Atlantic	3,648,000	Other mines	990,772
Kearsarge	1,731,075		
Total			109,370,000

* The statistics for 1892 at this writing are not available.

VALUE.

The proceeds from the sale of this stupendous output of copper cannot be very readily calculated, the fluctuations of the copper market ranging between a maximum of something over 60 cents per pound to a minimum of a trifle less than 9 cents. Some conception of the profits can be best gained from a statement of the dividends declared by the principal mining companies now in operation. In addition to this, it must be borne in mind that the majority of these companies are in possession of the most approved modern plants, which have cost vast fortunes; also immense tracts of real estate acquired at comparatively low prices and now capable of realizing in cash many times the purchase price, to say nothing of the various other valuable assets and the stores of mineral still untouched.

The list of the active dividend payers, with the amounts paid by each to Feb. 1, 1893, is as follows:

Mine.	Dividend paid.	Mine.	Dividend paid.
Atlantic	$700,000	Osceola	$1,607,500
Calumet & Hecla	38,850,000	Kearsarge	80,000
Central	1,970,000	Quincy	6,470,000
Franklin	1,100,000	Tamarack	3,160,000
Total			$54,027,500

To these same mines there has been paid in assessments the sum total of $3,190,000.

To the total dividends, as above indicated, add the amounts paid by the great dividend payers of the pre-Portage period—the Cliff, $2,280,000; Minnesota, $1,820,000, total, $4,100,000—and we have a grand total of $58,127,500. There are numerous other mines that, though never or but for a short time on the dividend list, have nevertheless greatly enriched those interested in them by their output and the amounts realized upon their available assets.

COST OF MINING.

Only the most careful and intelligent management can wrest a profit from copper mining at the prices prevailing during the past five years, except in case of mines which, like the Calumet and Hecla, are in a position to almost dictate the market value of the metal. Some of the best results are achieved in mines like the Atlantic. Though that mine's vein in matter averages but seven-eighths per cent mineral, the mine has steadily maintained a dividend of $1.00 per share yearly and has lately entered upon an immense construction account involving the building of a new stamp mill and railroad. The Tamarack is one of the cheapest producers, and it has been said that company can sell its product in New York at six cents per pound and make a profit. In 1890 that company actually accomplished the feat of producing and marketing copper at 5.9 cents per pound. But $11\frac{1}{2}$ cents per pound represents about the maximum of cost in mines now operating; in fact a higher cost would necessitate suspension of operation or continuation at a loss. The Calumet and Hecla and the Tamarack, Osceola combination (the latter controlling the Tamarack, Tamarack Jr., Osceola and Kearsarge mines and known locally as the Clark-Bigelow syndicate), have effected a great saving in their cost sheet by erecting smelting works of their own, and their example is about to be followed by the Quincy.

It is known that the veins that follow the formation extend to a great depth, far beyond any yet attained, and that the copper in them is more evenly distributed than in the fissure veins which also extend to unknown depths but are so irregular and "faulted" as to render necessary a greater relative amount of "dead work."

The formation extends in a slightly sinuous course from northeast to southwest, the strata dipping northwestward at an average angle of about forty-two degrees. On its western side lies Lake Superior, while on the east it rests upon the Potsdam sandstone. The average width is about 14,000 feet and the length about six miles. The main body is a lava formed rock called "trap" in which are imbedded the amygdaloids and conglomerates which now form the commercial sources of supply, with the single exception of the Central mine which, as has been stated, is on a famous fissure vein crossing the formation at right angles.

The copper is disseminated in the form of masses, sheet copper, "barrel work," and fine copper. Some masses have been formed many tons in weight and have had to be cut with chisels into smaller bodies in order to permit removal from their matrix. This process is laborious and tedious, and instances are on record where in old times the discovery of a mass has been too much of a good thing, the cost of getting it to the surface exceeding the value of the metal. Masses and sheet copper are largest and most numerous in the fissure veins. Sheet copper is found in large flat pieces, generally very thin, but sheets have been found eight inches in thickness. "Barrel work" consists of lumps of metal from the size of a fist to that of a foot ball and of ragged pieces too large to run through the stamp mill. The formation on Isle Royale is the reverse of that on Keweenaw Point as to relative position of the strata, sloping southeasterly and indicating the continuity of the Keweenaw stratification, Lake Superior occupying the depression. The strata are mose nearly horizontal, however, rarely tilting over thirty degrees.

Though the prehistoric miner seems to have wrought successfully in that field, his latter day successor has been unable to wrest any great wealth from Isle Royale. It has not been through lack of endeavor, for explorations are still under way. The intermediate Indian avoided the island whenever he could, believing it to be the abode of the "Gitchi Manitou," or Great Spirit.

THE IRON COUNTRY.

Three well defined districts—ranges—constitute the source of the Michigan iron ore supply. They lie in the western half of the northern peninsula and trend nearly east and west. They are designated in the order of discovery and development, the Marquette, Menominee and Gogebic ranges.

They each have a number of exceptionally large producing mines. The Marquette range in 1892 produced 2,606,856 tons of ore from twenty-eight operating mines, or an average of 95,000 tons from each; the Menominee range produced 2,261,499 tons from twenty-nine operating mines, or an average of 78,000 tons; while that portion of the Gogebic range lying wholly within the limits of this State produced 2,563,229 gross tons (the balance of this range upon the Wisconsin side of Montreal river shipped 405,764 tons) from seventeen reporting operations, or an average of 151,000 tons for each enterprise. Of course this enormous average output is due to the phenominal deposits operated by the Metropolitan Land & Iron Company and generally known as the Norrie and East Norrie mines, which have made the hitherto unapproached output from an all underground mine of 985,216 tons. Its total output since 1885 has been 4,114,623 tons, or an average of over half a million tons per annum, including the year of its discovery. There are only three mines in this State whose output exceeds that of this mine, and the youngest of the three, the Chapin, is over thirteen years old and has shipped 4,367,344 gross tons. The Lake Superior mine has shipped, including output of 1892, 5,718,007, and the Cleveland mine 5,027,606 gross tons.

GENERAL GEOLOGY.

These several deposits of iron ore in the upper peninsula have thus far been found only in the Huronian series of rocks. This series consists of quartzites, schists, banded ore and jaspers, greenstones, limestones and iron ore, and contains in all, according to Brooks, twenty distinct members.

The Marquette region embraces the Huronian rocks, extending from the city of the same name westward to L'Anse, a distance of about forty miles, and contains all the iron mines that shipped ore previous to 1877. Geologically, the strata form a broad synclinal trough corrugated and folded in the direction of its axis, resting upon Laurentian rocks. The general trend of the formation is east and west, with the exception of a tongue of Huronian rocks south of Lake Michigamme and extending into the Laurentian, in which the Republic mine is located, and an isolated patch about twenty miles south of Marquette in which the Cheshire mine is found. The mines of this region are in one comparatively compact belt. The most easterly of the deposits of ore known (except the Cheshire) are in the Negaunee basin, about a mile west of that town; the ores are of the soft hematite nature, readily mined and occur in enormous deposits. At the Buffalo company's property the ore was found to lie in a basin having a pitch to the north and west. This basin consisted of hematite and banded jasper schists. Hard hematite first shows itself in the Jackson mine immediately west of the Negaunee. Here the basin holding the hard hematites is narrow but widens towards the west, and at Michigamme lake the northern and southern veins are three miles apart. The first occurrence of magnetite is at the old Washington property, just south of the village of Humboldt, thirteen miles west of Negaunee. At this locality specular hematite, or slate ore, is also present in considerable quantities, but further west the ore mass is almost entirely magnetite.

The mines of Ishpeming, which lie about three miles west of Ishpeming, are famed for the quality and continuous output they have made, and are the main reliance upon which the reputation of this range will depend for years to come. Beginning their shipments a few years after the Jackson, they have maintained a regularity and uniformity of product that is nothing short of wonderful, and what is of full as much importance, they give every evidence of their ability to maintain their output for many more years. The names of the larger producers are familiar as household words the iron world over. Lake Angeline's phenomenally high percentage of iron and exceedingly low phosphorus gives it a unique position. The Cleveland and Lake Superior have been sending their high grade ores to the eastern furnaces for over thirty years. Barnum, Salisbury, Winthrop and Mitchell are in the list of active producers and will remain there in spite of predictions made by those interested in newer ranges.

The hard ore mines, specular slate and magnetite, of the western end of the county (from the Republic and Champion mines) have been the standards of their respective classes for about twenty years, and their total output foots up in the millions of tons. Mining of these ores is accomplished by ways and means to which the peculiar nature of the deposits lend themselves. For instance, at the Buffalo group, the North-of-England, or caving system, is adopted and operated with marked success, both in the cost of product and amount of ore recovered, the losses being very light. In this system of mining the ore body is cut into prisms by raises and drifts. In the center of a block of ore a winze is raised and up to the crushed and broken roof of rock and timbers, a horizontal cut is then taken from the top of the ore body for say eight to ten feet in height, and starting from the edge furthest from the mill-hole or winze, the ore is drawn, thus allowing the roof of sand and rock to fall upon a floor of solid ore, which had, before the roof fall, been covered with logging of old mine timbers, poles, slabs, etc., by means of which protection the roof, in course of a few falls becomes a woven mattress of timber, which keeps the surface sands from mixing with and thus lowering the grade of the ore.

In other mines, when the covering of rock will not fall regularly 'as it does here and the ore body is soft, the Nevada system of timbering is used. This consists in large posts from two to three feet in diameter, so framed as to form the skeleton of a cube. These frames reach from one side of the deposit to the other and offer a means of attacking and removing the ore and at the same time supporting the roof; at intervals pillars of ore are left in the mine to help support the roof and keep it from caving in unexpectedly. When the roof is about to fall, it is shown by the pressure of one set of timbers upon another, a "cap" or piece of timber resting upon and connecting two posts, being at times cut half through by the weight it is bearing. This is the warning given the miner to keep out of harm's way. In bodies of soft ore the evidence of these timbers bearing great weight is very frequently seen, but it is not necessarily a signal of danger, for these crushed, bent or broken timbers are often removed while the ore remains in place and a new set of timbers put in. These very often hold the passage ways open, as the movement of the ore may have taken place previous to the placing of the later timbers. In some mines this renewal of timber is constantly going on to keep main gangways open. Sometimes two gangways, or levels, are maintained to insure access to the shaft at all times, or during repair of one of the levels, which of course would be apt to stop work at the point of repair for the time being.

The removal of the pillars, after the sets of timbers have been placed in position, then follows. This is done in the case of some of the Gogebic mines by cutting into the center of the pillar at right angles to its length and directly across it, then driving a drift in the direction of its main axis, i. e., at right angles to this cut, to the hanging wall, and drawing back from this wall timbering to support the ore above. Two sets, or fifteen feet, are taken off in this manner, and if the wall shows signs of weakening, the ore is logged up and the place vacated for a week, when, after the fall of rocks, the same general scheme of removal takes place.

In hard magnetite and specular hematite ore mines the ore occurs in lens or bean shaped masses, and is removed by aid of power or air drills. No timber of any amount is called for in these mines, save in places where the walls are largely composed of a talcose schist, or soaprock as it is locally termed. These places are treacherous and large masses are apt to fall if heavy timbers are not placed to support them. These timbers are of all lengths, depending on the distances between the foot and hanging walls, and are usually of pine; hemlock is being used at times, but it is heavier and somewhat brashy, breaking across the grain under heavy stress.

This outline of the uses of timber and method of mining will serve as a description of the three ranges, with the exception of a few of the hard ore mines which have a solid and compact hanging wall or roof requiring no timbers for support, such as the Barnum mine, whose workings lie directly under the main streets of the city of Ishpeming. Little does the average visitor to this city think, as he walks the streets or rides in the railroad or electric cars, that hundreds of feet below him is another city with its streets laid out with greatest care by the engineer, whose cars are running day and night, and where the electric light burns practically twenty-four hours each day; and yet such is a fact. It is a sight that should not be missed, as an opportunity to visit and inspect the mines is usually accorded to the inquiring and intelligent traveler.

In this summary of the ores of the Marquette range, it is seen there is every known variety found within its limits. Large beds of limonite are known to exist in the vicinity of Michigamme, but owing to the low metallic contents, averaging fifty-three to fifty-six per cent, they will not stand the cost of lake transportation. Many of the mines possess immense reserves of low grade oar, which cannot be shipped for the same reason. The question then naturally occurs, why not utilize them at some point where fuel can be cheaply obtained, and where the ore can be brought to the furnace at low cost? Marquette, with its harbor and shipping facilities, offers more inducement to the steel and iron manufacturer than any other point on the lake, Chicago not excepted, as the same materials can be assembled at a lower cost than at that or any other lake city. Coke has been made from Connelsville, Pennsylvania, coal, of eminently satisfactory quality, and can be made at a cost about equal to that paid by Chicago. Vessels loading with ore from this point to Lake Erie ports will carry a return cargo of Connelsville coal at rates varying from thirty-five cents to forty cents per ton. Ores of every kind and grade for foundry or steel mixtures are available by a short twelve to twenty mile haul, the shortest to a manufacturing point, from any of the ranges. By using low grade ores, i. e., from fifty-two (furnace yield) to fifty-eight per cent, obtaining them at a price far below the normal market, with a short haul, and coke made upon the ground, utilizing the waste heat from the ores, there is no point today in the central west that can produce as high grade pig metal at the same cost as can be done here. This is worthy the serious consideration of all interested in the production of pig iron, and figures are to be had which will demonstrate the truth of this statement.

Menominee range lies about forty miles south of the Marquette range, runs about parallel with it, and is separated from it by a horizon of Laurentian granites, gneisses and schists. It includes two ranges of iron ore, separated by a belt of

silicious dolomite. In the southern range of deposits the iron ore consists principally of a soft specular, blue (red) hematite which runs high in iron and low in
phosphorus. Although quite soft the ore rarely changes color except on handling,
when it soon becomes coated with its own red powder; by the time the ore reaches
Cleveland, its texture is ·apparently earthy. The ore usually occurs in irregular
pockets or lens-shaped masses in a banded quartzose ferruginous schist, which is
often magnetic, and thus enables the ranges to be traced with the dip-needle.
The ore itself does not affect the compass needle.

The Chapin mine at Iron Mountain is the phenomenal property upon this range.
This reputation has been acquired by reason of the enormous size of the deposit,
its high grade and its reducability in the furnace owing to its peculiarly combined
elements, which have made it a general favorite with furnace men. The deposit
is lens-shaped in plan; that is, it appears as two wedges placed back to back. It
varies from three feet at the extreme ends to something over a hundred feet in the
widest portions, and is about two thousand feet long. It has been continuously
operated since 1880 when it sent to market 34,556 gross tons of ore. Its total output is over four million tons, and it has reserves which will enable it to maintain
its position as the leading shipper of this range for many years. To put before the
reader an illustration that may be grasped by the imagination it may be stated
that to convey the total product of this one mine in railroad cars, such as are used
for carrying ore from the mines to the docks, would require a train of 218,367
20-ton cars, which at twenty-three feet in length would cover a distance of 5,022,441
feet, or 951 miles. About the distance between New York city and Chicago.

The Gogebic range deposits vary in their mode of occurrence and contents from
those of the other two that have been described. The same series of rocks are
found, but occur in a reverse order. For instance, while quartzite forms the hanging wall of the Marquette ores, it is the foot wall of the Gogebic. Lying upon
the granites and schists of the Laurentian rocks, the Huronian quartzite dips to the
north at an angle of sixty to sixty-five degrees; north and conformable to this are
banded jasper schists varying in thickness from 600 to 1,500 feet; north of this are the
red and black slates. Then follow the traps and conglomerates from the northeast,
in which, at Keweenaw Point, the great native copper mines are located.

The ore is found lying in a V shaped trough, the left leg of the V being quartzite, the right a more or less decomposed diorite dyke, which are found underlying
each other and cutting through the ore formation to the granites, the covering or
capping of the ore being the banded jasper schist. The probable origin of the ore
has been closely studied by Prof. J. R. VanHise, of the University of Wisconsin.
Briefly, it is the result of a concentration of the ore that decomposition of the
banded jasper schists has liberated. Exploration has proved the existence of four
or five of these dykes upon which ore in varying amounts has been found.

In several places the ore came to the surface, and notably at the Colby mine at
Bessemer and the Aurora mine at Ironwood, where large quantities were obtained
at a very low mining cost. The ore is very uniform physically and chemically. It
is a soft red hematite with moisture varying from five to fourteen per cent; a typical
analysis of the better grade would be sixty-three per cent of iron, five per cent of
silica and about thirty-five thousandths per cent phosphorus. The general mode of
mining is by means of rooms and pillars, the ground being supported by sets of timbers
as elsewhere described. At the Brotherton mine the caving system has been used

since the opening of the property, and it has proved economical and safe and yields a large percentage of the ore. The ore is sent mainly to Ashland (forty miles west of Ironwood) docks when it is sent by lake to Cleveland, Ashtabula (Ohio ports), or to Buffalo, N. Y., for transportation to the furnaces of the Ohio valley and Pittsburg.

IRON PRODUCT BY RANGES.

The product of these three ranges is shipped from Marquette, Gladstone, Escanaba, Michigan, and Ashland, Wisconsin. A small quantity is sent by rail to the dock at St. Ignace. Considerable ore is locally used and cast into pig at the charcoal furnaces of Ishpeming, Negaunee, Marquette and Newberry.

The aggregate production of the three ranges, exclusive of the mines in Wisconsin, is shown in the following tables. The mines named in the tables are those which have produced upwards of 100,000 long tons each.

MARQUETTE RANGE.

Name of mine.	Output previous to 1892.	Output for 1892.	Totals.
Lake Superior	5,351,292	366,715	5,718,007
Cleveland	4,716,699	310,907	5,027,606
Republic	3,739,094	167,991	3,907,085
Jackson	3,162,615	92,567	3,255,182
*Iron Cliffs	2,427,693	289,385	2,717,078
Champion	2,654,527	109,979	2,764,506
Pittsburg & Lake Angeline	2,044,062	287,517	2,331,579
†Buffalo	1,155,932	379,719	1,535,651
‡Winthrop	1,199,799	191,658	1,391,457
New York	1,055,395	11,220	1,066,615
Volunteer	753,646	127,130	880,776
Michigamme	872,719	1,894	874,613
Humboldt	717,093	4,571	721,664
Cambria	623,871	41,549	665,420
Lucy (McComber)	445,990	26,326	472,316
Saginaw	451,424		451,424
Milwaukee	375,431		375,431
Negaunee	269,587	85,846	355,433
Lillie	262,521	29,005	291,526
Samson (Argyle)	267,205	600	267,805
Rolling Mill	234,625		234,625
Cheshire (Swanzy)	161,997	29,403	191,400
East New York	130,157	35,175	165,332
Spurr	164,244		164,244
Marquette	143,352	9,555	152,907
National	150,216		150,216
Detroit	140,841		140,841
West Republic	133,077		133,077
American	97,857	15,076	112,933
Other mines	1,332,774	53,058	1,385,832
Grand totals	35,250,735	2,666,856	37,917,591

*Consolidation of Barnum, Salisbury, Cliffs Shaft and Foster.
†Schlesinger group.
‡Braastad group.

MENOMINEE RANGE.

Name of mine.	Output previous to 1892.	Output for 1892.	Totals.
Chapin	3,707,292	660,052	4,367,344
Vulcan	1,488,750	179,904	1,668,654
Norway	1,246,585	44,767	1,291,352
Ludington	985,278	15,777	1,001,055
Iron River	903,411	1,176	904,587
Dunn	614,285	133,666	747,951
Curry	291,155	125,773	416,928
Perkins	394,064	----------	394,064
Mastodon	369,250	9,150	378,400
Great Western	284,952	87,487	372,439
Aragon	145,983	167,948	313,931
Cyclops	284,396	1,697	286,093
Quinnesec	283,323	----------	283,323
Sheldon & Shafer	196,498	57,682	254,621
Paint River	203,981	18,390	222,371
Pewabic	91,498	115,273	206,771
Youngstown	150,751	----------	150,751
Mansfield	68,139	69,259	137,398
Nanaimo	127,566	----------	127,566
Millie (Hewitt)	109,121	6,780	115,901
Monitor	69,713	42,819	112,532
Hemlock	35,531	65,459	100,990
Other mines	498,016	161,081	659,097
Grand totals	12,550,009	1,961,140	14,511,149

GOGEBIC RANGE.

Name of mine.	Output previous to 1892.	Output for 1892.	Totals.
Norrie	3,129,407	985,216	4,114,623
Ashland	1,371,952	231,896	1,603,848
Colby	1,255,059	304,241	1,559,300
Aurora	964,972	319,482	1,284,454
Pabst	507,626	113,245	620,871
Newport	379,070	165,962	545,032
Cary	293,931	106,484	400,415
Brotherton	251,567	130,833	382,400
Palms	129,215	102,382	231,597
Anvil	127,514	42,090	169,604
Sunday Lake	101,417	56,046	157,463
Other mines	321,534	79,001	400,535
Grand totals	8,833,264	2,636,878	11,470,142

AGGREGATE PRODUCTION OF MICHIGAN MINES.

Name of range.	Previous to 1892.	1892.	Totals.
Marquette range	35,250,735	2,666,856	37,917,591
Menominee range	12,550,009	1,964,140	14,514,149
Gogebic range	8,833,264	2,636,878	11,470,142
Grand totals	56,634,008	7,267,874	63,901,882

The rate of production indicated by the foregoing tables would seem at a casual glance to fix not a very remote limit to the supply. But the recent successful ventures in deep mining, and the now well established fact that many of the lenses of ore continue to great depths, the immense area still awaiting a thorough exploration, and the promise of electrical concentration to render valuable the all but inexhaustible stores of lean ore, place the limit beyond calculation.

By the Edison process of electrical concentration iron ore containing but twenty per cent metallic iron has been profitably treated and raised to a grade of seventy per cent, or within two per cent of chemically pure magnetite, while the phosphorus has been reduced so as to permit the use of such concentrates for still making. One carload at the experimental station near Humboldt attained seventy-one and four-tenths per centum of iron. The station was consumed by fire in 1891 while experiments were still in progress. It is understood, however, that Mr. Edison regards the process as an established success and has effected a lease of the Spurr mine near Michigamme for the purpose of beginning the concentration of ores on a commercial scale.

THE SHIPPING PORTS.

The Lake Superior region furnished nearly 55 per cent of all the ore mined in the United States in 1892, and of that quantity Michigan furnished 86 per cent. In no other part of the world are there equal facilities for the handling and transportation of such vast quantities of ore. A practically all-water route from the mine to the furnaces makes possible the transportation of ores in great bulks. In fact, but for this provision of nature, the district would be almost worthless on account of the prohibitory cost of railway transportation in carload lots. The great extent of coast line and its deep indentations afford a number of fine harbors which have been equipped expressly for the handling of iron ore. A brief account of these harbors will be of interest.

The first Lake Superior iron ore was shipped from Marquette early in the fifties, and up to the close of 1892 a total of 18,614,203 tons had passed from its docks into the holds of vessels. The amount shipped in 1892 was 1,027,323 tons. Until 1879 Marquette held the lead in quantity of ore handled, but in that year Escanaba gained it. Three docks, one recently built and another greatly extended, together with their incidental rolling stock, constitute the equipment for transferring the ore from the cars into the holds of lake carriers. No. 4 dock, built in 1889-90, is a specimen of the most modern and perfect structure of its class, and cost $250,000. It was fully described and illustrated with the designer's drawings in the New York Engineering and Mining Journal of January 10 and 17, 1891. Herewith is a brief description of the three docks, all owned by the Duluth, South Shore & Atlantic Railway Company:

No. 1. Height of dock above water 42 feet for first 1,300 feet of its length; the new extension of 600 feet is 44 feet above water; number of pockets, 270; number of tracks, 3; capacity, 27,000 long tons.

No. 2. This was a small and antiquated structure; in 1892 it was dismantled and a merchandise pier was erected on the piles.

No. 3. Height of dock above water, 44 feet; length, 1,600 feet; number of pockets, 300; number of tracks, 3; capacity, 25,000 long tons.

No. 4. Height above water, 47.5 feet; length, 1,400 feet; number of pockets, 200; number of tracks, 4; capacity, 30,000 long tons.

L'Anse became an ore shipping port in 1873 by the building of a dock, owned by the D. S. S. & A. Railroad Company, for the handling of the product from the west end of Marquette range. The dock is 38 feet high, 1,000 feet long, contains 100 pockets and has a capacity of 8,000 long tons. No ore has been shipped thence since 1885; the total reached 744,607 tons.

St. Ignace has been a shipping port on a small scale since 1882, and has handled 610,315 tons of ore. In 1891 the dock was shortened 400 feet, the material being removed to Marquette for the extension of dock No. 1 there. As constructed, it was 800 feet long, 42 feet high; contained 100 pockets and 3 tracks, and had a capacity of 10,000 long tons.

Escanaba has maintained the lead she won in 1879 and her aggregate tonnage of iron ore in 1891 and 1892 led the world. Shipments began in 1865 by putting the Marquette range under tribute; in 1877 the new Menominee range began to empty her treasures into the lap of the coming iron port of the world; in 1892 her shipments were 4,012,197 tons, nearly half the entire ore shipment of the whole Lake Superior region, and the stupendous total of 33,-875,451 tons of iron ore has passed through her gates en route to lower lake receiving ports. The Chicago & Northwestern railway company is the owner of the five immense docks at Escanaba. These docks, together with their equipment of cars, cost $2,200,000, and are described as follows:

No. 1. Height, 46 feet; length, 1,104 feet; pockets, 184; tracks, 2; capacity, 23,000 long tons.

No. 2. Height, 39 feet; length 1,082 feet; pockets, 192; tracks, 2; capacity, 19,300 long tons.

No. 3. Height, 39 feet; length, 1,212 feet; pockets, 202; tracks, 2; capacity, 20,000 long tons.

No. 4. Height, 46 feet; length 1,500 feet; pockets, 250; tracks, 2; capacity, 33,200 long tons.

No. 5. Height, 51 feet. 10 inches; length, 1,392 feet; pockets, 232; tracks, 2; capacity, 40,000 long tons.

At Ashland the Wisconsin Central railroad has one dock 46 feet high, 1,404 feet long, with 234 pockets, 3 tracks, and a capacity of 28,250 long tons. With its equipments the total cost was $644,000. The Milwaukee, Lake Shore and Western has two docks there, one 40 and the other 45 feet high, each 1,404 feet long, with 234 pockets; one has 4 and the other 3 tracks; their capacity respectively is 23,000 and 27,000 long tons. The total cost of equipment was $813,000.

Gladstone, Michigan, shares with Escanaba the care of the Menominee range product, and an occasional cargo of Gogebic and Marquette ore goes out of that port. Shipments began in 1889, and attained an aggregate of 458,711 tons at the end of 1892. The Minneapolis, Sault Ste. Marie & Atlantic (Soo line) is the owner of the dockage facilities, which consist of one dock 47 feet high, about 1,200 feet in length, with 120 pockets, 5 tracks and a capacity of 16,000 long tons.

The docks are all wooden structures. The upper dock or floor is from 40 to 50 feet above water level, sufficient to accommodate bins of 15 to 20 feet depth with outward sloping bottoms below the floor level, and yet high enough to be well above the rail of the largest vessel lying alongside. Plate iron chutes or spouts are hinged beneath small doors at the bottom of the pockets. The doors are controlled from the top of the dock, and when opened they discharge the ore through the chutes into the hold of the vessel. In this manner a cargo of three thousand tons is often loaded in three hours. As many pockets can be simultaneously discharged as there are hatchways in the vessels. As the principal mining companies are the owners of fleets of modern and capacious lake carriers employed exclusively in the ore transport business, the product of the mines thus receives most expeditious conveyance to the furnaces.

BILBOA AND LAKE SUPERIOR COMPARED.

The Bilboa district in Spain is the only iron producer in the world which will stand comparison with the Lake Superior district, with great disparity as to quantity. The output, previous to 1860, of the Bilboa district is not known. For the same period the production of the Marquette range, the only producing range in the Lake Superior district to 1860 and for many years after, is estimated at 203,676 long tons. The figures for the Bilboa district are given in metric tons; but as the metric ton has an advantage of only thirty-four pounds over the long ton, the quantities, as reported by the chief mining engineer of the province, may be compared with the Lake Superior figures as shown in the following table prepared by John Birkinbine for embodiment in his 1891 report on mineral resources to the census bureau of the United States:

Years.	Bilboa.	Lake Superior.	Years.	Bilboa.	Lake Superior.
1860	69,818	114,401	1876	432,418	993,311
1861	54,869	49,909	1877	1,040,264	1,023,129
1862	70,460	124,169	1878	1,305,625	1,127,593
1863	70,720	203,055	1879	1,262,671	1,420,745
1864	120,479	247,059	1880	2,658,627	1,962,477
1865	102,390	193,758	1881	2,620,626	2,828,640
1866	89,912	296,713	1882	3,855,000	2,982,958
1867	126,075	565,504	1883	3,627,752	2,580,223
1868	154,120	510,522	1884	3,216,321	2,321,582
1869	164,800	639,097	1885	3,311,419	2,445,855
1870	250,337	859,507	1886	8,185,228	3,684,201
1871	403,142	813,984	1887	4,198,696	4,728,695
1872	402,000	948,553	1888	3,631,593	5,006,896
1873	365,340	1,195,234	1889	3,001,511	7,519,614
1874 a	10,821	899,934	1890	4,326,933	8,944,031
1875 a	34,296	851,166			
Total 1860 to 1890				45,099,253	57,549,860

Yearly average for thirty-one years: Bilboa district, 1,451,815 metric tons; Lake Superior, 1,856,445 long tons. Output for 1891 of Bilboa district, not known; Lake Superior, 7,621,405 long tons. Output for 1892 of Bilboa district, not known; Lake Superior, 9,074,243 long tons.

The important position held by Michigan is well illustrated by comparing her singly with the Lake Superior district's great Spanish competitor from 1885 to 1890, the year 1885 being the first that the Gogebic range appeared as a producer of any importance. · The following table is also taken from Birkinbine's compilation:

Years.	Bilboa.	Michigan.
1885	3,311,419 metric tons.	2,203,199 long tons.
1886	3,155,228 "	3,179,511 "
1887	4,198,296 "	3,934,339 "
1888	3,631,593 "	4,113,803 "
1889	3,901,511 "	5,856,169 "
1890	4,326,933 "	7,141,654 "
1891		6,127,001 "
1892		7,287,874 "

UPPER PENINSULA SANDSTONE.

The sandstones of the upper peninsula are all located in the Potsdam horizon and quarries are operated at four points, all located upon the south shore of Lake Superior. They are composed of rounded and angular grains of sand rock. The cementing material of sandstones very largely affect the color of the stone and may be either silica, carbonate of lime, or oxide of iron, the colors of the stone in a measure determining the nature of the cement. Silica alone produces a whitish, hard, compact stone; carbonate of lime a blue or gray, soft and easy to work; while iron oxide yields the red and brown sandstones, usually working very free. This is particularly true of the sheets of Lake Superior stone. It cuts freer and easier in all directions than any other stone that may be regarded as a competitor in the market.

The grain of the stone is usually quite fine, so much so that in the case of the rock produced in the vicinity of Portage Entry it is said to have a liver texture. The most important producing locality is Portage Entry, sixteen miles southeast of Houghton. Here are four large quarries operating. The sheet of stone has a soil covering of from sixteen to thirty feet, then four feet of broken rock or rubble, then the eight-foot sheet of clear brown stone. The stone is very uniform in color and texture, as indeed it is at all the quarries.

The Portage Red Sandstone Company holds the land adjoining the above described property and the rock is the same in both. It may be of interest to those interested in quarries to know the composition of this rock and herewith is given an analysis, which may be taken as typical:

	Per cent.
Silica	94.73
Protoxide of iron	2.64
Aluminum	0.36
Carbonate of magnesia	0.75
Carbonate of lime	0.69
Water	0.74
Loss, etc.	0.09
Total	100.00

The Lake Superior Red Sandstone Company is close neighbor to the foregoing operators, has an average of thirty feet of stripping and a sheet of clear stone eleven feet thick; while another quarry in the same vicinity, the Kerber-Jacobs, has twenty-five feet of covering and a sixteen-foot sheet; in places it has been found twenty feet.. A cone four inches in diameter and fifteen feet, seven inches long, has been taken from this sheet and will be found exhibited in the Michigan department of the mining building. The magnificent triumphal arch found at the entrance to Michigan's mineral exhibit, is built of Portage Entry stone. It speaks for itself in its color, texture and carving qualities and a visit to it will well repay those interested in ornamental building stones.

This stone is shipped as far west as Kansas City, Mo., south to St. Louis, and as far east as New York city and Philadelphia; Duluth, Chicago and Buffalo being the three lake ports used for distributing inland. The finest quality of the redstone sells for ninety cents per cubic foot, delivered at any lake port, and variegated, *i. e.*, streaked or mottled with white, for seventy-five cents per foot. Chicago, St. Louis and Buffalo each receive about twenty-five per cent of the annual shipment; Duluth, as a shipping point to St. Paul, Minneapolis and Kansas City, fifteen per cent, while the remaining ten per cent is shipped to Cleveland.

OUTPUT OF THE SEVERAL QUARRIES IN CUBIC FEET DURING 1892.

Portage Entry	226,000
Portage Redstone Co.	275,000
Lake Superior Redstone Co.	10,000
Michigan Redstone Co.	50,000

At Marquette the stone is of a different color. While retaining the same texture and weathering qualities as the redstone district, it is of brown and purplish hues, the former being the handsomest stone quarried on the lake, though the amount, unfortunately, is limited. A peculiarity of the purplish stone is the rain drop effect. When viewed in certain lights the stone appears as though a few heavy drops of rain had fallen on it and the moisture partly absorbed. It is a very general favorite with Chicago builders, and the palatial home of the Hon. J. M. Longyear, of the city of Marquette, is built of it. There are three or four sheets having an average of three and one-half feet thickness, and covered with four to forty feet of soil, the quarry being located on a hillside. It sells for 65 cents at the lake ports, while the variegated stone is worth 40 cents, the clear brownstone selling for $1.30 per cubic foot. At Rock River, 25 miles east of Marquette, a new purplish stone has been found and partly developed last year. It promises exceedingly well, as there is a clear sheet of redstone seven feet thick, overlaid by nineteen feet of soil and two of shaley stone. About 1,000 cubic feet were shipped last year.

NOTE.—It is impossible to describe accurately these stone formations without at the same time making mention of special quarries and companies, and it is not intended to be understood that the wonderful sandstone formation of the upper peninsula is confined to places mentioned. It is confidently asserted that the richness, variety and extent of hidden formations is untested and unknown. Each year develops some hidden deposit far beyond even the suspicion of its existence. Neither was it intended that any one person should hold a master key to all the hidden recesses of nature's great storehouse.

The upper peninsula is one of nature's great banking houses, whose capital stock is its deposits, subject to be drawn only by the pick and shovel; with no exacting cashier to count, no identification required, no security asked; simply locate the funds; open the doors; help yourself.

THE GOLD MINES.

As if the upper peninsula were not sufficiently blest in its mineral resources, with its vast treasures of iron ore that years will not suffice to exhaust; with its unique and wonderful deposits of native copper, the only occurrence of its kind in the world; with its stores of building stones, slates and clays, it must needs be further blest by the glittering of gold in veins. About four miles northwest of the city of Ishpeming is located the Ropes gold mine, so named after its discoverer, which has been in operation for 12 years. It offers to the visitor a trip of more than ordinary interest. Its 65 ponderous stamps dropping incessantly crushing the quartz and liberating the precious yellow metal, its vibrating vanning machines which save the baser metals with their share of gold—these all add features of interest to a trip to the mining regions of the upper peninsula.

As has been stated by the commissioner of mineral statistics for 1885, a great deal has been said from time to time and innumerable conjectures made respecting the existence of gold among the mineral deposits of the Lake Superior region. The discovery of veins of quartz fabulously rich in this precious metal has been so often reported and investigated that something more than the mere claims of interested parties were needed to establish public confidence, or even awaken interest in the reported finds of deposits rich in gold. Gold-bearing quartz veins are not of infrequent occurrence; specimens of gold have been found in this district that for richness could not be excelled by any found in this country. The exhibit made a year or two ago of cabinet specimens was truly a remarkable one, both in point of number and value.

Early geologists are said to have made verbal reports respecting their belief in the existence of gold, and among the earliest companies organized were those which intended to explore for gold or silver. It was not before 1886 that this district attracted wide-spread attention owing to the phenomenal showing made upon the Michigan Gold Company's land and that of its immediate neighbors. These discoveries are about three miles west of the Ropes mine and are located in hills of serpentine and marble, many specimens of which had been collected and polished by Mr. Ropes. Great ridges of serpentine and marble may be traced for miles. These minerals, as they are there found, are possessed of qualities of color, grain and texture that render the formation of great economic value. Slabs and pieces of this rock may be seen in a polished state at the exhibit in the mines and mining building. The whole formation has an east and west trend and is composed of bare, sharp ridges of serpentine, marble, magnesian schists, greenstone and quartzite, all correlated under the general term serpentine formation.

Gold was first found in 1881 near the east line of the present property (S. $\frac{1}{2}$ of the N. W. $\frac{1}{4}$ Sec. 29, T. 48, R. 27) and 500 feet south of the northeast corner. To the west is greenstone, and south of it the massive serpentine, followed by magnesian schists, in which latter are found the various quartz seams, including the one in which the original discovery of gold was made. Regular mining was begun in 1882, and during the winter following a shaft was sunk 80 feet. The succeeding summer saw a 5-stamp mill erected, and it has continued its operations of sinking, drifting and topping ever since, with practically no stoppage. The five stamps have given place to a magnificent modern 65-stamp mill and today the mine and surface equipments are in admirable shape and reflect credit upon the management. The mine is developed by two shafts, one of which is about 700 feet deep. They mill them locally.

Following is a statement of the annual product of the Ropes Gold and Silver Company:

Years.		Bullion.	Concentrates.	Totals.
1883	Bullion and concentrates			$1,286 74
1884	Bullion and concentrates			4,183 56
1885		$24,380 31	$3,210 09	27,590 40
1886		38,499 93	4,653 92	43,153 85
1887		32,338 63	2,592 03	34,930 66
1888		45,183 78	5,047 95	50,231 73
1889		75,927 69	9,540 96	85,468 65
1890		56,548 10	8,697 66	65,240 76
1891		55,373 66	7,535 51	62,909 17
1892		42,208 06	8,253 77	50,461 83
Total				$425,407 35

The above figures are the net proceeds, after deducting refining charges, mint charges, freight charges and expenses. The gross product of the mine to date is $484,906.84.

SERPENTINES.

The serpentine group, incidentally mentioned when describing the occurrence of gold, deserves more than a passing notice. The number of places in which this rock is found in the United States is quite large, but they do not all contain the precious serpentine, or what is known as *verde antique*. This field contains both the ordinary and the precious. The latter is a beautiful stone when polished, with its deep greens of all shades, while veinings or markings give it an added value. Large columns and slabs of it have been cut and polished, showing its susceptibility to such treatment and proving its adaptability for interior decorations. From the nature of the stone it is not at all fitted for exposure to the elements; but this statement is true of every rock having the same composition. It is a silicate of magnesia, carrying a considerable amount of water, and usually has a notable percentage of iron protoxides, together with chrome iron, hornblende, olivine, and minerals of the pyroxene group. It is a soft though somewhat tough rock of variable color, usually greenish, though often variously streaked and spotted with yellow, brownish, or more rarely red, its color depending upon the degree of oxidation undergone by the included iron minerals.

There is a wide field here awaiting the advent of capital that is familiar with material of this kind, as the amount is inexhaustible. It can be readily reached by railroad, thus offering ready access to markets. A short haul of twenty miles would bring the rock to Marquette, whence it could be shipped to Buffalo for eastern markets or to Duluth for the western trade.

WAVERLY STONE, HOLLAND.

Quarries of Waverly stone are located at Holland, Ottawa county, State of Michigan and are in the sub-carboniferous sand rock, known to geologists as the Waverly formation from its extensive development at Waverly, Ohio. The stone is bluish gray, uniform in color, free from stains and spots, and from the iron pyrites which deface and stain the stone from some of the other localities in this formation. The cement is silica and when the stone is exposed to the air it hardens and becomes practically indestructible by heat, frost and atmospheric influence. It has an average crushing strength of 8,200 pounds to the cubic inch, as tested at the State University at Madison, Wisconsin.

Its uniformity of color, fineness of grain and strength make it a superior stone for cutting, it being susceptible of the most delicate carving.

Although the quarries have been very recently opened, the stone has been extensively used in western Michigan. In Muskegon, South Haven, Allegan and Holland some very fine and expensive buildings have been erected entirely of this stone and excite the admiration of all who see them, and the stone is being freely used in all the best structures for foundations and trimmings, the greater share going to the cities of Grand Rapids and Muskegon.

GRINDSTONE.

The grindstone quarries of Huron county were first discovered by Capt. A. G. Peer about the year 1850. These quarries are situated at Grindstone City, on the shores of Lake Huron, twenty-four miles northeast of Bad Axe, the county seat, and ninety miles above Port Huron. The stone of Huron county is the most valuable for wet grinding found in the United States. Lake Huron blue stone is known in every market in the United States and in some foreign countries. The demand for scythe stones and grindstones, from the five pound kitchen stone to those used in large factories and weighing nearly 9,000 pounds, exceeds the supply and this, notwithstanding increased facilities have been added each year. About 10,000 tons of grindstones and 12,000 gross of scythe stones are manufactured annually and the supply is unlimited. These quarries are operated by the Cleveland Stone Company and the Lake Huron Stone Company.

About twenty-four miles south and west from Grindstone City, near Bay Port, on Saginaw Bay, are located the Bay Port quarries, which, though not at present actively engaged in the manufacture of grindstones, have several layers of coarse and fine sandstone, six to ten feet in thickness, and similar in quality to the renowned grindstone of Grindstone City.

CHARCOAL PIG IRON.

In the production of charcoal pig iron, Michigan leads all the states as well as in iron ore. The census of 1890 report in operation in twenty-four states, one hundred and nineteen charcoal plant furnaces, representing a total capital of $20,008,-715, with a total product in the year of 661,497 tons of charcoal pig, valued at $11,985,103. Of these values Michigan's twenty-one furnaces produced $3,982,287, almost one-third, Alabama and Wisconsin coming next with $1,910,875 and $1,461,-775 respectively. Michigan's capital united in 1890 was $5,689,701, more than a quarter of the whole, an increase over 1880 of $2,500,000, while the value of the output increased $837,000 over 1880 despite the great fall in prices. There was an increase in 1890 over 1880 in the total product of charcoal pig iron in the United States of 229,479 tons, or fifty-two and three-quarters per cent, and yet the value of the total product for 1880 exceeded that for 1890 by $890,893.

The Michigan furnace companies employed six hundred and seventy-five hands in 1890 exclusive of officers, clerks and salesmen, and paid to them $321,032 in wages.

RIVERS AND WATER POWERS IN MICHIGAN.

BY S. B. M'CRACKEN.

It would be impossible without a scientific survey to give a full presentation of the water power facilities of Michigan. The plan pursued in compiling the matter herein was by circulars addressed to members of committees working in conjunction with the Michigan World's Fair Managers and others, in the various localities. The replies to these circulars were in many cases prompt and quite full, while in very many other cases no replies were received. The matter as presented herein makes the best showing possible under the circumstances. The compiler's personal acquaintance with the lower peninsula (more especially the southern part of it), has made possible a fuller report upon that section than upon other parts of the state.

It should be borne in mind, however, that the reports from which the matter is made up are merely the conceptions of those having but a practical knowledge of the several localities, and are largely little else than guess work. It is believed that the estimates are in most cases below the facts. To be accurate and reliable the facts should be ascertained by scientific methods which alone are exact.

In treating of the different rivers much use has necessarily been made of the maps, and it is proper to say that these do not in all cases agree. The altitudes given have reference to lake levels and are on the basis of railroad surveys. These do not in all cases show the water levels, as the point from which they are computed sometimes lie considerable higher than the mean levels through which the streams flow.

Prof. F. W. Denton, of the Mining School at Houghton, very kindly undertook to make report upon the water power of the upper peninsula. He writes, however, that the responses to the circulars sent out by him have been very meagre, not more than three or four having been received. He adds, "The trouble has been largely, I think, because the data called for was not commonly known, and few understood enough of the subject to risk an estimate. Such a report as this, to be of value requires some one to travel and collect the data on the spot." Prof. Denton's report, however, will be found of interest, as it is hoped the matter as a whole may be.

THE EASTERN WATERSHED OF THE LOWER PENINSULA.

Dividing on the straits of Mackinac and following the east coast line of the State southward, as the Pigeon, Cheboygan, Sturgeon, Rainy and Ocqueoc all rising in Otsego and Montmorency counties, and emptying into upper Lake Huron. At Alpena is Thunder Bay river, with numerous branches, draining Alpena county, the eastern portion of Montmorency and the more northern portions of Oscoda and Alcona counties. It is an enduring stream being fed by numerous lakes and affords many water power sites of ten to sixteen feet fall each and of six hundred to one thousand horse power.

The powers are not much developed for manufacturing purposes, although there are many drains built for log floating. Of equal importance with the last named is the Au Sable river which with its branches chains the counties of Otsego, Crawford, Oscoda and portions of Alcona and Iosco, emptying into the lake at Au Sable. At Grayling, in Crawford county, the railway survey shows an altitude of 553 feet above lake level, and at Bagley, in Otsego county, of 703 feet. This elevation, with a stream of considerable volume, must afford an immense hydraulic force. The Pine river, a comparatively small stream, enters the lake a few miles above Au Sable. Emptying into the north side of Saginaw bay are the Au Gres and Rifle rivers, both considerable streams. Passing the Saginaw river and its confluents, which are treated of under the head of the "Saginaw Valley," a number of small streams enter Lake Huron at the upper point of the "Thumb." Belle river, rising in Lapeer county, with an elevation at Imlay City of 218 feet above lake level and with a traverse distance of over forty miles, empties into St. Clair river, a short distance below the city of St. Clair. Other streams on the eastern slope are treated under separate heads.

THE SAGINAW VALLEY.

The Saginaw Valley will be understood to embrace the region of country the drainage of which finds its way into Saginaw bay through the river of the same name. The valley may be said to have a length of about one hundred and forty miles from Oakland and Livingston counties on the south to Roscommon county on the north, where the Tittabawassee river approaches nearly to Houghton lake, the main source of the Muskegon river which flows in the opposite direction. The valley has a breadth nearly equal to its length from the head waters of the Cass river in Huron county to the eastward to a point where the Chippewa becomes a near neighbor to the Muskegon in Osceola county on the west. The Saginaw river proper is a short stream, scarcely more than twenty miles in length, and it is formed by the junction of the Cass, Shiawassee and Tittabawassee rivers, the latter also receiving the waters of the Chippewa, Pine and Tobacco rivers. The Saginaw itself affords no water power.

John Larkin of Midland, Hon. B. W. Huston of Vassar, Thomas D. Dewey of Owosso, Hon. J. W. Begole of Flint, and J. K. Tisdall of Davisburg, furnished the information under this head.

The Tittabawassee river rises in Roscommon county and is more than a hundred miles in length as the river runs. At its source the elevation above the lake level is nearly 400 feet. The river is navigable for small craft as far up as Midland city, some 30 miles from its mouth, and was so used up to 1861, since which time it has been used only for log running and storage. The fall below Midland city is only some ten feet, affording no water power. From a considerable distance above Midland the river to its mouth is 250 to 300 feet wide, with an average summer depth of two to three feet. Above the confluence of the Chippewa the average depth is one-half to two feet. There are available but unimproved water power sites the entire length of the river above Midland every ten or twelve miles.

The Chippewa rises mainly in Clare county, runs south and east through Isabella into Midland county and has a traverse distance of fully 100 miles until it empties into the Tittabawassee at Midland. It ranges in width from 100 to 150 feet, with a summer depth at its mouth of one and one-half to two feet. There is a fine water power in operation at Mt. Pleasant in Isabella county and there are available sites at short distances its entire course. The elevation above lake level at the source of the Chippewa is 400 to 450 feet. The Pine river rises in Mecosta county, makes a southern detour into Gratiot and Montcalm, and discharges into the Chippewa near its mouth. There are fine water power improvements at St. Louis and Alma, in Gratiot county. The river, as to its length, volume and water power capacity, is about the same as the Chippewa. The Tobacco river rises in Clare county, has a flow of 50 to 75 miles, passes through the southwest corner of Gladwin county and empties into the Tittabawassee near the north line of Midland, and affords a number of available water power sites. Dams have been built on all of the four streams as aids to log driving in low water, so that the sites are but little used for mill purposes. The streams drain near 4,000 square miles and are fed from springs and beautiful clear lakes, the latter mainly in Clair, Isabella, Roscommon and Gladwin counties.

Cass river rises in Sanilac county, runs southeast, and empties in Saginaw river. It is fed by springs and small streams. There is improved water power at Vassar, in Tuscola county, and at Frankenmuth, in Saginaw county, with six feet fall and 100 horse power at Vassar. There are eligible sites at Tuscola and at Wahjamega, both in Tuscola county, that were formerly improved, but the dams have been washed away and they are not now used. The river has a descent of 61 feet from Vassar to its mouth.

The Shiawassee river rises partly in Oakland and partly in Livingston county, and has a northward course of 50 to 60 miles. It is fed by springs and lakes. There is improved power of fourteen to 16 feet fall at Davisburg and Holly in Oakland county. In Shiawassee county there is improved power at Byron, Nogs Bridge, Newburg, Shiawassee Town, Roberts Mills, Corunna and New Haven.

During summer the water supply is limited and the dam at Owosso has for some years been disused for this reason. At other seasons the volume of water is ample. The altitudes above the lake level are: Davisburg, 377 feet: Holly, 356; Corunna, 194; Owosso, 163.

Flint river is one of the most important of the single confluents of the Saginaw. It has its source in four small lakes in Lapeer county, giving it a permanent and comparatively full volume of water, though the supply is somewhat limited in summer. It is a remarkably crooked stream, making first northward some twenty miles then southward by a zigzag course through Genesee county half the distance and then northwestward to the Saginaw.

12

The first power in Genesee county is the Genesee mills, flouring, ten miles above the city of Flint, with a fall of eight feet. There are within the corporate limits of Flint a flouring mill with a capacity of 100 barrels of flour per day (besides custom work) and a large paper mill. The Thread river, which comes in at Flint, formerly carried a 300-barrel flouring mill, which was recently burned. Three miles below Flint is a 100-barrel flouring mill, and at Flushing, ten miles below, a 200-barrel mill. The head at these sites is from 7 to 10 feet. The altitudes above lake level are, Lapeer 248 feet, Flint 233. Farmers and Kearsley creeks are tributaries of the Flint river, each affording water power sites.

WATER POWER OF OAKLAND COUNTY.

With no large rivers passing through it, the county of Oakland yet holds within herself an immense hydraulic force, while she gives rise to streams that expend their force in different directions in other counties. The county is really the divide from which flows the Huron to the southwest, the Shiawassee to the north, the Clinton to the east and the Rouge to the south.

The divide as to the three first named rivers embraces but a small radius, with its center near the village of Clarkson, with an elevation of 356 feet above lake level. There also flows northward from the same divide the Kearsley creek, which empties into the Flint river, and furnishes a power at Ortonville in Oakland county and at points in Genesee county. The number of lakes in the county, large and small, is variously estimated at 250 to 400 and are unfailing feeders to these rivers.

The rivers named, except the Clinton, are mentioned under the proper heads. The Clinton, being so largely an Oakland county stream, is included under this head.

The Shiawassee river affords power at Holly and Davisburg in Oakland county and the Huron at Commerce and Milford. The Rouge also affords several small powers in the county. Pettibone creek is a small stream about eight miles long, rising in a lake in the town of Highland, passing through a chain of lakes and emptying into the Huron at Milford village. It has a fall of about a hundred feet in the eight miles. It furnishes two powers of 20 feet fall and 30 horse power, each in Highland township, one of 18 feet fall and 40 horse power at Commerce village, and three at Milford of 10, 20 and 23 feet, and 15 to 40 horse power each. At the village of Orion, near the northeast corner of the county, is a unique water power formed by throwing a dam across a small stream, Paint creek, at the foot of a cluster of small lakes, throwing the lakes into a common pond covering some 1,600 acres, dotted with a number of islands, the largest containing some 30 acres. The extent of the water surface gives a steady flow little affected by drouth. The power carries a large flouring mill at Orion with 13 feet fall, and another a mile below with 22 feet fall. Some five miles southeast from Orion, at Goodison's, the same stream carries another flour mill, and supplies another power also at Rochester.

At Ithaca, in Macomb county, is a fine power furnished by the Old Clinton and Kalamazoo canal, the water for which comes from the Oakland county reservoirs.

The Clinton river has its rise in two branches, one in the township of Independence and the other in the township of Springfield, Oakland county. It traverses nearly the entire width of Oakland county and runs through three townships in Macomb county, and empties into Lake St. Clair, four or five miles below Mt Clemens. It passes over a land surface of about fifty miles, although describing a water-course much greater.

It is fed by a chain of lakes until it reaches Pontiac. It affords about a dozen sites for water power, as follows:

Location of power.	Altitude feet.	Fall feet.	Horse power.
Springfield branch		10	20
Independence branch, Clarkston		22.6	35
Deer Lake		6	40
Waterford	406	8	30 to 40
Clintonville		6	30 to 40
Drayton Plains		6	25
Dawson's mill		12	50
Pontiac	352	16	75
Paddock's mill		10	
Amy (formerly Auburn)		16	
Rochester	165	13	
Utica	78	22	

Oliver A. Smith, of Clarkston, and J. A. Andrews, of Milford, supply information under this head.

THE BLACK RIVER.

This river rises in two branches, the north branch in Sanilac and the south branch in Lapeer county. It is a very crooked stream and enters St. Clair river at Port Huron. The following figures are compiled from information furnished by J. L. Paldi, civil engineer, and the Hon. W. L. Bancroft:

Location of power.	Fall feet.	Horse power.
Wadham's (abandoned)	8	40
Beard's mill	10	60
Comstock's (abandoned)	8	56
Comwell's (abandoned)	6	28
Pack's mill	6	28
Abbotsford on Mill creek	10	40
Brockway "	10	18
Yale (abandoned)	7	12

The descent from Crosswell to lake level is 148 feet.

THE HURON RIVER.

There are few streams carrying the volume of water that the Huron does that furnish so large an amount of water power. It has its direct rise in Oakland county, among the numerous lakes of that region, and receives an accession at Milford through the Pettibone creek, which also drains a chain of lakes and affords some water power at Milford, and at other points in Oakland county, which are noted under that head. Below Milford the Huron passes through a corner of Livingston, and thence into Washtenaw county, draining in its course a number of lakes. The largest of which is Portage lake, near the south line of Livingston county. The elevation above lake level at this point is about two hundred and eighty feet. The lake area is estimated at fifty square miles, and the watershed (by census report of 1880) at nine hundred and fifty square miles. Passing out of Washtenaw county below Ypsilanti into Wayne, the river reaches Lake Erie a few miles below the mouth of the Detroit river. The Huron passes through a land surface measuring about seventy miles, but its river course cannot be estimated at less than one hundred miles, and may considerably exceed that. The river was navigable for small craft as far up as Ypsilanti in the earlier days, but the railway connection with that place and the building of dams below it closed it for transit purposes. The water power below Portage Lake amounts to sixteen or eighteen, with horse power from sixty to six hundred, in all about two thousand three hundred horse power. Mill creek, a small stream comes in at Dexter with twelve feet fall and about fifty horse power, furnishing power for a flour mill; and at Ann Arbor a spring brook from the westward furnishes power for a small machine shop and a flour mill, and another small stream from the east supplied a small flour mill.

Col. H. S. Dean of Ann Arbor, who supplied the information above in connection with Thomas Beckett writes: "The course of the river through the numerous lakes affords much beautiful scenery, the wildness of some of the lakes (and surroundings), being almost beyond belief in counties as long settled as Oakland, Livingston and Washtenaw. From Unadilla to Milford one may pass in a small boat from lake to lake, through one portion of the Huron to another a distance of many miles, through constantly changing scenery. This region is each year becoming more of a pleasure resort, and numerous club houses and cottages are being erected on the shores of the various lakes. The whole course of the river is very irregular and winding. The Michigan Central railroad crosses it fifteen times between Dexter and Ypsilanti, a distance of seventeen miles.

RIVER ROUGE.

This is a small stream, but with a descent of nearly two hundred feet to the lake level in a distance of less than forty miles, it affords a valuable power. It has two branches, both rising in Oakland county. One branch, rising in Bloomfield, affords five small powers, namely: Morris' grist mill (unused), W. H. Smith's saw and cider mill, two and two and one-half miles, respectively, north of Birmingham, Birmingham flour mill, Frity's flour and saw mill two miles south of Birmingham, and the Southfield flour mill. The other branch springs from Walled lake, in the township of Commerce. The course of the stream is southeasterly until it empties into the Detroit river four miles below the city. It is fed in addition to its lake source by springs and small streams, and has an estimated water shed of three hundred and sixty square miles. It affords power in addition to above for five establishments of from twelve to forty-five horse power each.

C. B. Crosby, of Plymouth, and A. Partridge, of Birmingham, supply information in the above.

THE RIVER RAISIN.

This important milling stream of southeastern Michigan has its rise in Jackson, Lenawee and Hillsdale counties. It drains the greater part of Lenawee, the southeastern portion of Jackson, northeastern part of Hillsdale, and southwestern part of Washtenaw, and traverses the width of Monroe county to its mouth on lake Erie, a short distance below the city of Monroe. For the information regarding this stream and its water power capacity the compiler is indebted to Andrew Spalding and J. Robison, of Manchester. From their report the following facts are elicited:

Location of power.	Fall feet.	Horse power.	Altitude feet.
Brooklyn	8	25	
Norvel mill	7	40	382
Manchester, first fall	14	170	334
" second fall	7	60	
" third fall	12	125	
River Raisin, Bridgewater township	6	40	
Sharon	6½	50	
Norris (unused)	6	40	
Iron Creek (unused)	6	40	
Clinton	11	60	259
Newburg	5	30	
Tecumseh (paper mill)	11	60	234
" (Hayden's mill)	17	100	
" (Boyd & Root's mill)	8	50	
Adrian	16	60	190
Palmyra	7	222	
Blissfield	7	222	
Deerfield	7	222	
Petersburg	8	260	
Dundee	6	168	108
West Raisinville	9	370	
East "	6	200	
Frenchtown	6	200	
Monroe (Waterloo mills)	9	370	
" (unused power)	8	300	

In transmitting his report of power below Adrain, Mr. Spalding says: "I have submitted my report to various mill men and they all say that it is below the actual capacity of the stream."

THE WESTERN WATER SHED OF THE LOWER PENINSULA.

Up the eastern shore of Lake Michigan are three streams called Black river, the first with three important branches emptying at South Haven, the second at Black lake, and the third at Crimea. The first of these furnishes small powers at Bredsville, Bangor, Jerico, and at two or three other points in Van Buren county. The White river rises near the center of Newaygo county, passes through a corner of Oceana into Muskegon county, and empties into White lake, an arm of Lake Michigan, at Whitehall and Montague. Its descent from source to mouth is estimated at two hundred to two hundred and fifty feet. It has developed water powers at Whitecloud, Alleyton, Ætna and Hesperia in Newaygo county. The Pentwater river enters Lake Michigan at Pentwater, the Big Sable at Point Sable, and the Manistee at Manistee. The Betsie river traverses portions of Benzie and Manistee counties and empties into Lake Michigan at Frankfort, affording a water power at that point. The Platte river enters the lake some miles above, but its water power capacity is unknown. The Bear river, Rapid river and Bear creek find their way into the waters of Traverse bay at various points and the Maple river empties into the Straits of Mackinaw.

THE ST. JOSEPH VALLEY.

The St. Joseph river drains the southern tier of counties in Michigan from Hillsdale county, where it has its rise, westward to Lake Michigan. Within a small radius from where the corners of Lenawee and Hillsdale join Jackson county, is an elevation of nearly four hundred feet above lake level, from which flows the St. Joseph river to the west, the Kalamazoo and the Grand to the northwest, the Raisin to the east and the southwest, and several small streams southward into Ohio. The St. Joseph furnishes power with eleven feet fall at Jonesville, at Genesee mills below Jonesville, and at Litchfield in Hillsdale county. The outlet of Baw Beese lake draining into the St. Joseph furnishes a power at the city of Hillsdale. At Union City in Branch county the St. Joseph receives the waters of Coldwater river, on which there are four powers reported; two at Coldwater city with seven and one-half and sixteen feet fall, respectively, and one in Coldwater township, and one at Hodunk of eight and nine feet fall. There are light powers arising from creeks in other parts of Branch county.

At Three Rivers, in St. Joseph county, the St. Joseph river receives the waters of the Portage and Rock rivers. Three Rivers is an important manufacturing point, having a combined water power from the three streams that meet there of five hundred and twenty-five horse power. The Portage river has but one power and that at Three Rivers. The Rock river has besides that at Three Rivers a fifty horse power at Flowerfield and Howardsville. The St. Joseph affords power in St. Joseph county, in Park township, at Three Rivers and at Constantine of seventy-five, two hundred and fifty and two hundred horse power, respectively. At Niles, in Berrien county, there is a fine power capacity not stated. From the southwest corner of St. Joseph county the river passes into the state of Indiana and bending again northward gives the name to the flourishing city of South Bend, at which point, and at Elkhart and Mishawauka, in Indiana, it affords valuable power. Returning to Michigan it flows through the city of Niles and thence finds its way into Lake Michigan at St. Joseph and Benton Harbor.

The altitudes above lake level at the principal points named above are: Hillsdale, 513 feet; Jonesville, 495; Union City, 318; Three Rivers, 223; Constantine, 221; Niles, 115.

The information under this head is supplied by Hon. E. O. Grosvenor, of Jonesville, Hon. C. D. Randall, of Coldwater, and E. B. Linsley, of Three Rivers. Hon. J. J. Woodman, of Paw Paw, supplies some statistics of the Paw Paw river, a tributary of the St. Joseph, which rises in Van Buren county and empties into the St. Joseph near its mouth, being fed by springs, tributary streams and lakes.

There are five improved powers at Paw Paw with from twenty-five to fifty-three horse power, one at Watervleit of six hundred, and one at Hartford with one hundred horse power, and two unimproved.

THE KALAMAZOO RIVER.

This important Michigan river rises in two branches near the boundary line between Hillsdale and Jackson counties and runs diagonally through portions of Jackson, Calhoun, Kalamazoo and Allegan counties, emptying into Lake Michigan at Saugatuck. Its general course gives it a traverse route of about one hundred and twenty miles, the stream measurement, however, by its windings being much more. The information regarding its tributaries is incomplete. At the city of Battle Creek the stream of that name enters the Kalamazoo from the northeast. It affords a power at Bellevue, in Eaton county, as reported by Wm. Merritt, of Battle Creek, of twelve feet fall and one hundred horse power, and at Verona mills, three miles above Battle Creek city, of six feet fall and one hundred horse power. The other information under this head is derived mainly from Geo. S. Pierson, a civil engineer at Kalamazoo, and Hon. W. B. Williams, of Allegan, and the following statement is made from these sources. We have between Jackson and Allegan seventeen powers ranging from seventy-five to three thousand horse powers, as follows:

Location of power.	Altitude feet.	Fall feet.	Horse power.
Bath Mills, Jackson county			
Homer, Calhoun county	890		
Albion	361		
Marshall	316	18	250
Ceresco			
Battle Creek	237		
Augusta, Kalamazoo county	207		
Galesburg	206		100
Comstock	200		100
Kalamazoo	195	22	200
Yorkville			125
Painesville, Allegan county	162		600
Otsego	128	12	3,000
Allegan	126	8 to 12	1,200

The figures are necessarily but approximations only. In transmitting his report Mr. Pierson says: "There is still undeveloped power at Otsego and above Kalamazoo on the main river, and at numerous points on the tributary streams."

The water shed of the river and its tributaries has an area of about four hundred and fifty square miles. The flow of the river at Kalamazoo, October 23, 1880, was 567,879,840 gallons per day, which is about the average stage of the river at this point. The Hon. W. B. Williams adds: "There is small power at Mill Grove, on the outlet to Demerest lake, and at Pine Creek, near Otsego, on a creek by that name, and also on Swan creek about seven miles northwest from Allegan. There is also a good water power at Hamilton, in Allegan county, on the Rabbit river."

Persons familiar with the hydraulics can form some estimate of the immense water power afforded by the Kalamazoo river by comparing the flow of the river as given by Mr. Pierson with the altitudes as given in the table.

THE GRAND RIVER VALLEY.

The Grand river and its tributaries form one of the most extensive water systems in the lower peninsula. The Grand river itself traverses five counties from its rise, near the southern line of Jackson county, being northerly through Jackson, Lansing and Grand Ledge to the city of Ionia, whence its course is westward to its discharge into Lake Michigan at Grand Haven. Measurements by fairly straight lines the river would have a course of fully 200 miles, while its windings would give nearly, if not twice, that distance. Its drainage above Grand Rapids is computed to be more than 4,800 square miles.

At Lansing the Grand river receives the water of Cedar river, at Portland the Lookingglass river, at Muir the Maple, at Lowell the Flat, at Ada the Thornapple, and near Grand Rapids the Rouge river, besides a number of smaller streams at different points.

WATER POWERS OF THE GRAND RIVER.

Water powers varying from 75 to 2,000 horse power are found at Leoni, Michigan Center, Liberty, Summit and Jackson, in Jackson county; Onondaga, in Ingham county; Dimondale, in Eaton county; North and South Lansing, in Ingham county; Grand Ledge, in Eaton county; Portland and Lyons, in Ionia, and the greatest of all at Grand Rapids, in Kent county. Besides these the tributaries in many cases furnish powers of from seventeen to three hundred horse power. H. A. Hayden, of Jackson, gives the fall at Jackson at seven and one-half feet, Onondaga six, Eaton Rapids eight, Dimondale six and one-half.

E. W. Sparrow, of Lansing, states the fall at North Lansing to be eight feet, and at South Lansing five feet. L. B. Townsend, of Ionia, states the fall in two dams at Hubbardston, on Lookingglass river, to be eighteen feet, and at Dixon's creek ten feet. The fall of Prairie creek, emptying into the Grand river at Ionia, in a distance of about four miles, is about forty-one feet, making several fine water powers ranging from seventeen to forty-five horse power. Neal McMillan, of Rockford, states that from Child's Mill to Briggs Reef, on Rogers river, the fall is forty feet, with horse power from seventy-five to one hundred and seventy-five. On nearly all the tributaries emptying into Grand River there are falls capable of being utilized into powers. A very satisfactory peculiaritay of these streams is the even flow of water, varying but little through the year. Michigan very rarely suffers inconvenience from floods, there being no mountain sides to shed a deluge of water into the valleys and streams. Grand river carrying off the surplus of more than 4,000 square miles seldom gets out of its banks. It pursues its winding way from Jackson to Lake Michigan, creeping through valleys, rolling over rapids, tumbling over falls, meandering majestically through romantic scenery, occasionally dividing itself, forming beautiful little islands, frequently deepening to make homes for the finny tribe, with which it is abundantly stocked.

Fishing in Michigan streams is and always will be pre-eminently great sport, unlike fishing in canals and navigable streams where it is about as good one place as another. To catch fish you must go where they are. An Irishman speaking of the fishing in Michigan said it was just as good in one place as another, and a great deal better.

THE MUSKEGON RIVER.

This is the greatest water power river of Western Michigan, larger in its own volume than the Grand river except as the latter approaches the lake, and but for the larger and more numerous confluents of the Grand, would rank first in the river systems of the State. It rises in Higgins and Houghton lakes in Roscommon county, passes through portions of six counties and empties into Muskegon lake at Muskegon, the latter being joined with Lake Michigan by a short connecting strait. Roscommon station, on the Michigan Central railroad, within the width of a township of the headwaters of the Muskegon, according to the survey, lies five hundred and forty-six feet above lake level, and Big Rapids lies three hundred and thirty-four feet above the lake. The windings of the river cover about three hundred miles from head to mouth. Hon. Michael Brown, of Big Rapids, supplies the following statistics of water power in Mecosta county:

Location of power.	Fall feet.	Horse power.
Montague (Muskegon river)	10	200
Paris	9	150
Upper Big Rapids (Muskegon river)	9	175
Lower Big Rapids (Muskegon river)	6	150
Rogers farm	9	200
Mitchell's farm (Muskegon river)	10	240
Paris (Paris creek)	24	75
Ryan creek (near Big Rapids)	20	100
Ryan creek (at fork of Chippewa river, Mecosta county)	12	

Judge Brown adds: Paris creek is a short stream fed entirely by springs and spring brooks, never failing as a water power, and with the large fall reported, furnishes a very excellent power.

Ryan creek is the outlet of two small lakes in this county.

Of course the Muskegon river furnishes by far the largest amount of water power of any stream in the county. I do not believe that there is a river in the State that will equal it. The flow of water is regular and constant, the river never rising more than three feet. In fact the flow does not vary so as to cause any danger whatever to dams and manufactories. The flow of water at different points in Mecosta county ranges from 3,800 to 5,800 inches. At Newaygo village is a dam with 12 feet fall (which could be raised higher), giving a present horse power of 1,500, low water run. Pennoyer Creek and Brooks creek both come in at Newaygo, the former furnishing a 75 horse power dam and the latter 50 horse power, both improved. On the Muskegon river dam is a large saw mill, flour mill, planing mill and tub and pail factory. On Pennoyer creek is a furniture factory, and on Brooks creek a flour mill. Below Croton there is a heavy fall in the Muskegon where a 30-foot head could be obtained. At Bridgton, below Newaygo, there is also a fall which could be developed.

It is said that by building a dam at Muskegon a head of 16 feet could be had, giving over 20,000 horse power. Other statistics of the Muskegon and its tributaries are wanting, but from those given above some estimate can be found of the value of this stream for hydraulic uses.

13

MASON COUNTY.

George N. Stray and John L. Woodruff, of Ludington, write of the water power in Mason county: Lincoln river is fed by a lake three miles by one-half mile in extent and has a water shed of about 3 by 15 miles. It affords an 80 horse power site two miles north of Ludington. Hamlin river has a lake reservoir of 10 square miles and a water shed of 150 square miles, and 7 miles north of Ludington has a 160 horse power site. The powers on the two rivers have been used, but are not now. Baldwin, Kinnie and Weldon creeks, tributaries of the Pere Marquette, have improved powers in Mason county, and the Sweetwater, Winnippesogee, Beaver and Cedar creeks are susceptible of improvement. Also the middle and south branches of the Pere Marquette.

WATER POWER AT THE SAULT STE. MARIE.

The fall or rapid at the foot of Lake Superior is known by the French designation of the Sault Ste. Marie, which takes the briefer and more familiar form of the Soo. John G. Stradley, of the city of Sault Ste. Marie, writes of the possibilities of the water power at that point.

In the fall of 1890 a survey of the river St. Marys was made to ascertain the actual flow of water over the rapids. The amount per second is over 100,000 cubic feet, and the estimated horse power is so near 300,000 that it is fixed at that figure for the whole river. The river being an international boundary line the Canadians would probably be entitled to one-half of the power if they saw fit to develop it. The full flow of the river can be used for power, less the amount required to operate the locks in the ship canal. The length of the rapids is about three-quarters of a mile, and the fall eighteen and one-half feet. If little rapids is included, the fall will be about twenty feet. This head can be raised two and one-half or three feet by building a dam across the head of the rapids, which would raise the entire of Lake Superior. This would make a large increase in the power and is pronounced practical by both government and civil engineers, and the cost would be nominal compared with the benefits. A small part of the power is already developed by throwing a wing dam out into the rapids running an embankment up to the head. This wing dam is only about half way down the rapids and is called the Chandler-Dunbar water power. This has nothing to do with the large water power and does not interfere with it. The plans for the development contemplate a canal over three miles in length, six hundred feet wide and carrying eighteen feet depth of water its entire length. This would develop the largest water power in the world, and is so situated that every mill or factory built on it can have a train of cars at one door and the largest steamer that runs the lakes at another. There is no other place on the continent where this can be done. If the canal is constructed on the plan contemplated it will cost $5,000,000.

WATER POWER OF THE UPPER PENINSULA.

BY PROF. F. W. DENTON, OF MICHIGAN MINING SCHOOL.

The upper peninsula of Michigan comprises 22,580 square miles of area, and its topography may be classed as rough, it being largely made up of hills and ridges. The shore along Lake Superior is steep and rocky throughout, reaching elevations of four hundred to six hundred feet above the level of the lake in distance from the shore usually under fifteen miles. The main river systems have their sources near the south side of the northern range of high land, and flow in a southerly direction, approximately at right angles to the south shore of Lake Superior, and empty into Lake Michigan. The peninsula being long and narrow, the lengths of the watersheds are necessarily very limited, and owing to the numerous lesser ridges and ranges of hills running parallel to the rivers, the widths of the watersheds are likewise very limited. In fact there is but one river in this territory, which can be said to furnish first class water power, and that is the Menominee river, which is formed by the junction of the Bois Brule and the Michigamme rivers, and flows southeast and empties into Green bay. The Menominee throughout its length forms the boundary between the upper peninsula and the state of Wisconsin. It therefore flows across the base of the peninsula, thus draining a much larger territory than any other river in this district. Its feeders in Michigan are classed among the largest streams. Although the Menominee is the only river that furnishes a large amount of water power there are a number of lesser streams which undoubtedly furnish power which might be economically used.

RAINFALL.

The late Professor Winchell, in his report upon the topography, climate, and geology of Michigan (1873), gives the following figures for the upper peninsula:

Copper Falls, five years ------------------------------------- 37.23
Ontonagon, twelve " ------------------------------------- 24.20
Marquette, thirteen " ------------------------------------- 31.02
Sault Ste. Marie, thirty-three years--------------------- 30.28

The Ontonagon record is exceptionally low, and neglecting it as being due to local or other causes, the average of the remaining three yearly means 32.84 inches. This record cannot be considered as giving a fair average for the whole upper peninsula, for two reasons. First, the records were all taken at the lake shore where the average precipitation is probably less than that of the interior. Second, the measurement of the snowfall, which in these latitudes form so large a portion of the total precipitation for the year, is difficult to determine accurately. It has not been possible in the limited time allowed for this report, to investigate the rainfall down to the present time. The average for the district herein covered is probably about 32 inches, and this fall will be used in the calculation of the flow of the streams. In the report upon the water powers of the United States, prepared for the tenth census, the average rainfall taken for the district is 35 inches. It will be seen from the columns headed "ratios, with the mean for three months," that the precipitation is fairly uniform, ranging form .70 in the spring and winter to 1.4 in the autumn. This, however, is deceptive since the snow collects upon the ground in the winter months, only a small percentage reaching the streams at that time. During the thaws of the spring months this snow rapidly melts, producing freshets. The flow fluctuates considerably as an actual fact on this account, and there are usually two periods of very low water, one in summer and the other in winter. These conditions of small drainage areas, of small annual rainfalls, and of large fluctuations in the flow are therefore very unfavorable to the occurrence of first class water powers. The total fall, however, is as a rule considerable, the average height of the high land which divides the drainage into Lake Superior and from that into Lake Michigan being about 1,500 feet above the sea. The level of Lake Superior is 600 feet above the sea, and therefore the main streams have a total fall of about 900 feet in short distances. This fall does not take place uniformly as a rule, but occurs either in the form of rapids or natural waterfalls, where the streams cross the trap or granite ranges. The character of the surface varies in the different parts of the peninsula. The average condition will give probably a flow in the streams, equivalent to sixty per cent of the rainfall upon the respective watersheds. The available flow for the entire year is estimated to be twenty per cent of the mean annual rainfall. Regarding the more important streams a few figures, which however are only approximate, are given.

THE MENOMINEE RIVER IN MICHIGAN.

(Extracts from the "Report upon Water Powers" of the 10th United States Census.)

Dimensions of the Drainage Basin.—The drainage basin of 4,113 square miles is very irregular in outline. Narrow at the mouth, it widens out to an average of about 40 miles across, and sends an arm away north, so that the extreme sources are within ten miles of the waters of Lake Superior in Huron bay. Thus it nearly extends clear across the center of the upper peninsula of Michigan. At the nominal head of the river it already has a drainage area of 1,760 square miles, for the Bois Brule and the Michigamme are each large streams. Further down it receives the Pine and Pike rivers from Wisconsin, and the Sturgeon and Little Cedar from Michigan, besides numerous smaller streams. No gaugings have been made of the river, but the calculations of the water powers have been based upon a low water flow of 0.34 cubic feet per second per square mile of watershed, which is equivalent to 17.8 per cent of the total volume of precipitation, which is here taken as 35 inches.

In high water the power of the river is immensely increased. The river is not especially uniform in its flow, although running in a timbered country, but it cannot be considered an unsteady stream, its character being medium in this respect. The superintendent of the paper mill at the mouth said that after a heavy rain the river would rise to a maximum in about four days, stay at that stage about four days and then fall to about the usual level in about four days more.

Fall of the River.—The extreme sources on the west are within two miles of the Lac Vieux desert, the source of the Wisconsin, which is 951 feet above Lake Michigan, and on the north they are at least 990 feet above Lake Michigan, as Lake Michigamme is 952 feet above the level of Lake Superior. Thus the river may be considered to fall about 975 feet from its source to its mouth, in a distance by water of about 160 miles. This descent is scattered in local concentrations all along its course, and rapids characterize the river from the source to the mouth. The elevation of the river at the railroad crossing, three miles above the mouth of Pine river, is given by the Chicago and Northwestern railroad as 475 feet above Lake Michigan, and at Sturgeon river at the crossing, two and one-half miles above the mouth, 253 feet above the lake.

From this data the fall between the railroad crossing and the mouth of the Sturgeon is approximately 225 feet, an average of 12½ feet per mile. In this distance occur the Big and Little Quinnesec falls. In the 72 miles from the mouth of the Sturgeon river to the lake, the Menominee falls about 250 feet, an average of three and one-half feet per mile. The fall in these stretches is not uniform, but occurs irregularly, as rapids or waterfalls, forming numerous, cheap and good water powers. Sixteen principal rapids and falls are enumerated in the census report, the natural falls ranging from 12 to 60 feet. Among this number are two which are classed under "large undeveloped water powers of the United States." They are known as the Big and Little Quinnesec falls. Since the publication of the census report, the Big Quinnesec falls has been utilized by the Chapin & Ludington Iron Mining Company of the Menominee Range. A large plant of air compressors, operated by turbins, is located at the falls, and the compressed air is conducted through a large pipe to the mines three miles away, where it is made to operate surface and underground machinery.

Main tributaries of the Menominee in Michigan: Michigamme river, seventy-two miles, drains 756 square miles; Sturgeon river, five miles, drains 409 square miles.

MICHIGAMME RIVER.

This is the largest tributary of the Menominee. Its drainage basin reaches nearly across the upper peninsula, the extreme sources being within ten miles of the waters of Lake Superior, in Huron bay. The head of the river, however, is considered to be Lake Michigamme, which is the largest lake of the Menominee

NOTE.—This information regarding the tributaries of the Menominee river in Michigan is taken from the census report already referred to, except that twenty per cent instead of seventeen and eight-tenths is taken as giving the proportion of the total annual rainfall probably available throughout the year.

basin. The length of the river to the extreme source is seventy-two miles (map measurements), to Lake Michigamme fifty-one miles. The ordinary low stage power at the mouth, under ten feet head, is estimated as four hundred and six theoretical horse power, and the average width at the mouth is two hundred and fifty feet, and at the head eighty feet. Lake Michigamme is nine hundred and eighty feet above Lake Michigan. There are several prominent falls and rapids on the river, and all the falls are over rock ledges with rocky banks. About one thousand three hundred feet from the mouth is a perdendicular fall of thirty feet, with steep, rocky banks. Four miles from the mouth is another vertical fall of six feet. Fifteen miles from the mouth and three miles below the mouth of Deer river is a vertical fall of ten feet over a rocky ledge. Six miles above Fence river is Long Corry rapids, one and three-quarters miles long with about forty feet fall. Next there is a fall and a rapid three miles below Republic mine, three-quarters of a mile long, with about a fifteen feet fall. Lake Michigamme is eight miles above this place.

STURGEON RIVER.

The basin of this river is in Michigan and its length (map measurements) to the extreme source is fifty miles. The area drained is four hundred and nine square miles and the power under ten feet head at an ordinary low stage of the water is two hundred and nineteen theoretic horse power. The average width at the mouth is one hundred feet. The general course is south southwest, nearly at right angles to the general slope of the country, and hence the fall of the river is very slight. Ten miles above the mouth is a descent of sixteen feet in three pitches.

There are a number of other streams of about the same importance as possible sources of water power, as the tributaries of the Menominee river. These are tabulated as follows:

Name.	Drainage, square miles.	Theoretical horse power under 10 feet fall.
Manistique river	1,460	785
Ontonagon river	1,344	722
Escanaba river	971	522
Sturgeon river	763	410
Paint river (not before mentioned)	570	306
Ford river (not before mentioned)	480	258

It is impossible to give definite detailed information regarding these rivers. There are, however, undoubtedly many small water powers on these and other still smaller streams that have not been mentioned, which can be cheaply utilized. The rivers fall irregularly, forming rapids in some places and abrupt falls at others. This is shown by the government plats, and also by reports that have been received concerning these rivers. The fall of the streams through all parts of the upper peninsula, with the exception of those occurring on the narrow stretch near Sault Ste. Marie, is of a character that permits of a cheap utilization of the power. The factor wanting generally is not head, but quantity. The difficulty of the lack of volume is enhanced by the irregularity of the flow, caused by the snows of winter melting rapidly during a short period of time in the spring. On the other hand the localities are often very favorable for the construction of cheap dams, which can be made to impound the water and so regulate the flow. In conclusion we may say with certainty that there exists on the streams directly mentioned, and on numbers of others that have not been named, numerous small water powers furnishing from 50 to 200 horse power throughout the year, that could be cheaply utilized. A considerable number are already used, but the meager and inaccurate returns received do not warrant an attempt at tabulating them.

THE SOO WATER POWER.

BY C. H. CHAPMAN.

The great water power at Sault Ste. Marie is at the falls of the St. Mary's river. This river is the only known outlet for the greatest of all bodies of fresh water; and the assertion that this is the greatest and best water power in the world is occasionally contradicted by those who are unfamiliar with the requirements for good power. With consumers the greatest objection to water powers are the fluctuations in the head or power producing quantity. On smaller streams the spring freshets and summer droughts are serious obstacles to steady and even power, such as is required by nearly all manufactories; and steam, though much more expensive, is frequently adopted where water power would be utilized under more favorable conditions. The water power at Sault Ste. Marie has for its direct source of supply Lake Superior, with its thirty-two thousand square miles of solid water. The average variation of the depth of water in this great lake is one foot in a year. The low water season occurring in spring at the time and immediately following the freshets. From low water mark in April the lake gradually rises until about September when the highest point is reached, a difference of but twelve inches. There are some slight variations from this rule, but it is the average.

During the summer of 1890, a syndicate was organized in London, England, composed of English and Scotch capitalists, for the purpose of developing this great power to its fullest capacity. Colonel W. Hope, of the corps of civil engineers of the English army, visited Sault Ste. Marie in the interests of the syndicate. He remained several months and completed a minute survey of the falls. His charts show the depth variation and velocity of the water at every point, and when he finished, his report to the syndicate was to the effect that this was the greatest and most practicable water power on earth. John Best, of Edinburgh, Scotland, one of the largest and best known contractors in Great Britain accompanied Colonel Hope to Sault Ste. Marie, and made a careful examination of the entire locality. A few months since, Mr. Best was visited at his Edinburgh home by ex-general superintendent Watson, of the Duluth, South Shore and Atlantic Railway, and stated to that gentleman that the water power at the Sault was the grandest he had ever

THE SOO CANAL - VESSEL LOWERED, READY TO LEAVE.

seen, and the purchase and development would have been made by his syndicate, had it not been for the failure of the Barings of London.

One of the features of Colonel Hope's plan of development was to place a dam across the river at the head of the falls to raise the water in Lake Superior and hold complete control over the head and prevent the slightest variation in its flow, thus the steadiest known power would have been equaled, if not excelled. This plan was approved and pronounced practicable by the United States corps of engineers. In considering great water powers one's first thought is of Niagara as the greatest, but there the most puzzling problem with the engineers is, how to overcome and utilize the fall. It is too great and no practical machinery will stand the continuous strain of more than twenty-five foot of a head. The head at the Soo is about twenty feet and the supply is one never failing for twenty-four hours a day and three hundred and sixty-five days in a year. There is now completed here a development of ten thousand theoretical horse power. This was made quite easily and at comparatively small cost by building a wing dam in the rapids. The average power at Minneapolis, from the falls of St. Anthony, is five thousand theoretical horse power, while at the Soo twice the amount is already developed and ten times more is awaiting development.

14

LUMBER INTERESTS.

Although agriculture is the chief producing interest of this State, and engages the attention of the largest share of its people, fertile farms and prolific orchards have not alone contributed to its prosperity. Noted for its wheat, its wool and its fruit, it is also the first of the United States in its production of lumber, salt, charcoal pig iron and copper, and in the extent of its fresh-water fisheries. Certainly first in the value, and probably first in the amount, of its yield of iron ore, and among the most advanced in its general manufacturing and commercial development. While a few states excel it in the volume of their crops, and some in the aggregate of their industrial statistics, none can equal it in the magnitude and diversity of its resources, taken together. Its forests, mines, mills and factories, while offering employment to all grades of labor, from the unskilled worker with the pick and shovel to the most expert mechanic, also create a large and constant local demand for the farm products of the State, and thus doubly promote the general progress. The full extent of the invitation Michigan thus proffers to the laborer and the artisan in search of work and to the farmer of small means who desires to purchase new lands, and to secure a home market for his surplus produce, can be best made plain by brief accounts of the history and condition of its leading industries.

Before the ax of the lumberman commenced its work on the forests of Michigan, the northern part of its lower peninsula surpassed any known region of the same area in the richness of its stock of timber. Interspersed with the best varieties of pine were extensive growths of oak, maple, beech, ash, walnut, cherry, whitewood, hickory and elm, while the less valuable cedar, hemlock, basswood and tamarack grew, in some sections, in equal abundance. In the upper peninsula and northern part of the lower peninsula pine existed also in large quantities, and broad tracts of hard wood invited the erection of furnaces for the manufacture of the best grades of charcoal iron. Magnificent forests of hard timber covered the greater part of the southern counties, now so rich in agricultural wealth. A more comprehensive account of the timber resources of the State is printed on succeeding pages, from the pen of Prof. W. J. Beal, the accomplished botanist of the Agricultural College.

Much of the timber product of the State has been of an exceedingly superior quality. Its cork pine ranks among the best of the soft woods, and commands the highest market price. Its common grades of white and Norway pine are of standard value, while its harder woods are in demand in the ship-yards, factories and cabinet shops of this and the European continent.

THE CHIEF MANUFACTURING INTEREST OF THE STATE.

For many years lumbering has been the chief manufacturing interest of Michigan, and no American state equaled it in the extent and value of its lumber product. The State has never collected and compiled the annual statistics of this industry, and the most trustworthy sources of information upon the subject are the elaborate publications of journalists connected with papers representing that interest, or issued at the centers of the manufacture. Even these are deficient in statistics covering the trade in spars, staves, heading, and long timber, and the thousands of cords of fuel chopped and sold annually have gone unrecorded, as also have the heavy shipments of railroad ties, cedar telegraph poles, piles, paving blocks, spool stock, and hardwoods for the furniture maker.

GROWTH AND MAGNITUDE OF THE LUMBER BUSINESS.

The history of this great industry covers a period of only about thirty years. In 1854 the Hon. Wm. L. Webber, of East Saginaw, made the first estimate of the extent of the operations of Michigan lumbermen whose activity was then chiefly confined to the valley of the Saginaw river. He reported the existence of sixty-one mills, many of them using water power, and placed their entire annual product at but 108,000,000 feet. Eighteen years later, in 1872, it was estimated that the lumber product of Michigan for twelve months included 2,560,000 feet of oak timber, 12,700,000 staves, 300,000,000 lath, 400,000,000 shingles, and 2,500,000,000 feet of sawed pine. The number of saw mills in the State at that time was about fifteen hundred, employing more that twenty thousand persons, and representing $25,000,000 of capital. There were also two hundred shingle mills and eighty stave and hoop factories, with an annual product of $4,000,000 in value. The lumber trade suffered materially during the following years of commercial depression, but in 1879 the total amount sawed in this State reached 3,100,000,000 feet, and Gov. Jerome in his inaugural message estimated the value of the entire timber product of that year at $60,000,000. The product of 1881 is estimated by the lumber journals to have been:

Lumber product for 1881.

Location.	No. Feet.
Upper Peninsula	450,000,000
The Saginaw Valley	1,011,000,000
The Lake Huron Shore	320,000,000
The Lake Michigan Shore:	
Manistee	225,000,000
Ludington	120,000,000
White Lake	120,000,000
Muskegon	632,500,000
Grand Haven and Spring Lake	191,000,000
Miscellaneous	75,000,000
Interior Mills:	
Chicago & West Michigan R. R.	65,000,000
Grand Rapids & Indiana R. R.	196,000,000
Detroit Lansing, and Northern R. R.	84,000,000
Michigan Central R. R.—Mackinac and Bay City Divisions	85,000,000
Flint & Pere Marquette R. R.	145,000,000
Miscellaneous	200,000,000
Total	3,919,500,000

This large total is that of sawed pine lumber alone and is exclusive of shingles, lath, staves and long timber, whose product possesses an annual value of many millions. An ingenious calculation shows that the work of the Michigan mills during that year in sawed lumber would load a train of cars 2,470 miles in length, each car carrying 10,000 feet and occupying thirty-three feet of track, and would build a city of handsome frame houses capable of furnishing comfortable homes for more than a million of people. The aggregate value of the forest products of this State already marketed is in excess of $1,000,000,000. These totals far outstripped those of any other timber producing state, or of any country of like area.

The production of lumber increased until about 1883, when it seemed to receive a check. Many small timber claims were worked up and mills were idle. It was then claimed by some that the great lumber producing State was weakening. The output was visibly decreased, but that the pine timber was exhausted was by no means true. In 1892 the lumber production was, lumber 3,794,256,751 and shingles 2,140,800,000, and the price much better. This included hardwood lumber, of which there is an immense amount in the State. A large proportion of the lumber produced in Michigan is being manufactured within the State and the manufactured articles shipped instead of raw lumber.

THE GREAT CENTERS OF MANUFACTURE.

The distribution of the lumber manufacture of Michigan is determined by its rivers and railroads. Below the valleys of the Saginaw and the Grand, little else than a mere local trade now exists. The Saginaw receives the waters of the Tittabawassee, the Cass, the Flint, the Shiawassee, the Bad, the Pine, the Chippewa, the Tobacco, and their numerous tributaries, draining a vast and magnificently timbered region. At its mouth is the thriving city of Bay City; sixteen miles above, at the head of steam navigation, is Saginaw. At these cities and in the flourishing villages between them are collected the finest lumber manufacturing establishments in the world, whose total yearly product surpasses that of any other single district. The river which brings the logs to their booms also bears large vessels to their docks, and they have under absolute control all the advantages of cheap water transportation. The Saginaw valley is also connected by several first-class lines with the railway system of the continent, and with this multiplied outlet commands access to all the markets of the world.

The Lake Huron shore, including Saginaw bay, counts its saw mills by the hundred. The Au Sable and Thunder bay are important logging rivers of that part of the State, and lumbering is also extensively carried on along the Rifle, the Aux Gres, the Cheboygan, the Black, and many smaller streams. Alpena, Tawas City, East Tawas, Cheboygan, Oscoda, Au Sable, Harrisville and Black River are important manufacturing or shipping points.

The chief lumbering rivers emptying into Lake Michigan are the Muskegon, the Manistee, the White and the Pere Marquette. Many millions of feet are also cut annually along the banks of the two Sables, the Aux Becs Scies, the Pentwater, and other lesser streams. The Muskegon, after draining a broad valley extending far into the interior, expands into a handsome lake close upon the shore of Lake Michigan. No natural provision could be more favorable for the handling of logs and the shipment of the sawed product, and the city of Muskegon, located upon the south shore of the lake, has the distinction of having annually cut more lumber than any other single city in the world. Manistee possesses a similar eminence in the manufacture of shingles. Montague, Whitehall, Pentwater, Ludington, Frankfort, Elk Rapids and Traverse City also contribute to swell the total of the forest products of the Lake Michigan shore.

There are many inland towns, situated upon railway lines, which are important centers of this industry.

Lumbering is yet in its infancy in the upper peninsula, but the value of the sawed and square timber product of that region in 1881 must be estimated at over $4,000,000. Saw mills are scattered along the shores and the railways of Menominee, Delta, Mackinac, Marquette, Schoolcraft, Baraga, Houghton and Ontonagon counties, but the chief centers of lumber production in that section of the State are Menominee, Escanaba, Manistique, St. Ignace, Ford River and Munising.

Menominee is claimed to be the greatest lumber producing city in the State at this time.

HARDWOODS IN NORTHERN MICHIGAN.

BY J. G. RAMSDELL, TRAVERSE CITY.

That portion of the lower peninsula of Michigan lying north and west of the Manistee river, and embracing the counties of Benzie, Leelanau, Grand Traverse, Antrim, Charlevoix and Emmet, the west half of Kalkaska, and the north halves of Manistee, Wexford and Missaukee, was originally covered with a dense forest growth of valuable timber. Along the river valleys and around the smaller inland lakes, pine, hemlock and cedar were the prevailing timbers. On the high table and rolling lands, around the borders of the larger inland lakes, and along the shore of the great lake and bays, the forest was composed of deciduous timber, interspersed with hemlock, maple and elm being the predominating varieties. About one-tenth of the whole area above described was occupied by pine or cedar, covered with water or was waste land. Of the pine about one-half has been cut; most of the cedar is still standing. The other nine-tenths were heavily timbered with hardwoods of uncommon height and size, of thrifty growth and excellent quality. This hardwood area is mostly owned by actual settlers; a large quantity, however, is still held by the Grand Rapids & Indiana Railroad and the Michigan Agricultural College.

About one-eighth of the hardwood lands have been cleared for agricultural purposes, leaving seven-eights of the natural forest still standing. As this hardwood land is all excellent farming land, in estimating the amount of timber available for manufacturing purposes, one-fourth of the hardwood area must be deducted for farm reserves. The whole number of acres in the territory under consideration is about 3,000,000; deducting one-tenth for pine, cedar, water and waste leaves 2,700,-000 acres as the amount of hardwood land. Estimating one-eighth of this as already cleared for agriculture, leaves as the amount of uncut hardwood land 2,362,-500 acres, and deducting from this one-fourth of the whole hardwood area leaves 2,025,000 acres of uncut hardwood available for commercial purposes.

From evidence before me, recently taken in a chancery cause, where the question of the amount per acre of merchantable deciduous saw timber on a certain half section of land in Benzie county became an important factor, I find that the testimony of timber experts placed the estimate at 8,000 feet of merchantable lumber per acre from the deciduous timber, 6,000 feet of which was surface clear; and it also showed that the half section in question was a fair average of the hardwood lands in this region. This estimate would make the amount of deciduous merchantable saw timber 1,620,000,000 feet. Nine-tenths of this is maple and elm, and the rest is beech, basswood, birch, ash and red oak in the order named. The foregoing estimate I consider too high; I would place the total at about 1,500,000,-000 feet of deciduous timber available for lumber.

I have consulted experts in the cordwood business, and they estimate the amount of timber available for charcoal wood, remaining after the saw timber is taken out, from twenty-five to thirty-five cords per acre. Taking the mean of thirty cords would give 60,750,000 cords that might be utilized for that purpose; enough to manufacture 25,000,000 tons of charcoal pig iron, or enough to furnish fifty charcoal furnaces of an average annual capacity of 20,000 tons for twenty-five years.

In making these estimates no account is made of hemlock, which is interspersed among all classes of timber and is valuable for both tan bark and lumber. The quantity is large, and for the whole region might be safely placed at one-tenth as much as the hardwood.

Of the territory embraced in the foregoing estimates, about twenty-two townships are directly tributary to the head of Grand Traverse bay as its natural outlet, the artificial outlet over the four railroads centering at Traverse City greatly enlarging the advantages of manufacturing at that place. There are but two charcoal furnaces in the whole region and consequently a large portion of the charcoal timber left after the removal of the saw timber goes to waste. The vast amount of this timber is to be had for the cost of cutting and transportation, the short and cheap water freight from the ore docks of Escanaba and St. Ignace, and the abundance of lime for flux cropping out in ledges on Grand Traverse bay should at once attract the charcoal iron manufacturers of the United States to this region, as combining advantages for this industry unequaled elsewhere, and suggesting an economy of production that would defy all competition in the production of charcoal iron.

The Onondaga salt formation underlies this whole territory at a depth of from 1,200 to 1,800 feet below the level of Lake Michigan. This formation has a stratum of pure rock salt from thirty to three hundred feet in thickness. The late Prof. Alexander Winchell, state geologist for Michigan, in his report of this region estimated the depth of boring to reach the salt rock at the head of Grand Traverse bay at about 1,200 feet.

No attempt has been made to test the accuracy of Prof. Winchell's survey at this place. The business men of Traverse City and vicinity have become impressed with the great advantages which the production of salt would be to the hardwood manufacturing interest and incidentally to all other business, and are taking steps to test the geological prediction referred to. Undoubtedly within the next six months the matter will be definitely determined by the sinking of a well. Should the salt rock be reached by such boring, the advantages of Traverse City and vicinity for working up the vast quantity of hardwood in the northwest portion of the lower peninsula of Michigan from stump to finish will be unequaled. For those who desire to enter into any branch of the hardwood industry, the forests of northwestern Michigan afford the most abundant supply of excellent timber of any portion of the United States. Its railroad facilities and numerous lake ports give superior advantages in the matter of freight. The numerous well tilled farms scattered through the region afford an abundance of cheap and excellent provisions for the household, and the free school system gives the best educational advantages to working men's children. Capacious and well furnished school houses are found in every neighborhood. The leading denominations have erected churches in all the villages, and many out among the farmers where villages are distant, and keep their pupils well supplied with an able and earnest ministry. In this country the new and old are most fortunately blended; the new in the advantage of cheap raw material, and the old in all the advantages of modern improvements.

THE BROAD-LEAVED TREES OF MICHIGAN.

BY W. J. BEAL, AGRICULTURAL COLLEGE, MICH.

"Hardwood" is a very indefinite and unsatisfactory term popularly employed, not only to designate the timber of oaks, sugar maple, beech, the hickories, etc., which is truly hard, but that of basswood, whitewood, butternut and cottonwood, which is truly soft. The term at the head of this article is easily understood by everyone and has the advantage, at least so far as Michigan is concerned, of being strictly accurate without exception.

The term "hardwood" implies another term, "softwood," which is not uncommonly employed to designate the timber of white pine, Norway pine, cedar, spruce, balsam, etc. These are all evergreen, with narrow leaves, but the timber of Norway pine is nearly on the dividing line between hardwood and softwood, and is certainly harder than that of basswood and cottonwood, which is usually included in the hardwoods. Tamarack, or larch, is not an evergreen, but is nearly related in a scientific way to the pines, cedars and spruces. Instead of the term "softwood" it would be preferable to use the term

CONE-BEARING OR PIN-LEAVED TREES.

Our trees belonging to this list are white pine, Norway pine, jack pine, hemlock, black spruce, white spruce, balsam fir, white (yellow) cedar, red cedar and tamarack.

Timber is relatively hard or soft nearly in proportion to its specific gravity when dry. From the forest report of the tenth census I give the specific gravity of the woods of some well-known trees. The heavier the wood the more valuable it is for fuel, the heating capacity when burned corresponding very closely to the weight:

15

Chestnut oak	.8605	Canoe birch	.5955
Shagbark hickory	.8372	Black cherry	.5822
Ironwood	.8284	Sycamore	.5678
White oak	.7470	Silver maple	.5269
Swamp white oak	.7453	Norway pine	.4854
Rock elm	.7263	Jack pine	.4761
Sugar maple	.6912	Basswood	.4525
Beech	.6883	Chestnut	.4504
White ash	.6543	Black willow	.4456
Red oak	.6540	Hemlock	.4239
American elm	.6506	Tulip tree (white wood)	.4230
Tamarack	.6236	Butternut	.4086
Red maple	.6178	Cottonwood	.3889
Black walnut	.6115	White pine	.3854
White (yellow) cedar	.3164		

The wood of the same species, or closely allied species, is harder in proportion as it grows in a dry climate. For example, the wood of white ash grown in dry portions of Texas is twenty per cent heavier than that grown in damper climates, like that of Michigan, while the wood of black walnut is thirty-three per cent heavier.

Michigan once contained, by estimate, 150,000,000,000 feet of pine, board measure. It is safe to say seven-eighths of this has been cut, or in some way destroyed. Since the petted "rabbit" has escaped it may now be a satisfaction to quote the opinion of Hon. Perry Hannah, that the State would have been better off had she never possessed a foot of pine, but had possessed only hardwoods instead. The reasons for this statement are as follows: Pine often grows on poor land, the dead leaves and brush and tops of trees encourage fires which devastate large areas, spreading to living trees and often beyond, destroying fences, dwellings and crops. The stumps are durable, and troublesome to cultivate among or expensive to remove. Desolation too often follows the track of the man who secures and cuts pine or other evergreen trees; but where hardwood is cut cultivated fields soon appear. Broad leaved trees are much less liable to suffer from fire, or lead to the spread of fires; they more frequently grow on good soil, and the stumps in a not remote period decay and disappear, leaving good farms to recruit and sustain the country.

For nearly all purposes the timber of some one or more of our numerous broad leaved trees is just as good as that of pine and even better. Timber of white and Norway pine is very pretty and suitable for many purposes, but with it we cannot acceptably fill so great a variety of places, especially in unpainted surfaces, or where strength or durability is required, as can be filled by timber of our broad leaved trees. The wood of many of the latter trees is most admirable for veneers, or for cutting in special ways to show the grain to the best advantage. The reasons why the broad leaved trees have not been removed as fast as the pine are these: The timber is harder and heavier, not so easily worked and more costly to transport. These slight barriers may have been an advantage to delay the rapid slaughter of this timber, which will take the place of pine when gone.

The main bulk of marketable timber of the cone-bearing trees consists of white pine, Norway pine, white (yellow) cedar, hemlock, with a little black spruce, white spruce and balsam fir; while the species of our broad leaved trees which furnish timber in the market are ten to twelve times as great.

The sugar maple is perhaps the most generally distributed and the most abundant of the native trees of our State, while beech is very widely distributed, red oak probably next. The white oak is abundant, well known and valuable, but disappears to the north as we enter the pine.

If we follow in nearly a direct line from the lower point of Lake Huron across the State to the mouth of the Kalamazoo river, in latitude a little north of 43 degrees, we will find at the south, three tiers of counties producing scarcely any other species of trees than those with broad leaves; while at the north, extending into the upper peninsula, are mixed tracts of both classes of trees as above defined. In this northern region may yet be found many cone-bearing trees of white and Norway pine, jack pine, hemlock, white (yellow) cedar, tamarack, black spruce, white spruce and balsam fir, while intermingled with them or in separate lots, are broad-leaved trees as follows: Sugar maple (including bird's eye), white oak, beech, American elm, (including gray), basswood, rock elm, red oak, black oak, swamp white oak (usually classed with white oak), black ash, yellow birch, red maple (one of the soft maples), silver maple (another soft maple), hackberry, butternut, bitternut, canoe birch, black birch, aspen, balm of gilead, black cherry, white ash, hickory, ironwood, burr-oak and scarlet oak.

In the region including the southern three tiers of counties spoken of, the number of species of broad-leaved trees is much increased, though in many counties this is all needed to supply the wants of the people living in the vicinity. In this southern region may be found white oak, swamp white oak, red oak, burr-oak, chestnut oak, black oak, beech, sugar maple, black maple, red maple, silver maple, basswood, black ash, white ash, red ash, blue ash, sycamore, American elm, rock elm, red elm, hackberry, mulberry, tulip tree, black cherry, Kentucky coffee tree, honey locust, downy thorn, dogwood, pepperidge, sassafras, black walnut, butternut, shagbark hickory, western shellbark hickory, small fruited hickory, mockernut, pignut, bitternut, black birch, black willow, aspen, large toothed aspen, cottonwood, downy poplar, balsam poplar, red cedar, black spruce, tamarack, and rarely a few trees of white pine, hemlock and jack pine. In all, native to the State, there about seventy kinds of trees.

Michigan has for a long time taken first rank among the northern central states for the value of her lumber product, and it is evident from the foregoing statements she must long hold a prominent place. But with the increased population of the State and surrounding states, greater inroads must be made on our forests. With improved modes of cutting and transporting this timber, it must go more rapidly than did the pine. As it takes a long time to grow a crop of timber, it stands us in hand to husband our present supply, using it all to best advantage, taking some pains to save unmolested in suitable places the groves of young trees already coming on to supply the demands of the future.

Hewing farms out of the forest, here and there, let in the winds and otherwise disturbed the natural condition of things. One of the consequences most apparant was the decay of trees at the top; slowly at first, but more and more apparent as more trees in the neighborhood were hewn down. There is no hope of reviving such trees; they must be cut, the sooner the better, and some returns obtained for the timber. In many cases when the primeval forest is left in isolated blocks, trees are turned up by the roots; various kinds of insects attack the decaying trees, and the work of destruction goes on rapidly. Not so with the second growth, which adapts itself to the changed conditions of surroundings. Our native forests are to be considered as exhaustible.

It is not pleasant to consider that the end is rapidly approaching, unless we begin to give more attention to the study of the subject and see to it that some of the youngest and smallest trees are spared for another crop. In most cases, very likely, those who cut the first crop will leave the recuperation to other hands. The history of other countries has repeatedly shown that "no system of agriculture can be long successful and profitable which ignores the necessity of renewing and cultivating trees;" and, we might add, that fails to give attention to the needs of the trees which remain.

THE SALT PRODUCT.

The manufacture of salt was inaugurated in Michigan in Saginaw ... 1860. It required a large expenditure in money and much experience before the industry had passed the experimental stage and reached substantial footing as a foremost industry. Between 1860 and 1866 not less than $200,000 were invested in the great salt scheme on the Saginaw, and men were bankrupted. It is safe to say that prior to 1870 not a dollar was made in manufacturing salt in Michigan because of the inexperience of the men engaged in the work, and because of the greed to get all the salt there was in the brine. The brine as it comes from the earth on the Saginaw contains iron, which made the salt rusty; bromide of sodium that made it bitter, and gypsum that made it cake, and all of which made it practically useless except as a fertilizer. The wiser men saw that it was a losing game unless they could get rid of these impurities and compel all manufacturers to do so. In 1869 a law was enacted by the legislature making it compulsory that all salt manufactured in the State should be inspected. To secure this enactment the saltmakers imposed upon themselves a special tax to cover the expenses of the office. That worked well and the quality of Michigan salt rapidly rose. But there were obstacles in the way of putting it on the market. In 1876 an association was formed, including all the prominent manufacturers, whereby all were bound to observe certain rules and regulations that were thought to be conducive to the success of Michigan salt. The association handled all the salt produced by its members, and thus secured uniform prices.

Salt works in the Saginaw valley are operated in connection with steam saw mills, and the refuse from the manufacture of lumber and shingles is used for fuel in evaporating the salt brine. By this method the production of salt is the most economical in the United States.

The following table prepared by William A. Raborg gives the amount produced in the various states and territories in 1890.

The production of salt in the United States during the years 1889 and 1890 was as follows: In 1889, 8,005,565 barrels, valued at $4,195,412, and in 1890, 8,776,991 barrels, valued at $4,752,286. The amount and value of the salt produced in the various states and territories in the latter year, 1890, is given in the following table:

Quantity and value of salt produced in the United States during the year 1890.

States and territories.	Production, Barrels.	Value.
Michigan	3,837,632	$2,302,579
New York	2,532,036	1,266,018
Ohio	231,303	136,617
West Virginia	229,938	134,638
Louisiana	273,553	132,000
California	62,363	57,085
Utah	427,500	126,100
Kansas	882,666	397,199
Nevada, Illinois, Indiana, Virginia, Tennessee, Kentucky, and other States and Territories, estimated	300,000	200,000
Total	8,776,991	$4,752,236

With a production of 3,837,632 barrels of salt, valued at $2,302,579, Michigan headed the list of salt producing states and territories in 1890. In 1889 the production was 3,856,929 barrels, valued at $2,088,909. Since 1887 there has been a yearly decrease in the production, although the amount of salt made continued to represent over one-half the product of the United States.

The average depths of the wells in the different counties were as follows: Mason, 2,200 feet; Manistee, 2,000 feet; St. Clair, 1,700 feet; Huron, 1,200 feet; Midland, 1,200 feet; Bay, Saginaw, and Iosco, 850 feet.

During 1890 there were one hundred and twenty-two salt producing companies in the State, ninety-seven of which were in operation, having a capacity of production of 5,950,000 barrels.

Product of Michigan salt in 1890, by districts.

Counties.	Fine.	Bulk.	Fine packers.	Packers.	Solar.	Second quality.	Total.
	Barrels.	*Barrels.*	*Barrels.*	*Barrels.*	*Barrels.*	*Barrels.*	*Barrels.*
Saginaw	655,293	305,127	308	1,659	18,896	25,571	1,006,854
Bay	581,072	214,787	462	3,138		20,644	820,103
Manistee	826,293	84,527	3,716	12,691		79,298	1,006,525
Mason	333,871	16,013	2,270			15,463	367,617
Huron	32,676	22,968		37			55,681
St. Clair	155,754	81,123	1,619	2,812		703	242,011
Iosco	289,232						289,232
Midland	46,812	1,353	55			1,389	49,609
Total	2,921,003	725,898	8,430	20,337	18,896	143,063	3,837,632

In 1892 State Salt Inspector Michael Casey reported the following salt manufacturers, with capacity of each by districts:

District No. 1, Saginaw County.

	Total barrels.		Total barrels.
A. T. Bliss, U. M.	40,180	Whittier Co.	6,193
A. T. Bliss, L. M.	25,712	G. B. Wiggins	6,607
Bliss & Van Auken, No. 2	39,688	A. W. Wright Lumber Co.	42,779
Bliss & Van Auken, No. 1	17,769	Wylie Bros.	13,432
Briggs & Cooper	11,575	S. C. Stone	8,044
Green, Ring & Co.	26,193	Linton Co.	18,725
Gebhart & Estabrook	15,197	Merrill & Ring	2,108
C. L. Grant & Co.	14,216	Tyler & Son	24,264
Nelson Holland	34,835	E. O. & S. L. Eastman	26,058
Mitchell, McClure & Co.	34,968	D. Hardin & Co.	8,470
Melchers & Nerreter	3,236	D. Hardin	2,594
C. Merrill & Co.	53,183	Brand & Hardin	11,671
W. B. Mershon & Co.	27,863	E. F. Gould	4,505
Rust Bros. & Co.	36,754	C. K. Eddy & Son	27,257
Rust, Eaton & Co.	35,963	E. R. Ayers & Co.	24,352
Sample & Camp	1,568	Wall & Webber	24,189
C. M. Hill	14,594	Cambray & Co.	3,940
Saginaw Lumber & Salt Co.	42,241	Ed. Germain	15,320
W. F. Stevens	4,891	G. B. Wiggins, Stevens block	5,793
Whitney & Batchelor	83,691	L. McLaughlin	2,410
			842,235

District No. 2, Bay County.

	Total barrels.		Total barrels.
F. B. Bradley & Co.	26,371	S. McLean & Co.	49,425
Butman & Rust	5,749	Pitts & Cranage	45,731
Dolsen-Chapin Co.	38,528	Sage & Co.	67,753
Eddy, Avery & Eddy	51,650	W. B. Rouse	82,350
Eddy Bros. & Co.	40,206	Kern Manufacturing Co.	32,347
Folsom & Arnold	28,680	Hine & Lederach	14,750
E. Hall	32,512	N. B. Bradley & Son	2,287
J. R. Hall	33,537	William Peter	19,019
Hargrave & Son	1,502	C. C. Barker	7,551
Carpenter & Co.	27,909	J. Boyce	22,083
Michigan Pipe Co.	12,965	Smalley & Woodworth	8,806
Miller & Turner	31,715	T. H. McGraw & Co.	11,771
McEwan Bros. & Co.	45,822		
			691,834

District No. 3, Huron County.

	Total barrels.		Total barrels.
Port Hope Salt Co.	831	R. C. Ogilvie	440
Curran, Flash & Conly	823	Huron Dairy Salt Co.	29,065
			31,159

District No. 4, St. Clair County.

	Total barrels.		Total barrels.
St. Clair River Salt Co.	1,183	Vacuum Salt Co.	77,521
Thompson Bros.	93,979	Walton Salt Co.	75,272
Diamond Crystal Salt Co.	18,466	Marine City Stave Co.	80,821
			347,242

District No. 5, Iosco County.

	Total barrels.		Total barrels.
Temple Emery	41,549	Gratwick, Smith & Fryer Lumber Co.	69,815
Iosco Brine Supply Co.	14,442	Pack, Woods & Co.	89,486
Winona Salt Co.	15,605		
			230,897

District No. 6, Midland County.

	Total barrels.		Total barrels.
William Patrick	21,573	Midland Salt & Lumber Co.	11,807
			33,380

District No. 7, Manistee County.

	Total barrels.		Total barrels.
Canfield Salt & Lumber Co.	110,705	Louis Sands	124,282
Canfield Salt & Lumber Co., East Lake.	54,478	Stronach Lumber Co.	198,936
Canfield & Wheeler Co.	71,690	E. G. Filler & Son	100,573
Michigan Trust Co.	382,137	C. Reits & Bro.	13,100
State Lumber Co.	186,941	Eureka Lumber Co.	141,196
			1,294,139

District No. 8, Mason County.

	Total barrels.		Total barrels.
Butters & Peter Salt Lumber Co.	68,931	Pere Marquette Lumber Co.	90,918
Thomas Percy	181,819		
			341,668

Recapitulation.

	Total barrels.		Total barrels.
Saginaw District, No. 1	842,235	Iosco District, No. 5	230,897
Bay County District, No. 2	691,334	Midland District, No. 6	33,390
Huron District, No. 3	31,159	Manistee District, No. 7	1,294,139
St. Clair District, No. 4	347,242	Mason District, No. 8	341,668
			3,812,054

THE SALT MARKET.

The manufacture of salt of late has not been very profitable, and but for the fact that it has been produced in connection with the manufacture of lumber products, the refuse from the logs furnishing the fuel for evaporating the brine, the production of salt in this State would have been comparatively on a limited scale. The impression has gained a foothold throughout the country that the salt industry is a monopoly, and that every person who engaged therein was inevitably to become a millionaire. That such is not the fact is shown by the following comparison of net prices obtained by the manufacturers, based on a barrel of 280 pounds, with a 20-cent package included:

Average price per barrel, 1866	$1 80	Average price per barrel, 1879	$1 02
" " " " 1867	1 77	" " " " 1880	75
" " " " 1868	1 85	" " " " 1881	83 2-8
" " " " 1869	1 58	" " " " 1882	70
" " " " 1870	1 32	" " " " 1883	81
" " " " 1871	1 46	" " " " 1884	75 2-3
" " " " 1872	1 46	" " " " 1885	70
" " " " 1873	1 37	" " " " 1886	66
" " " " 1874	1 19	" " " " 1887	57 4-10
" " " " 1875	1 10	" " " " 1888	58 5-10
" " " " 1876	1 05	" " " " 1889	54 3-10
" " " " 1877	85	" " " " 1890	54 7-10
" " " " 1878	85	" " " " 1891	55

There is no commodity of general domestic consumption so cheap as Michigan salt.

COAL.

BY S. G. HIGGINS, SAGINAW.

Coal is found in this State over a pretty wide area, in Huron, Arenac, Shiawassee, Clinton, Ingham, Eaton, Jackson, and in other counties; but it has only been extensively mined in Shiawassee and Jackson counties, principally in the latter. Coal mining has for many years been a prominent industry in and about Jackson. (Extract Report Mineral Statistics.)

[Extract from Review of Saginaw Board of Trade.]

It has been known for many years that coal beds existed in the Saginaw valley, but no practical efforts were made to develop them until about three years ago, when two mines were opened at Sebewaing, forty miles northeast of Saginaw, on the line of the Saginaw, Tuscola & Huron railroad, one by the Saginaw Bay Coal Company, controlled by Saginaw capitalists, and the other by the Sebewaing Coal Company, controlled by Bay City and Tuscola county capitalists. The coal has found a ready market, the demand being greater than the companies were able to supply, owing to the scarcity of labor to work the mines. During 1892 there were shipped from Sebewaing. eight hundred and six cars of coal, being an average of sixty-seven cars per month, which went to various points in the State. The demand for the coal is rapidly increasing, and during the present winter the companies were compelled to decline many orders.

The coal is found at Sebewaing about one hundred feet from the surface, in a bed averaging four and one-half feet in thickness. It is an excellent quality of bituminous coal. Owing to its cokeing qualities, it has a tendency to run together and form a mass on the grates, unless properly handled. At first this was a serious drawback to the use of the coal, but now that it is better understood, the firemen have no difficulty in using it. The coal possesses more heat units than the Ohio coal, and is a cheaper fuel for the Saginaw valley.

16

The following diagram of stratification was furnished by Saginaw board of trade:

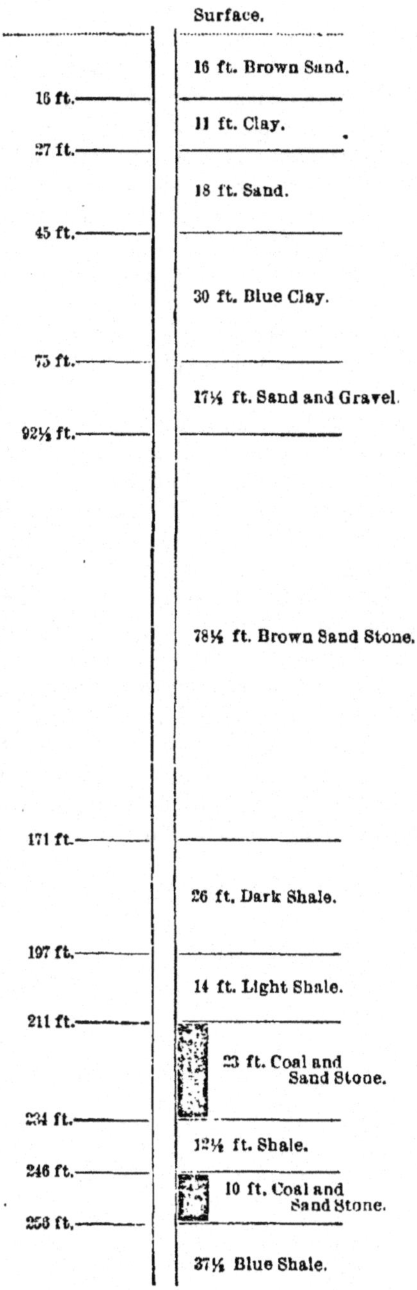

Diagram of a part of the first Salt Well put down in the Saginaw valley, drilled by the East Saginaw Salt Manufacturing Co., in 1859, at Saginaw, showing beds of coal passed through.

Surface.

16 ft. Brown Sand.

16 ft.———

11 ft. Clay.

27 ft.———

18 ft. Sand.

45 ft.———

30 ft. Blue Clay.

75 ft.———

17½ ft. Sand and Gravel.

92½ ft.———

78½ ft. Brown Sand Stone.

171 ft.———

26 ft. Dark Shale.

197 ft.———

14 ft. Light Shale.

211 ft.———

23 ft. Coal and Sand Stone.

234 ft.———

12½ ft. Shale.

246 ft.———

10 ft. Coal and Sand Stone.

256 ft.———

37½ Blue Shale.

This salt well, as will be seen by the diagram, passed through two coal bearing strata, one 23 feet in thickness, at a depth of 211 feet, and the other 10 feet, at a depth of 216 feet. This salt well was located in the city of East Saginaw, now a part of the city of Saginaw. The accompanying diagram is reproduced from the record made of the well at the time it was put down. It is somewhat remarkable that this coal has not yet been opened up, and is an illustration of the fact that we have not yet begun to comprehend the great natural wealth and resources of the Saginaw valley.

In 1875 coal was discovered five miles west of Saginaw, on section 12, town 12 north, range 3 east. A report of the discovery, printed at the time, states as follows:

"Two holes, one-fourth mile apart, were sunk to the depth of one hundred and sixty-four feet, resulting in finding a superior article of bituminous coal. During the past summer another hole was bored nearly a fourth mile distant from the others, and the following is the log of the borers:

	Feet.
Sand	16
Clay and hard pan	85
Sulphuret of iron	2
Sandstone and slate	23
Coal	4½
Sandstone, slate and shale	24
Coal	7
Total	161½

"The following analysis was reported by the chemist to whom the coal borings were submitted:

	Per cent.
Carbon	73.3
Ash	5.7
Sulphur	.68

"The almost entire absence of sulphur and the large preponderance of carbon render this, it is claimed by those who claim to be posted, fully equal to the product of the celebrated Blossburg and Cumberland mines."

The report goes on to say that drillings at a point southwest from the holes above mentioned, on the banks of the Tittabawassee river, struck a bed of coal seven feet thick, one hundred and fifty-eight feet from the surface.

During the past year coal has been discovered at numerous places in Saginaw county, south and southwest from Saginaw, from forty to fifty feet below the surface, with good roof, and in beds of five to seven feet in thickness, and of a most excellent quality.

There is no reason to doubt but the whole Saginaw valley is underlaid with rich deposits of coal, which will furnish an unlimited supply of fuel for the great manufacturing industries to be developed.

It is said by experts who have examined the coal, that it is what is called a "caking" or coking coal, and suitable for use in smelting iron ore. This is the nearest coal to the rich bessemer ores of the upper peninsula, and these ores could be hauled in cars direct from the mines to Saginaw for smelting, saving the long journey to Cleveland and Pittsburgh, and the numerous transfers from cars to boats and from boats to cars. Furthermore, the cars could run winter and summer, and save the expense of piling the ore on the surface at the mines during the winter while navigation is closed. It requires two tons of coke to smelt one ton of ore, and hence the ore must come to the coke for smelting. The great deposits of iron ore in the Duluth region cannot be utilized there, for want of fuel, but with a good coke at Saginaw we could smelt a large part of these ores.

This is an essential element of independence in the State. While the State is not far from Ohio and Pennsylvania and transportation is not exhorbitant, without a home supply we would be subject to accidents and at the mercy of combines. If the coal supply develops, as anticipated by the more sanguine and enterprising, Michigan takes one step upward.

RAILROAD DEPARTMENT — THE COMMISSIONER OF RAILROADS.

BY E. A. RUNDELL.

The Commissioner of Railroads is appointed under the provisions of act No. 79, session laws of 1873. He holds his office for the term of two years upon appointment of the Governor by and with the advice and consent of the Senate, and until his succeesor is appointed and qualified.

It is the duty of the Commissioner of Railroads generally to examine into the condition and management of the business of the railroads in the State, so far as the same affects or relates to the interests of the public, and to ascertain whether such railroad companies and their officers and employés comply with the laws of the State in force concerning them.

It is also his duty to require annual reports from all railroad companies doing business in the State on the first day of April of each year, showing their condition and traffic operations for the year ending on the 31st of December preceding.

At least once each year to visit every county in the State having a railroad station within its limits, and to inspect and examine the tracks, bridges, buildings, and other structures, so as to know that they are in safe and effective condition, and managed in accordance with the police regulations of the State.

To order safety gates or flagmen at highway and street crossings; to prescribe a uniform code of signals at all crossings and junctions of railroads within the State; to inspect and determine upon the sufficiency of all fences and to prescribe the manner of constructing the same; to require and receive reports of all accidents resulting in a loss of life or otherwise, and to investigate the causes of the same; to direct the erection of safety guards at overhead obstructions; to provide a uniform system of accounts for all the railroad corporations of the State; to regulate the speed of trains upon defective tracks and to stop them entirely if in his judgment the public safety requires. To direct prosecutions for infractions of the railroad laws; to compute and report to the Auditor General on the first of July of each year the taxes due and payable from each railroad company, and from all palace-car companies, fast freight lines, etc., doing business in the State, upon their gross receipts for the preceding year; to make an annual report to the Governor, on or before the first day of January of each year, of his doings for the preceding year, or for the time intervening since his last report, containing such facts, statements and explanations as will disclose the actual workings of the system of railroad transportation of freight and passengers, and its bearings upon the business prosperity, personal convenience and safety of the people of the State, with such suggestions in relation thereto as to him may seem appropriate.

He is empowered to appoint a deputy, with the approval of the Governor, whose powers are defined by law, and in case of the death, resignation or removal of the commissioner, the deputy performs the duties of the commissioner until a successor shall be appointed. (See 3235 to 3312 a inclusive, Howell's annotated statutes.) He shall also appoint a mechanical engineer. (See act 247, laws of 1887.)

It will be seen from the above that the office of Commissioner of Railroads is a very important and responsible position. It is ably filled by the present incumbent, Hon. S. R. Billings, of Davison, Mich.

The duties and work of the department of the Commissioner of Railroads will be more readily understood when it is remembered there are 79 railroad companies operating in this State with a mileage of 7,502 of main line track, exclusive of spurs and side tracks, and 1,489 railway stations required to be inspected every year. There are also 773 wood and iron bridges, 30 draw bridges, 2,302 combination and trestles, 340 railroad crossings at grade, 40 railroad crossings over or under, 7,282 highway crossings, 495 highway crossings with gates or signals, 318 highway crossings over or under, 9,712 miles of fencing, 75 interlocking and derailing switch and signal systems. These all require the constant attention of the Commissioner.

The railroads operating in and partly within and partly without Michigan are a very important factor in connection with the business commerce of the State. They employ 26,838 persons in the State, carry about 34,208,271 passengers and move 57,852,628 tons of freight per year. The total income from all sources amounts to $96,682,121.41, and the total amount paid out for operating expenses, interest and rentals amounts to $87,141,330.11. The amount of authorized capital stock and debt is $767,663,559.30. The total cost of the railroads and equipments for Michigan to December 31, 1892, is $294,611,753,84; 3,222 locomotives, 1,650 passenger cars and 108,246 cars of all other kinds are used in conducting this vast amount of business, which is steadily increasing. It required 65,547 tons of new rails and 2,370,130 new ties to keep the railroads in Michigan in repair for the year ending 1891.

The amount of taxes for the year ending December 31, 1892, due the State from the railroads and payable July 1, 1893, is $893,762.01, an increase of $39,-427.89 over the year 1891. The taxes paid the State by railroads is steadily increasing, and for the past five years shows an average increase of $36,328.69. If this increase is maintained, the amount will soon reach $1,000,000.

A little study of the above will show the necessity and importance of the duties of the Commissioner of Railroads and his department.

Railroads are in close touch with the pulse of the nation. They throb and beat with every fluctuation of business. The volume of business done by the railroads indicate the prosperity of the State and country.

Several important bills were passed by the legislature of 1893 affecting the railroads operating in this State. The two most important are as follows: A bill to provide separate grades for railroads and public highways and streets where railroads intersect such highways and streets; also a bill to regulate the construction of the tracks of railroads and street railroads across each other, and stringing of wires, electric or other, above railroad tracks, and relative to the maintenance of such tracks heretofore so constructed and wires heretofore so strung.

Great credit is due to the officers managing the railroads in this State for the constant care and efficient manner in which they are operated, and it is only fair to state that the management and officers of the railroads doing business in Michigan are ever desirous and willing to obey and comply with the laws. They cheerfully coöperate with the Commissioner of Railroads in carrying out recommendations or instructions given by said commissioner tending to promote the safety or the protection of life and property.

The figures given in this article are chiefly taken and compiled from the annual reports ending December 31, 1891.

At this date nearly every county in the State is traversed by railroads. A glance at the map in the front of this book will show how well the State is supplied with this convenience, and the competition is so great the fare for passenger and freight is reasonable if not low. It is deemed unnecessary to make special mention of each road.

TRANSPORTATION.

Besides a network of railroads no country in the world of equal magnitude will show equal facilities for water transportation. All cities on the coast of the great lakes surrounding Michigan have communication with the world. Vessels carrying 1,000,000 feet of newly cut lumber clear from ports on Lake Michigan. A moment's reflection will surprise you. A freight car will carry 10,000 feet of lumber. It would require one hundred cars full loaded to carry one vessel load; five full trains of twenty cars each, with the necessary expense of five conductors, five engineers, five firemen, and a number of brakesmen, taking this with stationmen, roadmen, trackmen, all to be paid from the profits, makes it necessary as a business to charge higher freight rates than vessels. Saginaw is miles inland and yet is connected by river navigable by large vessels. Grand Rapids will in the course of time be linked to Lake Michigan by a deepening of Grand river. New York has a few cities which are favored by water transportation. Ohio has Cleveland, Cincinnati and Toledo. Illinois has Chicago and cities on the Mississippi. Wisconsin has Milwaukee and other cities of less importance, and many other states a mere taste of water transportation. Michigan has Ontonagon, Marquette, the "Soo," Escanaba, Menominee, Muskegon, Grand Haven, Alpena, Port Huron, Saginaw, Bay City, St. Clair, Detroit, and others of smaller importance. More than any other country in the world, and in order to compete with this the railroads must offer great inducements in the way of cheap rates and accommodations.

THE ST. CLAIR TUNNEL.

The United States and the Dominion of Canada are divided by the St. Clair river, which great stream is the connecting link of the greatest group of lakes in the world. Through this river the waters of Lakes Michigan, Superior and Huron

TUNNEL PORTAL, AMERICAN SIDE

APPROACH TO TUNNEL, CANADIAN SIDE

INTERIOR OF
TUNNEL

MAMMOTH
TUNNEL ENGINE
IN
AMERICAN PORTAL

flow onward toward the great tumble at Niagara, eventually to reach the briny Atlantic through the wild, majestic St. Lawrence.

It is by nature as well as by adoption the great artery or canal of inland commerce, national and international in importance, hence to obstruct would be a national and international interruption. Across this great highway of navigation, the interchanging inland commerce between east and west, a way must be provided. A bridge was impractiable, ferries difficult and uncertain on account of ice and interruption. The problem was solved by the Grand Trunk system by the construction of, in many respects, the greatest tunnel of modern history, virtually leaving the grand St. Clair river clear to navigation uninterrupted by ferries. While it is intended to do no advertising in this work it would be impossible to make mention properly of the great St. Clair tunnel without mentioning the Grand Trunk railroad, the designer and finisher of the work.

A few statistics, only a few of special interest, may be given here. The length of the tunnel proper is 6,025 feet, and of the open portals or approaches 5,603 feet additional, or more than two miles in all, the longest sub-marine tunnel in the world. It is a continuous iron tube, nineteen feet ten inches in diameter. put together in sections as the work of boring proceeded, and firmly bolted together, the total weight of the iron aggregating 56,000,000 pounds.

The work was commenced in September, 1888, and it was opened for freight traffic in October, 1891, a little more than three years being required for its completion. Passenger trains began running through it December 7, 1891. The work was begun on both sides and carried on until the two sections met in mid-river, and with such accuracy that they were perfectly in line as they came together. Throughout its entire length it perforates a bed of blue clay, and with the exception of an occasional pocket of quicksand and water, with once in a while a rock or bolder, the clay was the only material met. The borings were made by means of cylindrical steel shields with cutting edges, driven forward by hydraulic rams and as fast as the clay was cut away a section of the iron wall of the tunnel was bolted to its fellow section, and thus the wall was completed as the work progressed. The rails of the track rest upon cross ties only six inches apart, laid on stringers which in turn rest on a bed of brick and concrete, filling the bottom of the tube.

The engines used for pulling the trains through the tunnel and up the steep grade after emerging, are the largest in the world, having ten drive wheels, and weighing nearly 200,000 pounds. The boilers are 74 inches in diameter, the fireboxes 132 and one-half inches long and 42 and one-eighth inches wide, and the cylinders are 22 inches in diameter, with 28-inch stroke.

The cost of the great tunnel was $2,700,000. and when it is understood that 4,000 cars can be daily moved through it and this is contrasted with the slow, laborious and dangerous transfers by ferries, it will readily appear that the enormous expenditure was a wise undertaking and will yield profitable returns.

We cannot give the G. T. R. R. Co. too much credit for the undertaking, when the expenditure and risk is considered. At its own expense it demonstrated the fact that capital and engineering skill will accomplish most anything. No one can pass through this tunnel without being impressed with the permanent character of its construction and the safety, speed, and certainty of travel and transportation. It will remain a lasting monument to its projectors.

THE SHIPPING PORTS.

BY RICHARD A. PARKER, C. E., OF MARQUETTE.

The Lake Superior region furnished nearly fifty-five per cent of the ore mined in the United States in 1892, and of that quantity Michigan furnished eighty-six per cent. In no other part of the world are there equal facilities for the handling and transportation of such vast quantities of ore. A practically all water route from the mines to the furnaces makes possible the transportation of ores in great bulks. In fact, but for this provision of nature, the district would be almost worthless on account of the prohibitory cost of transportation in carload lots.

The great extent of coast line and its deep indentations afford a number of fine harbors, some of which have been equipped expressly for the handling of iron ore. A brief sketch of these harbors will be of interest. The first Lake Superior iron ore was shipped from Marquette early in the fifties, and up to the close of 1892 a total of 18,644,203 tons had passed from its docks into the holds of vessels. The amount shipped in 1892 was 1,027,323 tons. Until 1879 Marquette held the lead in quantity of ore handled, but in that year Escanaba gained it. Three docks, one recently built and another greatly extended, together with their incidental rolling stock, constitute the equipment for transferring the ore from the cars into the holds of lake carriers. No. 4 dock, built in 1889-90, is a specimen of the most modern and perfect structure of its class and cost $250,000. It was fully described and illustrated, with the designer's drawings, in the New York Engineering and Mining Journal of January 10 and 17, 1891.

Herewith is a brief sketch of the three docks all owned by the Duluth, South Shore and Atlantic Railway Company.

No. 1.—Height of dock above water forty-two feet for first thirteen hundred feet of its length; the new extension of six hundred feet is forty-four feet above water; number of pockets two hundred and seventy, number of tracks three, capacity twenty-seven thousand long tons.

No. 2.—This was a small and antiquated structure. In 1892 it was dismantled and a merchandise pier was erected on the piles.

No. 3.—Height of dock above water forty-four feet, length sixteen hundred feet, number of pockets three hundred, number of tracks three, capacity twenty-five thousand long tons.

No. 4.—Height above water, forty-seven and one-half feet; length, fourteen hundred feet; capacity thirty thousand long tons.

L'Anse became an ore shipping port in 1873 by the building of a dock owned by the Duluth, South Shore and Atlantic Railroad Company for the handling of the product from the west end of the Marquette range. The dock is thirty-eight feet high, one thousand feet long, contains a hundred pockets, and has a capacity of eight thousand long tons. No ore has been shipped thence since 1885. The total reached seven hundred and forty-four thousand six hundred and ninety-seven tons.

St. Ignace has been a shipping port on a small scale since 1882, and has handled six hundred and ten thousand two hundred and fifteen tons of ore. In 1891 the dock was shortened four hundred feet, the material being removed to Marquette for the extension of No. 1 dock there. As constructed it was eight hundred feet long, forty-two feet high, contained one hundred pockets and three tracks, and had a capacity of ten thousand long tons.

Escanaba has maintained the lead she won in 1879 and her aggregate tonnage of iron ore in 1891 and 1892 led the world. Shipment began in 1865 by putting the Marquette range under tribute. In 1877 the new Menominee range began to empty her treasures into the lap of the coming iron port of the world. In 1892 her shipments were 4,012,197 tons, nearly one-half the entire ore shipment of the whole Lake Superior region. The stupendous quantity of 33,975,451 tons of iron ore has passed through her gates en route to lower lake receiving ports.

The Chicago and Northwestern Railway company is the owner of the five immense docks at Escanaba. These docks, together with their equipment of cars, cost $2,290,000. They are described as follows:

No. 1.—Height, forty-six feet; length eleven hundred and four feet; pockets, one hundred and eighty-four; tracks, two; capacity twenty-three thousand long tons.

No. 2.—Height, thirty-nine feet; length, ten hundred and eighty-two feet; pockets, one hundred and ninety-two; tracks, two; capacity, nineteen thousand three hundred long tons.

No. 3.—Height, thirty-nine feet; length, twelve hundred and twelve feet; pockets, two hundred and two; tracks, two; capacity, twenty thousand long tons.

No. 4.—Height, forty-six feet; length, fifteen hundred feet; pockets, two hundred and fifty; tracks, two; capacity, thirty-three thousand two hundred long tons.

No. 5.—Height, fifty-one feet ten inches; length, thirteen hundred and ninety-two feet; pockets, two hundred and thirty-two; tracks, two; capacity, forty thousand six hundred long tons.

At Ashland the Wisconsin Central railway has one dock forty-six feet high, fourteen hundred and four feet long, contains two hundred and thirty-four pockets and three tracks, and has a capacity of twenty-eight thousand two hundred and fifty long tons. With its equipments the total cost was $644,800. The Milwaukee, Lake Shore & Western has two docks there, one forty and the other forty-five feet high. Each is fourteen hundred and four feet long and contains two hundred and thirty-four pockets. One has four and the other three tracks. Their capacity respectively is twenty-three thousand and twenty-seven thousand long tons. The total cost with equipments was $813,000.

Gladstone, Michigan, shares with Escanaba the care of the Menominee range product and an occasional cargo of Gogebic and Marquette ore goes out of this

17

port. Shipments began in 1889 and attained an aggregate of 458,711 tons at the end of 1892. The Minneapolis, Sault Ste. Marie and Atlantic (Soo Line) is the owner of the dockage facilities, which consist of one dock forty-seven feet high, about twelve hundred feet in length, contains one hundred and twenty pockets and five tracks and has a capacity of sixteen thousand long tons. The docks are all wooden structures. The upper deck or floor is from forty to fifty feet above water level, sufficient to accommodate bins of fifteen to twenty feet depth with outward sloping bottoms below the floor level, and yet high enough to be well above the rail of the largest vessels lying alongside. Plate iron chutes or spouts are hinged beneath small doors at the bottom of the pockets. The doors are controlled from the top of the docks and when opened they discharge the ore through the chutes into the hold of the vessel. In this manner a cargo of three thousand tons is often loaded in three hours. As many pockets can be simultaneously discharged as there are hatchways in the vessels. As the principal mining companies are the owners of the fleets of modern and capacious lake carriers employed exclusively in the ore transportation business, the product of the mines receives most expeditious conveyance to the furnaces.

BILBOA AND LAKE SUPERIOR COMPARED.

The Bilboa district in Spain is the only iron producer in the world which will stand comparison with the Lake Superior district with great disparity as to quantity. The output in 1860 of the Bilboa district is not known. For the same period the production of the Marquette range, the only producing range in the Lake Superior district to 1860, and for many years after, is estimated at 203,676 long tons. The figures for the Bilboa district are given in metric tons, but as the metric ton has an advantage of only thirty-four pounds over the long tons, the quantity making, as reported by the chief mining engineer of the province, may be compared with the Lake Superior figures, as shown in the following table prepared by John Birkinbine for embodiment in his 1891 report on mineral resources to the census bureau of the United States:

Year.	Bilboa.	Lake Superior.	Total, 1860 to 1890 inclusive.	
			Bilboa.	Lake Superior.
1860	69,816	114,401		
1870	250,337	859,507		
1880	2,683,627	1,962,477		
1890	4,326,983	8,844,031	45,099,253	57,549,800

EDUCATIONAL.

MICHIGAN'S SYSTEM OF COMMON SCHOOLS.

BY J. E. HAMMOND, DEPUTY SUPERINTENDENT OF PUBLIC INSTRUCTION.

The State of Michigan has an excellent school system. No State in proportion to the wealth gives a more generous support to its common schools, and the denominational colleges and normal schools take high rank among the educational institutions of the country.

CLASSIFICATION OF THE SCHOOLS.

The common schools are known as graded and ungraded. The ungraded schools exist in the smaller country districts, and still preserve some of the chief features of the original primary school.

Within the past ten years a large number of the ungraded country schools have been graded by the teachers and school officers, under the supervision of the county board of school examiners, and now have prescribed courses of study similar to those of the villages and cities. The work of grading all the country schools is well begun and in the near future it may seem advisable to make another classification than graded and ungraded.

The districts are well distributed throughout the State, two or three miles apart, containing from three to nine sections of land, and there is no considerable village or city within the boundary of Michigan which cannot point to its substantial school buildings as one of its most attractive features. The statistics gathered by the Superintendent of Public Instruction for 1892 show that every organized county in the State was provided with school houses and that with very few exceptions all districts maintained school during the year

The number of school houses reported for 1892 was 7,666, of which 5,897 were frame buildings and only 390 were log structures. The whole number of districts in 1892 was 7,145, and in the district were employed 16,100 teachers, receiving an aggregate of $2,639,301.54, not including the cost of buildings and the salaries paid in seventeen incorporated institutions within the limits of the State.

HIGHER INSTITUTIONS OF LEARNING.

The institutions above referred to may justly be considered a part of our school systems, as into them annually are received thousands of the best students of the State. These institutions supported by the State being noticed in another part of this work we speak briefly of them here. Aside from the school for dependent children, for the deaf, dumb and blind, reformatory for boys, and reformatory for girls, Michigan has reason to be proud of her mining school which is situated in the richest copper bearing region of the country. The Agricultural College, near Lansing, the State Normal School at Ypsilanti, and above and greater than all, the great University, at Ann Arbor.

INCORPORATED INSTITUTIONS.

It is eminently proper in this connection to accord a little time and space to a part of an educational system that may not be included elsewhere and which should not be overlooked.

Statistics of the denominational schools of Michigan in 1892.

Name.	Where located.	Denomination.	Name of President.	No. of instructors.	No. of students.	Endowment.	Value of property.
Albion College	Albion	Methodist Episcopal	L. R. Fiske	26	610	$230,000	$125,000
Alma College	Alma	Presbyterian	A. F. Bruske	13	172	81,000	150,000
Adrian College	Adrain	Protestant Methodist	J. F. McCulloch	13	137	48,000	200,000
Battle Creek College	Battle Creek	Seventh Day Adventist	W. W. Prescott	25	612		105,508
Benzonia College	Benzonia	Congregational	S. B. Harvey	9	96	33,000	14,000
Detroit College	Detroit	Catholic	M. P. Dowling	16	310		160,000
Hillsdale College	Hillsdale	Free Baptist	G. F. Mosher	26	524	202,000	75,000
Hope College	Holland	Dutch Reformed	Charles Scott	12	264	136,000	40,000
Kalamazoo College	Kalamazoo	Baptist	Theodore Nelson	9	177	195,685	60,000
Olivet College	Olivet	Congregational, Presbyterian	W. G. Sperry	20	407	142,252	174,320
St. Mary's Academy	Monroe	Catholic	Mother M. Clotilda	22	176		90,294
Spring Arbor Seminary	Spring Arbor	Free Methodist	A. H. Stilwell	4	100		10,000

PRIVATE AND OTHER SCHOOLS.

There are in Michigan a number of schools under private control of some merit. The Catholic church maintains parochial schools in all of the larger cities. At Kalamazoo is located a female seminary, and at Orchard Lake, near Pontiac, is a military academy, whose course includes instructions in military tactics. There are two medical colleges located in Detroit, and a number of private institutions throughout the State especially devoted to commercial training, prominent among which is the Ferris Industrial School at Big Rapids, Cleary's Business College at

Ypsilanti, and Parson's Business College at Kalamazoo. The number of private schools in the State reported to the Superintendent of Public Instruction in 1892 was two hundred and eighty-eight, giving instruction to 26,614 pupils.

FUNDS FOR THE SUPPORT OF EDUCATION.

There are several sources of revenue for the support of the primary school.

1. *Taxes voted by school districts.* The voters of each district have authority to vote amounts for the support of schools during the year, under certain provisions of law imposed with the view of preventing extravagance. The taxes thus voted are reported by school officers to township officers and by them spread upon the tax roll for collection. The total taxation in Michigan in 1892 was $3,826,315.63, or about one-third of a cent on a dollar of the assessed valuation of the State.

2. *The one mill tax.* Beside the so-called district tax mentioned above, each township raises annually a tax of one-tenth of a cent on each dollar of its assessed valuation, and this is apportioned to the school district in which it was raised, provided such district has maintained at least the minimum school term required by law. Such part of this tax as may have been raised in unorganized territory, or in districts not maintaining the required school term, is apportioned to those districts which have complied with the law, according to the number of children in the school census. In 1892 the amount realized from the one mill tax was $661,804.53.

3. *The Primary School Fund.* This amount is paid to the schools twice each year, on the tenth day of May and November. The Superintendent of Public Instruction apportions this fund to the various counties in proportion to the number of children of school age—5 to 20—in the county. The amount for each county is apportioned to the township and school districts, so that every county, township and school district receives now from the State in 1893 an amount equal to three-fourths of the entire State tax paid. Upon the organization of Michigan as a State, the moneys derived from the sale of section 16 was made a permanent school fund, and controlled by the State as a whole, and not by each individual township, as in some states. Another source of revenue to this fund is the money received from the sale of swamp lands. Formerly only one-half received from the sale of swamp lands went into the school fund; now the whole amount is made available for the use of the schools. The extinguishment of the State debt has also left the specific tax paid by the corporations, to be added to the income of the primary school fund. The amount per capita of the primary school fund twice each year is about 75 cents per pupil. Total amount received in this way in 1892 was $906,810, while in the May apportionment alone in 1893 nearly $520,000 was distributed.

4. *Aid comes to the schools from various other sources.* The tuition of non-resident pupils amounts to a considerable in many graded village schools, and by a law of the legislature of 1881 all the money received from the dog tax in excess of $100 goes into the fund for the support of schools. The total amount received from miscellaneous sources in 1892 was $279,683.

The entire sum realized for school purposes in 1892 was $5,738,222.69.

SCHOOL YEAR REQUIRED BY LAW.

In section V of article XIII of the constitution of the State is found the following provision: "A school shall be maintained in each school district at least three months in each year." Also in section XIV of chaper IV of the school laws will be found the statutory provision concerning the number of months to be taught in a school year, to entitle districts to their share of the school funds. Districts having less than thirty children are required to maintain school at least three months; districts having thirty and less than eight hundred children, five months, and nine months in all districts having more than eight hundred children. The penalty for non-compliance with this requirement is the forfeiture of the primary money and mill tax. Very few districts in Michigan are deprived of money for these reasons.

SUPERVISION.

The head of Michigan's school system is the Superintendent of Public Instruction, whose duties are too numerous to be enumerated here. One of the most important of the duties of this official is the preparing of an annual report containing:

A statement showing the condition of the State and incorporated institutions, also the primary, graded and high schools.

Estimates and amounts of expenditure of all educational funds.

Plans for the management of all educational funds and the better organization of the educational system.

Abstracts of the annual report of the school inspectors of the several townships and cities of the State.

TEACHERS' INSTITUTES.

He is authorized by law to conduct teachers' institutes in various parts of the State, or if unable to attend in person, to appoint a suitable person or persons to conduct the same, subject to certain regulations which the superintendent may prescribe. Such institutes are held annually in nearly every county, and are of much practical value to those who avail themselves of the advantages thus afforded. During the year 1892 institutes were held in sixty-nine counties of the State, with an aggregate attendance of 6,346 teachers. All male teachers are required to pay an annual institute fee of one dollar, and all female teachers a fee of fifty cents. This amount with a State appropriation not to exceed $1,800, is used for the support of teachers' institutes. The Superintendent of Public Instruction is elected at the November election for a term of two years and receives a salary of $2,000 per year.

CITY SCHOOLS.

The control of the city schools is in the hands of a school board, consisting of five or more members, elected at the annual school meeting for terms of three years. The supervision and government of each school is in the hands of a superintendent of schools, who is elected by the school board annually for a period of one year, although many city boards make contracts with the superintendent for two or three years. The superintendent of schools is held responsible to the school board for the care and management of all the schools of the city district and makes reports to the school board and Superintendent of Public Instruction. The schools in most cities are not under the supervision of the

COUNTY COMMISSIONER OF SCHOOLS.

This officer is elected by the people of each county at the spring election for a term of two years. His salary is fixed by the board of supervisors limited by certain provisions of law, relative to the number of schools under supervision. The minimum salary in counties containing fifty schools is $500, and maximum salary paid in any county is $1,500. He visits all the schools of the county, receives reports from townships and district school officers and transmits them to the county clerk and Superintendent of Public Instruction; he also makes such reports to the Superintendent of Public Instruction as may be required by that official. As assistant conductor of the institute he is expected to take an active part in the work of the institute and is usually appointed on a committee of local management. Perhaps the most important of the duties of the commissioner is the

EXAMINATION OF TEACHERS.

In this work he is assisted by two school examiners, who are appointed by the board of supervisors for terms of two years. This board of examiners conducts the examinations and grants certificates to successful applicants. Questions for examination are all prepared by the Superintendent of Public Instruction and sent to the commissioner under seal with instructions that seal shall not be broken until the morning of the examination in the presence of the teachers. Applicants for all grades of certificates are examined on the last Thursday and Friday of March and the first Thursday and Friday of August of each year, and for those who apply for third grade only, special examinations, not to exceed four in any year, are conducted by the board of examiners.

In addition to the common branches persons desiring second grade certificates are required to pass an examination in algebra and natural philosophy. Those who apply for a certificate of the first grade are examined in geometry, general history and botany, also all of the branches mentioned above.

The work of candidates for the first grade must be examined, approved and countersigned by the Superintendent of Public Instruction, to be valid throughout the State. First grade certificates are valid for four years, second grade for three years and third grade for one year, unless sooner revoked for cause by the power granted them. The institute fee is usually collected at the time of examination. For their services the two examiners each receive four dollars per day.

THE TOWNSHIP BOARD

is composed of the township clerk and two school inspectors. This board has control of the township library, establishes the boundaries of school districts, may make alteration in the boundaries of the same, make a report to the county commissioner and Superintendent of Public Instruction of the schools of the township, and hear and settle disputes from district officers.

THE DISTRICT OFFICERS

are three in number, namely, director, moderator and assessor. The director is secretary and the chief officer. The moderator is chairman of the board, also of the district meetings. He countersigns all orders drawn by the director. The assessor is the treasurer of the board and pays out the funds of the district on order of the other officers. To this board is entrusted the care and management of the schools, such as keeping district property in repair, employing teachers, etc., subject to certain limitations which cannot be enumerated here.

TEXT BOOKS.

Michigan has no adopted series of text books. This question is left mainly to local control with certain instructions of law. The district board is authorized by law to specify the studies to be pursued in the schools of the district and said board is required to make a record of the adoption of text books, and it is unlawful for them to change such books within five years, except by the consent of a majority of the qualified voters at a regularly called meeting. This is a wise provision and prevents the too frequent change of text books by district officers. Books to indigent children may be furnished by the district board to children whose parents are unable to buy the necessary books and the expense thereof paid the same as any other district expense.

FREE TEXT BOOKS

may be provided by a district board to all the children of the district if so authorized by a majority of the qualified voters.

LIBRARIES

are found in many Michigan schools. There is scarcely a school in the State employing more than one teacher that does not possess a few books of reference, and many schools possess large and well arranged libraries. In 1892, 520 townships and 1110 districts reported libraries, while the whole number of volumes reported in both township and district libraries for the same year was 518,652. The amount paid for the support of district libraries was $76,575.33, and for township libraries $5,860.12. A tax for the support of a township library may be voted by the voters at the annual meeting and raised in the same manner as any other township tax, but more than four-fifths of the whole amount are penal fines, obtained according to the provisions of Section XII of Article XIII, of the constitution of the State.

"SECTION 12. The legislature shall also provide for the establishment of at least one library in each township and city; and all fines assessed and collected in the several counties and townships for any breach of the penal laws shall be exclusively applied to the support of such libraries, unless otherwise ordered by

UNIVERSITY OF MICHIGAN, ANN ARBOR.

MICHIGAN SCHOOL FOR THE BLIND, LANSING.

STATE PUBLIC SCHOOL, COLDWATER.

the township board of any township, or the board of education of any city: *Provided*, That in no case shall such fines be used for other than library or school purposes."

READING CIRCLES.

Another great factor for good we mention the reading circle which has been formed in many schools in the State, and in the hands of energetic commissioners, superintendents and teachers are doing much to keep out the hurtful, trashy reading and supply in its place books of travel, history, science and choice gems of literature before stories of train robberies and murder are thought of.

NORMAL SCHOOLS AND PROFESSIONAL INSTRUCTION.

No sketch of the primary school system of the State would be complete without at least a mention of our Normal School, at Ypsilanti.

This institution is included in the article on the State institutions, but a few facts even if repeated will be of interest. Organized in 1852 it is now in the forty-second year of its usefulness. In 1892 one hundred and seventy-eight students graduated from its courses, thirty-seven instructors were employed and one thousand three hundred and eighteen students were in attendance during the year. The estimated value of the buildings and grounds of this institution is nearly a quarter of a million dollars, and over twelve thousand books are found in the library. For the support of the school the legislature appropriates about $50,000 annually and the income from productive funds is about $5,000 per year. In all two thousand two hundred students have graduated from the school, besides many others who, not having completed the course, are numbered among the progressive teachers of the State. Michigan is justly proud of the work of this great institution, and its influence is felt in almost every village and city through the entire State.

THE UNIVERSITY AND COLLEGES

of the State recognize the value of professional training for teachers and nearly all have normal departments under the charge of practical and scholarly common school men. Recognizing such instruction as of real merit the legislature in the season of 1893 passed an act making it lawful for the State Board of Education to grant teachers' certificates to the graduates of certain colleges which give the required amount of normal instruction. In this connection it should be stated that graduates from the State Normal School are legally qualified teachers, as are the graduates of the literary department of the University.

The demand for trained teachers is such that in several localities normal schools under private control are conducted by able, experienced educators and are doing good service to the schools of the State. Among the foremost of such schools are mentioned the Business and Collegiate Institute at Benton Harbor, Normal at Fenton, Industrial School at Big Rapids, Normal School and Business College, at Mt. Pleasant.

18

THE SUMMER SCHOOLS

at Bay View, Agricultural College and Alma, should not be forgotten by those who desire instruction during the long vacation. The State teachers' institute already mentioned, also county teachers' association, are doing much and stimulate to better and more professional labor.

KINDERGARTEN METHOD

for the children of the lower grades. The introduction of this kind of instruction is of comparatively recent date and its value to the schools of the State cannot be overestimated. The legislature of 1891 very wisely passed an act making it lawful for any school board in the State to provide a suitable room and necessary apparatus for this work. The same act provides that the district board may require teachers to be qualified to give such instruction in addition to the other qualifications required. By this act children between the ages of four and seven are entitled to instruction in the kindergarten department.

The education of the body should go hand in hand with the training of the mind, for worse than an untrained mind in a healthy body is an educated mind in a body broken down with overstudy, poor ventilation and improper light. The educators of Michigan, aware of the fact that good health is necessary for happiness, have adopted

PHYSICAL TRAINING

as a part of high school and college courses and no school course is considered symmetrical or complete without exercise with dumb bells, Indian clubs, marching, calisthenics, drill, etc., and to the credit of our law makers we may add that $20,000 for a building for physical training at the State Normal School was appropriated during the session of 1893. The health of the Michigan boy and girl has become the first question to be considered by the professional teacher.

MUSIC AND DRAWING

is fast becoming a part of the course of study in our larger graded schools. Besides being taught to some extent in nearly all graded schools, forty villages and cities in the State in 1892 employed special teachers in music and about the same number of schools employed special drawing teachers. In a nut shell we have:

Seven thousand one hundred and seventy-five school districts.

Seven thousand six hundred and sixty-six school houses.

Sixteen thousand one hundred teachers employed.

Six hundred and seventy-four thousand, two hundred and seventy-nine children of school age.

Parochial schools in large cities.

Twenty or more private schools (business colleges, normal schools).

Seventeen incorporated colleges and schools.

School for Feeble Minded and Epiletic (established in 1893).

School for Dependent Children.
Industrial Home for Girls.
Industrial School for Boys.
School for the Blind.
School for the Deaf and Dumb.
Mining School.
Normal School.
Agricultural College.
University.

In considering what has been accomplished and what is being done in the line of progress in the State, we feel that educational interests have not suffered and that the founders of our State government did their work wisely. To them we say, "well done." Men or institutions founded by them are not perfect. Conditions change and the system so nearly perfect must undergo changes to keep pace with the progress of the age. Schools in cities and villages are kept abreast of the times by election of capable men to places on the school board while in many country districts men who can be persuaded to accept the offer are selected. Such selections many times are made from the ranks of those who have only an indifferent interest in the welfare of the school. For this and other reasons the schools should be changed from district to

TOWNSHIP CONTROL.

This change in our school system is desirable and when the people of a township can be convinced that their schools will be better managed by a board of five or more representative men elected by the people of the township instead of three school officers in each of the several districts, making in some townships thirty or forty school officers, we may hope for better schools without necessarily incurring greater expense.

Last, but by no means least, children in the schools of Michigan are taught

PATRIOTISM.

In the reading books, in stories of American history, in patriotic recitations and songs, in exercises with flags, and in pole raisings, the boys and girls are taught a reverence for "Old Glory," and over many a school house from the fertile fields of the south to the pines and mines of the north "The Star Spangled Banner Triumphantly Waves."

THE STATE UNIVERSITY.

BY J. H. WADE, SECRETARY.

The University of Michigan has for years maintained its position as one of the first of American educational institutions. It is strong in the breadth of its fundamental plan, the practical usefulness of its work, the value of its contributions to the general stock of knowledge, the ample character of its equipment; the cheapness with which its advantages can be enjoyed and its thoroughly democratic atmosphere.

ITS REMARKABLE DEVELOPMENT.

It was first opened to the public in 1811, and hence has had an active existence of fifty-two years. Within that time its corps of three instructors has grown to one hundred and sixty-five instructors and assistants, and its list of students, which in its first catalog contained about fifty-three names, has reached nearly twenty-eight hundred. Originally a more local school, unknown beyond the limits of the State, it has won an international reputation, and its rolls have borne the names of students from all parts of the United States and from many foreign countries.

ITS LOCATION, BUILDINGS AND DEPARTMENTS.

The University is located in the city of Ann Arbor, thirty-eight miles west of Detroit, on the Michigan Central railroad. Fifteen buildings are situated upon a high plateau in a campus of forty acres in extent. The astronomical observatory and the two hospitals are on the high bluff overlooking the Huron valley. The University now contains the following departments: 1. The department of literature, science and the arts, embracing, *a*, graduate school; *b*, the collegiate work; *c*, the work in engineering. 2. The department of medicine and surgery. 3. The department of law. 4. The school of pharmacy. 5. The homeopathic medical college. 6. The college of dental surgery. Each of these departments has its faculty of instruction, who are charged with its special management.

TERMS OF ADMISSION.

All students on entering pay a matriculation fee, which to residents of the State is $10, and to non-residents $25. This fee entitles the student to all the privileges of permanent membership. The annual fees are as follows: In the literary department, $20 for residents and $25 for non-residents; in the professional schools, $25 and $35. When a degree is taken a diploma fee of $10 must be paid. Board and rooms are obtainable in private families at Ann Arbor at from $3 to $5 per week; rooms without board at from 75 cents to $2 per week. Students by forming clubs can bring their expenses within the weekly range of from $2 to $3. Those who do not care to become candidates for regular degrees may take optional courses, pursuing only such studies as they may select. Women are admitted to all branches of the University on the same terms as men.

LENGTH OF TERMS.

The regular term in the collegiate department covers four years, in the medical schools four years, in the dental school three years and in the law school and in the pharmacy school two years each.

THE MUSEUMS AND LABORATORIES.

The museums contain large collections in natural history, agriculture, archæology, ethnology, the fine arts, history, anatomy and materia medica. In the laboratories opportunities are provided for practical instruction in physics, chemistry, geology, zoölogy, animal morphology, botany, physiology and dentistry.

THE HOSPITALS.

In the hospitals facilities are afforded to medical students for instruction by clinics. Patients are received in them and treated without charge except for medicines and board, and all persons suffering from diseases of any kind, except those of a contagious character, are granted admission.

ATTENDANCE IN 1893.

The total enrollment of students in all departments in March, 1893, was as follows:

Department of literature, science and the arts	1,491
Department of medicine and surgery	344
Department of law	639
School of pharmacy	82
Homeopathic medical college	63
College of dental surgery	189
	2,808
Deduct for names counted twice	30
Total attendance	2,778

Of the foregoing 1,105 were residents of Michigan; the others came not only from other states and territories, but from foreign countries, including the British North American provinces, the Hawaiian islands, the Burmuda islands, England, Japan, Germany, China, Italy, Barbadoes, Bulgaria, Costa Rica, Porto Rico, Scotland and South Africa.

THE POOR MAN'S UNIVERSITY.

This institution, with its ample equipment and its numerous courses of study, is emphatically the poor man's university. All its advantages are open at merely nominal fees to any qualified applicant. With personal economy the student can support himself during the collegiate year with but small expenditure. Not a few of those today in attendance there are paying their own way without assistance from parents or others. Labor is not despised at the University, and the cases have been numerous where young men in straitened circumstances have sought and obtained employment at Ann Arbor and with the wages thus earned aided materially their struggle after knowledge. Among the chief sources of the University's strong hold upon the affections of the people who have so liberally supported it must be reckoned this fact, that it shares so fully in the thoroughly democratic spirit of the primary schools.

THE MICHIGAN AGRICULTURAL COLLEGE.

BY PRESIDENT O. CLUTE.

The Agricultural College was incorporated in 1855. A few months later the present site was chosen, which is three and one-half miles east of Lansing. Contracts were soon let for a main building, a boarding hall, a small brick barn and four small cottages for professors' residences. These buildings were so far completed as to enable the college to open in May, 1857, under the presidency of Hon. Joseph R. Williams.

President Williams was a modern man. In him the ideas of the new education had come to full growth. He believed in a healthful, well trained body, a carefully educated mind in which all the faculties should be thoroughly trained, and a keen moral nature, no less willing to grant to others their rights than to claim its own. He had been an early friend of the Agricultural College before the law was passed for its organization. He desired that the school should educate *men*, give them strong bodies, skillful hands, well trained minds, pure morals.

To train the body he relied on the farm and garden work, where young men should come into direct contact with soil and sun and by struggle with nature learn to conquer nature. To train the mind he looked to the study of the native tongue, of the great laws of mathematics permeating all nature through the power of the omnicient geometrician, and to a study of those great sciences which do but reveal to us the thoughts and methods of the omnipresent energy. To train the morals he depended on attrition of man with man and on the ever present influence of pure character in companions, professors and instructors.

He was followed in the presidency by Dr. T. C. Abbot, whose convictions were in the same channel, whose methods were similar. To those two men the college owes its modern spirit, its rational methods, its success which has been slowly won, but which is as solid as the hills.

When the college was first established it was an agricultural school, but after congress passed the Morrill act of 1862, its provisions were accepted by Michigan, which made it necessary to add a course in mechanic arts to the course in agriculture, and now the college has these two courses and no others. Its "leading object" is to teach agriculture and the mechanic arts.

For this work it is now well equipped. In the thirty-five years of its life it has subdued the forest and made fertile farm, gardens and orchards. Gradually there have grown up many laboratories, barns, dormitories and dwellings. Its land, buildings and equipment have cost $450,000. Its library has 18,000 volumes. The facilities for imparting instruction in all its departments are superior. Its professors are strong men, devoted to their work.

The value of its work is shown by results. The students trained in its classes become men of force. They can work and win. A large per cent of them become agriculturists or mechanics Those who take up other branches have the constant industry and the trained judgment that bring success.

Those desiring further information are invited to address the president, Agricultural College P. O., Michigan.

COLLEGE HALL

AGRICULTURAL LABORATORY

CHEMICAL LABORATORY

HORTICULTURAL LABORATORY

AGRICULTURAL COLLEGE, LANSING.

MICHIGAN AGRICULTURAL COLLEGE.

MICHIGAN MINING SCHOOL.

BY M. E. WADSWORTH.

This institution was established by the legislature of Michigan in 1885, and first opened for the admission of students Sept. 15, 1886.

The object of the school is to give instruction in all subjects relating to the development of the mineral wealth of the country, and it has confined itself strictly to its original purpose. In carrying out the designs of its founders, both theoretical and practical instruction is provided for in the various subjects of mathematics, physics, drawing, blue printing, graphical statics, designing, chemistry, assaying, ore dressing, metallurgy, properties and mechanics of materials, mechanism, shop practice, mechanical, electrical, hydraulic, structural and mining engineering, surveying, mining, crystallography, mineralogy, petrography, paleontology, and structural, physical, economic and field geology.

The laboratories, shops, and mill are well equipped for giving instruction in the subjects named, and every advantage practicable is taken of the location and equipment of the school to make the instruction practical, and enable the student to learn that which he can use in his subsequent work. On account of this, the Mining School is conducted strictly as a professional school, the same as are the theological, law and medical schools of the country, and no encouragement is given to any student to enter or remain in it who is not thoroughly in earnest to master the studies relating to his chosen profession.

Its course of instruction comprises three or four years, at the option of the pupil.

The three years course embraces most of the subjects required in the ordinary work of the mining engineer, and on its completion the degree of bachelor of science (B. S.) is given. For those who desire it an additional year is taken, making the four years course, which comprises many of the advanced and higher subjects of the mining engineer's profession.

The course of study requires from the pupil from six to seven hours a day, five days a week, in the class room, laboratory, mill or mine, and all preparation for his daily work has to be done outside of these hours, hence a student needs to give nearly all of his available time to his work if he expects to do well. The course in its first and third years occupies forty-five weeks of the year, and in the second and fourth years forty-four weeks of the year; but in the fourth year six of the weeks are devoted to the preparation of a thesis, which is required before the student can receive the degree of mining engineer.

The Michigan Mining School has advanced more rapidly than any other State or independent school of mining engineering in the United States, having for some three years more students in mining engineering than any other school in the country. During the past year ninety-two pupils have been enrolled from twenty different states and foreign countries.

The demand for its graduates has been good and in advance of the supply, and every effort practical has been made to give the kind of an education that the modern mining engineer needs at the present time.

The Mining School is under the direction of a board of control consisting of six

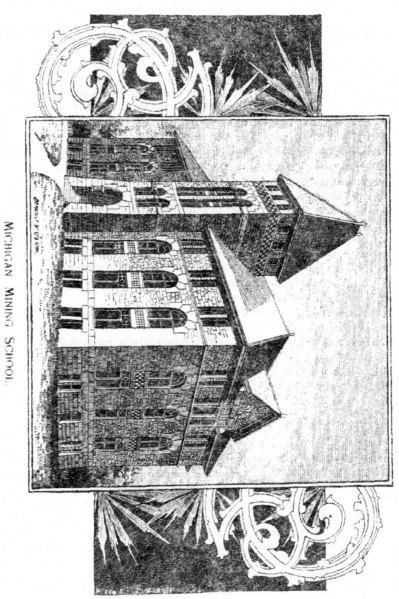

MICHIGAN MINING SCHOOL.

members appointed for a term of six years, the terms of two members expiring every second year. The present board is constituted as follows:

Hon. John Monroe Longyear, Marquette	June 9, 1895.
Alfred Kidder, Marquette	June 9, 1895.
James Renrick Cooper, Hancock	June 9, 1897.
Preston Capenter Firth West, Calumet	June 9, 1897.
Hon. Jay Abel Hubbell, Houghton	June 9, 1899.
Hon. Thomas Bree Dunstan, Hancock	June 9, 1899.

OFFICERS OF THE BOARD OF CONTROL.

President of the Board of Control—Hon. Jay Abel Hubbell.
Secretary of the Board of Control—Allen Forsyth Rees.
Director of the Mining School—Marshman Edward Wadsworth.
Treasurer and Purchasing Agent of the Mining School—Allen Forsyth Rees.

During its first year the school was under the direction of Albert Williams, Jr., and since then under that of M. E. Wadsworth.

The main building now occupied by the Mining School was completed by the State in 1889, at a cost of $75,000. The building is constructed of Portage entry sandstone, with a tile roof. It is heated and ventilated by steam, having two large boilers for heating and an extra boiler for driving machinery.

The main building is one hundred and nine feet by fifty-three feet, with a wing thirty-seven feet by twenty-five feet. A well appointed stamp mill and ore dressing works, a small metallurgical building, etc., complete the structures belonging to the Mining School.

A new building for the accommodation of the mechanical, electrical and mining engineering, and drawing and surveying will be erected in 1893-1894, and the interior of the main building remodeled to meet the increasing needs of the school developed by its rapid increase in numbers.

The library has been especially selected for the technical and other needs of the school and numbers some nine thousand volumes, while the reading room contains all the important and technical periodicals that bear on the subjects taught in the school.

The physical laboratory is well equipped with the special apparatus needed in the student's practical work, like galvanometers of various kinds, calorimeters, resistance boxes, spectragonimeters, spherometers, balances, bridges, sextants, sonometers, polariscopes, electric motors, photometers, etc., etc.

In chemistry there are two laboratories, one for general chemistry and qualitative analysis, and the other for quantitative analysis. These laboratories are well equipped with gas and water supplies, with filter pumps for each student, as well as with all the needed modern apparatus for chemical work, including thirteen analytical balances, spectroscopes, Hempel's and Bunsen's apparatus, etc.

The assay laboratory is fitted with ten large crucible furnaces, eighteen Brown's muffle furnaces, sixteen Hoskin's gasoline crucible and muffle furnaces; Blake's and Gates' crushers, large buck plates, large and small mortars, sieves, etc., as well as six pulp scales and five button balances. The mill and ore dressing works are well equipped with one 650-pound three-stamp battery, for wet or dry crushing, furnished with copper plates, one Blake crusher, one sample grinder, one pair of rolls, one amalgamating pan, one settler, two jigs, one Calumet separator, one spitzkasten, one Frue vanner, apron tables, screens, precipitating tanks, and settling tanks, sufficient to enable the student to check all his results by assay.

For metallurgical purposes, there has been erected a 7x10 reverberatory roasting furnace, which will enable the students to treat their concentrates and refractory ores.

The mechanical laboratories are well equipped with apparatus for the scheduled work. Among the instruments on hand are one Crosby and one Tabor indicator, with full complement of springs, Heath stop-watch, two polar planimeters, Ashcroft revolution counter, Schaeffer and Budenberg tachometer, lazy tongs and other reducing gears, Ashcroft pyrometor, set of Green's standard thermometers, Haisler and Barrus clorimeters, water meters, Ashcroft boiler test pump, steam gauge testing machine, etc. There are also on hand a number of cut models of injectors, etc., for illustrating lectures.

The mechanical laboratories are further provided with a 100,000-pound machine fitted for tests in tension, compression, cross breaking and shearing, a Thurston autographic tension machine, an Olsen 2,000-pound cement tester, and an Ashcroft oil testing machine. There are also on hand a Henning electric contact micrometer, for measurement of extension, an electric micrometer for compression tests, a B. and S. vernier caliper, and several micrometer calipers, a 24-inch by 16-foot New Haven Tool Company's engine lathe, Prentice screw-cutting lathe, two hand lathes, a 34-inch automatic feed Blaisdell drill press, a 20-inch Lodge & Davis drill press, a 16-inch Gould and Eberhardt chaper, a Whitcomb planer of capacity 8x2x2 feet, a Brainard No. 4 Universal milling machine, one wet and two dry emery grinders, and several smaller machine tools. The assortment of chuncks, taps, drills, reamers, and general tools is very complete. For practice in pipe fitting a separate bench has been provided, and a complete set of pipe tools and fittings up to two inches inclusive is in stock. The pattern shop contains two Clement wood lathes, a 33-inch Fay hand saw, Beach jig saw, emery wheels and grindstones, Pedrick & Ayer gouge grinders, a very complete assortment of hand tools and appliances, a 9x9 inch New York safety vertical high speed engine, an 8x12 Buckeye automatic engine, a 12k Edison dynamo, a 2HP. Sprague motor, several Ayrton & Perry ammeters and voltameters, Beyman ammeters, storage cells, etc.

The Mining School has a complete outfit for its work in plane, railroad and mining surveying, including one plane table, from Buff & Berger; nine transits, three from Buff & Berger, three from Heller & Brightly, two from Gurley; five Burt Solar compasses; five magnetic compasses; fifteen Locke hand levels. In addition to these more expensive instruments, the school owns the necessary number of mining lamps, chains, steel tapes, poles, rods, etc.

Two of the transits are provided with three tripod outfits for mine surveying, and all the transits are adapted to mine as well as surface work.

The laboratories for crystallography, mineralogy, petrography and geology are well equipped and prepared for both elementary and advanced students. Amongst other material these laboratories have the following:

Crystals and crystal models 4,104
Mineral specimens 27,310
Rock specimens 11,575

Also thirty-eight petrographical microscopes with accessories, spectroscopes, goniometers, polariscopes, etc.

The Michigan Mining School is located at Houghton, the county seat of Houghton county, a county which stands third in valuation in the State. Houghton is easily reached by rail from Detroit, Grand Rapids, Lansing, Chicago, Milwaukee, St. Paul, Superior and Duluth, and by steamer from all the important ports on the chain of the great lakes.

In the immediate vicinity of the Mining School are located the Quincy, Atlantic, Franklin and Huron copper mines, while within a distance of fifteen miles are situated the Calumet and Hecla, Tamarack, Osceola and other copper mines, with their machine shops, smelting works, rolling and stamp mills, etc. In the iron mining regions lie numerous great iron mines, prominent among which are the Cleveland, Jackson, Lake Superior, Lake Angeline, Champion, Republic, Chapin, Vulcan, Cyclops, Colby and Norrie.

From this location the student of the Michigan Mining School is placed in a mining atmosphere, in which all his surroundings and associations are in conformity with his present and future work. He is thus enabled to see in actual operation some of the most successful and extensive mining operations now conducted anywhere.

No fees of any kind are charged, the school being absolutely free to all persons from whatsoever state or country they may come.

Catalogs containing full particulars concerning the requirements for admission, course of study, etc., can be obtained by an application by mail or in person to the director at Houghton.

MICHIGAN STATE NORMAL SCHOOL.

BY DANIEL PUTNAM, YPSILANTI, MICHIGAN.

This institution is located in the city of Ypsilanti. It was opened and its first building was dedicated on October 5, 1852, being the first normal school established west of New York. It is under the control of the State Board of Education, and its sole purpose is to prepare teachers for all grades of the public schools of the State.

Its buildings are ample and are well adapted to the work of the school. Its general assembly hall affords seating for nearly a thousand persons; the chemical, physical and biological laboratories are excellent, and are supplied with the best of apparatus. It has a carefully selected general library of thirteen thousand volumes, and a reading room supplied with all the leading literary and educational magazines of this country, and a considerable number of foreign educational periodicals. In addition to the general library there are departmental libraries selected for special use in teaching the various branches.

The training department, embracing a kindergarten and all the grades of the primary and grammar departments of a regular public school, affords students an opportunity to observe model teaching, and also to apply in practice, under care-

STATE NORMAL SCHOOL, YPSILANTI.

ful supervision and criticism, the principles and methods in which they receive instruction.

Connected with the normal school, though not organically a part of it, is a conservatory of music which affords most excellent facilities for the study of that important branch of a teacher's education. Vocal music and voice culture are regular studies in the normal courses.

Several courses of studies are provided to meet the wants of the various grades of schools. Courses of one and two years are provided for graduates of approved high schools; and it is the policy of the school to encourage those who enter to complete as much as possible of the academic work before entering. A purely professional course of twenty weeks is offered to graduates of colleges. This course leads to a life certificate and to the degree of bachelor of pedagogics. Students completing a regular three years course receive a legal certificate entitling them to teach in the schools of the State for a period of five years; graduates from a four years course receive life certificates. An advanced course is provided which gives the graduate from it the degree of bachelor of pedagogics.

The faculty, including professors, assistants and instructors, numbers thirty-seven, and will probably be increased during the next year. It is the purpose of the board to secure first-class instruction in all departments.

The demand for graduates of the normal in the schools of the State is beyond the capacity of the school to supply and is constantly increasing.

The school year is divided into two terms of twenty weeks each, the first term beginning early in September, the second early in February.

No tuition fee is charged; but students not holding appointments from a member of the Legislature pay an incidental admission fee of five dollars each term. Members of the Legislature are authorized to appoint two students from their own districts. Such students pay no fee.

The living expenses of students are very moderate. Furnished rooms can be had for 75 cents to $1.25 per week. Board in "clubs" costs about $2 per week. Board, with furnished room, in private families can be obtained at rates varying from $3 to $4 per week.

MICHIGAN SCHOOL FOR THE BLIND

was established at Lansing in 1879. It had formerly been connected with the deaf and dumb institution. The number of students in 1892 was 85, number of instructors 9. It is under the management of the special board of control. No one possessing fully developed feelings of humanity can visit this institution without experiencing sensations of pity upon seeing so many innocent youths deprived of the greatest of all blessings, with the sunlight and beauties of God's universe eternally shut out, groping their way in physical darkness through life in presence of the fact that it is a question with many whether life is worth living. If there are any deep grounds for this question with all the senses and faculties to enjoy life it would seem to be easily settled by the deprivation of the sense of sight.

The object of this institution is to so train the intellect, through which alone the other senses would be reached, that great pleasures may be experienced by these unfortunates. They learn to read by the sense of touch and become excellent musicians. They are also trained to make many articles useful and ornamental. With the many attainments and accomplishments acquired at the school, life is relieved of the monotonies of an uneducated blind person.

MICHIGAN SCHOOL FOR DEAF MUTES.

This institution was established in 1854. Prior to 1879 the blind as well as deaf mutes were instructed in the same building, but provisions were made to separate them.

The institution for the deaf mutes is located at Flint, in Genesee county. The total value of the property is about 450,000, which includes eighty-eight acres of land and excellent buildings.

The object of the institution is to educate deaf mutes and fit them for useful and remunerative occupations, thereby rendering them independent.

The State maintains this institution with the same liberality it extends to all its similar institutions and the result commends the plan. Many who would be burdens on their friends or the State are instructed and trained so skillfully that they become educated and competent to earn good livings. No charge is made to pupils in Michigan and, indeed, the State authorizes the trustees to assist the poor unfortunates when needed. The institution accomplishes what it would be almost utterly impossible to otherwise do. The State will never forget or neglect its unfortunates.

STATE PUBLIC SCHOOL.

The State Public School is located at Coldwater, Branch county, and was established in 1871 and opened in 1874. It is a temporary home for dependent and ill-treated children, between the ages of two and twelve years.

The object of the institution is to take care of and educate such children until homes can be found for them in good families.

Since the institution was established 3,331 children have been received, most of whom have been provided with good homes. There are now about two hundred in the school. There is a farm of 130 acres connected with the institution. The management is vested in a board and there are six teachers and three officers. Two hundred and fifty children can be accommodated. Two thousand five hundred and ninety-one have been indentured, one hundred and fourteen have died, four hundred and seventeen returned to counties.

The State may well be proud of an institution having for its object the care and training of poor, homeless, destitute waifs, snatching innocents from the recruiting sources of vice and crime and placing them on the road to virtue and usefulness. In the future our citizenship must necessarily be composed of the children of today. Michigan is proverbial for helping those who cannot help themselves.

SCHOOL FOR THE DEAF, FLINT.

MICHIGAN MILITARY ACADEMY.

The Michigan Military Academy was incorporated September 4, 1877. The aim of this institution is to give young men an education, both physical and mental, which shall develop them into the fullest and highest manhood; an education which shall produce, as far as possible, full and perfect men. To this end, the school is established upon a system that combines military instruction with the ordinary courses of high schools and academies.

The Academy is situated twenty-six miles from Detroit and four and one-half miles from Pontiac, with which it is connected by railroad. The grounds, comprising one hundred and twenty acres, are on the shore of Orchard lake, in one of the most beautiful and healthful localities in Michigan. The buildings are all new, of brick, and built expressly for the purpose for which they are used. There are already six modern buildings, well lighted and ventilated, and complete in every respect. Value of buildings and grounds, $300,000.

From the location of the Academy all the benefits of country life are secured, and the cadets are free from the temptations and distractions of the city. The Academy has every advantage to make it especially good—location, healthfulness, rational methods, thoroughness and progressive spirit.

The special work of the Academy is to prepare for our best universities, and to give an extended course to those not intending to go to college. Courses of instruction are offered in the preparation for the college courses leading to the degrees of bachelor of arts, philosophy, science, letters, and for the courses in civil, mechanical, mining and electrical engineering. In chemistry, electricity, law, history, mathematics, English, Latin, Greek, French and German, opportunity is given at the Academy for advanced work.

Students in attendance, one hundred and forty. Number of graduates, one hundred and ninety-five.

Col. E. M. Heyl, U. S. A. Inspector General, Division of Missouri, in his annual report for 1892 to the Inspector General at Washington, says in regard to this Academy:

"The Michigan Military Academy at Orchard lake, has, by its high grade of scholarship and its strenuous efforts for the best success, achieved a place second to none in the country."—*Extract from Contributions to the American Educational History, 1892, Bureau of Education, Washington, D. C.*

This Academy still maintains its place as the leading military institution of the country outside of West Point, and in all its details it is the most complete and thorough school of the kind I have ever inspected. The State may well be proud of Orchard Lake Military Academy, and the young men it graduates, as they will be the material on which the country can rely in the event of war.

The site is most excellent and the sanitary condition and sewerage perfect."

MICHIGAN MILITARY ACADEMY.

AKELEY INSTITUTE.

This institute was founded by Hon. H. C. Akeley and is located at Grand Haven, on the banks of Lake Michigan. It was Mr. Akeley's belief that girls should not obtain classical education at the expense of physical strength and development. Three principal features are cared for: Mental advancement, physical development and moral culture; and the regime in all departments is so interwoven and blended that the results are remarkably satisfactory.

BATTLE CREEK COLLEGE.

Battle Creek College was founded in 1874, by the Seventh Day Adventists Educational Society, and was duly incorporated in the same year, according to the laws of the State of Michigan providing for the incorporation of institutions of learning. It is a denominational institution, designed to give young people a liberal education and prepare them for usefulness in the different lines of religious work. Its managers aim to make moral and religious influences prominent, and thoroughness of instruction, solidity of character and usefulness in life the principal objects of attainment. They hope to have a school where the fear of God will prevail, where His holy word will be reverenced, and where His worship and service will be respected; where the young will receive discipline and instruction which will qualify them for the duties of life, and make them a benefit to their fellow men. Such as desire to be in harmony with these objects are heartily invited to attend.

LOCATION.

The college is situated in Battle Creek, a city of about 15,000 inhabitants and one of the most active and enterprising towns in the peninsular State. Being at the junction of the Chicago & Grand Trunk, Michigan Central, and Cincinnati, Jackson & Mackinaw railroads, about half way between Detroit and Chicago, the city is easy of access from all parts of the country. The site of the college is on a fine eminence in the western part of the city, about one-half of a mile from the business center.

GROUNDS AND BUILDINGS.

The college campus consists of seven acres, about half of which is taken up with buildings and the lawn, and the remainder gives abundant room for out-of door sports.

THE HOME LIFE.

Past experience has demonstrated that the school can be more successfully carried on by having the students board and room in the college buildings, with the members of the faculty, thus constituting a large school family. The

20

young people should receive a much broader training than that which comes merely from the study of books. It is the best time for them to form habits of neatness and christian courtesy, and to obtain that general culture which comes from daily and intimate association with educated christian teachers. Much care is taken to render the home life not only attractive, but efficient in the cultivation of those habits of life and graces of character which distinguish the refined christian man and woman. Teachers and students share one family life, with common aims and interest. The regulations are reasonable, and are adapted to secure trust, freedom and happiness. It is intended that every student shall enjoy the pleasant associations, and receive the personal care of a true home. All the students in the college buildings will be required to aid in part payment of their expenses, in the work connected with the boarding hall and the laundry and in the care of the grounds and buildings. This service will occupy one hour each day. Much valuable information and discipline are thus secured to the student. Sharing the daily duties, and bearing mutual responsibilities for the common good, have proved to be of great educational value in establishing health and developing character. The influence of this service, rendered heartily, is invaluable in producing, during the years of mental training, habits of accuracy, self-reliance, unselfishness and genuine sympathy with all workers.

After several years of experience with the present plan of the home life, the managers of the college are convinced of its great value as an aid in the proper development of christian character and they earnestly recommend that all parents residing out of the city, who send their sons and daughters to the college, make provision for them to live at the school home.

Parents are assured that those who are sent here to work for their board are by that arrangement deprived in a large degree of the special privileges and benefits which they might otherwise enjoy. In such cases the faculty cannot be expected to take that responsibility for the general welfare of the student which they are willing to assume in the home.

MUSEUM.

In addition to many curious and interesting articles donated by friends of the college in different parts of the world, the museum contains a set of Ward's casts of fossils, and quite a complete line of specimens illustrating mineralogy and geology. The college desires to acknowledge its obligations to those who have contributed to the museum in the past and to request a continuance of their favors. A brief sketch of any article forwarded will add to its interest and value.

LIBRARY.

The library consists at present of about 2,000 volumes and new books are constantly being added to its list. The student finds this medium of information valuable for research in the different branches of study. In connection with the library is a reading room, supplied with secular and religous papers and magazines for the use of the students.

DISCIPLINE.

Battle Creek College aims to develop character of the highest type as well as scholarship of the best quality, and its discipline has respect to these ends. Every effort is given toward making the student self-reliant, self-controlled men and women. But it is not a reform school and its patrons should not send to this institution young people too incorrigible to be governed at home. If any of this class gain admittance they may expect to be summarily dismissed as soon as their true character is discovered.

HOPE COLLEGE.

Hope College is located at Holland City, Ottawa county. The college campus contains about sixteen acres and is beautifully situated in the center of the city, adjacent to Macatawa bay, on which is located Macatawa park and Ottawa Beach, popular summer resorts. The location is remarkably healthy, is easy of access by rail and water, being on an arm of Lake Michigan and close to the great lake. The prevailing wind is from the west and consequently the college is, with breathing air fresh from the lake, always pure and healthy.

The college buildings are eight in number and more are being built. It is an institution of the reformed church largely under supervision of Hollanders, who are noted for sobriety, honesty, industry and enterprise. Catalogs furnished by college.

ALMA COLLEGE.

BY AUGUST F. BRUSKE, PRESIDENT.

This is the youngest of the family of christian colleges in Michigan. It was founded in the year of our Lord 1886, by the synod of Michigan representing the Presbyterian church of the United States of America. The decision to establish it in Alma, Gratiot county, was reached because such an institution was most needed by the central and northern portions of our State. Almost all the colleges are in the southern and eastern parts of Michigan, leaving over one million of people without the advantages of the higher christian education. These people had almshouses, jails, asylums, penitentiaries, and now they have also a college. Some of the principal promoters of the enterprise were A. W. Wright, Esq., of Alma, who gave thirty acres of land, two substantial brick buildings at the beginning and has been a continual giver to the library and the other departments of college work; Alexander Folsom, Esq., of Bay City, who gave $80,000 toward endowment; Thomas Merrill, Esq., of Saginaw; C. W. Wells, Esq., F. C. Stone, Esq., Charles Davis, Esq., all of Saginaw, and Hon. John Longyear, of Marquette. By the munificence of these gentlemen the college was permitted to open its doors in 1887 and start at once upon a thrifty and vigorous life. Thirty-five students registered on the first day. The total attendance last year was one hundred and seventy-two.

The faculty for instruction is composed of thirteen ladies and gentlemen, all having enjoyed special training and having demonstrated their fitness by previous experience and success in teaching elsewhere. The institution has thirty acres of land, four brick buildings, substantial and essentially fire proof. It has an excellent library of 23,000 volumes and pamphlets, most of the books being obtained by purchase.

Among the advantages claimed for Alma College are:

1. Its central location, easily accessible, being at the junction of two important railroads; far enough from any similar institution to deliver it from unhappy rivalries, in a region of fertile country, high and free from malaria.

2. To thoroughly competent teachers, to the best of facilities by way of library and apparatus, there are added the best opportunities for moral and religious training. A course of bible stories embracing the geography, biography and books of the bible, the contents of sacred scripture, and finishing with natural theology and the evidences of christianity. This, it is believed, must stimulate the religious energies and build up character as is not possible in institutions under the control of the State.

3. The members of the faculty are in daily and familiar association with the students so that the personal wants of each student are recognized and provided for.

The following are the courses of study: 1. The classical. 2. Scientific. 3. Philosophical. 4. The literary. 5. Training department for kindergarten teachers. 6. The commercial for those wishing a business education. 7. The musical deparment. 8. The art department. 9. The college preparatory. 10. The academic for those desiring a short course of two or three years.

CATHOLIC SCHOOLS AND CHARITIES IN THE DIOCESE OF GRAND RAPIDS, MICHIGAN.

The diocese of Grand Rapids, Michigan, lies in the lower peninsula of Michigan and north of the southern boundaries of Ottawa, Kent, Montcalm, Gratiot and Saginaw counties. .

Every parish in the cities and towns has a school attended by nearly all the Catholic children who are of the school age. The total number of school houses is forty-two. The attendance at these during the year 1892 was a little over ten thousand, taught by one hundred and eighty teachers, all of whom, except eighteen, are members of religious orders. In the upper classes of several schools in the cities the course of studies is the same as that of the high schools.

Grand Rapids and Saginaw have each six school houses; Bay City, four; Muskegon, Manistee and Alpena, three; West Bay City and Au Sable, two; Big Rapids, Ludington, Traverse City, Provement, Petoskey, Harbor Springs, Cross

Village, Cheboygan, Essexville, Mount Pleasant, Maple Grove, Alpine and Wright are each supplied with one school. The value of the buildings ranges from one thousand dollars to twenty thousand.

Grand Rapids has a home for the aged poor, with nearly one hundred inmates, in charge of the Little Sisters of the Poor. Less than one-half of the projected building, three stories with a basement, has been erected.

The Sisters of Mercy conduct two hospitals, the one in Big Rapids, the other in Manistee. The patients in both are mostly from the lumber camps. Mr. John Canfield, of Manistee, donated the magnificent hospital in the city of his residence to the Sisters of Mercy.

The Sisters of Charity have a hospital in Saginaw. The old hospital is a frame building, the new, of which one wing is complete, will be of brick and cost not less than one hundred thousand dollars.

St. John's Orphan Asylum, in Grand Rapids, is in charge of the Sisters of St. Dominic. It is the gift of the late John Clancy. Only one wing is built, housing about ninety-five children. In St. Vincent's Orphan Home, in Saginaw, the Sisters of Charity care for fully ninety.

HILLSDALE COLLEGE.

Hillsdale College is situated in Hillsdale, on the Lake Shore railroad. It was founded in 1855, to furnish an opportunity for a liberal education to all persons, "irrespective of nationality, color or sex." It has a classical, scientific, normal, theological, music, art and commercial department, with a well selected library, biological and chemical laboratories, and a well equipped gymnasium. Its literary societies are among the prominent features of the college. Since its organization there have been over ten thousand different students in attendance in its various departments, of whom over six hundred have been graduated from its regular courses. It exists under the auspices of the Free Baptists, but it is not sectarian. It has an endowment fund of about $210,000, and a set of fine brick buildings well adapted to college uses. Its president is Hon. George F. Mosher LL. D.

DETROIT COLLEGE.

BY C. COPPENS, S. J., VICE PRESIDENT.

This college was founded in 1877, by the fathers of the Society of Jesus, at the invitation and with the aid of the Rt. Rev. Bishop C. Borgess, of Detroit. It was incorporated April 27, 1881, according to the general law of the State of Michigan, with power to grant the usual literary honors and degrees.

It embraces a classical, a scientific and a commercial course. Its president, the Rev. M. P. Dowling, is assisted by sixteen professors and instructors. Its students during the last scholastic year numbered 310, those entered upon the college register from the date of its foundation to the present, number 1,340. The value of its grounds, buildings, library, apparatus, etc., is $160,000; its liabilities are $60,000. The institution has never received any aid from the State or city, but to erect this beautiful structure, built three years ago, kind patrons among the Catholics of Detroit contributed about $50,000. The tuition paid by each student is put down at forty dollars yearly; as a matter of fact the income from that source was last year $9,520.

The college has no other resources. But then there are only four instructors to draw salaries. The president and all the remaining members of the faculty, being Jesuits, devote their whole time and labor to the welfare of the students without any other remuneration than their mere support, and as they all live in the college buildings and lead a community life, by means of tuition fees and occasional perquistes they are enabled to pay the current expenses, meet the interest on the large debt and add every year some improvements for the benefit of the students.

There are no boarders at the college except the faculty. There is no female department. The graduates so far count sixty-eight. The library counts 8,100 volumes and about 250 are added yearly.

All the members of the faculty and nearly all the students are Catholics, although others are admitted. The main purpose of the school is the thorough education of its pupils in scholarly attainments, strict moral and religious principles and habits of correct conduct.

ADRIAN COLLEGE.

This institution is delightfully located in the western suburbs of the city of Adrian. The buildings are among the best college buildings in the State. They are four in number and built of brick, heated with steam, are large, well planned and contain well furnished, roomy dormitories. The grounds include twenty acres. The grounds, buildings, museum, libraries, apparatus, musical instruments, furniture and endowment are valued at $300,000.

It is controlled by a board of thirty trustees, twenty-four of whom are elected by the Methodist Protestant church and six by the alumni association of the college.

There are four four-year courses and a preparatory department with three-year courses. The degrees conferred are Bachelor of Arts, Bachelor of Science, Bachelor of Philosophy and Bachelor of Letters; also Masters' and Doctors' degrees.

There is a school of theology with complete course leading to the degree of Bachelor of Divinity.

There is a school of music, with instruction in instrumental music, vocal music and musical composition. Degree, Bachelor of Music.

PENAL AND CHARITABLE INSTITUTIONS.

BY L. C. STORRS, SECRETARY STATE BOARD OF CHARITIES AND CORRECTIONS.

PRISONS.

Michigan has three penal institutions. One at Jackson, one at Ionia and one at Marquette, in which for the fiscal ending June 30, 1892 there were confined an average 1,188 prisoners. The city of Detroit has a house of correction, in which during a like period the average was 708 prisoners, a total during 1891-2 of 1,896 prisoners.

The prison property of the State is estimated at $1,531,416.98, and there was expended in operating them during 1890-2, $214,037.10.

The prisoners are provided with chapels and school rooms, and with chaplain and teachers.

An industrial home for discharged prisoners is in active operation, situated in Detroit. This is not a State institution, but was founded and is now directed by Mrs. Agnes L. d'Arcambal.

The home is incorporated by the State, controlled by a board of trustees and supported largely by the avails of the products of its industries.

REFORMATORIES.

Michigan has two, the Industrial School for Boys at Lansing, and the Industrial Home for Girls at Adrian. For the fiscal year ending June 30, 1892, there were confined in these two institutions an average of 709 children. The State has invested in them $428,246.05 and the expense of operating them in 1891-2 was $98,500.00. The system of parol is in operation and large numbers from these schools have found homes with good families throughout the State and are doing well.

21

DEPENDENT AND NEGLECTED CHILDREN.

Michigan maintains a school and temporary home for such at Coldwater called the State Public School. During the eighteen years of its existence 3,261 children have been received into such institution. June 30, 1892, there were in the school and out on trial (but still belonging) 283 children; out under indenture (but under the control of the school), 1,069; of the total number received, only 402 were returned to the counties from which received (unfit under the law to remain); the balance had been adopted, married, become self-supporting, etc. The State has invested in this school $227,816.22. The current expenses for 1891-2 were $33,570.75.

COUNTY AGENCY SYSTEM.

An agent is appointed in each county in Michigan by the Governor. His duties are, in a general way to examine and report on the home of each applicant for children from the industrial school, and from the school for dependent children. To supervise such children after being placed in homes. To examine the case of each and every child under sixteen years of age who has been arrested and to counsel with, and recommend to the court, what disposition shall be made of a child so arrested. These agents report for the fiscal year ending June 30, 1892, 812 children arrested, of whom 230 were committed to reformatories and 396 were placed in homes; 596 visits were made to children placed in homes.

THE BLIND, THE DEAF AND DUMB.

Michigan has an institution for each of these two classes of defections. There was an average attendance during 1892 at the School for the Blind of seventy-four pupils. The State has invested in these two institutions $715,619.34. The operating expenses were $75,357.89.

INSANE.

Three State asylums exist in the State, besides an asylum for the Dangerous and Criminal Insane. There were under treatment at the three, during the year 1892, 2,914 patients. There are the two private asylums in Michigan, in which there were 191 patients, and one county asylum (Wayne), in which there were 245

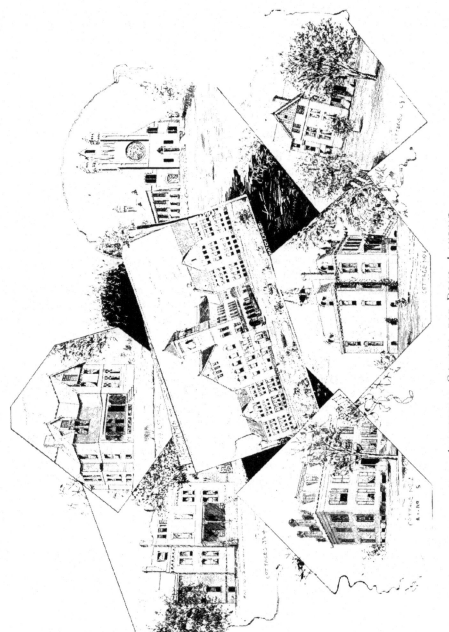

INDUSTRIAL SCHOOL FOR BOYS, LANSING.

There is a normal department for the benefit of teachers in the public schools. The course of instruction extends through two years, Certificates of completion are given. Instruction is also given in painting and drawing.

The number of instructors is twelve; average number of students, 175.

J. F. McCulloch, B. Ph., A. M., is president, and Geo. B. McElroy, D. D., Ph. D., is dean of the school of theology.

ALBION COLLEGE.

Albion College was projected in 1833 as a seminary or academy by Rev. Henry Colclazer, Rev. Elijah H. Pilcher, and Benjamin H. Packard, M. D., who were residents of the territory of Michigan. The measure was endorsed by the Ohio conference of the Methodist Episcopal church then having ecclesiastical jurisdiction in the State; and in 1835 an act was passed chartering the institution under the name of Spring Arbor Seminary, and locating the same at Spring Arbor in Jackson county. In 1839 the charter was amended, the corporate name changed to Wesleyan Seminary, and the same removed to Albion in Calhoun county.

The first building was erected in 1843, and the Seminary was opened for reception of students in November of that year under the supervision of Rev. Charles F. Stockwell as principal. In 1849 the powers of the institution were enlarged by the conversion of the seminary into a female college, with authority to grant degrees to women. In 1861 general college powers were granted by the legislature under the corporate name of Albion College.

The institution occupies a campus of about fifteen acres just east of the business portion of the city of Albion. On these grounds there are now standing six buildings—three of these used for general college purposes, and containing, aside from class and lecture rooms, the chapel, the library, museum, chemical laboratory, biological laboratory, conservatory of music, studio of the school of painting and society rooms. The fourth building in the order of erection is the astronomical observatory, fully equipped and next in size in the State to the observatory at Ann Arbor. A gymnasium, seventy by ninety-three feet, was erected in 1892. At the extreme eastern point of the campus stands the Sigma Chi hall, built by the chapter three years ago.

The McMillan chemical laboratory, the gift of Hon. James McMillan, senator in congress, costing $25,000, aside from plumbing and special fittings, is in process of erection, the same to be finished as early as September 15, 1893.

Hon Aaron T. Bliss, of Saginaw, ex-member of congress, is erecting a $50,000 library building, the same to contain a war memorial hall.

PROPERTY AND ENDOWMENTS.

Buildings, grounds and appliances	$200,000
Endowments	400,000
Endowment of library	30,000
Library—bound volumes	9,000
" unbound volumes	2,500
Museum—specimens in mineralogy, conchology, natural hist., etc.	10,000

Four new chairs, just endowed, three of them to be filled in 1895 when the funds become due.

Board of instructors consists of 28; students in attendance, 625.

The president is Rev. Lewis R. Fiske, D. D., LL. D.

The following are the names of the principals and presidents from the opening of the institution:

Rev. Charles F. Stockwell, A. M.

Rev. Clark T. Hinman, D. D.

Hon. Ira Mayhew, LL. D.

Rev. Thomas H. Sinex, D. D., during whose incumbency the school became a college of liberal arts.

Rev. George B. Joslyn, D. D.

Rev. J. L. G. McKeown, D. D.

Rev. William B. Silber. Ph. D.

Rev. Lewis R. Fiske, D. D., LL. D.

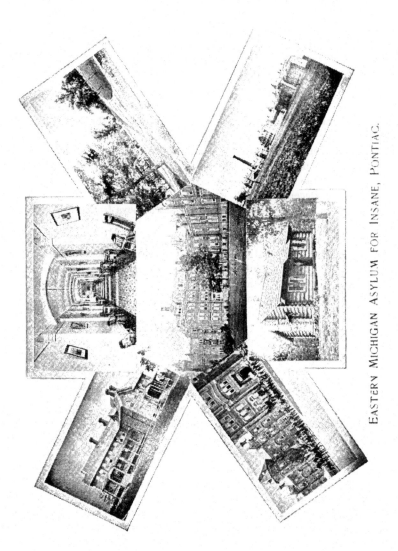

EASTERN MICHIGAN ASYLUM FOR INSANE, PONTIAC.

patients. The State property in her three asylums aggregates $2,384,374.08, and the operating expenses for the year 1891-2 were $514,239.03.

Insane convicts in Michigan prisons are transferred to her Asylum for Criminal and Dangerous Insane, where they are cared for as all others like afflicted. To this institution are also tranferred from her other asylums all inmates of homicidal tendencies.

THE INDUSTRIAL SCHOOL FOR BOYS

is located at Lansing, Michigan. It was formerly called the Reform School and was established in 1855, costing $25,000. With the institution is a farm, in all 261 acres, and upon this a large amount of crops are produced, serving the double purpose of furnishing vegetables, grain, hay and fruit for the use of the institution and at the same time employment and instruction to the boys. The number in school December, 1892, was 413. The object of this institution is to reform, educate and make useful men of a class of boys from which the criminal and vicious element is recruited.

Boys made bad by circumstances are arrested in their criminal course and by discipline, instruction and good example are directed into honorable channels and many become respectable, useful and wealthy citizens. The State recognizes the fact that it costs less and is much better to reform and check the growth of criminals than to manage them after made.

THE INDUSTRIAL HOME FOR GIRLS.

Located at Adrian, in Lenawee county, was established in 1879.

The object of this institution is the reformation of juvenile females who have by force of circumstances got started on a career which would almost certainly result in crime and abandonment.

The cost of maintaining this institution for two years ending June 30, 1892, was $72,123.23, and the result proves the wisdom of the expenditure. Two hundred and seven girls were provided for, taken from their demoralizing surroundings and halted in their short, rapid race to infamy. Too little genuine sympathy is manifested for this class. Many poor, unfortunate girls are driven forward in their downward course by unkind and unchristian treatment from those who utter long prayers in churches, who might reform and ought to be aided and encouraged.

The institution deserves credit and support.

ASYLUMS FOR THE INSANE.

The State is provided with four institutions and an act passed the legislature in 1893 establishing the fifth in the upper peninsula. Michigan asylum for the insane, the oldest, is located at Kalamazoo and was established by an act passed in 1848. It cost $572,000, and was opened in 1859.

The disbursements for two years ending January 3, was $422,470, a considerable portion of which was paid by individuals and counties.

The number of patients, males, 520; females, 527; medical attendants, 6; employés, 198.

Eastern Michigan Asylum is located at Pontiac, Oakland county. It was opened in 1878 and cost $467,000.

Number of patients under treatment in 1892 was, males, 449; females, 444; medical attendants, 5; employés, 163.

Northern Michigan Asylum, established in 1881, is located at Traverse City, Grand Traverse county, and cost $522,430.

Michigan Asylumn for Dangerous and Criminal Insane was established in 1883, and is located at Ionia, in connection with the reformatory. It cost $91,750. Number of patients in 1892, 164; number of employés, 31.

The legislature of 1893 made appropriations for an asylum for the insane in the upper peninsula. Each institution of this kind is managed by a special board of trustees appointed by the Governor, and is managed in the best possible manner.

MICHIGAN ASYLUM FOR THE INSANE, KALAMAZOO.

NORTHERN MICHIGAN ASYLUM FOR THE INSANE, TRAVERSE CITY.

TOTAL VALUE OF PROPERTY IN STATE INSTITUTIONS EXCEPT CAPITOL.

University of Michigan, Ann Arbor_____ $1,300,617 18
Agricultural College, Lansing_____ 459,131 69
State Normal School, Ypsilanti_____ 234,479 11
Michigan Mining School, Houghton_____ 150,000 00
Soldiers' Home, Grand Rapids_____ 168,990 00
Michigan Asylum, Kalamazoo_____ 950,507 60
Eastern Asylum, Pontiac_____ 793,245 30
Northern Asylum, Traverse City_____ 650,621 18
Michigan Asylum for Dangerous and Criminal Insane, Ionia_____ 138,736 58
State House of Correction, Marquette_____ 255,361 78
State House of Correction and Reformatory, Ionia _____ 416,802 02
State Prison, Jackson_____ 887,033 12
Industrial Home for Girls, Adrian_____ 172,708 18
Industrial School for Boys, Lansing_____ 255,477 87
Michigan State Public School, Coldwater_____ 227,816 22
Michigan School for Deaf and Dumb, Flint_____ 494,133 52
Michigan School for Blind, Lansing_____ 221,485 71

$7,777,212 06

STATE INDEBTEDNESS AND TAXATION.

BY E. J. WRIGHT, TAX DEPARTMENT, AUDITOR GENERAL'S OFFICE.

Michigan is practically free from debt, the entire amount of outstanding State bonds being $10,992.83, on which interest ceased long since. By the conditions of the grant of certain lands to the State by the United States the proceeds of the sale of the lands so granted are held by the State as a perpetual trust for the benefit of its grand system of public schools, the State assuming the obligation to pay the interest thereon annually for the support of the schools. The moneys to the credit of the several funds at the commencement of the present fiscal year were: Primary school fund, $4,466,090.06; University fund, $522,211.93; Agricultural College fund, $401,414.63; Normal School fund, $64,622.62. The equalized valuation of the State ten years ago was $810,000,000; the last equalization made it $1,130,000,000. An average tax of but a small fraction over one and one-half mills per annum has sufficed to amply sustain the State government, the asylums, reformatory and penal institutions, to pay the State's obligations to its educational institutions, and to liberally provide for every demand upon the State's resources.

The census of 1890 gives the combined State, county, municipal, and school district indebtedness of the State as $8.09 per capita, divided as follows: State, combining the trust funds as a debt of the State and including $31,992.83 of the State bonds then outstanding, $5,308,294; county, $1,257,698; municipal, $8,510,430; school district, $1,865,497. The nominal debt was $2.54 per capita, or in reality the entire liability of each citizen to the State, in addition to his share of the current requirements, being to pay annually 7 per cent on $2.54.

Local taxation is proportionately light, the economy of government being such that the requirements of the counties, townships and school districts, are far from burdensome. Even in the cities and villages where municipal luxuries are sometimes liberally indulged in, taxation is rarely excessive.

Railroad and express companies, insurance companies (exclusive of mutual benefit associations and farmers' mutual fire insurance companies), and some other corporations, pay tribute to the State by specific taxes, licenses and incorporation fees, etc.

The tax on liquor dealers is a considerable amount. While these taxes are by no means restrictive, they materially reduce the amount required to be raised by general taxation. The last legislature enacted a law providing for a graduated tax upon inheritances the effect of which cannot be determined yet.

All property real and personal, within the jurisdiction of the State, is subject to taxation, unless expressly exempted by law, and assessors are required to assess all property at its cash value. Real property belonging to the United States, to the State, or to counties, townships, cities, villages, or school districts, and used for public purposes, is exempted. Real and personal property owned and occupied by library, benevolent, charitable, educational and scientific institutions, incorporated under the laws of the State, is exempted while occupied solely for the purposes for which such institutions were incorporated. Houses of public worship, with the land on which they stand, the furniture therein, and all right in the pews, and parsonages owned by religious societies, and occupied as such; all lands used as burial grounds, and the tombs and monuments therein; the real property of corporations paying specific taxes (except that railroad properties are liable to assessment for local improvements in cities and villages, and all railroad lands not adjoining the tracks of the company, are subject to all taxes); property owned exclusively by State, county, or district agricultural societies, and used exclusively for fair purposes; the real and personal property of persons who in the opinion of the supervisor and board of review, by reason of poverty are unable to contribute toward the public charges; lands dedicated to the public and used as public parks, and monument grounds or armories belonging to military organizations, and not used for gain, complete the list of exemptions of real property. The other exemptions of personal property are: So much of the credits due, or to become due, as shall equal the amount of bona fide and unconditional debts of the person owning household furniture, provisions and fuel, to the value of five hundred dollars to each household, the library, family pictures, school books, one sewing machine, used and owned by each individual or family, and the wearing apparel of every individual, farm implements and machinery or personal property of any farmer to the amount of $200, the working tools of any mechanic not to exceed in value $100; all mules, and horses and cattle, not over one year old, all sheep and swine not over six months old, and all domesticated birds; pensions receivable from the United States, the personal property of library associations, circulating libraries, libraries of reference, and reading rooms owned or supported by the public and not used for gain, and all posts of the G. A. R., tents of the S. O. V., of the W. R. C., the Y. M. C. A., the W. C. T. U., Y. P. C. U., and similar associations; the property of Indians not citizens, and all fire engines or other implements for extinguishing fires, when owned or used by any organized or independent fire company. Personal property is assessed where found in April, and the assessment roll is made by the supervisor or assessor in May. All persons may be required to furnish sworn statements of their property. The assessment is open to inspection, and is subject to revision and correction by the board of review as may appear equitable and proper. At their annual session the board of supervisors of each county equalizes the value of real property in the several assessment districts and determines the amount to be raised by taxes for current purposes. Taxes assessed become a debt to the township and a lien upon the property assessed on December 1, and the township treasurer or village collector is required to collect and pay over the taxes before March 1 following. A collection fee of four per cent is added to taxes unpaid after December and interest at eight per cent after March 1. No personal property is exempt from seizure and sale to satisfy unpaid taxes. Unpaid taxes on real property are returned to the county treasurer and by him to the Auditor General, and if not paid to the Auditor General or the county treasurer within one year after return the lands are subject to sale for taxes and charges, including seventy cents for the expense of advertising and sale of each description. The Auditor General files with the circuit court of each county a petition for decree, and the delinquent taxpayer is notified of his day in court by publication. A decree having been obtained, sale is made on the first Monday in December at the county treasurer's office. After sale one year is allowed for redemption, after which a deed is issued to the purchaser on demand, unless bid in to the State, in which event the land is subject to sale by the Auditor General as State tax land, a deed being issued to the purchaser. All State tax lands unsold are offered at the annual sales of delinquent tax lands.

Lands subject to sale for taxes are sold for the taxes, charges, and accrued interest, and the purchaser may be put in possession by writ of assistance issued out of the circuit court.

All conveyances of land, except those executed by law, must be accompanied by certificates from the Auditor General or county treasurer, showing that the taxes thereon have been paid for the five years preceding the date of the instrument when presented to the register of deeds for recording. The experience of the State in the State system for the collection of delinquent taxes on lands, in contradistinction from the county system, is that a larger proportion of taxes are collected by the State system, and at a much less expense than in the states which adhere to the county system, which has been twice tried by Michigan and as often abandoned because of its proven undesirability, uncertainty and lack of uniformity.

MICHIGAN: ITS RESOURCES, BANKING LAW, AND FINANCES.

BY HON. T. C. SHERWOOD, BANK COMMISSIONER, MICHIGAN.

NOTE.—On account of the failure of some Michigan banks, a feeling of distrust was created against the entire system in the minds of many citizens, which caused a great deal of needless anxiety and suspicion. For the benefit of persons not understanding the banking laws and financial resources of the State, we copy the following article by permission:

Michigan, the beautiful Peninsular State, to be known needs but to be mentioned. With its two and one-half millions of inhabitants and its 58,915 square miles of territory, it comprises not only a wide region of abundant natural resources but also those industries and improvements that make her the peer of any State in the Union. The coal fields and beautiful farms of the southern part of the lower peninsula, the forests of the northern portion, together with the copper, iron and forestry of the upper peninsula, combine to make Michigan rich in natural resources to which when added the manufacturing industry, which the enterprise, thrift and industry of the citizens has built up, together with her excellent system of free schools, all tend to give Michigan a world-wide reputation in all that adds to the material, industrial and intellectual wealth of the nation.

Time will not permit me to fully discuss the resources of Michigan, and I will therefore call your attention to but a few industries, the development of which has made Michigan famous the world over. I will only refer to the copper, iron ore, lumber, shingles, salt and furniture industries, at this time, and hope you will become sufficiently interested to visit us and make a personal tour of inspection.

For the year 1892 the output of copper in Michigan, as compiled by the Mining Journal, was 107,200,000 pounds of refined copper, which at twelve cents per pound, the average price during the year, amounts to $12,864,000.00, and yet we are not asking that copper be coined into pennies and made a legal tender for debts.

The output of iron ore in 1892, according to the Iron Herald, amounted to 7,824,-556 tons, the average price being $4.00 per ton, making the total value $31,298,624.00.

22

The total quantity of lumber manufactured in Michigan in 1892 was 3,794,256,751 feet which at $15.00 per thousand amounts to $56,913,851 00.

The total number of shingles make in 1892 was 2,140,647,875, the average price as to grades being $2.50 per thousand, makes the total value $5,351,620.00.

The number of barrels of salt produced in Michigan in 1892 was 3,812,000, which at sixty cents per barrel amounts to $2,287,000; and last though not least comes the furniture industry, which in Michigan in increasing each year. The city of Grand Rapids, which today is perhaps the most noted furniture manufacturing city in the United States, in 1892 manufactured furniture valued at $10,864,000.

From these six industries alone (one of which is incomplete, as I have only given the furniture product of one city) Michigan offers to the markets of the world, in one year, goods amounting to over $119,500,000.

I have not mentioned the great agricultural interest of Michigan, not because it is insignificant, for it is not. It far exceeds every other industry, and compares favorably with any other of our sister states in its production of hay, grain, wool, fruit and vegetables.

I have simply mentioned those industries that have made Michigan known abroad and gained for her an enviable reputation among the sisterhood of states.

Notwithstanding Michigan is rich in agricultural, timber and mineral resources, until a few years we have had to depend upon outside capital for the development of these resources, and this brings me to the second part of the subject assigned me, viz.:

ITS BANKING LAW AND FINANCES.

Michigan in common with other states has had a varied experience in banking and banking laws, and has dearly paid for that experience in the losses she has sustained, as have other states in the union, as well as the nations of Europe.

It seems strange that the states and nations will not be benefited by the experience of others, but they will not. The John laws of today are just as positive that something can be made out of nothing as was the original John in France in 1718. Each individual thinks his financial policy the correct one, and the reason it failed of success 173 years ago was because the system was in advance of the times, which the changes in the manner of transacting business and the increased intelligence of the people will now make successful. We admit that the business methods have changed within the past few years, and will necessarily change as business increases and our facilities for exchanging the products of the different countries multiply. We also realize that there is a marked advancement in the intelligence of our business men, but we must not forget that the great fundamental principles of finance never change and the more intelligence we possess the more careful we will be to have a sound foundation for the support of the financial system which is the life blood of the nation.

The Michigan banking law of 1837, under which the notorious "wildcat" money was issued, was repealed in 1841, but it was not until 1857 that the State had a banking law that was at all satisfactory to the public; this law provided for banks of issue, in fact up to the close of the civil war the name bank carried with it the idea of an issue of paper currency rather than for the transacting of the business of the commercial world, and for the safe deposit of the surplus funds of our citizens. The passage by congress of the national banking act in 1863 and the law passed in 1865 imposing a tax of ten per cent on the amount of the notes of any State bank or banking association, effected a complete change in the system of banking in our State.

Instead of being banks of issue and depending largely upon circulation for their profits, our banks became commercial associations or, if you please, clearing houses, where our business men made their exchanges, discounted their commercial paper and deposited their surplus money; the banks' profits being derived from loans made with these deposits (upon which no interest was paid) and from exchange bought and sold.

The law of 1857, although reasonably satisfactory in the transaction of commercial business, even in the changed condition of business affairs, failed to provide for small depositors who desired to deposit their savings and receive interest thereon. Hence, in 1873, the law was amended providing for the incorporation of savings banks. But the State has outgrown the law. It was incomplete and defective and many of its provisions obsolete.

The business men of the State urged upon the legislature of 1887 the necessity of a new banking law that would satisfy the demands of the constantly increasing business of the State.

The legislature enacted such a law, which was adopted by the people at the general election of 1888, and became operative January 7, 1889.

Michigan's present general banking law provides for a banking department charged with the execution of the law, and its chief officer is called the Commissioner of the Banking Department.

He issues authority for the incorporation of banks, calls for at least four reports annually, at such times as he deems necessary, causes examinations to be made of each bank under his supervision, at least once in each year, and has the same authority over the State banks of Michigan that the Comptroller of the Currency at Washington has over the national banks of the United States.

In fact our banking law is copied largely from the national bank act, with several additional amendments, applicable to the business necessities of our State.

Michigan State banks are capitalized and the stockholders are each liable for an amount equal to the par value of their stock in addition to the said stock. At least fifty per cent of the capital must be paid in before the bank is authorized to commence business, and the remainder in monthly installments of at least ten per cent of the capital stock.

The amount of capital required of a State bank is regulated by the size of the city or town where the bank is located, the smallest capital being $15,000 in towns whose population does not exceed 1,500.

Michigan's banking law differs from the national bank act in that it is a dual law. It recognizes two classes of business—commercial and savings—both separate and distinct, and yet both embodied in one with separate restrictions.

The commercial department of our State banks is especially for the accommodation of business men. They are exclusively devoted to the collection, safe keeping and the employment in temporary loans the floating capital of the country.

Every merchant, miner, manufacturer and farmer is dependent upon the commercial bank for funds to enable them to market their products at the earliest moment. Hence, Michigan's law restricts the loaning of the deposits of commercial banks upon mortgage or any form of real estate security to fifty per cent of its capital stock, and then only upon a two-thirds vote of its directors, except to secure a debt previously contracted in good faith.

This restriction is simply to prevent the tying up of capital by long time loans, and by so doing embarrass the commercial and manufacturing enterprises of the State.

The savings department of our State banks is the depository for the surplus money not needed in active commercial business.

Deposits in this department are generally made by mechanics, who have not the time or opportunity to make investments, and by laborers and servants, who have not the education or ability to engage in active business.

They deposit their money for safe keeping and for interest under such rules and regulations as the board of directors of the bank prescribes.

One of the rules governing savings deposits adopted by nearly every savings bank in the State, provides that the cashier may in all cases require ninety days' notice to him in writing, before a depositor will be entitled to withdraw his deposit or any part thereof.

This rule is enforced only in case of financial excitement and has been resorted to with good effect by many banks in our State during the past few weeks.

People withdraw their money from banks in times of financial excitement not because they doubt the solvency of the bank, so much as they fear that others will get ahead of them and secure the money the bank has on hand. When they find that *none* are allowed to draw their deposits they go away satisfied that their chances are as good as others, and usually at the end of sixty days thank the cashier for enforcing the ninety day rule.

Michigan's banking law recognizes the fact that banks are but the custodians of the people's money and therefore prescribe the amount, quality and kind of securities that may be taken with the deposits in the two departments of our State banks.

In the commercial department, as I have already said, money can not be loaned on real estate security except by a two-thirds vote of its directors and then not more than fifty per cent of its capital.

It can not loan to one individual, company, corporation or firm more than ten per cent of its capital and surplus, except by a two-thirds vote of its directors, in which case the limit is twenty per cent.

This limitation does not apply to loans upon real estate or other collateral security, or the discounting of commercial paper owned by the person negotiating the same, or bills of exchange drawn in good faith against actually existing values.

Commercial banks or banks with commercial departments are required to keep on hand at all times at least fifteen per cent of their total deposits, except that in cities of over one hundred thousand population, each of such banks shall keep on hand twenty per cent of its deposits, one-half of which reserve shall be in lawful money, and the balance may be in funds, payable on demand, deposited in banks in cities, approved by the Commissioner as reserve cities.

The savings department is required to keep on hand at least fifteen per cent of its deposits, one-third of which reserve shall be in lawful money in its own vaults, and the balance on deposit payable on demand with banks, national or State, in reserve cities or invested in United States bonds.

Three-fifths of the remainder, or fifty-one per cent of the deposits, must be invested in bonds or in negotiable paper secured by bonds, or upon notes or bonds secured by mortgage lien upon unincumbered real estate, worth at least twice the amount loaned.

The remainder of the deposits, or thirty-four per cent, may be invested in notes, bills or other evidences of debt, the payment of which is secured by the deposit of personal property as security, or may be deposited in banks in reserve cities, providing the amount does not exceed ten per cent of the total deposits, capital and surplus of the depositing bank, and an amount not exceeding the capital and additional stockholders' liability may be invested in negotiable paper approved by the board of directors.

This 34 per cent investment of collateral and short time commercial paper, acts as a sort of financial safety valve. Being readily converted in money, it enables a bank to meet unusual demands without being compelled to dispose of its mortgage securities.

At the time our banking law was being discussed in the legislature, I had some doubt of the wisdom of allowing banks to incorporate with savings and commercial departments for the transaction of both classes of business, but after four years of trial, I see no reason for changing, especially in small towns and villages where the two classes of business could not profitably be carried on in two separate institutions.

Many business men now have two bank accounts, one commercial and one savings. The bank combining both classes of business can accommodate this class of persons, and there is no excuse for a bank's customer going elsewhere for an accommodation, unless at the request of the bank.

The relations between a bank and its customer should be as close and private as between physician and patient. No man in ill health would think of consulting and taking prescriptions from three or four physicians at the same time unless he expected to die, and no man should have accounts at several banks, especially if he is a borrower, unless he expects to die a financial death and wants a large number of mourners at his funeral. It is a fact that no banker can deny, that the heaviest losses banks sustain are by those who are customers of several banks at the same time.

Michigan's law does not permit the issuing of any bill, note or certificate intended to circulate as money, neither can a bank issue post notes.

All debts due to any State banking association on which interest is past due and unpaid for a period of six months, unless the same are well secured or in process of collection, are required to be charged off at the expiration of that time.

The expenses of the banking department are paid by the State from the general fund, but each State bank is required to pay into the State treasury for the credit of the general fund, one-hundredth part of one per cent of the gross amount of the assets of said bank at the time the examination is made, provided that the examination fee of any bank shall not be less than ten dollars.

Michigan's banking law does not provide for the supervision of private banks.

These banks are without any supervision whatever, and so far as the public knows, the amount of capital invested, methods of business and investments made, they are what their name indicates, *private.*

Our law provides the usual penalties for its violation, giving the commissioner power to take immediate possession of a bank for any violation of its provisions, and under the direction of the court wind up its buisness.

This in brief is Michigan's banking law, and in the four and one-half years it has been in operation, its adaptability to the varied business demands of our State, is amply proven by the fact that over eighty banks have incorporated under its provisions within that time.

On May 4 last, the one hundred and forty-nine bank and three trust companies then incorporated, reported their assets as $84,276,584.34 at the same time the one hundred and three national banks reported total assets as $75,722,412.09 making the total assets of the incorporated banks of the State $160,000,000.00'

The deposits of the State banks May 4 were $65,533,057.93 and the national banks $41.056,961.88 make a total of more than $106,590,000.00.

Rather than weary you I have briefly alluded to the resources of Michigan, and pointed out the salient points of its banking law and bank resources, and can only add that if you desire a closer acquaintance with us Wolverines, visit our State and study for yourselves our marvelous resources, our wonderful lakes and rivers, our health restoring summer resorts, and our beautiful scenery. I can assure you a hearty reception and a royal welcome.

FISHERIES.

HERSCHEL V. WHITTAKER, OF STATE FISH COMMISSION, DETROIT.

"Mich-sawg-ye-gan," the "Land of the Lakes" was the somewhat poetic and significant name given by the Ojibways to that territory lying within the present borders of the State of Michigan.

From the earliest that is known of this territory it was the favorite hunting and fishing ground of the savages. Here nature seems to have provided every variety of landscape from the heavily timbered mountainous districts of the extreme north to those lovely natural parks called oak openings of the southern peninsula, carpeted with flowers and verdant grasses and dotted everywhere with magnificent oaks. Here and there, in natural basins between the gentle swells of the rolling prairies nestled beautiful sparkling lakes, and on their limpid bosoms were reflected the beauties of their surroundings, which seemed fittingly placed as mirrors in which nature might admire her own loveliness. Floating lazily over them were innumerable wild fowl, while their depths swarmed with the king of fresh water game fish, the black bass, the muskallonge, the pike, and scores of other kinds of edible fish.

The silver threaded brooks and streams filled each valley with their murmurings, and the Indian gliding from lake to lake and stream to stream in his bark canoe, had but to stretch forth his hand and partake of their bounties.

More than five thousand of these beautiful lakes bountifully stocked with excellent fish, lie within the present limits of the State, and while the aborigine, the original proprietor of it all, has long since departed for his "Happy Hunting Ground," the finny denizens of these waters still delight the angler and fill his days with pleasure.

Bordering the two peninsulas of the State and almost surrounding them, lie the great fresh water seas of the northwest, the largest body of fresh water on the globe. Michigan with two thousand miles of lake coast holds preëminence over all her sister states in the importance of her commercial fisheries. These lakes have an area or 97,000 square miles and a total length of about 1,500 miles with a varying depth of from 100 to more than 900 feet, and all of them are filled with the purest water.

Upon these waters the missionary, filled with religious zeal for the salvation of souls, launched his frail birch bark canoe. Confiding his body to the mercies of the savages, and commending his soul to his Maker, he set forth for the conversion of the savages. Following him came the hardy adventurer and explorer, who through lack of opportunity for military distinction in the armies of France in time of peace, sought in the wilds of America to extend the domain of his king and to mend his own personal fortunes, and hoped to discover a way to Far Cathay. The fur trader and the courrier-du-bois followed close upon his footsteps and penetrated every cove and inlet of the lakes, to barter their cheap and tawdry gewgaws with the redskin for the valuable peltries of the beaver, mink, otter and other fur bearing animals.

All these found these lakes teeming with the choicest varieties of fish. Here was the "attikumaig," the "deer-of-the-water," that most excellent of fishes, the whitefish, the "salmo namaycush" or salmon trout whose proportions are said to have reached the weight of seventy pounds, the pike, perch or pickerel, the doré of the French, the lordly sturgeon which exceeded in size all others, often reaching a weight of one hundred and twenty-five pounds; the siskowet, the muskallonge, the white and black bass, the rock bass, pike, catfish, mullet, perch, sun fish, gar and other varieties abounded everywhere, and in their season the multitudes of herring or ciscoes exceeded belief.

For years after the white man settled on these lakes these storehouses of food remained untouched save for the small demand made upon them by the scattered settlers for daily food, and for the small quantities which were salted for winter use.

In the decade between 1830 and 1840 fishing as an industry first began to assume some importance and a few persons engaged in it as a business, but the product was largely salted and put up in packages for shipment.

About 1850 the fishermen on the Detroit river constructed in connection with their fisheries where the whitefish was taken in the fall season, pens for the confinement alive of whitefish until December and later, and when the glut consequent upon large catches had been disposed of, the penned whitefish were taken from the pens and shipped to distant markets. The severe weather of winter served to keep them in a fresh condition. The profits derived from this mode of procedure were large, and these advantages ultimately led to the invention of the method of artificially freezing of fish by which fish might be kept for an indefinite time, and from this was evolved the modern methods now pursued all over the lakes of holding fish in freezers. This discovery gave to the fishing industry a great impetus and the business was suddenly revolutionized. From being prosecuted with small gangs or strings of nets and with sail and row boats by a few individuals, the fishing being confined to a few months in the year, it has now grown to such proportions that frequently a single fisherman controls nets extending twenty-five, fifty and seventy miles in length, following his business with the use of steam craft and fishing during all seasons of the year, unless interfered with by the rigor of the season.

During the season of 1891 there were fished in the waters of this State 2,632 miles of gill nets, sufficient in length to encircle the entire State with nearly seven hundred miles to spare. There were 2,028 pound nets fished, having leaders measuring 316 miles, and ninety seines with a length of 8,175 fathoms.

There were about twenty-five freezers with a capacity of 2,500 tons of frozen fish and the industry employed upwards of 4,000 men.

The boats in use were seventy steamers, five hundred and seventy-four sail boats, three hundred and three pound boats and five hundred and forty-six skiffs.

The total amount invested in nets, boats, lands and buildings was $1,104,960.50.

The following table shows the number of pounds and the total value of all kinds of fish taken in this State for the year 1891:

Summarized report of all districts.

Fish caught.	Pounds.	Value.
Whitefish	8,110,387	$351,196 67
Lake trout	9,132,770	375,202 05
Pike perch	2,791,188	93,623 51
Herring	7,522,900	117,319 75
Sturgeon	831,606	34,188 48
Bass	95,318	4,472 00
Sangers	70,150	1,124 50
Perch	2,017,300	21,191 75
Suckers	1,392,150	17,132 50
Catfish	159,290	8,699 55
Caviare	58,999	13,383 50
All other kinds	1,232,310	28,494 15
Total	$3,714,868	$1,058,028 41

The vigorous prosecution of the fisheries, without any restraint upon the methods pursued, has resulted in a depletion of the waters, and they are threatened with decay and perhaps absolute extinction unless some steps are taken by the State to arrest it. Those interested in these matters have sought to propose means by which the fisheries may be conserved in the interests of the people, and the means suggested are as follows:

1. The passage of necessary restrictive legislation to control the fishermen in methods of capture;

(*a*) By making it unlawful to take at any time or in any season of the year young and immature fish which have not reached the spawning age, and

(*b*) The establishment of a close season during the spawning period, which will allow the fish to perform the function of reproduction undisturbed.

2. The impregnation of the ova artificially and the hatching of the eggs in suitable hatcheries, whereby the loss of ova may be reduced to the minimum, such operations to be conducted on a liberal scale.

Artificial impregnation has been demonstrated to be highly successful, the history of the treatment of the ova of the salmonidæ for a series of years showing that with proper care the percentage of loss on ova taken will not exceed ten per cent.

The State of Michigan at an early period became impressed with the importance of fish culture and has made liberal appropriations for the conduct of this work.

It has now, established and in operation, four hatcheries. Two of these hatcheries are devoted to the propagation of commercial fish, like the whitefish and pike perch or wall-eyed pike, one for the propagation of brook trout, California or mountain trout, and the brown trout of Europe, and one for the cultivation and

23

breeding of carp. It is intended soon to established a station for the culture and propagation of the black bass.

The annual output of whitefish fry for the past four years has been upwards of 100,000,000, and during the spring of 1893 it will reach nearly if not quite 200,000,000.

The average output of pike perch or wall-eyed pike for the same period has been upwards of 30,000,000.

The output of all varieties of trout averages about 3,000,000 yearly, and of carp about 5,000.

In addition to this there have been distributed about 200,000 salmon trout fry annually for the last two years, 2,500,000 white bass and 273,000 silver eels.

The success of these operations have been eminently satisfactory. Before the year 1840 the brook trout was unknown in the waters of the lower peninsula, with the exception of one or two streams. Today there is excellent fishing in more than fifty counties, and the work is popular everywhere.

STATE BOARD OF FISH COMMISSIONERS.

BY GEO. D. MUSSEY.

In 1873 an act was passed by the legislature creating this board and the Governor appointed two commissioners, who, with himself, constituted the board. In 1875 the board was reorganized, the statute having been so amended as to provide for three commissioners, one for two years, one for four years and one for six years, and their successors to be appointed to a term of six years each. The present board consists of Hoyt Post and Herschel Whittaker of Detroit and Horace W. Davis of Grand Rapids. The commissioners receive no compensation whatever, but are allowed their actual expenses when traveling on the business of the board. The work is a labor of love, which every commissioner can testify is an expensive one for him.

The duty of the board is to conduct the artificial propagation of such varieties of food fish as it may deem best and to distribute the same gratuitously in the waters of the great lakes and the rivers and straits connecting them, or in the inland lakes and streams upon the application of some person interested in the waters sought to be stocked; the only condition being that the waters thus supplied with fish by this board shall be open to the public for fishing by lawful methods and at lawful times.

The varieties now propagated are the whitefish, lake or salmon trout, pike-perch or wall-eyed pike, brook trout, California or mountain trout, the brown trout of Germany, and the German carp. The distribution of whitefish fry is confined exclusively to the great lakes and rivers connecting them; all other varieties are furnished upon the application of those interested in the stocking of the inland waters in their immediate vicinity. Those wishing fish for stocking streams, lakes or ponds should write to the Michigan fish commission, Detroit, for blanks, which will be furnished on request and which when filled up and returned will enable the board to determine the kind and quantity needed for the waters to be supplied.

Previous to the organization of this board there were very few streams in the lower peninsula of this State in which brook trout were native, and below a line from Petoskey to Saginaw absolutely no brook trout were to be found. There are now nine hundred and seventy-six streams in the lower peninsula, distributed through fifty-six counties, which have been stocked by this board, all open to fishing and in which this most valuable of game fishes may be found in comparative abundance. Besides this, a large number of streams have been partially stocked with brook trout in several other counties of the lower peninsula and in a number of counties in the upper peninsula. These streams will be open for fishing in from one to two years.

The State is rapidly acquiring a wide reputation for its splendid trout fishing and the amount of money brought into the State every season by sportsmen and tourists on account of the trout fishing is enormous, aggregating many thousands of dollars. No enterprise in which the State is engaged returns so directly to every class of its people such large and important benefits as do the results of the work of the Michigan fish commission. No other State in the union propagates so large a number of fish each year, and no State produces fry at so small a cost per thousand.

The State now has four hatching stations, located at Detroit, Paris, Sault Ste. Marie and Glenwood. At Detroit is the whitefish and wall-eyed pike hatchery. This is the largest and most complete whitefish hatchery in the world. It contains 1,050 hatching jars, each capable of running four quarts of eggs; a total capacity of over 150,000,000 of whitefish eggs.

At Paris, Mecosta county, is the hatchery for all varieties of trout. This is one of the best hatcheries in the United States, and while there may be one or two larger ones, there are none which excel it in its construction or adaptability for the hatching of trout. Its capacity is about 5,000,000 of fry per year. It has never been filled to its fullest capacity.

At Sault Ste. Marie is a hatchery for whitefish and trout. It was built as an experiment and after having been run two years has proved a success for both varieties. It will undoubtedly be continued at Sault Ste. Marie, or at some other point in the upper peninsula.

At Glenwood are the carp and goldfish ponds. This station has always been successful and the State now breeds more carp than is needed to supply the demand. The hatching of goldfish at this station has also been attended with success and soon this beautiful fish will be ready for public distribution.

The following is a statement of fry of all kinds hatched and distributed since the organization of the board up to January 1, 1893:

Whitefish	740,965,500	Schoodic salmon	329,618
Wall-eyed pike	170,723,256	California trout	83,475
Brook trout	15,097,900	Lock leven trout	43,000
White bass	2,500,000	Cary	26,868
Lake trout	2,080,301	Black bass	12,215
California salmon	1,304,651	Eels	2,211,000
Brown trout	507,500		
Total			935,885,314

In addition to the work of propagating fish, the board some years ago inaugurated an examination of the inland lakes of the State, commencing with the southern tier of counties, intending eventually to examine all the lakes in the lower peninsula at least. This work has been continued for seven years and accurate and complete records of the examination of each lake are kept, each year's reports being bound in separate and permanent volumes, so that in the end a complete history of each lake will be on file and the board will thereby be enabled to accurately determine what fish are best suited for the waters of any given lake. This board was the first to undertake this work, and it is a feature that has met the approval and high commendation of all the fish commissioners from other states who have learned of it.

For nearly two years the board has employed a statistical agent whose business it is to visit all of the fisheries of the State and get from the proprietors a report of their catch, which the law requires them to furnish to this board. A very competent man was secured and the statistics now obtained are of great value, showing, as they do, notwithstanding the greatly improved methods of fishing and the acknowledged destruction of immense numbers of immature whitefish, that through the constant replenishing of the waters by this board the annual catch of whitefish falls but little short of that of the much hardier and naturally more numerous salmon trout. Without the efforts of the Michigan fish commission very few whitefish would now be caught in the waters of this State.

The capital invested in the commercial fisheries of the State exceeds one million of dollars. The annual catch exceeds thirty-five millions of pounds, having a wholesale value of over one million of dollars. More than twenty-nine hundred miles of nets are in use every year, and employment is furnished to about forty-five hundred men.

This board has, for the last two years, also employed a scientist, who has made investigations as directed by the board, and who has already largely increased the knowledge of certain fishes. His investigations so far have been confined principally to the wall-eyed pike, one of the most valuable, as well as one of the most difficult fish to handle and propagate, on account of the great loss in hatching. The investigations of this gentleman have not only led to improved methods of handling, but have also added largely to the literature on the subject, articles on the development of the wall-eyed pike having been written by him and published by this board, which have met with the flattering approval of scientists in all of the states and in many foreign countries.

This board provides fish for the farmer, the mechanic, the laborer, the sportsman and for commerce. The rich and the poor are benefited alike by the work of the board. It has always been true that the Michigan fish commission is the friend of all the people; it is rapidly becoming true that all the people are friends of the Michigan fish commission.

MICHIGAN SOLDIERS' HOME.

———

The Michigan Soldiers' Home, established in 1885, is situated on Grand river three miles north of the center of the city of Grand Rapids, on a plat of ground containing 132 acres, which was donated by the city of Grand Rapids at a cost of $16,500. The building, which will accommodate 400 members, was completed December 1, 1886, at a cost of $99,667.57. The legislative appropriations were: For maintenance of inmates for 1885, $10,000; for 1886, $40,000; and for the erection of buildings and preparing of grounds, $100,000. The home has at present 335 inmates; on leave of absence, 35. Total enrollment for last fiscal year, 212; present value of its property, $168,990. The institution is designed to furnish a home for "all honorably discharged soldiers, sailors and marines, who served in the army or navy of the United States in the late war of the rebellion, and who are disabled by disease, wounds or otherwise, who have no adequate means of support, and by reason of disability are incapable of earning their living, and who would be otherwise dependent upon public or private charity." To be entitled, however, to the privileges of the home, applicants, must have resided in Michigan one year preceding the passage of the act establishing the home, or they must have served in a Michigan regiment, or have been accredited to Michigan.

The supervision and government of the home is vested in a board of managers consisting of the Governor, who is *ex officio* chairman, and six members, appointed by the Governor, for a term of six years. Public acts No. 152, 1885. The legislative appropriation for 1891 and 1892 was $175,750 for the two years; 1891 the amount was $91,000, and 1892, $84,750.

BOARD OF MANAGERS.

	Term expires.
Governor John T. Rich	March 1, 1895
John Northwood, New Lothrop	March 1, 1895
L. W. Sprague, Greenville	March 1, 1897
L. G. Rutherford, Grand Rapids	March 1, 1897
Rush J. Shank, Lansing	March 1, 1897
James A. Crozier, Menominee	March 1, 1899
Loomis K. Bishop, Grand Rapids	March 1, 1899

OFFICERS OF THE BOARD.

Governor John T. Rich .... Chairman, *ex officio*
L. G. Rutherford, Grand Rapids .... Clerk
James A. Crozier, Menominee .... Treasurer

OFFICERS OF THE HOME.

Capt. B. F. Graves .... Commandant
Maj. J. W. Long... Adjutant
Col. Chester B. Hinsdill... Quartermaster
Dr. D. C. Spalding .... Surgeon

MICHIGAN AS A SUMMER RESORT.

No state in the union offers equal advantages to the resorter, with its 5,000 small lakes and web work of streams all stocked with gamy fish, and beautiful and healthy surroundings all easy of access, and at the same time as wild as the most romantic could desire. Streams filled with trout, running through a country where deer and bear are to be found, with surroundings as wild and primitive as though the destructive hand of man had never touched it, and at the same time so close to excellent hotels and camping grounds that no hardships need be experienced as is so often necessary in order to enjoy such things in other places.

We have one thousand six hundred miles of coast line, with hardly a stretch of five miles without a grand location for camping or a resort already established. The variety of "outing places" is so complete that to fail to be pleased in Michigan would indicate the impossibility to please. All classes of entertainment are found, from the grand modern hotel, as fine as the most lavish could wish, to the small fishing camp; the fashionable resorts where expenses are not considered, to the small camp with expenses cut down to less than fifty cents per day all told. As an evidence of the popularity of Michigan resorts, the number of resorters are largely increasing each year and an annual visit to the old camping ground is looked forward to with pleasure. Thousands of beautiful sites on quiet little lakes or on rivers are being bought by clubs and club houses built. This is within reach of everybody, as the land can be bought for from $1.25 to $25 per acre and a small outlay in buildings will furnish accommodations to a club.

In the north half of the lower peninsula and in the upper peninsula there is not a county that has no lakes or streams. The southern part of the State is equally well provided with lakes and rivers, but lacks the wild element and cheapness of land, being more thickly settled. The western shore of the lower peninsula is dotted with resorts from Berrien to Emmet county. Many have been improved at large expense. Macatawa park at Holland is a very elegant resort and is largely patronized by excursions from Grand Rapids and other cities. Hackley park assembly is located near Muskegon and has connection with the city by railroad, boats, etc. It is located on beautiful bluffs, with a grand view of Lake Michigan. Charles Hackley, a very liberal gentleman of Muskegon, with a keen sense of the beautiful, donated a large amount of money to be used in beautifying this place, and it was named by Bishop Newman of Washington, D. C., the "Gem of the Chautauquas." The grounds are owned by the

Methodist association who have a splendid auditorium and other buildings, water works and electric light plant. The W. C. T. U. and teachers' association also are erecting buildings. From here to Grand Traverse we have no means of knowing how many resorts and club houses are located. Going north, the tourist on a vessel can hardly get out of sight of one resort or club house before another comes in sight. Many church organizations and societies have established resorts. Many old ones, such as Old Mission, We-que-ton-sing, Omena, Harbor Point, Bay View. We will not attempt to mention each, for want of space, but the tourist need experience no difficulty in finding a place enchanting. The group of islands forming Manitou county are all interesting and many lovely locations are there. Across the water, from Menominee, passing Mackinac Island, the Les Cheneaux, St. Marys river, passing into Lake Superior, and coasting on the borders of the State, the most romantic and daring could be satisfied. There are beauties and wonders on the shore of Lake Superior but few know anything of.

All points are reached by rail or water to within a few miles and the trip to and from all such places is made cheaply and with comfort. On the east border of the State the same condition is found. Lake Huron, a grand body of water, St. Clair river, St. Clair lake, Detroit river—a thousand pages would not be sufficient to thoroughly describe all the interesting locations.

Deer, bear, porcupine, badgers, wild cats, foxes and small game are here but are not plenty, only in certain localities. Of wild geese and ducks and other feathered game there is a fair supply. Of snakes there are some, but not near so many as in states farther south. The fish and game laws of the State are calculated to protect and increase, making the sport better each year.

TRANSPORTATION.

Resorts are reached by water from all directions, on elegant vessels, and on land by railway. Very few stage coaches or canals. It costs but little more to enjoy the luxury of a steamer trip than to stay at home.

EMIGRATION.

Emigrants who float in with the tide will not find Michigan their El Dorado. While Michigan is an open field for intelligent, enterprising and honest workers, it has no department for the indolent or vicious class. The long winters admonish us that preparations must be made during summer for the coming winter.

This proves a great incentive to exertion, and the work of preparing for winter creates a habit of preparing for coming winters in the future. Michigan is a poor place to idle away time and trust in providence for the future supply until you have positive assurance that providence will trust you. The lazy, indolent and dishonest class will find no opening in Michigan.

The Lord hates a lazy man and the law takes care of the dishonest. Michigan is a hive of industry, with no use for drones. The object in migrating is generally to better the situation. The capitalist may see better investment for his money, the manufacturer advantages justifying removal, the laborer remunerative employment, the farmer land within his power to own. For such investigation, we offer this book as a guide or help. To induce immigration is not the prime object of this work. While additions to our population, if of the right kind, are always desirable and welcome, we desire to hold out no false inducements.

Skilled labor in Michigan is remunerated much the same as in other states. Although manufacturing is carried on largely, and the products of the mines and manufactories are almost unlimited, it is not intended to convey the idea that labor, skilled, clerical or common, is demanded at exorbitant salaries and wages. It is much the same as in other states. Let no one suppose that elegant positions, fat jobs or first-class employment at big wages await all comers. Such is not the case. Many stranded wrecks result from false impressions. After reading booming articles in which the truth is entirely ignored, with feverish haste sacrifices are made, little savings are used, in the senseless rush to worse than fairy lands, only to find nothing as represented and anticipated, but simply to realize that somebody lied. The finely written and elaborately illustrated matter published by railroad land agents and land companies to induce buyers, should be taken at a very large discount, and statements allowed a large percentage for shrinkage. The luckless immigrant with false impressions, induced by misleading statements, cuts loose his moorings and joins the ranks of the seekers of some "*ignis-fatuus,*" many to strand in some unpromising or uninhabitable country, without friends or means of support, with no bright prospect ahead. With inevitable ruin, want,

24

`deprivation, and destitution surrounding him, family begging for the most meager necessities of life, cold, hungry, disappointed, and, if possessing less than iron nerve, completely demoralized. No situation can be more terrible. He retraces his weary way to his former home and, if of the right sort, devotes the balance of his life to repair his loss. This is not fiction; many, too many, can attest its truthfulness. Michigan has its share of paupers and unfortunates and we sincerely and earnestly desire to avoid making more. If you desire to locate in Michigan, for whatever purpose, we advise investigation, full and satisfactory. The State will bear it. If what you want is not found here, no passport is required to pass on. If Michigan does not suit you, shake its dust from your feet and seek your tenting ground in some other part of the earth. The Creator providentially ordained that mankind should be constituted with different likes and dislikes. While the Floridian loves his sunny home and orange grove, the northern Michigander will travel miles on his snow shoes to inform you that he would not exchange. First determine what you want, then learn where it is to be found.

INVESTIGATION.

Many do not investigate at all, but accept the gilded statements of the boomer with blind faith and repeat the drama of the spider and the fly. Others investigate, but how? With a map spread out before them a bird's eye view of the State is had and they know all about it. They read the report of a potato crop, possibly the report of some choice acre, and immediately jump at the conclusion that that locality is the great potato country. Maps and statistical reports are good as far as they go, but when you arrive at any certain locality and look around, you can see but a short distance, beyond which you know nothing, and in many cases no one can tell you. Of the whole number of sections of land in a state no two are alike. They may be similar. Thousands of acres are used for farming in Michigan not fit for the business, and at the same time thousands of acres of first class land remains unused. Proper investigation would have reversed this matter. No State in the union possesses the variety of soils and location that Michigan does, from the extremely poor to the best. But you cannot look over soils and compare them as you would the wares in a tin shop. Location without proper investigation is a leap in the dark. It would not be policy, if possible, to sell by forced sale and have occupied every acre of vacant or unused land in the State. No state can prosper and flourish with a dissatisfied citizenship, no more than can a manufactory flourish with dissatisfied workmen. The same condition pervades all the ramifications of business and social life, even from the general government down to the humblest home. Success has and always will be the American's watchword. Hence, individual success portends State and national success. Success depends upon exertion, exertion upon opportunity, opportunity upon investigation, plain, positive and personal.

SHIP YARDS.

The great and increasing commerce of the lakes makes vessel building an important factor in the industries of the State. When it is taken into consideration that a large part of the labor of ship building is skilled labor, for which wages much better than common labor is paid, it will readily be seen that a vast amount of money is distributed through this channel.

In ship building, Wayne county leads as to numbers but Bay very far exceeds any other as to tonnage. The following tables show the kind of vessels, tonnage, etc.:

Where and by whom built.	Number and kind of vessels.					Tonnage.	Total tonnage.
	Steamers and propellers.	Lake barges.	Tugs.	Schooners.	Whole number.		
DETROIT AND WYANDOTTE:							
D. D. D. Co.	65	5			70	71,245	
Cooper	1		3		4	146	
Thos. Davis				1	1	79	
J. Oads	6			5	11	3,561	
Campbell & O.	4	2	2	6	14	4,956	
J. N. Jones	2	3	4	11	20	9,472	
McDonald	1			3	4	670	
Garrett				1	1	75	
W. H. Baker			1		1	22	
Stapiniski	1		1	1	3	234	
Dean & Co.		1	2		3	252	
Hicks				1	1	85	
Clark	3	2		1	6	3,670	
Irwin	2				2	234	
Ellenwood			1		1	16	
Thurston	1				1	33	
Miscellaneous	1		1	2	4	249	
Kirby	3		1		4	1,985	
Total	90	13	16	32	151		97,084

Table showing kind of vessels, tonnage, etc.—Continued.

Where and by whom built.	Steamers and propellers.	Lake barges.	Tugs.	Schooners.	Whole number.	Tonnage.	Total tonnage.
BAY CITY AND WEST BAY CITY:							
F. W. Wheeler & Co.	61	11	10	5	87	84,313	
J. Davidson	18	5	3	6	32	33,217	
Crosswaithe	3	1			4	2,326	
Beebe			1		1	11	
Rose	1		1		2	1,281	
Boston		1			1	250	
Hitchcock	1	1	1		3	452	
Jones	1				1	1,158	
Wheeler	1		1		2	1,049	
Crosswaithe		3		1	4	2,179	
Tripp & Co.		1			1	370	
Dickson				1	1	640	
Miscellaneous	2				2	108	
Total	83	23	17	18	141		127,351
SAGINAW, EAST AND WEST:							
Smith & W.	2			1	3	897	
Barbage			1		1	41	
Tripp		1	5	1	7	925	
Kelly	1				1	218	
Kirby & T.	1	1		1	3	912	
C. Wheeler	1	1	5	1	8	2,408	
Doherty			1		1	62	
Elmwood				1	1	150	
Dickson		1			1	583	
T. A. Estes				1	1	165	
Morgan		1			1	592	
Arnold	3	11			14	7,803	
Lester		1			1	246	
Carpenter				1	1	191	
Pendell		1			1	389	
Crosswaithe		1		2	3	1,969	
Fox		1			1	206	
Campbell		1			1	493	
Kenson		1			1	328	
Lutts		1			1	847	
Miscellaneous	1	1	2		4	465	
Total	9	24	14	9	56		19,455
PORT HURON:							
Bedford				1	1	102	
Jenks & Co.	1				1	268	
Barber		1			1	212	
Dunford & A.		4		1	5	2,085	
Arnold				2	2	819	
Leighton			2	3	5	1,376	
L. Fitz					1	886	
D. D. Co.	1				1	1,383	
Murr & Co.	1	3			4	3,577	
Herrick			1		1	19	
Hardison	1			2	3	792	
Stewart		1	2		3	564	
Fitzgerald			1	6	7	3,130	
Total	5	9	6	15	35		14,683

Table showing kind of vessels, tonnage, etc.—Continued.

Where and by whom built.	Number and kind of vessels.					Tonnage.	Total tonnage.
	Steamers and propellers.	Lake barges.	Tugs.	Schooners.	Whole number.		
MARINE CITY:							
J. J. Hill	2				2	251	
Rogers		1			1	858	
Holland	1	1			2	651	
Rice	1	1		1	3	671	
Morley & Hill	14	1		1	16	13,330	
Leeter & Co.	16	12	2	2	32	15,144	
Kanyon	1				1	213	
Wolverton		1			1	953	
J. H. Jenkins		1			1	739	
Luff		2		1	3	638	
Gardiner	1				1	296	
Arnold	1	2			3	1,404	
Kung	7	3			10	2,560	
McDowell		1	1		2	310	
Bushnell		2			2	935	
Anderson	7	1			8	3,612	
A. Pope				1	1	42	
Langell	1				1	593	
Kelsey		1			1	268	
Gallagher			1		1	26	
Miscellaneous			1		1	15	
Total	52	30	5	6	93		43,359
SAUGATUCK:							
Mastell	3		16	1	20	2,147	
J. Elliott	5		2	1	8	1,181	
Donnelly			1		1	20	
McMillan				1	1	121	
Keith				1	1	465	
Rogers	1			1	2	441	
Brittain	1				1	118	
Miscellaneous	1		1		2	226	
Total	11		20	5	36		4,699
GRAND HAVEN:							
Callister	1	2	1	1	5	814	
Kirby	6		4		10	2,207	
G. H. S. Co.	1				1	608	
Robertson	19	2	10	4	35	6,162	
Pierson			2	2	4	374	
Litchfield				2	2	376	
Kelly	1				1	117	
Vantall			1		1	6	
Total	28	4	18	9	59		10,664
MT. CLEMENS:							
W. Dulac	6	4	1		11	6,282	
Chabideaux	1				1	97	
Stewart		1			1	400	
Saunders	2				2	142	
Hall & Kent	1				1	209	
Leighton	1				1	124	
Daily & S.	1				2	468	
Duprus	1	1			2	407	
Wardell	1				1	79	
Total	14	6	1		21		8,208

Table showing kind of vessels, tonnage, etc.—Continued.

Where and by whom built.	Number and kind of vessels.					Tonnage.	Total tonnage.
	Steamers and propellers.	Lake barges.	Tugs.	Schooners.	Whole number.		
ST. CLAIR:							
Langell	8	7		1	16	9,939	
Cornwall		1			1	273	
Bower			1		1	326	
Dulac		1			1	511	
Miscellaneous				1	1	52	
Total	8	10		2	20		11,106
MUSKEGON:							
Arnold	1		7	1	9	301	
Foolander	1		2	3	6	314	
Notler			1		1	20	
Mitchell			1		1	8	
Total	2		11	4	17		643
TRENTON:							
Craig & Son	10				10	7,581	
Turner	6	6		1	13	4,100	
Calkins		1			1	225	
W. N. S.				1	1	115	
Total	16	7		2	25		12,021
GIBRALTER:							
Linn	6	5		3	14	9,873	
Calkins		1		1	2	534	
Total	6	6		4	16		10,407
ALGONAC:							
Pangborn				1	1	146	
Chas. Cash			1		1	18	
Smith	1	3	2		6	1,283	
Harman	2		1	1	4	1,110	
St. German				1	1	119	
Barker		1			1	283	
Navaugh				1	1	300	
Williams			1		1	119	
Total	3	4	5	4	16		3,381
SOUTH HAVEN:							
Wilkes				1	1	99	
Winter			2		2	23	
Hancock					1	126	
Perene	1				3	678	
Martell	2			1	1	172	
Finch	1			1	1	96	
Total	4		2	3	9		1,163

Table showing kind of vessels, tonnage, etc.—Continued.

Where and by whom built.	Number and kind of vessels.					Tonnage.	Total. tonnage.
	Steamers and propellers.	Lake barges.	Tugs.	Schooners.	Whole number.		
HURON:							
Squires	1	1	1	3	6	1,886	
E. Bates				1	1	222	
Barker				1	1	193	
Kelly		1			1	868	
Ketchum				2	2	320	
Total	1	2	1	7	11		2,989
BENTON HARBOR:							
Burgoyne	1			1	2	169	
Randall	4				4	+851	
E. W. Heath	1				1	178	
Total	6			1	7		+1,198

Vessels were built at other places as follows:

Where built.	Number and kind of vessels.					Tonnage.
	Steamers and propellers.	Lake barges.	Tugs.	Schooners.	Whole number.	
St. Joseph	2		1	4	7	293
Manistee	1	2	1	1	5	1,146
Bangor	2	2		2	6	3,876
Ludington	1		1	1	3	132
Pentwater			2	1	3	124
Sebewaing	1			1	2	315
Cleveland	2				2	3,121
Marysville	2				2	394
Allegan	1			1	2	573
Charlevoix				2	2	124
Fair Haven	2				2	281

One vessel was built at each of the following places: Oscoda, Portsmouth, Cheboygan, Caseville, Sand Beach, Wenona, White Lake, Eastmanville, Baraga, Au Sable, North Baltimore, Escanaba, Ferrysburg and Salina. In all three propellers, five barges, two tugs and four schooners, with 3,276 tons burden.

Whole number steam vessels and propellers	360
lake barges	147
tugs	123
schooners	133
Unknown	8
Whole number vessels of all kinds	771
Total tonnage	382,052

Over 1,000 tons burden, 132; over 2,000 tons burden, 7.

MICHIGAN STATE TROOPS

BY C. L. EATON, ADJUTANT GENERAL.

Michigan's military force comprises five regiments of infantry with an aggregate strength of nearly three thousand men. Each regiment has eight companies and is divided into two battalions. The personnel of the men comprising this force is first class. A large majority of its membership is made up of our successful, energetic and pushing young business men, who manifest deep interest in the organization. The first regiment has one company at each of the following places, viz.: Ann Arbor, Adrian, Tecumseh, Lansing, Mason, Ypsilanti and two at Jackson.

The second regiment has three companies at Grand Rapids and one each at Coldwater, Kalamazoo, Three Rivers, Grand Haven and Ionia.

The companies of the third are located respectively at Flint, Alpena, Bay City, Saginaw, East Saginaw, Port Huron, Owosso and Cheboygan.

The fourth regiment, with the exception of one company (G, of Monroe), is located in the city of Detroit.

The fifth regiment has five companies, located at Calumet, Menominee, Houghton, Marquette and Ironwood in the upper peninsula, but three of its companies, those at Big Rapids, Manistee and Muskegon being below the straits. The brigade is under command of Brig. Gen. E. W. Bowen, of Ypsilanti. The regiments are commanded in their numerical order by Col. John E. Tyrrell of Jackson, Col. C. H. Rose of Grand Rapids, Col. C. R. Hawley of Bay City, Col. P. J. Sheahan of Detroit and Col. F. B. Lyon of Calumet.

Money for the support of our military system is raised by an annual tax of four cents per capita. It is believed by the writer that the Michigan State troops are as well officered as are those of any state in the union, and that in discipline, personal appearance, gentlemanly and soldierly conduct, the Michigan boys are not excelled by those of any of our sister states.

HEALTH IN MICHIGAN.

BY HENRY B. BAKER, M. D., SECRETARY OF THE STATE BOARD OF HEALTH.

Man makes most rapid and greatest progress in that belt or zone within which
the average annual temperature does not much exceed 60° F. or fall much below
45° F. As regards productiveness of soil, and consequent prosperity in food supplies, the warmer portion of the zone is believed to be favorable, but the evidence
seems conclusive that for hardiness of constitution and general and special healthfulness the coldest portion excels. The average annual temperature in central
Michigan is about 46.5° F. But Michigan is exceptionally well situated for climatic influences. Extreme heat and extreme cold endanger life and health. Michigan being surrounded, except on the south, by large bodies of water, the temperature in summer is not as high as it otherwise would be, and in winter it is not as
low. How this is favorable to human health may perhaps be better appreciated
by noticing how it affects tender plant life; it is well known that peach trees are
easily killed by extreme cold, yet western Michigan is remarkable for its peach
crops, made possible in this latitude by the mildness of the winter climate, modified as it is by the large bodies of water in the great lakes which nearly surround
the State. This modification of the winter climate in Michigan is undoubtedly
favorable to human health, by lessening the danger from inflammation of the
lungs, bronchitis, influenza, etc.; and the cooling of the air in summer by the
water of the great lakes is favorable by lessening the danger from diarrhea, dysen-
tery, and the other diseases which are usually coincident with high temperatures.

Many of the diseases which most commonly kill people are spread by ignorant
and careless disregard of sanitary law. Safety from such diseases is impossible in
states and in communities where such disregard is common. In Michigan the people are fast becoming active in efforts for the general promotion of the public
health. It was one of the first states in the union to establish a State Board of
Health, and local boards of health are now quite generally organized throughout

25

the State. The people seem to place a high estimate upon the value of human life and health; during the session of 1881 the State legislature passed forty-eight acts bearing directly or indirectly upon this subject. No man can live to himself alone,—he is greatly dependent upon his surroundings and fellow citizens for safety to life and health. One of the greatest recommendations for Michigan as a State to *live* in is the intelligent regard of its citizens for human life and health.

The conditions in Michigan being favorable for public health and happiness, what is the positive evidence of the general result, as shown by the death rate? Is it possible to compare the death rate in Michigan with that in other states and countries? Unfortunately for our present purpose, governments have nowhere paid sufficient attention to this subject of life and health to enable one to make accurate and complete comparisons of different states or countries. Considering such masses of statistics as are supplied by the census of Great Britain and of the United States, etc., this may seem strange, but it is true. The actual death rate in these countries has not yet been learned, though for many cities it is quite closely ascertained. Censuses of states and countries collect statements of deaths which occurred during the year preceding the census, and many deaths are omitted because of movements of relatives and friends, and the forgetfulness of other people. The omissions are probably not the same in all states, because the movements of the inhabitants are not equal. According to the United States censuses preceding that of 1880 (the results of which are not yet published) Michigan has had a very low death rate, lower than that of most other states. After the census of 1870, the writer undertook to ascertain, by means of statistics collected for the same time by another set of men than the census marshals, what proportion of the deaths in Michigan were omitted and what the actual death rate was. A "Life Table," similar to those employed by insurance companies was then made, showing for Michigan the average years of life after each age, and for persons of each sex and at every age the probable duration of life in Michigan. Obviously it will not do to compare a death rate thus obtained with the death rate of any state ascertained directly from the United States census, because, to make my life table for Michigan, the deaths by the census were nearly doubled—being multiplied by 1.86; but even then the death rate was so small that it became desirable to compare it with an exceptionally low one. Dr. Wm. Farr, the most eminent vital statistician, has constructed a life table for the healthy districts of England, concerning which he has said:

"We have no means of ascertaining what the rate of mortality would be among men living in the most favorable sanitary conditions; otherwise observations for a term of years on a considerable number of such persons would supply a standard rate with which other rates could be compared. In the absence of such a standard, the districts of England in which the mortality rate did not exceed seventeen annual deaths in 1,000 living have been selected as the basis of a new life table."

Comparing my life table for Michigan with Dr. Farr's life table of the healthy districts of England it is found that they are almost identical, for all ages except under five years and over eighty years, the exception under five years being explained in part by the fact that for the Michigan table the still-births were counted as deaths, while in England they were not; the exception over eighty years being that among both males and females the death rate seemed to be less in Michigan than in England. The total annual death rate in all England is about twenty-two per thousand inhabitants. The total annual death rate in Michigan was, according to my life table, about seventeen and four-tenths per thousand inhabitants. The inhabitants of Michigan now number nearly 1,700,000. In that number of people the difference between a death rate of twenty-two and one of seventeen and four-tenths per thousand amounts to over 7,500 lives; and according to the Michigan life table, this number of persons are saved in each year over what would die if the death rate in Michigan equaled that in all England.

The foregoing was written in 1881, and the statement which I then made, that "one of the greatest recommendations for Michigan as a State to *live* in is the intelligent regard of its citizens for human life and health," is amply borne out by the following evidence of the great number of lives saved and cases of sickness prevented by public health work, which could only have been accomplished by the intelligent coöperation of the people with health officials.

PUBLIC HEALTH WORK—RESULTS.

The public health work in Michigan is well advanced and has strikingly reduced the amount of sickness and deaths in the State.

Legislative enactments provide for the establishment of local boards of health in all townships, cities and villages in Michigan. Each of these local boards is required by law to appoint a health officer, who shall be an executive officer of that board. Part of the duty of the health officer of each local board is to report, to the Secretary of the State Board of Health, every outbreak of a communicable disease which occurs in his jurisdiction; and to keep the secretary of the State board constantly informed respecting every outbreak of such disease. On receipt of outbreak reports from health officers (or from other sources), the secretary of the State board immediately sends the health officer in whose jurisdiction the disease is reported to exist, instructions in regard to preventing the spread of the disease, and recommends measures to be adopted to prevent its recurrence. Isolation of those sick with dangerous diseases, and disinfection of all clothing and other articles liable to have become infected with the germs of those diseases, are two of the most strongly emphasized recommendations of the State board to local health officers. At the end of an outbreak of a communicable disease, the health officer in whose jurisdiction it occurred is required to make a final report to the office of the State board, stating the number of cases and deaths which took place during the outbreak, the source of the contagium which caused it, whether or not the preventive measures of isolation and disinfection were resorted to, etc. The information thus obtained is compiled in the office of the Secretary of the State Board of Health, and from this the first diagram in this article in constructed. The following diagrams graphically illustrate the great reduction in the number of cases and deaths from several diseases in Michigan.

The first diagram, relative to "isolation and disinfection," shows a very great reduction of cases and deaths from scarlet fever and diphtheria in Michigan during the five years, 1886–90, accomplished by isolation of the sick, and disinfection of infected rooms, clothing, bedding, furniture, etc., there having been on the average about six times as many cases and six times as many deaths in each of the

683 outbreaks in which isolation and disinfection were neglected as in each of the 613 outbreaks in which isolation and disinfection were enforced. As stated in the foot note of the first diagram, during the five years, the total number of outbreaks of scarlet fever was 1,857, total number of cases 11,312, and total number of deaths 591. If no efforts at isolation and disinfection had been made and the averages had remained the same as in the 366 outbreaks in which isolation and disinfection were neglected, the number of cases would have been 24,680 and the deaths 1,281. Taking from these respectively the number of cases and deaths which occurred and there remains the indicated saving from scarlet fever of 690 lives and 13,368 cases in the five years. By the same method there is indicated for the five years a saving from diphtheria of 2,722 lives and 15,302 cases, making a saving during the five years from the two diseases, scarlet fever and diphtheria, of 3,410 lives and 28,670 cases of sickness.

The next diagram, "Lives Saved by Public Health Work," compiled from the State department's vital statistics of Michigan shows a great reduction in the death rate, indicating a saving of over ten thousand (10,851) lives from the three diseases, scarlet fever, small-pox and typhoid fever, by public health work since the State Board of Health was established, in the year 1873. Diagram number sixteen shows a reduction of over half in the sickness from scarlet fever during the five years, (1887-91, compared with the five years, 1877-81, these two periods being ten years apart.

LIVES SAVED BY PUBLIC-HEALTH WORK. COMPARISON OF DEATH-RATES IN MICHIGAN FROM SCARLET FEVER AND SMALL-POX BEFORE AND SINCE THE STATE BOARD OF HEALTH WAS ESTABLISHED AND FROM TYPHOID FEVER BEFORE AND SINCE ITS RESTRICTION WAS UNDERTAKEN BY THE STATE BOARD. COMPILED FROM STATE DEPARTMENT'S "VITAL STATISTICS" OF MICHIGAN.

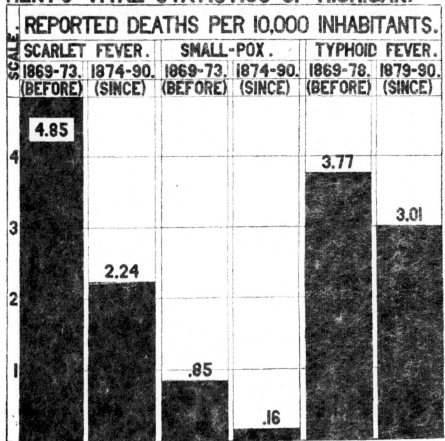

	REPORTED DEATHS PER 10,000 INHABITANTS.					
	SCARLET FEVER.		SMALL-POX.		TYPHOID FEVER.	
SCALE	1869-73. (BEFORE)	1874-90. (SINCE)	1869-73. (BEFORE)	1874-90. (SINCE)	1869-78. (BEFORE)	1879-90. (SINCE)
	4.85	2.24	.85	.16	3.77	3.01

LIVES SAVED FROM: SCARLET FEVER (17 YEARS) 7,265; SMALL-POX (17 YEARS) 1,921; TYPHOID FEVER (12 YEARS) 1,571.

MICHIGAN STATE BOARD OF HEALTH EXHIBIT.

ISOLATION AND DISINFECTION RESTRICTED SCARLET FEVER AND DIPHTHERIA IN MICHIGAN DURING THE 5 YEARS 1886-90.

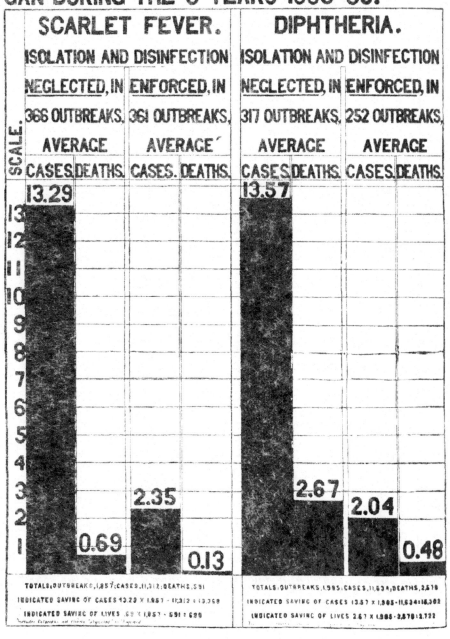

SCARLET FEVER.

ISOLATION AND DISINFECTION

NEGLECTED, IN 366 OUTBREAKS. ENFORCED, IN 361 OUTBREAKS.

AVERAGE CASES. DEATHS. AVERAGE CASES. DEATHS.

13.29   0.69   2.35   0.13

DIPHTHERIA.

ISOLATION AND DISINFECTION

NEGLECTED, IN 317 OUTBREAKS. ENFORCED, IN 252 OUTBREAKS.

AVERAGE CASES. DEATHS. AVERAGE CASES. DEATHS.

13.57   2.67   2.04   0.48

TOTALS, OUTBREAKS, 1,857; CASES, 11,912; DEATHS, 591

INDICATED SAVING OF CASES 13.29 X 1,857 = 11,912 = 13,358

INDICATED SAVING OF LIVES .69 X 1,857 = 591 = 690

TOTALS, OUTBREAKS, 1,905, CASES, 11,634, DEATHS, 2,878

INDICATED SAVING OF CASES 13.57 X 1,905 = 11,634 = 14,202

INDICATED SAVING OF LIVES 2.67 X 1,905 = 2,878 = 2,722

MICHIGAN STATE BOARD OF HEALTH EXHIBIT.

NO. 16.—DECREASE OF SICKNESS FROM SCARLET FEVER, IN MICHIGAN

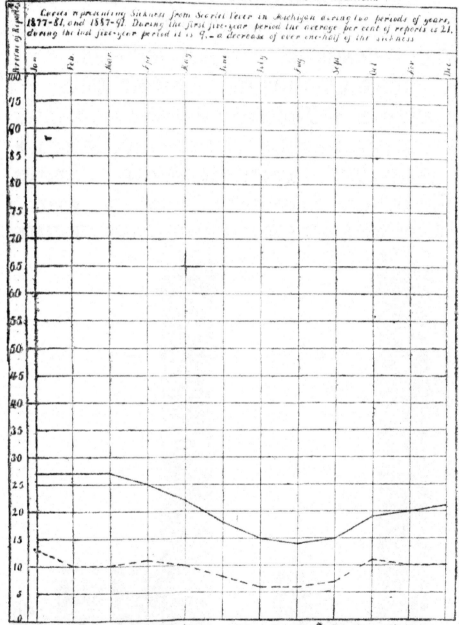

Curves representing Sickness from Scarlet Fever in Michigan during two periods of years, 1877-81, and 1887-91. During the first five-year period the average per cent of reports is 21, during the last five-year period it is 9,—a decrease of over one-half of the sickness

Sickness from Scarlet Fever, 5 years. 1877-81 _____ Sickness from Scarlet Fever, 5 years, 1887-91 _ _ _ _

Indicating what per cent of all reports received stated the presence of scarlet fever then under the observation of the physicians reporting

Over 17,000 weekly reports of sickness were received for the first period, and over 24,000 for the last period.

SAULT STE. MARIE.

BY C. H. CHAPMAN.

Sault Ste. Marie has been, is now and will continue to be a favored locality; a place wherein large public expenditures will be made, so long as navigation and railway traffic continues. The State of Michigan began large public expenditures here as early as 1837. Stevens T. Mason, the first Governor of Michigan, after its admission into the union as a state, urged in his message to the legislature the importance of building a ship canal around the Ste. Marys rapids. March 21, 1837, an act was approved by the Governor appropriating $25,000 for a survey, providing for maps, profile, etc., to be made, together with an estimated cost of the construction. The survey was completed that year, but the State and general government authority came into conflict over the right to pass through certain lands, and the actual construction, of what has since grown to be the greatest ship canal in the world, was not begun until sixteen years after Governor Mason first called public attention to this needed improvement of the great water-ways. Congress appropriated 750,000 acres of land to aid the State in building the canal and locks. Work was begun June 4, 1853, and finished on the 21st of May, 1855. The canal was three-fourths of a mile in length, one hundred feet wide and contained two consecutive locks, each 350 feet long, 70 feet wide and 13 feet depth of water. The actual cost of the canal was $999,802.46. From the date of its opening the lake traffic increased annually at such a rate that in 1870 the United States government began its improvements of the canal. A new lock, 515 feet long and 80 feet wide, with 17 feet of water on the miter sills and with a lift of 18½ feet, was built at a cost of $2,150,000. This lock was completed and opened to navigation September 1, 1881. June 9, 1881. the canal was transferred to the general government from the State. This work had barely been completed when the demands of commerce, so enormously increased, compelled further improvements, and on May 4, 1887, work was begun on another new lock, now nearly completed, on the site of the old State locks. The lock now in operation at the Soo is the largest in the world, and the new one, when completed, will be nearly double its capacity. The lock now being constructed will have a length of 800 feet between gates, a width of 100 feet throughout, a depth of 21 feet of water on the miter sills, with a lift of 18½ feet. The estimated cost of this canal improvement is $4,738,865. It is expected that it will be completed and ready for operation in 1891. The following comparative statement of the traffic through the canal for the years 1855 and 1892, will give an idea of the increase and development of lake navigation during the past thirty-seven years:

1855. Registered tonnage, 106,296—coal, tons, 1,414; flour, barrels, 10,287; iron ore, tons, 1,447.

1892. Registered tonnage, 10,647,203—coal, tons, 2,904,266; flour, barrels, 5,418,135; iron ore, tons, 4,901,132.

Another great improvement the government has undertaken at this point is the opening of Hay Lake channel, shortening the distance through the Ste. Marie river eleven miles and making it possible to navigate this river at night, a condition impracticable with the present channel. This work is now partially completed. The estimated cost of this improvement is $2,659,115.

The United States government is prosecuting another great improvement in the city of Sault Ste. Marie, now nearly completed, that of rebuilding and enlarging Fort Brady, at a cost of $250,000.

The International railroad bridge here, a mile in length and costing $1,000,000, was completed in 1888. It is the connecting link of three trunk lines of railroad centering here. The city is located at the junction of the three great lakes, Superior, Michigan and Huron, on the great water highway between the east, the west and the northwest, at the only point between Duluth and Buffalo where it can be easily bridged for railways. Three roads are built and other great trunk lines are centering here, which makes it a natural distributing point and gives it every advantage of rail and water transportation, insuring cheap freight rates, both for raw material and manufactured product.

The city when the United States census was taken in 1890 had a population of 5,760, which is steadily increasing. It is lighted by electricity, has a fine system of water works and sewers, and has four miles of electric street railway in operation. One-eighth of the commerce of the United States passes through the Soo canal and locks.

26

GEOGRAPHICAL AND GEOLOGICAL FEATURES

BY F. S. DEWEY, ALPENA, MICH.

[The following article was received almost too late for insertion, but it is considered too valuable to omit. The work was retarded by articles being withheld, while on the other hand the early issuance of the work was urged. This will, to some extent, explain any want of order in arrangement of subjects:]

On rowing a boat close to the beach along the shore of Thunder bay, one will notice that the water close to the shore is much deeper than it is a few rods further out. Still beyond is another deep depression and then again another shallow. On close observation it will be found that the shallow places are long ridges or banks of sand under the water running parallel with the shore. The constant action of the waves along the beach digs the sand away and the undercurrent carries it back and places it in these long parallel ridges. In going back from the water on the land one finds great numbers of long sand ridges, just the same as those in the bottom of the bay and which look like great earthworks thrown up by some ancient army in its gradual and stubborn retreat. These curious lines of embankment having their incipient growth beneath the waters of the lake are found all along the shore of the bay and lake, lying parallel and generally only a few rods apart and extending back from a mile to ten miles, and in some cases as far back as twenty or twenty-five miles from the shore. These formations are very marked in and about Alpena, and especially between Alpena and Ossineke. Two or three miles west of Alpena we find them crossing the road at intervals of a quarter to a half of a mile. Beyond or west of each of these ridges is a level plane or terrace just a few feet higher than its succeeding one to the east. Finally, nine miles west of Alpena, the State road comes to a hill, beyond which there are no more of these old lines of ancient earthworks. Along the foot of this hill or high bluff are great numbers of rounded stones or boulders all plainly worn and smoothed by the water long ages ago. Here it is very plain to see was once the shore of Lake Huron. These rounded boulders were sorted from the sand and pushed up in line along the shore by the ice and waves many thousand years ago. Farther to the northwest, along the shore of Presque Isle county, the work of the terrace epoch is beautifully illustrated, and particularly as one approaches Crawford's quarry from the south one may see these huge terraces developed in a most pronounced manner. While yet a mile or more away one suddenly comes in full view of Lake Huron, the blue waters of the lake appearing to rise like a distant bank or plain to blend and mingle with the blue sky above. While standing there on the ancient shore where the waters of Lake Huron beat and broke for ages, one sees before him a giant stairway with broad steps or terraces leading down to the lake. Just west of Crawford quarry the level road leads along one of these broad terraces. A hundred and eighty feet above and in plain view at the left is the ancient shore from which a great stairway leads abruptly two hundred feet down to the present water level. The boy with his hand sled in winter may leap with the speed of an arrow over the history of a hundred decades of centuries in much less than a hundred seconds. This old lake shore may be plainly traced not only along the shores of Lake Huron and Saginaw bay, but along Lakes Erie and St. Clair as well. Near Denmark junction, southeast of Saginaw, the

The Soo Canal—Vessel Entering Lower Gate of Lock.

old lake shore is plainly marked, so also just east of Yale, at Ridgway, Utica and at Lenawee Junction, near Adrian. Between these several points and the present shore may be plainly seen these ancient terraces or shore lines.

It need hardly be mentioned that when the lakes stood at this higher level they were all one excepting, of course, Lake Ontario. There was no Niagara river then and only Lake Ontario went down the St. Lawrence to the sea. All the rest had an outlet of their own down through Illinois and the Mississippi. Indeed much of the great prairies of Illinois were then the bottom of Lake Michigan. Once ages upon ages before there had been another Niagara gorge, much of its course lying to the west of the Niagara of today. For untold centuries the old river had flowed and worn a deep channel down through the rocks and another old Niagara falls had shaken the earth with its thunder.

For some reason perhaps not yet fully understood there came about a remarkable change in climatic conditions, but whatever the cause may have been the result was that the northern part of North America and of the old world as well became covered to a very great depth with ice and snow. Great glaciers were thus formed of very wide extent, at some period of their existence, in all probability, being as wide as the continent itself. This vast sheet of ice and snow swept slowly and with irresistible force in a direction generally southward, bearing before it and within its mass and along its under surface immense accumulations of debris, rocks, gravel, sand and mud, which, between the upper and the nether millstone of nature, were ground up and comminuted and prepared for tillable land. The same thing is going on in Greenland today, where the vast fields of ice sweep slowly over the surface of the land, push their margins gradually out into the ocean and finally as huge icebergs break off and float away. In the mountainous regions of Switzerland as well as in Alaska these glaciers are continuing their work.

How long this reign of ice continued is a matter of conjecture, but it is pretty certain that its history covered a vastly greater period than does the history of man. During all these thousands of years it carried on its work of breaking off huge fragments of rocks far to the north, grinding them up into rounded boulders, gravel, sand and clay and preparing them for the advent of civilized man. This immense sheet of ice extended certainly as far south as the Ohio river and perhaps at times very much farther. Then slowly year after year its southern margin began melting away. Sometimes its great nose full of sand and mud melted off just as fast as it pushed southward, thus forming a great bank of earth before it. These banks are the hills and knolls of our beautiful peninsula. As the springtime gradually dawned nothing was left of this ice field about Michigan except great tongues of ice several hundred miles in length pushing out of the cold north, one from the northeast along the bed of Lake Erie; one from the northwest, bending to the south down Lake Huron; a third coming straight down through the valley of Lake Michigan; while a fourth swept westward along the region occupied by Lake Superior. It is perhaps needless to add that these great inland seas were for the time being entirely swept out of existence, their beds being more than filled by these vast sweeping fields of ice. The glacier that plowed down through the bed of Lake Huron crowded up a somewhat irregular furrow on its western margin, a sort of lateral moraine which extends from about the middle of Alpena county southward more than fifty miles. It presents an almost unbroken line of hills from two hundred to three hundred feet above the level of Lake Huron, in some places presenting sides as steep as it is possible for the soil to lie.

Centuries after this a second furrow or moraine was formed, beginning between Devil lake and Hubbard river in Alpena county and extending generally parallel with the first, but in much more broken hills of varying heights. The lofty table land back of Ossineke rising to a height of two hundred and fifty feet, is a portion of this last moraine.

Of course the edges of this glacier were somewhat irregular and this was especially the case with its anterior margin, in consequence of which the earth which it transported was deposited in irregular heaps and banks and lines. It trickled and tumbled down out of the lofty, melting, jagged sides and prow of this ice plateau and was often nicely assorted by the creeks and rivulets thus formed from the melting ice into plainly distinguishable layers of sand and gravel and clay. These layers are found lying at every angle of elevation and in every corrugated form, wherever excavations are made through our hills for railroad or other purposes. Even ripple marks and little gravel beds show plainly where flowed out of the melting mass some turbid, rushing stream. In this manner were formed all the hills in Michigan south of Mackinaw, as well as the round tops and high ridges of Ohio and Indiana. Many of these hills attain almost to the dignity of mountains, but differ from them in one very important particular, which is that they are composed entirely of earth transported from the north by glacial action. None of them are built up of solid rocks elevated by some subterranean forces, as are all true mountains. While rocks, to be sure, underlie all of the southern peninsula of Michigan in superimposed, almost horizontal layers, still they are hidden from view except in comparatively few localities by the earth—or drift, as it is called—transported here by the glaciers. This drift is of wonderfully varying thickness. In the eastern part of Alpena county there are hundreds of acres with not enough drift covering the ledge rocks to make a garden, while west of the old shore line of the lake the thickness of the drift reaches from one hundred to three hundred feet, while in some portions of the State it reaches a depth of at least six hundred feet. It may not be generally understood how much of the beautiful and lovely scenery of Michigan is due to the action of these ancient glaciers. Their deeply serrated southern margins melting slowly or rapidly as the sun traveled high or low in the heavens, or, as the glacier moved more rapidly or slowly, left irregular and huge piles of drifts as are plainly observable about Ann Arbor and Hillsdale. Prospect Hill in Lenawee county reaches a height of six hundred feet above the general level, while Bundy's hills, farther to the west, are almost as high. These are fine examples of irregular terminal moraines. Nearly all of the thousand beautiful little lakes which add so much charm to the landscape simply occupy the hollows consequent on the irregular melting of the glaciers.

As would be natural to suppose, the underlying rock upon which these glaciers plowed and scraped their way southward show unmistakable evidence of the tremendous power of this moving sheet of ice. Wherever by excavation the rocks are exposed to view, they are found scraped, planed and polished almost as smooth as a marble table. The *striæ* or lines and furrows made by the scraping of the pebbles and boulders in the bottom of the glacier over the softer underlying rocks clearly point out the direction which the glaciers traveled. At Alpena they show the direction of the glacier to be southeast by east. In many places throughout Alpena county these glacial markings are beautifully exhibited. The Lockwood school in Alpena has more than twenty blocks of stone in its foundation cut by the chisel of this ancient artisan. Some of the boulders transported from Canada down into Michigan are of remarkable size, the measurement of several in the eastern part of Alpena county indicating a weight of more than a hundred thousand pounds. One of them, perhaps the largest, is a jasper conglomerate or pudding stone, closely similar to the class rock placed on the university campus by the class of 1862. It is, however, many times larger. Perhaps no finer specimen can be found in the State illustrating both the transported boulder and the action of the glacier, than the great black mass lying close by the Michigan Central railway station at Battle Creek. This was evidently transported from near Lake Superior and borne in the bottom of the glacier, as is evidenced from its polished surface, its glacial markings and flattened form.

As one contemplates the work performed by the ancient glaciers in and about Michigan, it seems almost impossible to fail to recognize a purpose in it all. The material ground up and transported by them and spread out over the hitherto almost barren rocks constitute a factor of the very highest importance. The scanty soil thinly sprinkled over the almost barren rocks would have given a very meager response to the labors of the husbandman. To them he is indebted for all the material out of which he has made the beautiful farms of Michigan, while the hard heads or boulders so extremely abundant everywhere throughout the State undoubtedly have a purpose besides that of a building material, but somehow heretofore a very shortsighted policy seems to have blinded the people's eyes to its value. To be sure they have for many years been extensively employed to make the most abominable street pavement that ever tortured the living or jostled the dead, but their value for roads and highways, when crushed into fragments, seems to have been very tardily appreciated.

As has just been stated, underlying the whole of Michigan south of Mackinaw are layers upon layers of different kinds of rock which was once sediment or mud deposited in the bottom of the ocean. These sedimentary rocks are of varying thickness and in the central portion of the State reach a depth of many thousand feet. Underneath them all lies the granite, the universal foundation of all sedimentary rock. These strata of sedimentary rock lie one upon the other like a pile of very flat plate with the center in Gratiot county. The top one or the last and smallest of all was formed at the very beginning of the coal period and is perhaps a hundred and fifty miles across. Its southern margin is close by the city of Jackson, while its northern extremity is a few miles north of the western end of Saginaw bay. All the coal of Michigan is found in that stratum. Any attempt to search for coal outside the limits here indicated would therefore be a waste of time and capital. Fragments and perhaps sometimes considerable masses of coal might be found in the extreme southern portion of the State, but its existence there is easily accounted for by the action of the glaciers. Small masses of copper and iron are also frequently found scattered over the surface of the southern peninsula, but it would be utterly useless to search for them anywhere south of Mackinaw. Each successive underlying plate or stratum of rock is larger and its edges crop out all around the edges of the smaller plate, except some of the lower ones, which dip down under the states of Indiana and Ohio. Long before the glacier epoch when Michigan was a gulf of the sea almost surrounded by land and as the sea retreated it left salt or brine in these plates or basins. In Saginaw brine is obtained from one of these basins and at Tawas from another and a lower one, while at Alpena at a depth of about 1,250 feet we strike a very thick bed of pure, solid rock salt. This is in a still lower basin and can be obtained only by letting in water from above and pumping it out as brine. The most of these sedimentary rocks are limestone, while some are shale, like that at Sulphur island in Thunder bay. There are strata of sandstone as at Ionia, where is found a beautiful mottled stratum colored with iron. This is a most elegant stone for building purposes and is the more valuable because of the ease with which it is cut. Another stratum crops out at Napoleon and Stony Point and would also if properly worked be found very valuable for building purposes. There is also a peculiar sandstone cropping out near Marshall which is very full of fresh water mussels, showing its origin to have been *la custrine*. Much of the limestone rock is literally full of the remains of animal life and there is one stratum at least of considerable thickness cropping out near Alpena that is composed almost entirely of marine shells. The oil of these animals is much of it still stored up in the rocks, and if there was only an impervious covering to keep the oil from escaping then we might in many localities obtain petroleum in large quantities and of the best quality. It oozes out of the ground in many places in Alpena county and at Alpena, while boring through the lower Devonian rocks, a very fine quality of oil was struck at a depth of 1,200 feet. In this region the rocks are all broken into fragments by the ancient earthquakes, so that water flows freely through them and forces the oil and gas out apparently as fast as it is distilled. In many places the surface water drops into holes and crevasses in the rocks, thus forming underground currents or streams. This is emphatically true of the western part of Presque Isle county and the northern half of Alpena. If, therefore, wells are bored anywhere along the shore southeast of these localities the drill would almost surely strike some of these crevices in the rocks and the water would come up to the surface. If the casing pipe is extended upward the water will still rise in it from thirty to seventy feet. In the city of Alpena are eight of these flowing wells, yielding not less than five million gallons daily. Five of them are only five or six hundred feet in depth, while two others about 1,300 feet deep yielded a very excellent mineral water which is very strongly impregnated with sulphur gas. This gas in the water has power to dissolve the limestone rock and constantly increase the size of the underground passages. In the region above named are a large number of remarkable illustrations of the corroding effect of this gas. Immense caverns have been formed down deep in the rocks, thus leaving an unsupported dome, which in hundreds of cases has dropped down into the subterranean cavern.

The gradual dissolving and wearing away of the fallen débris has left wells or pits of horrid depth and prodigious size, the existence of which very few people have any knowledge. In the northern part of Alpena county in the township of Long Rapids are some remarkable specimens of these giant wells. In one forty acre lot are five of these deep pits which are substantial types of all the rest.

They are in the midst of a grand old forest scarcely touched as yet by the hand of man, and so dense is it that one finds himself without any warning right on the very brink of the yawning abyss. The first at which one arrives is the type of all the rest throughout this region. It is partly full of water, how deep has not been determined, but it is a hundred and sixty feet from its ferned and flowered rim to the liquid mirror below, and across the top from rim to rim is about two hundred and fifty feet. The walls are perpendicular solid rock and grey dolomite Hamilton limestone with patches of moss, and here and there a lichen or a trailing vine clinging to the seams and crevices of the dark old walls. Twenty-five years ago a large tall white pine stood leaning so far out over the rim that it could not have been saved. When it was cut it swept over, down, and shot like a javelin head first into the water below and entirely disappeared from sight. It soon rose to the surface stripped of its branches, where it still remains floating in undisturbed tranquility. While many of these wells are partly filled with water at all seasons of the year, there are many others which are always dry and still others which are filled during times of freshet. Many of them receive brooks and creeks which plunge down in beautiful cascades and disappear among the jagged rocks at the bottom.

In the southern part of Presque Isle county is one of these pits which is worthy of more than a passing notice. While approaching by the main traveled road which leads close past the western margin, one is attracted by the sound of rushing waters long before arriving in sight of the pit. Leading down to it from the east is a long, narrow, rocky ravine more than a mile in length and perhaps an eighth of a mile wide, gradually deepening till at the western extremity it reaches a depth of at least 150 feet. This extremity is one of those giant wells like the ones before described. The general contour of this ravine is closely similar to the prostrate form of a man, the feet slanting upward to the east. Besides the well which represents the head, there is another at the shoulders, the two being joined together by a narrow channel which represents the neck. The north branch of Thunder bay river, sweeping around from the northwest, is one of the most beautiful streams in Michigan and millions of feet of forest timber are floated down its channel every year. It is a river about the size of the Huron at Ann Arbor and furnishes all the year round reliable water power for a good size saw-mill and also a grist-mill side by side, after passing which all its waters are poured into this ravine. The entrance is at the upper or easterly end, and the river comes rushing and foaming down along the rugged, rocky channel to the shoulders and through the neck into the head. Here in a great eddying whirlpool 250 feet across it sweeps round and round and is all swallowed up in this bottomless pit. During the freshets of the spring and autumn this ravine generally fills up with water, making a lake more than a mile in length and 150 feet in depth. The river then flows on over its hitherto dry bed beyond, not only undiminished in volume but, on the contrary, largely augmented by great volumes of water boiling up from the same subterranean caverns that had formerly swallowed it down. All logs, drift-wood and debris which have accumulated at the head are now swept by the force of the current out at the feet. This wonderful curiosity is popularly known as sunken lake.

The number of these giant wells in the region of Alpena county reaches close to three hundred. Most of them are very large and deep, with perpendicular lime-stone walls, and, of course, cannot be explored without the aid of a pulley and line. Some are churn shaped, increasing in size downward, and it is more than probable that careful exploration would reveal very interesting subterranean passage-ways. Indeed, the finding of large caves in rocks so full of fissures capable of swallowing up a large river, together with hundreds of creeks and smaller streams, could scarcely be a matter of surprise. Many of them bear the most undoubted evidence of having been very recently formed and one, on the line of the Au Sable and Northwestern railroad, was certainly formed in a single night. It is related by the foreman of the construction that a section of the road, all finished and ready for trains, dropped out of sight and there was left what appeared to be a bottomless pit filled with water which no amount of filling seemed to affect. It became necessary to change the line and pass around. Most of these pits seem to belong to a series which lie in a general line extending from Misery bay, five miles east of Alpena, to town 34-1, perhaps sixty miles northwest. They undoubtedly approximately indicate the course of the subterranean river. The fact that many of them are partly filled with water during times of freshet, together with great numbers of fish of considerable size, would certainly indicate some such subterranean connection. In one of these wells far to the northwest we learn, from the very highest authority, that a large number of fish, no less than twenty barrels, were left struggling in the bottom of the well unable to find their way out as the water sank away and left them. Near the head of Long lake is one from which considerable quantities of fish have been taken and trapped in small pools where the receding water had left them. As there are no surface streams whatever to either of these pits just named, they furnish the most positive proof of the existence of an underground river. Not only have we the proof of its existence, but its very course may be traced with a considerable degree of accuracy. Starting at the prime meridian in the middle of the west boundary of Presque Isle county, it takes a southeasterly course down into the township of Long Rapids in Alpena county, thence northeast across Maple ridge to Long lake, thence bending to the southeast and continuing along near the shore of this lake it flows in nearly a straight line to the southeast till it terminates in Misery bay. Just southeast of Long lake there is an extensive deep synclinal depression in the rocks, undoubtedly due to the river wearing away the supporting rocks below. This depression, known as the Narrows, is usually a lake a mile in length and sixty feet or more in depth and emptying by a large stream into Lake Huron. The outlet of Long lake passes through it, but in very dry weather all the water in this basin leaks out through the crevices in the clean, bare rock strata at the bottom, leaving only a small pool in one of these deep wells.

Misery bay, where this subterranean river empties, is really a small, shallow, inland lake of about two hundred acres in area, connected with Lake Huron by a narrow entrance, sometimes too shallow for even a fish boat to enter. Its western extremity is bounded by high bluffs, at the margin of which the ledges of rocks have pitched downward toward the water, leaving a rugged rim and a deep rift in the rocks one-half mile long and ten to twenty feet deep. The archæologist who will squeeze his way along this narrow rift will find between the strata a rich harvest of very perfect devonian fossils. In fact the whole State of Michigan does not afford another field that can compare with the Thunder bay region in the extent, variety and perfection of its fossil remains. In the bottom of this little bay are three of these giant wells, one of them larger and deeper than any heretofore noted. This is the one which constitutes the mouth of the underground river. In summer the water boiling up from this immense pit is cold as spring water, while in the coldest winters ice never forms on the surface, but a broad open river leads out through the narrow channel into the open lake. Even when the thermometer is far below zero and the ice outside along the shore is from two to three feet thick, flocks of wild ducks find this secluded spot an inviting place to spend the entire winter. A strange peculiarity of this subterranean river is its intermittent flow. Every twenty minutes an immense volume of water pours out from down below filling the little bay to a height of eight inches above the ordinary level, thus causing the water to rush out through the narrow opening into Lake Huron, and then for twenty minutes it rests again and the tide goes down, and thus the rising and the falling of the tide goes on as if from the mighty pulsations of some great heart down in the bosom of the earth.

Aside from the curious phenomena connected with the subterranean river here lies hidden, only five miles from the busy city of Alpena, the most secluded, the most charming spot on the whole west shore of Lake Huron. Several large springs boil up from the bottom of the bay, it is full of fish and in season fairly swarming with wild water fowl, many of which fondly tarry through the entire long winter. Out beyond this little inland lake is Little Thunder bay, of a thousand acres or more, fairly separated and protected from the open lake by the long, slender arm of Misery point, together with Round island and Crooked island, both these islands being very safe and delightfully charming camping grounds for the seeker after health, rest and recreation.

The question is very frequently asked what valuable minerals may we hope to find in the rocks of the southern peninsula. No doubt the reader has already learned enough of their character to enable him to answer this question for himself. The character of the rocks plainly indicates that at several different times in the early history of the globe the ocean covered the entire peninsula, and we further learn that most of these rocks are simply sedimentary deposits laid down as mud or sand in the bottom of this ancient sea. It would be quite unreasonable to presume that any considerable quantity of gold or silver, copper or iron, should ever have been floating around in the warm water of the old steamy ocean. These metals are never deposited in the mud or slimy ooze of the ocean's bed, and to search for them there would be the height of folly. It is true indeed that nuggets of copper and masses of iron have been often found in all parts of the southern peninsula and even in Ohio and Indiana, but having been brought down from the Lake Superior country by the force of the ancient glaciers, they possess no special significance. They have found their way there in the same manner as have the boulders and hard heads heretofore described.

While this peninsula has none of the metals referred to, it possesses a most extraordinary wealth in its mines of coal, its inexhaustible salt wells, its extensive and numerous stone quarries and alabaster beds, the remarkable variety and immense extent of its forest products, the charming beauty of its numberless crystal lakes and rivers, all peopled with swarms of fish, and wild fowl in almost endless variety; and, added to these, a depth and fertility and variety of soil which never for a single season fails to respond by abundant harvests to the labors of the husbandman. It seems no wonder that nature, casting about it her great protecting arms of Lakes Huron and Michigan, should hold it like a precious jewel in her fond embrace, cooling and moistening the heated air of summer and adding warmth and humidity to the cold blasts of winter. The intelligent foreigner contemplating removal from his fatherland casts his eye across the length and breadth of the checkered map of our country and finally, instinctively placing his finger on the picture of that beautiful spot of earth which is laved and kissed on all sides by those great inland seas, exclaims to himself: "There will I make my home." In like manner from many a thankless hillside and narrow vale in New England the weary husbandman has turned his footsteps toward the setting sun and found himself a happy home between those great warm arms. It is perhaps to this class of people, quite as much as to any other, that we are indebted for the intelligence, the energy, the versatility and prosperity of our people. It is fortunate indeed that where nature has placed her richest storehouses she has directed the steps of a people worthy of her treasures. In variety and extent of production her forests surpass any other state. In salt she takes the lead. In copper and iron she stands at the head and one almost wonders if the finger of the prophet was not pointed toward the occident when he spoke of that "land whose stones are iron and out of whose hills thou mayest dig brass."

Its extensive gardens of berries and vegetables, of celery and peppermint, its wide stretches of beautiful farms every year yielding a bountiful harvest, all challenge the admiration of every traveler across our State, while its vast orchards of peaches stretched along the shores of Lake Michigan stand without a rival in the world. In the northeastern quarter, especially in Alpena county, are great plum orchards, some of them containing many thousands of trees, whose fruit is absolutely without blemish and in every respect of the very highest possible degree of perfection. Even at Mackinac island, that gem of the northern lakes, this fruit grows in abundance, and no exhibit in wax ever showed fewer imperfections. It would seem that nothing could prevent this northeast quarter of the State from becoming in the near future one vast orchard of plums and apples and pears. Perhaps when the feast has been spread for years the enemy may find it out, but as yet he has not come and the experimental stage has long been passed. Besides sufficient for home consumption, large quantities are shipped for other markets every year, while the demand, like that for the potatoes of this northern region, refuses to be satisfied. Let the speculative genius figure out if he can how a hundred acres of land can be made to yield more round dollars with less hard labor than when planted to plums in a region where the tree and its fruit attain perfection and the curculio has not come. Let him who contemplates putting a little fortune into a pile of brick and mortar in the form of a great bleak mansion stop and consider what pleasure, what infinite delight may be his portion in his declining years if in close communion with a great orchard yearly loaded with sweet and tempting smiles of nature; and let him whose vague unrest might tempt him to forsake our shores stop long enough to contemplate the words on the seal of our commonwealth, "If thou seekest a beautiful peninsula, behold it here."

MICHIGAN BY COUNTIES.

To obtain reliable sketches of each county, the members of the legislature were requested to designate some suitable person resident of each county to write it up. To secure uniformity in the matter the sketch published in the issue of 1873 was mailed to the person so designated, together with a circular letter out lining the matter to be mentioned. In part of the counties this was well done; other persons did not respond and the compiler was forced to gather such facts as he could find.

There are few counties but have some local advantages not generally known which could be properly set forth but which are necessarily left out.

There are numerous locations in the State with superior advantages for certain kinds of manufacturing and said locations want the factories, while on the other hand there is capital seeking such places, neither knowing of the other; with a bare knowledge of facts both might be benefited. This was one of the objects of this work.

Neglecting to improve an opportunity of this kind is "hiding a light under a bushel," and those who would be benefited by the act are the losers by the neglect. Neglecting opportunities cripples enterprise. The press has been a great factor in the advancement of the State. Adverse criticism and erroneous statements made in the early history of the State or territory had much to do with stagnating State progress. Immediately after the war of 1812 an act passed congress giving each soldier a bounty of 160 acres of land, 2,000,000 acres to be located in Michigan. An examination was made into the quality of the land and in a report made by Edward Tiffin, Surveyor General, to Josiah Meigs, Commissioner General Land Office, November 30, 1815, he said the land was all either swamp or barren, sandy land on which nothing would grow. In finishing the report he said: "Taking the country altogether so far as has been explored and to all appearances, together with information received concurring, the balance is as bad; there would not be more than one acre out of a hundred, if there would be one out of a thousand, that would in any case admit of cultivation."

On February 6, 1816, the following message was issued by the president:

"To the Senate and House of Representatives of the United States:

"It is represented that the lands in Michigan territory, designated by law towards satisfying the land bounties promised to the soldiers of the late army, are so covered with swamps and lakes, or otherwise unfit for cultivation, that a very

27

inconsiderable proportion can be applied to the intended grants. I recommend therefore that other lands be designated by congress for the purpose of supplying the deficiency.

"JAMES MADISON."

How much the soldiers would have been wronged we will leave to the farmers in southern Michigan. Later statements have been made that the pine timber being nearly exhausted the land will be worthless. Now this statement is about as far off actual facts as Tiffin and President Madison. The pine timber has been slaughtered true enough, but there is more hardwood timber in Michigan than any other settled state. The upper part of the lower peninsula is full of it and the land that was stripped of timber is developing into excellent farming land.

Future history will likely record events or dates in Michigan as periods after the beginning of the nineteenth century, as the black swamp period, the lumber period, the iron and copper period, the manufacturing period, and finally the farming period.

ALCONA COUNTY.

Alcona county was organized in 1869. It is bounded on the north by Alpena, on the east by Lake Huron, on the south by Iosco and on the west by Oscoda. It has an area of about 720 square miles, and had a population in 1890 of 5,409. Harrisville, a town of 593 inhabitants, situated in the eastern part of the county, on Lake Huron, is the county seat. The surface of the county is comparatively level, with the exception of the townships along the lake shore, which are more or less rolling. Swamps are scattered here and there throughout the county, but most of them have their origin in springs and can be easily reclaimed. In the western portion of the county are found large tracts of sandy land, much of which is believed to have a soil suitable for agricultural purposes.

The county is well watered by the Pine, Au Sable and Hubbard rivers and their tributaries, ample water power for all milling purposes being found in a number of localities. The soil of the eastern townships is generally a heavy clay with a clay subsoil; while that of the "plains" is either a sandy loam or a clear sand. The timber consists of white and yellow pine, hemlock, beech, maple, cedar, oak and some black birch. The older portions of the county produce good crops of winter and spring wheat, oats, barley, etc., in fact few counties can show a larger yield to the acre, as wheat has been produced yielding an average of 45 bushels to the acre. Peas and all kinds of vegetables are also grown in great abundance. The experiments in fruit raising in this comparatively new county have been uniformly successful. Young orchards present a thrifty appearance, and the lighter fruits will, no doubt, amply repay those who attempt their cultivation. Berries are indigenous to the soil, and as a rule yield bountifully. The cost of clearing the heavier timbered lands will average about $18 per acre. There are good wood markets at various points, $2.50 being the uniform price for cordwood.

In 1891 there were subject to entry and sale 27,147 acres. A State road runs west from Harrisville 36 miles. Lands are accessible by good roads throughout the entire county. The climate is equable, the winters beginning about December 1, and continuing steadily up to March 15. The snowfall averages about eight inches in depth, the ground freezing but little. Plowing is usually begun by April 1 and seeding by May 1. The schools of the county are comparatively few, but are well sustained. The health of the inhabitants has been generally good, the invigorating influence of the lake breeze being felt to a remarkable extent, particularly during the summer months. Every branch of the lumber trade is carried on with success. Labor is in good demand, wages ranging from $28 to $33 per month with board. Improved land can be had at prices ranging from $10 to $25 per acre. Unimproved lands are proportionately less. A railroad from Standish, on the Mackinac division of the Michigan Central, to Alpena, extends along the eastern border of the county. Harrisville already enjoys an extensive lake commerce. Alcona county, with its cheap lands and productive soil, offers every inducement to the man with limited means, and a good class of immigrants would receive a hearty welcome from its inhabitants.

ALGER COUNTY

was organized in 1885 from Schoolcraft. It is bounded on the north by Lake Superior, east by Luce and Schoolcraft, south by Schoolcraft and Delta and west by Marquette. It has an area of 588,862 acres, being the 12th county in size, the 82d in population and 67th in wealth. Au Train, on Bay of same name, with population of 284 in 1890, is the county seat. The agricultural resources of the county are as yet but little developed, but the crops natural to the climate are good. The soil is rich and fruits of various kinds grow in abundance.

There are no navigable rivers; but the county is well watered and drained and has its share of inland lakes. It has about seventy-five miles of border on Lake Superior besides the border of Grand Island, behind which is the largest and best harbor on the lake and which is used as a harbor of refuge. The harbor at Grand Marias has been improved by the United States government, and is regarded as good.

The timber is principally beech, maple, birch, elm, pine, hemlock and cedar. Most of the pine lands have been lumbered but there remains about 200,000,000 feet yet standing. Unimproved lands are worth about $4 per acre and there is a large amount of this kind of land. There is about 28,400 acres of public land subject to sale or entry, besides railroad lands. Lumber, charcoal and brownstone are the principal industries of the county although the fishing interests at Grand Marias and Au Train are quite extensive. There are saw mills at Onoto and Rock River and shingle mills at Shingleton. Brownstone of excellent quality is quarried at Rock River and this promises to be the great industry, as the showing for fine stone is excellent in several localities. The Duluth, South Shore & Atlantic Railroad passes through the county, giving railroad communications and shipping facilities east and west.

Fish and game are plentiful, deer, fox, wolf and lynx. In inland lakes and streams trout, bass, pike, etc., abound.

There are good local markets for produce raised, good schools and church organizations.

ALLEGAN COUNTY.

BY J. F. HENRY, SAUGATUCK.

Allegan county was organized in 1835. It is bounded on the north by Ottawa and Kent, on the south by Van Buren and Kalamazoo, on the east by Barry, and on the west by Lake Michigan. It has an area of 828 square miles, divided into 24 townships and had a population in 1892 of 38,961. Allegan, an incorporated village of about 3,000 inhabitants situated on the Kalamazoo river near the geographical center of the county, is the county seat, and the largest town. Other thriving villages are Otsego, Plainwell, Wayland, Fennville, Martin, Moline, Hopkins, Hamilton, Graafschap, Douglas and Saugatuck. The latter two villages, situated near the mouth of the Kalamazoo river, are the only lake ports of the county, and a daily line of steamers to Chicago is maintained during the season of navigation. This part of the county is becoming quite a summer resort for Chicago and Grand Rapids people. Allegan, Otsego, Plainwell, Hamilton and other points enjoy the advantages of fine water power and considerable milling and manufacturing is done in the county.

The topography of the county may be described as level and rolling. There are several large swamps along the Black and Gun rivers, also smaller tracts of marsh land, most of which is reclaimable.

The county is well watered by the Kalamazoo, Black and Gun rivers and numerous little inland lakes. In the eastern part are many flowing wells.

Almost every variety of soil and some of the finest farms in the State may be found in this county.

The reclaimed swamp lands are well adapted to the raising of celery, onions and cabbages. In Clyde township the cultivation of pepperment has proved to be profitable. The southern part of the coast line of western Michigan is known as the "fruit belt," and that portion of it within Allegan county is not excelled in the production of peaches, grapes, apples, berries, etc. The great market which Chicago affords and opens up absorbs all the fruit which can be marketed, and the beautiful orchards and comfortable, not to say elegant, homes, which may be seen throughout the fruit belt, bear witness to the fact that fruit culture is both pleasant and profitable. In cereals, wheat is the principal crop, but large quantities of corn and oats are raised. There are now no lands in Allegan county subject to entry. Unimproved hardwood lands from which the timber has been taken off are worth from $15 to $30 an acre. Improved farms are held at from $25 to $100 per acre, according to location, soil, nature of improvements, etc.

The roads as a general thing are good, and in some parts of the county excellent. The climate is salubrious. In summer there are but few days which are oppressively hot, and the winters are not severe, the mercury seldom falling much below freezing point.

Churches and school houses are numerous throughout the county and in 1892 the certificate of Allegan high school admitted to the University of Michigan without further examination.

The Chicago & West Michigan, Lake Shore & Michigan Southern, Grand Rapids & Indiana, and Cincinnati, Jackson & Mackinaw railroads traverse the county and by lake and rail all productions of the county find a ready market in the cities of Chicago, Milwaukee, Grand Rapids and Muskegon.

ALPENA COUNTY.

Alpena county was organized in 1857. It is bounded on the north by Presque Isle, on the west by Montmorency, on the south by Alcona, and on the east by Lake Huron. Alpena, a flourishing city of 11,283 inhabitants, is the county seat. It has an area of 540 square miles, and had a population in 1890 of 15,581. The surface of the country is gently rolling, and is well watered by Thunder bay and Hubbard rivers, also by innumerable springs, brooks and lakes, which abound with all varieties of fish, and afford ample water power in many townships. There are but few sand plains in this county, but a considerable quantity of swamp land may be found, nearly all of which is subject to drainage. The soil in the western portion of the county is chiefly a dark loam with clay subsoil; in the eastern portion it is of a sandy nature, though quite fertile in many localities. The prevailing varieties of timber are beech, maple, elm, ash, hemlock, and large quantities of cedar. Winter wheat, oats, peas and barley are successfully grown. Corn, though not a staple product, often yields a large crop. Apples, pears and all varieties of plums are grown on every farm, and always find a ready market in Alpena. The cost of clearing averages about $20 per acre, and the wood cut brings from $2.50 to $3.50 per cord.

There are 22,320 acres of land subject to entry or sale. Plenty of desirable unimproved lands in the hands of private parties are to be had at prices ranging from $2 to $5 per acre. Some of the most valuable lands in the county have been pine lands originally. The best farming lands are located three or four miles back from the mouth of the rivers, and when improved are held at from $10 to $50 per acre. The Alpena and Torch Lake State road leads due west from Alpena, through the center of the county. There is also a good local State road system, which makes all parts of the county accessible.

Alpena has about six months of fair weather, three months of steady winter and three months of very broken weather in the spring and fall. Snow averages about one foot in depth and usually comes by December 1. Farmers begin plowing by April 1. The schools and churches are in a flourishing condition and the intelligence of Alpena county will compare very favorably with any locality in the State. The county is remarkably free from malaria and fevers, doubtless owing to the influence of the lake on its eastern border. Lumbering is carried on extensively, and labor is always in good demand. The fishing industry is by no means a small one, and a large number of men and boats are annually employed in catching and preparing fish for the Detroit and Cleveland markets. There is also a large traffic in cedar, used for posts, telegraph poles and railroad ties.

The road leading northward from Tawas City along the lake shore terminates at Alpena, but will eventually be built through Presque Isle to Cheboygan. It has been for some years an important lake port, vessels of every description being found in its harbor during the summer season, and there is no doubt but that the county will at once feel the impetus given it by this double outlet.

ANTRIM COUNTY.

Antrim county is situated on the east side of Grand Traverse bay and embraces sixteen townships lying in towns 29, 30, 31 and 32 north, in ranges 5, 6, 7, 8 and 9 west, and has an area of 581 square miles.

It is bounded on the north by Charlevoix county, on the east by Otsego, on the south by Kalkaska and Grand Traverse and on the west by Grand Traverse bay.

Antrim county was first settled by the whites in 1848, by Abram S. Wadsworth at the mouth of Elk river near the southwest corner of the county.

It was first organized as the township of Antrim, Grand Traverse county, in 1853. This name was changed to Megezee and then to Elk Rapids.

The county of Antrim was organized in the spring of 1863 and the first county election was held on the 6th day of April, 1863. The highest number of votes cast for any officer was 66. Bellaire, the county seat, is situated near the geographical center of the county and was first settled in 1879. It is pleasantly situated on the Intermediate river and has an excellent water power which is owned by Richardi & Bechtold, who have extensive woodenware works here.

Elk Rapids is situated at the mouth of Elk river, which is the outlet of the chain of lakes that traverse the county from northeast to southwest. It was originally the county seat, and is pleasantly located on the east arm of Traverse bay, and the most famous place in the United States for black bass fishing. Here are located the immense smelting works of the Elk Rapids iron company, and the Elk Rapids chemical works are the most extensive of any of the kind in the world. It has excellent school and church advantages and is one of the most delightful summer resorts in Northern Michigan.

Mancelona is situated in the southern part of the county on the Grand Rapids & Indiana railroad, and is a thriving manufacturing town, having extensive woodenware factories and the Antrim iron works.

There are now two railroads running through the county from north to south, to wit: The Grand Rapids & Indiana and the Chicago & West Michigan with a branch of the Chicago & West Michigan running to Elk Rapids.

The general surface of the county is rolling and in the northeastern portion it gets somewhat hilly. The soil is generally a sandy loam containing a large amount of lime with a clay soil in some localities. The timber contains a large variety, sugar maple, beech, elm, cedar and hemlock predominating.

The cereals yield very well, and for roots and vegetables the county is unsurpassed by any county in the State. In the western part of the county all kinds of northern fruit are a sure crop, apples, plums and pears producing very abundantly, grapes and peaches doing well in some localities.

The water of the inland lakes is of rare purity and abound in the finest of fish.

The climate is very mild, the ground seldom freezing in the winter, the snow falling early protects the winter wheat from the freezing and thawing that proves so destructive to winter wheat further south. The climate is free from malaria and bilious diseases are very rare.

During the season of navigation steamers and sailing vessels are constantly plying between Elk Rapids, Torch Lake and all lake ports. Roads are now getting good throughout the county and school advantages are unsurpassed by the older counties of the State.

Taking all things into consideration there is no better field for the merchant, manufacturer or farmer than Antrim county offers.

ARENAC COUNTY.

Arenac county was organized in April, 1883. It had a population of 5,683 in 1890, and has an area of 234,998 acres, with 1,035 acres subject to entry or sale. Lumber, farm products and fish are the chief products, and manufacturing is carried on to some extent.

Arenac is bounded on the north by Ogemaw and Iosco counties, on the east and south by Saginaw bay, and on the west by Gladwin county. Standish, a nice village of about 1,500 inhabitants, is the county seat. The Michigan Central railroad affords the chief means of transportation.

BARAGA COUNTY.

Baraga county was organized in 1875. It was taken from Houghton, and is bounded on the north by Houghton and Lake Superior, on the east and south by Marquette, and on the west by Houghton and Sturgeon river. L'Anse, a town of 1,500 inhabitants, is the county seat. It has an area of 900 square miles, and had a population in 1890 of 3,036. The surface of the country is generally undulating, although some level land is found in the Sturgeon Bay valley and in the southeastern townships.

The county is well watered by a number of streams, the Sturgeon river, on the western side, being the largest river in the upper peninsula. Ample water power is afforded by several of these streams. Nearly every variety of soil is found, the valley lands being particularly rich. The subsoil in most parts consists of gravel, sand and clay, underneath which can be found either slate rock or sandstone. The timber consists of sugar maple, pine, hemlock, birch. cedar, spruce balsam and Norway pine. Some wheat is raised, but the principal crops are hay, oats, potatoes, beans and garden vegetables, all of which find a ready market. Fruit growing is in its infancy, yet several varieties of apples and cherries are grown successfully. Clearing costs about $15 per acre. Hardwood brings from $3 to $4 per cord; softwood about $2. Farmers do not plow for the first crop.

There are 34,346 acres subject to entry or sale. Many of these lands are desirable for agricultural purposes, and can be had at prices ranging from $1.50 to $5 per acre. Three State roads lead out from L'Anse in different directions, rendering all parts of the county accessible. Snow falls in November and leaves about April 1. The winters are very steady and the climate may be said to be exceptionally fine. Farmers commence work about the 1st of May. Free schools are open ten months in the year.

A number of iron mines are in constant operation, and stone and slate quarries are being successfully developed. These, with the lumbering and fishing industries, cause a demand for labor at all times, which is often hard to supply. The Duluth, South Shore and Atlantic railroad crosses the county, also the Houghton branch passes through L'Anse. Railroads are projected which, with the excellent water communication (there being eighty miles of sea coast), will very materially aid the commercial enterprises of this new and rapidly developing county.

BARRY COUNTY.

BY M. L. COOK, HASTINGS, MICH.

Barry county was organized in 1839. It is bounded on the north by Kent and Ionia, on the east by Eaton, on the south by Calhoun and Kalamazoo, and on the west by Allegan. It has an area of 576 square miles, and a population in 1890 of 23,783. Hastings, a thriving and prosperous city of 3,500 people, is the county seat, where the county has just finished a beautiful court house and county jail at an expense of $75,000.

The surface is generally rolling, with occasional level tracts, but all parts of the county are tillable. It is watered mainly by the Thornapple river, a stream of considerable importance, affording several good water power privileges. Numerous small streams flow into the Thornapple. There are many picturesque and beautiful lakes, affording splendid opportunities for boating and fishing, some of them destined to be favorite resorts. The soil of ten townships is clay, with a gravel mixture. In the other six, the soil is more or less sandy, with clay subsoil.

Barry county can still boast of considerable hardwood timber, and lumbering is usually active in winter. Agriculture is the pursuit of the great majority of its inhabitants, and no county in Michigan can raise better wheat than this. While wheat is the staple, corn, oats, potatoes, beans and barley are successfully raised. Plenty of grasses are raised in all sections of the county, particularly on the heavy timbered lands of the eastern and northern portions.

Desirable farm lands can be purchased from $20 to $70 per acre, according to location and condition.

Like most counties, Barry county needs good roads. The old system of spring plowing and fall scraping of highways has not been known to make good roads in Barry or any other county. The county will average with its neighbors in the matter of roads, which is not the most complimentary thing to be said on the subject.

Barry has the usual climate of the southern tiers of counties in Michigan.

No county in Michigan takes more pride in her schools. The county is peopled almost wholly by native Americans, who value the school house and the church, and prize good citizenship, which can come only from the educated citizen. There are 150 school districts in the county, and 153 school buildings. There are over fifty church buildings in the county.

Two railroads traverse the county, the Grand Rapids branch of the Michigan Central from east to west, and the Chicago, Kalamazoo & Saginaw from southwest to northeast. Besides these, the Cincinnati, Jackson & Mackinaw and the Detroit, Lansing & Northern touch the county at the southwestern and northeastern corners respectively. These roads open up the county excellently, and place shipping facilities within easy reach of all.

While agriculture is the principal pursuit, manufacturing interests are becoming quite important in Barry county, especially at Hastings, which has the only whip factory in Michigan, and the largest wool boot factory in the world.

BAY COUNTY.

BY W. R. M'CORMICK, BAY CITY.

Bay county was organized in 1857. It is bounded on the north by Arenac, on the east by Tuscola, and Saginaw bay, on the south by Saginaw, and on the west by Midland and Gladwin. It has an area of 1,008 square miles and has a population of about 64,000.

The county has 67 miles of excellent stone roads and more are being built. These run in various directions to the farming districts from Bay City, the county seat. The county is level, with the exception of that part of the county north of Lincoln and Standish counties, which is slightly rolling. Although there is a large extent of coast line and many rivers flowing into the bay, there are but few water powers, and those are somewhat limited in capacity. The soil is a deep, rich loam with a clay sub-soil mixed with limestone. Oak, elm, basswood, ash, beech, maple and hemlock comprise the principal varieties of timber. The county is noted for its wheat. Hay, oats and corn are also extensively raised. Apples are grown in abundance. The fruit buds are retarded by the cool lake winds and thus escape the early frosts. The smaller fruits are a more uncertain crop, although grapes of the hardier varieties do well along the shore.

The cost of clearing averages $20 per acre, and the wood cut finds a ready market at a fair price. Good farms and homes in towns can be bought on easy terms. There are large tracts of timbered land, suitable for agricultural purposes, which can be had at prices ranging from $8 to $10 per acre. They are generally within easy reach of railroad towns. The climate is a variable one. Snow falls by December 1 and averages about one foot in depth during the season. The ground generally freezes from one to two feet in depth, hence farmers begin work about ten days later than in southern Michigan.

The privileges incident to schools and churches are unexcelled, the public schools of Bay City being especially fine.

All sorts of enterprises are engaged in successfully. Lumbering, manufacturing, fishing and ship building is carried on very extensively, over two thousand men being employed in the ship yards. The largest pail and tub factory in the world is located in Bay City. They also have the Water Pipe Company and the Crystal water works, bicycle factory, industrial works, planing mills, sash and door factories, saw mills and salt works.

Common labor is always in good demand, wages ranging from $19 to $30 per month, with board. The county is spending a large amount of money in macadamizing the principal thoroughfares of the county, and every portion of it can be readily reached by railroads, water or good roads.

The Flint & Pere Marquette, Michigan Central, Detroit & Bay City, the Cincinnati, Saginaw & Muskegon and the Grand Trunk railroads afford excellent outlets for all of the productions of the county.

Bay City is an important lake port, the largest vessels entering its harbor during the seasons for navigation.

BENZIE COUNTY.

Benzie county was organized in 1869. It is bounded on the north by Leelenau and Lake Michigan, on the east by Grand Traverse, on the south by Manistee and on the west by Lake Michigan. It has an area of 350 square miles, and had a population in 1890 of 5,237. Benzonia, a growing town of about 500 inhabitants, situated on Crystal lake, is the county seat. A strip of country about ten miles in width along the lake shore is of a hilly character, and is not as desirable for farming purposes as the land farther east, which is comparatively level, and is remarkably productive. The county is watered by two small streams running through it from east to west, also by several small inland lakes. A sandy, gravelly soil predominates, but there are large tracts containing clay, and on some farms the soil is little else than clay; on others it is a sandy loam, warm and highly productive. The sugar maple, elm, basswood, beech, birch, white oak, hemlock and cherry constitute the prevailing varieties of timber.

The soil seems well adapted to all root crops. Potatoes grow to the greatest perfection, and clover does remarkably well. In good seasons wheat and corn do well, although the lack of rains has caused some difficulty for a few years past, owing to the fact that the ground leaches rapidly. The ten-mile belt referred to above produces splendid fruit, and in fact the whole northern part of the county may be said to be a fruit growing district. Peaches, pears, apples, plums, grapes, cherries and berries of all kinds grow in profusion. Peaches have grown for twenty years without interruption.

The cost of clearing averages about $15 per acre, and wood finds a ready market in several localities. There are 5,630 acres of land subject to sale or entry. Good agricultural lands, well timbered, can be had at from $3 to $15 per acre.

Two State roads pass through the county, one from Manistee along the lake shore to Frankfort and Leland, and the other from Manistee to Traverse City, passing through Benzonia, Garfield, Almira and Homestead.

The climate is a very desirable one, the seasons following each other without the marked variations in temperature found in counties further south. The ground does not freeze and plowing begins in April. The average depth of snow is two feet.

The schools are very good, and a college at Benzonia prepares teachers for the common and graded schools.

There is a constant demand for labor, owing to the development of so many industries incident to a timbered country. Several lines of steamers touch at Frankfort, affording an outlet for the products of the county. A large iron furnace near Frankfort creats a. steady demand for harwood, and employs a large number of men. The Frankfort & Southeastern, the Manistee & Northeastern and Chicago and West Michigan railroads pass through the county.

BERRIEN COUNTY.

BY HENRY CHAMBERLAIN, THREE OAKS.

Berrien is the southwest county of the State. Its western boundary is Lake Michigan. Its principal rivers are the St. Joseph, Paw Paw, Dowagiac and Galien, with many minor streams. All of these streams furnish water power of great volume, about one-half of which is unimproved. All parts of the county are within seventy-five miles of Chicago, which is reached by two railroads and by vessels from the mouth of the St. Joseph river. The Michigan Central, Chicago & West Michigan, the Vandalia and the Wabash & Michigan railroads pass through the county. There are but few farms which are more than eight miles from a railroad station.

The county is generally level or gently rolling with no broken land except along the banks of the larger streams and Lake Michigan. The larger part of the soil is a rich gravelly or sandy loam; parts of six townships are clay or clay loam. A narrow strip along Lake Michigan is a thin, sandy soil. There are many small lakes and quite a number of marshes in the county. Some of the marshes have but little value except for pasture or wild hay; but many have great value for the production of celery, peppermint, onions, cabbage, potatoes and other vegetables.

The principal products of the county are wheat, corn, rye, oats, barley, potatoes and hay, with a fair amount of butter and cheese. The lands are all valuable for hay and pasture, and sheep and cattle are raised and fed for market.

All parts of the county grow apples, pears, quinces and grapes. The "fruit belt" on the lake shore grows peaches and the small fruits in large quantities.

A very large portion of the county was originally covered with heavy timber, beech, maple, walnut, hickory, ash, whitewood, elm, basswood and oak, much of it very valuable. A smaller part was openings upon which grew white, yellow, black and burr oak and hickory. There are a number of small prairies in the county. The lands are all now cleared, except small tracts connected with farms, kept for fuel and fencing. There is but little unimproved land in the county. The improved lands are held at from $30 to $125 dollars per acre for farm purposes; fruit lands $30 to $500 per acre.

The manufactures are wood pulp and paper, flour and meal, furniture, agricultural implements, machinery, etc.

Niles, Benton Harbor and St. Joseph are the cities. Buchanan, Berrien Springs, Three Oaks and Watervliet are the larger villages, with twenty or more other villages and hamlets with from 50 to 600 inhabitants.

The lake fisheries are principally located at St. Joseph, from the mouth of which river there is a large vessel interest.

The markets are the cities and villages of the county, Chicago and the world.

There is a school and school house in every rural district and a graded or high school in every city or village. Churches and church edifices are numerous enough to enable all the people to attend churches of their own faith. Wages of farm labor are $15 to $30 per month and board; common labor, $1 to $1.50 per day; skilled labor, $2 to $3.50 per day. There are fish in most of the lakes and streams. The larger game is all gone, and ducks, quail and squirrels are not at all abundant. There are no stone quarries or mineral lands in the county.

BRANCH COUNTY.

BY DWIGHT E. YOUNGS, UNION CITY.

Branch county's first permanent settler located where is now the village of Bronson in 1828. He was followed the next year by some who located at Girard and Coldwater. The county was formed by an act passed by the legislative council October 29, 1829, and named for Hon. John Branch, of North Carolina, President Jackson's Secretary of the Navy, but was associated with several other counties, known as the township of Green, until 1833, when, having about 70 voters, the county commenced its independent existence. It is bounded north by Calhoun, east by Hillsdale, south by Indiana and west by St. Joseph. It has an area of 516 square miles. Population, 1890, was 26,791. Coldwater, the county seat, with 5,247 inhabitants, was platted as a village in 1832, organizing with a charter, 1837. The years from 1831 to 1837 witnessed the advent of large numbers of permanent settlers in all parts of the county. Union City was platted in 1835 as Goodwinsville. Quincy had an existence as a little more than a country four corners until the advent of the railroad, but was incorporated in 1858; since then its growth has been rapid. Bronson was incorporated in 1866 and given the name of its first settler, who was Jabe Bronson, but a portion of its area was platted in 1833, as York. Sherwood, a lively little town on the Air Line railroad, has grown up since the building of that road, was platted while it was being graded.

The surface of the county is generally level, although a small portion is gently rolling, no hills. There are four streams passing through parts of the county, all, however, uniting their waters with the St. Joseph at Union City, which passes through the county in a southwesterly direction. About three-fifths of the county has a soil of a sandy or gravelly loam with a hard subsoil, the remainder a heavy clay especially adapted to grazing and stock raising.

The timber on the heavy soil was principally beech and maple, many maple orchards being retained to the present. There is also an abundance of ash, elm, basswood, with some cherry, black walnut and butternut, while on the lighter soil oak and hickory are found. Wheat, oats, corn and potatoes are extensively raised. Stock raising is receiving much attention, especially the finer breeds of horses and sheep. Of fruits, apples are extensively grown, as are all the small fruits, but peaches, owing to an occasional severe winter, are a failure in late years.

The land is mostly improved, a few tracts being left, for the timber is more valuable than that improved, which is valued from $20 to $125 per acre, according to location and buildings. Winter usually commences about December 20, lasting until March. Two or three exceptional years have given winter from the middle of November to the 10th of April. Crops are good with few exceptions in the past 55 years. May 1 generally furnishes an abundance of new feed for stock.

The best of water is supplied from wells, 15 to 45 feet in depth. For soft water cisterns are required.

The system of drainage adopted to dispose of any surplus water has made the county as healthy a region as anywhere found. Ague and fever being practically banished, leaves the principal diseases, such as are at times epidemic among children in all localities. Very many of the early settlers lived to pass fourscore years, a few fourscore and ten.

Branch county may be justly proud of her religious and educational advantages. There are large and commodious school buildings in the principal villages, while the country districts are supplied with neat and comfortable structures. Every village has churches for the different denominations, and many country four corners are supplied with the same.

Manufacturing is carried on quite extensively in the larger towns. Many inducements are held out to draw such industries to the villages, now largely dependent on the farming country around for support.

The Lake Shore & Michigan Southern railroad main line passes through Quincy, Coldwater, Batavia, a corner of Bethel and Bronson, while the Air Line of the Michigan Central passes through Union and Sherwood, the Fort Wayne, Jackson & Saginaw nearly touching the southeast corner of the county.

There are a number of beautiful inland lakes, one near the village of Quincy which has been connected with others to the south and west by means of a canal, with a view to navigation through a string of lakes to Orland, Ind., a distance of about forty miles.

A beautiful sheet of water eight miles south of Coldwater, through which the Coldwater river flows, giving it its name, is about six miles by one and a half in extent, in which is an island of 40 acres, is utilized as a summer resort by residents of the county. Cottages have been erected on its shores, to which they migrate during the heat of summer. Another similar resort is located about three miles north of the city on a lake provided with a small excursion steamboat to accommodate picnic and pleasure parties.

In the early days before the advent of steam in the State, the St. Joseph river was deemed a navigable stream and Union City the head of navigation, but its waters have never been turned to account for this purpose.

CALHOUN COUNTY.

Calhoun county was organized in 1833. It is bounded on the north by Barry and Eaton, on the east by Jackson, on the south by Branch and Hillsdale and on the west by Kalamazoo. Marshall, a city of 3,968 inhabitants, is the county seat. The surface of the county has an area of 720 square miles, and had a population in 1890 of 43,501. The surface of the county is gently rolling. The Kalamazoo river crosses the county from east to west, affording a number of water powers. There are several flouring mills in the county which are run by water. The county is otherwise well watered by a number of small streams. Nearly every variety of soil is found, a light, sandy loam characterizing some townships, and a strong clay others. A good clay subsoil generally underlies the surface at a proper depth.

Oak is the principal variety of timber, although there is some beech, maple, whitewood, elm and walnut. Wheat and corn are extensively raised. The soil produces wonderfully well, though of a light appearance in localities. Garden vegetables of every variety grow abundantly with little care. Apples are the principal fruit crop, though peaches and pears are raised to a limited extent. The smaller fruits are successfully grown in every township.

The timber on any available tract would pay for the clearing, as there is a good market for wood. There are no government or state lands on the market.

Improved lands are held at from $25 to $100 per acre. The unimproved lands are generally attached to improved farms and are not for sale. The seasons are well defined, snow rarely falling out of the winter months. The ground freezes to a moderate depth and spring work begins early in April.

The county schools are excellent and those of the larger towns are among the best in the State.

Agriculture is the principal industry, although large manufacturing interests are centered at Battle Creek and Albion. Labor is in fair demand particularly in the summer season, wages ranging $16 to $25 per month, with board.

The Michigan Central railroad main line, its Air Line, the Chicago & Grand Trunk, and the Lansing branch of the Michigan Southern, traverse the county.

Calhoun is one of the wealthiest counties in the State, being seventh in wealth, being equalized at $30,000,000, and is a very desirable county in which to locate, taking into consideration all of its resources and advantages. Albion College, a denominational institution under the control of the Methodists, is located at Albion, and has a large pupilage.

CASS COUNTY.

BY MRS. AGUSTUS JEWELL, OF DOWAGIAC.

Cass county was organized in 1829. It is situated in the beautiful St. Joseph valley, the scene of J. Fennimore Cooper's "Oak Openings" or "Bee Hunters," and was named in honor of Lewis Cass, who was governor of Michigan from 1813 to 1830. It is bounded on the north by Van Buren county, east by St. Joseph county, south by the State of Indiana and west by Berrien county. Contains 314,584 acres of land with a population of 20,953 in 1890.

Pre-historic remains are to be found through the county consisting of mounds and garden beds. The surface of the county, like all Michigan, is composed entirely of drift. A mass of debris, consisting of loose stones, gravel and sand, probably several hundred feet in thickness. It is gently undulating, thereby furnishing excellent surface drainage, making it healthful, and with the purest of water keeping it free from epidemics of any kind. The leading features may be classed under the headings of heavy timbered lands, oak openings and prairies. Three distinct varieties of soil are to be found, in these divisions: on the heavily timbered, gravely soil mixed with sand or clay; oak openings, a sandy loam; while that of the prairie is a black, sticky, soft soil, the richest and best in the county. A clay and gravely subsoil is usually underlying all. It is beautified and well watered with its 180 lakes and ponds, whose shores are skirted with beautiful farms alternating with primeval forests coming down to their very margins as when none other than the bark canoe skimmed the surface of their pure waters, thereby affording many beautiful summer resorts, and there are a number of small streams furnishing good water power. Fish abound plentifully in all the lakes and streams, and small wild game is in limited supply in the timbered tracts. The timber is mainly oak, hickory, beech, maple, ash elm, whitewood and basswood. Wheat, corn, hay, oats, barley, rye. and potatoes are the usual crops, and the soil is unsurpassed for the production of all cereals raised in the latitude, while hogs, sheep and cattle form no small part of its agricultural interests. Nearly all kinds of fruit and vegetables do well, a fair proportion of which are shipped.

There are no public lands of any description in the market. Snow falls the first of December and averages ten to twelve inches in depth. The season for plowing usually commences about the last of March. Labor is in fair demand, its manufacturing and agricultural interests employing several hundred hands. Wages on farms range from $16 to $25 per month, with board. School and church privileges are unsurpassed. The Michigan Central main line, its Air Line, the Cincinnati, Wabash & Michigan, and the Chicago & Grand Trunk railroads pass through the county, placing every township within easy reach of both eastern and western markets. Eight papers are published within the county, seven weekly and one monthly and has twenty-four postoffices.

A peculiar feature is attached to Calvin township in this county, not to be found in any other township in the State, that of a preponderance of colored people who far outnumber the white population. The primal cause of this condition was the residence here of a society of Friends who extended helping hands to trembling fugitive slaves as early as 1836, who soon became land owners and are among the thrifty population.

Cassopolis, situated on the bank of Stone lake, a half a mile distant from the beautiful Diamond lake, is the county seat with a population of 1,500 with two railroads, the Michigan Central air line and the Chicago & Grand Trunk, its manufacturing interests consisting of a bowl factory, foundry, saw and flouring mills. Dowagiac, situated on the Michigan Central main line, and commercially one of its most important stations, is in the northern part of the county, one hundred miles east of Chicago, has a population of 3,500. With the manufacturing industries of the famous "Round Oak" stoves, Dowagiac shoe grain drills, chair factory, marble works, sand bands, washing machines, saw and flouring mills, sash and door factory, planing mills and many other minor industries. The city contains the finest opera house in America for a town of its size, the "Beckwith Memorial Building," and with its thirteen miles of cement walks, well kept streets and homes, with its system of water works, supplied directly from artesian wells, and electric lights, its literary and musical societies and fine public library, all corroborate the unanimous statements of commercial travelers that it is the thriftiest, neatest and most attractive town of its size in the country and will bear the most thorough investigation if in pursuit of a place that combines rare advantages for business and a home.

CHARLEVOIX COUNTY.

Charlevoix county was organized in 1869. It is bounded on the north by Emmet and Lake Michigan, on the east by Cheboygan and Otsego, on the south by Antrim, and on the west by Lake Michigan. It has an area of 396 square miles, and had a population in 1890 of 9,686. Charlevoix, a flourishing village of 1,500 inhabitants, situated on Lake Michigan, is the county seat. The surface of the county is everywhere rolling, and in some parts decidedly hilly. The county is well watered. Pine lake, a beautiful sheet of water, stretching 14 miles in an easterly direction from Charlevoix village. Six miles from Charlevoix, a branch of the lake runs in a southerly direction eight miles. The branch is fed by the famous trout fishing stream, the Jordan. The Boyne flows in at the east end of the lake, and the county generally is covered with innumerable spring brooks of the coldest water. There is some available water power, particularly on the Jordan and Boyne rivers. The soil varies from a light sandy to a heavy clay, filled with calcareous matter. The subsoil is of as varied a nature as that of the surface.

Sugar maple, elm, beech, basswood, ash, hemlock, and cedar timber is found in great quantities throughout the county.

The principal crops are winter wheat, oats corn, hay, clover, potatoes, and root crops. The summer resorts at Charlevoix furnish an excellent market for all sorts of garden vegetables.

All fruits do well, excepting grapes and peaches. The hardier kind of apples are especially successful. Charlevoix county is at the northern extremity of the celebrated Michigan fruit belt. The cost of clearing averages $20 per acre, although the wood produced generally pays for the clearing.

There are no government lands in the market. There are 3,070 acres of land subject to entry or sale.

Unimproved lands are held at from $7 to $10 per acre, while improved farms average from $15 to $60, in the interior, and from $25 to $100 near Charlevoix. There is a State road from Traverse City to Petoskey, which crosses the county. There are a number of wagon roads traversing the county, most of which are new, but are steadily improving. There are also several tramroads built through belts of hardwood timber which facilitate travel. Much of the travel in summer is by water. The winter is very steady, snow falling by November 15, and lasting five months. The summer season is delightful, and the county is a great resort for invalids afflicted with asthmatic difficulties. The schools are very creditable for a new county.

As Pine lake is navigable for large vessels, the timber business is an important enterprise in this county. Wood, ties, fence posts, hemlock bark and logs are cut during the winter, and are shipped during the summer to Chicago, Milwaukee, Racine, and other lake ports. There are several saw mills in the county. An iron furnace at Ironton, on Pine lake, furnishes employment to a large number of men. The fishing industry is also a considerable one.

The Grand Rapids & Indiana Railroad passes through Charlevoix.

The famous resorts on Pine lake have contributed largely to the development of the county, and are thronged every summer with admirers of the beautiful scenery and delightful climate of Charlevoix county.

CHEBOYGAN COUNTY.

BY EDWARD FORSYTH, OF CHEBOYGAN.

Cheboygan county was organized in 1853. It is bounded on the north by Lake Huron and the Straits of Mackinaw, on the east by Lake Huron and Presque Isle county, on the south by Otsego and Montmorency, and on the west by Emmet and Charlevoix. Cheboygan, a rapidly growing town of 7,000 inhabitants, is the county seat. It is a live port, with all modern improvements, sewers, paved streets, street cars, electric lights, $10,000 opera house, splendid schools and churches. The county has an area of 792 square miles and had a population in 1890 of 11,145. The surface of the county is greatly diversified, level plains being found in some localities and rolling land in others, the hills on the borders of the lake sometimes rising to a height of 200 feet. It is watered by the Rainy, Black, Pigeon, Cheboygan and Maple rivers, also by Cheboygan, Black, Mullet, Burt and Douglass lakes. Several of these rivers and lakes are navigable, affording excellent opportunities for transportation of wood, bark, etc., and the rafting of logs. The streams furnish good water power in various places, and are alive with fish. The shores of these lakes are rapidly becoming popular summer resorts, which furnish splendid markets for all kinds of farm produce, butter, eggs, vegetables, milk, cheese, berries, etc., from June until October, at city prices. The region is a hay fever sanitarium, which keeps the resorts open until frost comes. Among these resorts are Topinabee, Dodge's Point and Koehler's on Mullett lake, Columbus Landing and Columbus Beach on Burt lake, Roose & Grace's hotel on Long lake, besides other resorts on Douglass, Black and Carp lakes. The soil is composed of red clay in some portions and sand and clay loam in others, generally rich and productive. The timber consists of maple, beech, pine, cedar, hemlock, poplar, elm and basswood. The principal crops are wheat, corn, oats, hay, potatoes and vegetables, all of which are successfully grown. Apples, plums, cherries and berries do well, but peaches and pears are not as successful. The wild berry crop nets $10,000 to $15,000 a year. Strawberries, huckleberries, raspberries and blackberries grow wild in abundance. Market now exists for every stick of timber grown in the county. Dozens of little hardwood mills exist all over the county, while a big tannery at Cheboygan consumes 20,000 cords of hemlock bark a year and a stave mill uses up from 3,000,000 to 6,000,000 of elm annually. All kinds of wood is in demand in the log, or as ties, posts, bark, cordwood or pulp wood and brings from $2.50 per thousand feet for basswood to $8.50 for elm and $50 for curly maple. Cordwood sells green at from $1.25 to $1.75 and dry for $2 a cord. There are 27,525 acres of public land subject to sale or entry beside railroad land claims. Government land for entry only can be had by application to United States land office at Grayling. State land can be bought or entered at State land office, Lansing. Improved farms, individual lands, can be had at reasonable prices, sometimes far below actual value.

A State road runs from Cheboygan to Petoskey and one from Cheboygan to Rogers City. Other roads of more recent construction cross the county in all directions and more are being built as the progress of the county demands, and for nine months in the year they are excellent. They are being rapidly improved and new roads opened. Snow usually falls about November 15. The average depth attained during the winter may be said to be about twenty inches. The ground seldom freezes and spring work commences early in May. Grass is king; one acre will support as much life as the best blue grass land of Kentucky. The schools of the county are numerous and of the best kind, with a competent county commissioner in charge and the people show great enterprise in building new school houses as fast as necessary. The county is, in the main, free from malaria. The great changes in temperature cause some rheumatic complaints, but as a rule, the county is very healthy. The lumbering interests are very extensive, employing at remunerative wages a great many men. Besides this industry, there is in Cheboygan a big tannery employing, all told, 250 to 300 hands the year round; a 125-barrel flouring mill and one of fifty barrels capacity, three foundries, three planing mills, electric lights, ship yards, etc., and as fast as land can be cleared new farms are being developed, which add yearly to the wealth and resources of the county. Fishing is also extensively engaged in. Labor is always in good demand.

The Michigan Central railroad (Mackinaw division) passes through Cheboygan, and the Detroit, Bay City & Alpena railroad will reach the southern borders of the county before snow flies, and will go north to the straits next year, opening up a magnificent railroad region. Lake vessels of the largest size enter its two harbors, one of which is in Cheboygan and the other at Duncan City, a mile distant.

CHIPPEWA COUNTY.

BY C. H. CHAPMAN, SAULT STE MARIE.

COURT HOUSE.

Chippewa county was organized in 1826, ten years before Michigan was admitted into the union as a State, and embraced nearly the entire upper peninsula of Michigan, all of the north part of Wisconsin and all of the north part of Minnesota east of the Mississippi river. It has been reduced from time to time until now it is bounded on the north and east by the St. Mary's river and Lake Superior, on the south by Mackinac and Lake Huron, and on the west by Mackinac and Luce counties. It is the second county in size in the State and has a total of 995,225 acres. The population in 1880 was 5,248, and in 1890 had increased to 12,019, an increase of 129.02 per cent, not including the county of Luce, organized out of this territory during this period. In 1891 this county contained 17,430 acres of improved farm land and 38,978 acres in farms partially improved. The average number of acres in each farm in the county was 131.49. The assessed valuation as equalized in 1890 was $5,000,000. The county now contains public lands subject to sale or entry, 121,009 acres; homes of 80 acres each for 1,512 families. Its population is largely of the best class of Canadians. Sault Ste. Marie, a city of 8,000 inhabitants, is the county seat. This city is located on the St. Mary's river at a point where the government canal around the rapids was constructed. It has three trunk lines of railroads and other lines are pushing in this direction. The river is spanned by the great international bridge at this point, making a short rail route between the Atlantic states and the great west.

The surface of this county is gently rolling. In the northern portion of the county there is considerable sandy land, also a few cedar swamps which are easily drained. The eastern portion, particularly that lying south of Sault Ste. Marie, comprising also a part of what are now known as the "burnt lands," is a very desirable agricultural region, the soil being a deep red clay, which is easily worked, and, after exposure to the atmosphere, pulverizes, and is not liable to become sun-baked or cracked. The soil is peculiarly adapted to the raising of peas, and the entire absence of bugs makes the crops much sought after by seedsmen. A small portion of the middle part of the county has a light sandy soil, timbered with scattering pine, and surrounded by fine bodies of hardwood land with a rich, sandy-loam soil. The western portion is timbered with pine of a good quality. There are also large tracts of choice hardwood land interspersed with scattering pine. The southern portion of the western part of the county is the valley of the Tahquamenon. The timber is cedar and pine. On the bottoms are extensive meadows of blue joint grass, the soil being a dark vegetable mould with clay subsoil. The county is well watered by the Tahquamenon and its many branches; also by the St. Mary's, Two-hearted, Munuscong, Carp and numerous smaller streams and inland lakes. Fine water powers are to be found on many of these streams. St. Mary's river has one of the finest water powers in the world, there being a fall of 18 feet between Lakes Superior and Huron.

The principal crops are wheat, oats, barley, peas, hay, and all sorts of root crops. Considerable attention has been paid to farming within the past sixteen years. The county took the first prize for spring and winter wheat at the State fair held at Jackson in the fall of 1882. Corn is not successfully grown. Peas, hay and potatoes are among the most profitable crops. The smaller fruits grow to great perfection and are of the finest flavor. All sorts of berries grow in abundance, but the larger fruits do not succeed as well, owing to the length of the winters.

There are large tracts of "burnt lands" which can be cleared at from $2.50 to $10 per acre. The cost of clearing the heavier timbered lands, however, will average $15 per acre. There are good wood markets at the Sault and at the towns along the Detroit, Mackinac & Marquette Railroad.

In addition to the public lands open for sale or entry as homesteads, there are about 400,000 acres of canal, railroad and lumbermen's lands subject to sale at prices ranging from $1 to $10 per acre, according to location. Along the lines of the railroads large tracts are being taken up, both by the settlers and by non-residents, who can foresee their future value. A State road connects St. Ignace with the Sault. There are also many local roads, newly made, which are opening up the country in every direction. Winter sets in early. The snow falls to an average depth of three feet, the ground seldom freezing. Plowing begins as soon as the snow is off the ground, generally by April 1. Crops mature rapidly, owing to a peculiarity of the climate. The atmosphere is remarkably dry, and is tempered and equalized by the great lakes to the north and south. The health of the citizens of this locality is materially improved by the entire absence of malaria.

The lakes and spring brooks are filled with every variety of brook trout, the best evidence in the world of the purity of their waters.

There are forty-three district schools in the county and many others in process of organization.

The principal industries are lumbering, agriculture, fishing, sawing, dressing and manufacturing lumber into boxes, sash and doors for eastern shipment.

Chippewa is a great county. It has the best of agricultural and timbered lands, a great variety of soil, fine water privileges, good society, available markets, and excellent shipping facilities. The attention of the immigrant has been turned in this direction, and its rapid development is an assured fact.

BY OTTO FOWLE.

Chippewa county lies at the extreme eastern end of the upper peninsula, extending from Lake Huron on the south to Lake Superior on the north, and from the St. Mary river on the east, including several islands still east of this, westward to range eight west of Michigan meridian; it contains, including fractional, a total of fifty-five surveyed townships, or approximately 1,600 square miles. This is all now remaining of the county which once comprised the greater part of the upper peninsula of Michigan, northern Wisconsin and most of the state of Minnesota.

The industries of the county are greatly diversified, including agriculture, manufacturing and fishing. The principal agricultural products being wheat, oats, rye, peas, of which a large amount and of a superior quality is raised; several large seed firms having warehouses at Sault Ste. Marie, the county seat, are obtaining a fine quality and large quantities of seed peas. Potatoes, turnips, parsnips, beets, carrots, squashes and pumpkins yield abundantly and of fine quality, while garden stuffs of all kinds are easily produced. Timothy, clover, red top and many of the wild grasses yield large cuts of hay and afford excellent pasturage. Horses, sheep, cattle, hogs and poultry are raised to a considerable extent. Chippewa county mutton stands the favorite in the local markets over anything imported from the south and west. Of wheat, both spring and winter are raised; the latter has lately obtained the preference. While farming is still in its infancy here, Chippewa county has twice taken the premium on wheat at the State fair. Corn, on account of early frosts, is not attempted, excepting garden varieties.

The surface of the county is, in the most, quite level, varying about the streams from light rolling to decidedly hilly; good drainage is everywhere admissible. The soil varies from lighty sandy to heavy clay, while loam tracts are abundant.

All small fruits are easily raised, of excellent quality and good yield. Strawberries, currants and raspberries especially thrive. Who has not heard of Lake Superior raspberry jam? Whortle and cranberries are shipped in large quantities. Plums are prolific, while apples with care can be raised.

Lumbering has been extensively carried on in this county for several years. The pine still standing is estimated at one thousand million feet, about one hundred million being manufactured annually. Large tracts of spruce and other pulp woods are found, of which twenty thousand cords are annually gotten out.

Interspersed with the pine and hemlock throughout the county are extensive tracts and belts of excellent hardwood. Running west from Waiskai river, the entire length of the county, about forty miles, is a belt of hardwood from sixteen to twenty miles wide, composed of beech, birch and maple; the maple is of superior quality running largely to bird's-eye, and grows large and thrifty. The birch is remarkable for its richness in color and grows very plentifully. This hardwood is found in smaller tracts on most of the islands and interspersed throughout the main land. The low lands and river bottoms have a heavy growth of poplar and spruce, while cedar is abundant. It is estimated that not more than one-third of the hardwood has been cut. The greater part of the county can be classed as unimproved, and varies from $1.50 to $6.00 per acre in value. It is estimated that of improved lands there are about 25,000 acres valued at from $6 00 to $20.00 per acre while the farms near the Sault run as high as $100.00 per acre. Much of the improvement is well and thoroughly done, good fences and buildings, while the latest farm machinery is extensively used.

The manufactures are mostly of lumber and its products. At Sault Ste. Marie and Bay Mills are extensive planing, sash, door and box factories. At Sault Ste. Marie are first class machine shops and foundries, while brick of good quality are extensively manufactured.

The chief streams of the county, after the St. Mary, the outlet of Lake Superior, on which the United States government locks at Sault Ste. Marie are situated are the Taquahmenon, Waishkai, and Monoskong, none of the latter being navigable, except for light tugs and flat boats, but affording excellent facilities for transporting timber, pulp, wood and cedar.

There are no mines in the county. Stone quarries are extensively worked at Drummond Island where the backing stone for the government lock and building stone is taken.

Sault Ste. Marie is the chief city, situated at the rapids of the St. Mary river. It has a population of 7,000 and is sustaining a substantial growth. It is the depot of supplies for the entire county and much beside. Here are the famous government locks, through which passes the entire Lake Superior commerce, the tonnage of 1892 being over 11,000,000 tons.

The money expended by the government to complete the work now projected, with that already spent, will approximate $10,000,000. The operation of the canal affords labor for a large force and is an important factor in sustaining the city. Fuel and food supplies for the boats afford a large trade which insures good prices to the farmers for their products. The government is also constructing the buildings for a military post at a cost of about $350,000 to take the place of old Fort Brady established in 1822. When completed this, it is conceded, will be one of the finest posts in the Union.

The fall of the St. Mary at this point is eighteen feet, thus affording one of the best water powers in the country. Of this the Chandler Dunbar Water Power Co. has utilized about 10,000 horse power, with which it lights the city, runs many electric motors, and proposes to pump the city water. Negotiations are pending by which a large pulp and flouring mill are to be located on their site. Running through the city from above the falls to Little Rapids extends the canal of the St. Mary's Falls Water Power Co., on which $400,000 has been expended, and when completed to the proposed dimensions will afford 30,000 horse power. One hundred acres for mill sites on the river front is owned by this company, which when in operation will have facilities afforded for having railway tracks and docks adjacent to the mills. There are at present three railways in operation at this point, the "Soo" line, the Duluth, South Shore & Atlantic, and the Canadian Pacific, all of which have an interest in the international bridge across the St. Mary.

Fish and game are abundant. The commercial fish include whitefish, herring, sturgeon, pickerel and lake trout. The fish annually shipped from this point, mostly whitefish and lake trout, is about 2,200 tons, valued at $231,000. The game fish are brook trout and bass, and are taken in large numbers.

The large game consists of deer, bear, wolves, foxes, lynx, and many fur-bearing animals such as otter, beaver, muskrat, skunk and rabbit. Of birds, partridges and ducks are most abundant.

CLARE COUNTY.

Clare county was organized in 1871. It is bounded on the north by Missaukee and Roscommon, on the east by Gladwin, on the south by Isabella and on the west by Osceola. It has an area of 576 square miles, and had a population in 1890 of 7,553. Harrison, a town of 800 inhabitants, is the county seat. The surface of the country is gently rolling, with some hilly sections in the center of the county. It is well watered by small streams, inland lakes and spring brooks. At Farwell and Clare a small water power is afforded by the Tobacco river which might be used to run several mills. The swamps are mostly cedar and ash, and are easily drained. A number of townships have a light, sandy soil with a clay subsoil. A large part of the county, however, has a good clay soil.

Pine, hemlock, beech, maple, basswood and elm comprise the principal varieties of timber. The crops are mainly wheat, hay and potatoes. Oats are successfully grown in some townships. The county being new, fruit raising has not as yet had a fair test. There are, however, thrifty young orchards which give promise of bearing large crops in the near future. The cost of clearing averages $20 per acre. There are convenient wood markets all along the line of the railroads.

There is 6,197 acres of State and Government land subject to sale or entry. There are large tracts of unimproved lands in the market, which can be had at from $3 to $10 per acre, while improved farms range from $15 to $60. There are also large quantities of stump lands, which will eventually make good farms, and which are held at from 50 cents to $6 and $7 per acre.

There are two State roads in the county, one running north from Farwell to Houghton lake, and the other running north and east from Clare to Gladwin. The local roads are generally in a fair condition. Snow falls by December 1, and attains a depth of from 12 to 18 inches. The ground does not freeze to a great depth, and spring work usually begins by April 15.

The schools are fair, considering the newness of the county. At the villages along the line of the railroads they are very good indeed.

The industries are lumbering and agriculture. Labor is always in good demand, particularly in the lumber woods, wages ranging from $23 to $30 per month with board. The Flint & Pere Marquette railroad and T. A. A. & N. M. railway and its branches cross the county, affording a good outlet for its vast lumber resources.

CLINTON COUNTY.

BY R. M. WINSTON, ST. JOHNS, MICH.

Clinton county was organized in 1839. It is bounded on the north by Gratiot, on the east by Shiawassee, on the south by Eaton and Ingham, and on the west by Ionia. It has an area of five hundred and seventy-six square miles, and a population in 1890 of 26,509. St. Johns, a thriving town of 3,132 inhabitants, is the county seat. The surface of the county is gently rolling and is well watered by the Lookingglass, Maple and Grand rivers, and many small brooks flowing into them. The swamp lands are well drained. Through the center of the county east and west the soil is a rich clay loam. North and south of the central belt there are belts of excellent sandy and gravelly loam. The greater part of the county was embraced in the heavily timbered land and timber openings, the open land or "prairies" being generally of small expanse. The lands from which heavy timber has been cleared are generally strongest and best. There is, however, but little poor soil in the county.

The prevailing varieties of timber are oak, maple, basswood, beech, ash, hickory, elm and walnut. The forests are being preserved for farm use and but little lumbering will be done in the future.

The Detroit, Grand Haven & Milwaukee railroad crosses the county from east to west while the Detroit, Lansing & Northern, Jackson, Lansing & Saginaw and the Toledo, Ann Arbor & Northern Michigan cross the southwestern, southeastern and northeastern portions of the county respectively.

Agricultural products peculiar to this latitude can be successfully produced in Clinton county, and it is a matter of record that Clinton county has raised in one year, more wheat than any other county of equal area in the United States. Oats, corn, barley and potatoes are also successfully grown; and from the reclaimed swamp lands, bountiful crops of garden products and hay are produced. Apples, pears, peaches, plums, berries and grapes do well. The apple crop is becoming an important source of income. Good lands with a fair improvement are held at from $30 to $40 per acre, while farms with excellent buildings, good fences, etc., are held at from $40 to $50 per acre; some farms near railroad towns bring $75 per acre. These farms are near good markets reached by roads unsurpassed by those of any county in the State.

Every part of the county is well supplied with schools and churches, the rural schools being well graded and provided with a uniform course of study; the teachers

29

are enthusiastic and competent. In the villages are excellent graded and Union schools.

Stock raising is an important industry, and farmers are taking great interest in improving their horses, cattle, sheep and swine by purchasing and importing stock for breeding purposes. It is undoubtedly a fact that farmers are making more money from stock than from grain products. We now have five creameries and two cheese factories in active operation. One mercantile firm in St. Johns alone purchased last year butter and eggs to the amount of $60,000. A dealer in eggs purchased and shipped 270,000 dozen, valued at $50,000. These facts from two firms show the importance of our small industries.

Manufacturing is also quite an important industry, St. Johns claiming the largest exclusive table factory in the world, the firm carrying a stock of hardwood lumber of 9,000,000 feet. The Ovid carriage works are also well known.

The merchants carry large stocks of goods, one firm doing a business of over $200,000 sales in 1892.

The inhabitants are principally of American descent except in the townships in the west central part where an industrious German population can be found.

For miles one may travel through Clinton county and see a succession of well cultivated farms with neatly painted and constructed farm buildings, showing conclusively that the people are industrious, intelligent and live in a county second to none in such material resources as a fertile soil, mild climate, and good markets can give.

CRAWFORD COUNTY.

BY R. HANSON, GRAYLING, MICH.

The principal industry of Crawford county is lumbering, largely in the logs put into the Manistee and Au Sable rivers. Manufacturing into lumber is also carried on at the principal town of the county, Grayling, which is also the county seat; also a small amount at Frederic and Roscommon, making a total of about seventy-five millions a year manufactured, and the probable amount of logs as much more.

Geographically the county is located on the head waters of two of the finest rivers in the State, starting a few miles north of the county. These two rivers run parallel for a distance of nearly twelve miles, only one and one-half to three miles apart, then dividing, one, the Manistee, flowing toward the west and emptying into Lake Michigan, and the other turning toward the east, emptying into Lake Huron.

As to agriculture considerable has been done, and all kinds of grain raised, but owing to the cold and late frost, is not generally considered a success.

The soil is light and sandy, being open plains or covered with pine largely, except two towns in the northwest corner, which is hardwood, such as beech, maple, basswood and birch. About two-thirds of the wood lands of the county are cut. The unimproved land is worth 50 cents per acre, and the improved land $20 to $30 per acre. On both the Manistee and Au Sable there are some splendid water powers undeveloped. Both the Manistee and Au Sable abound with the celebrated grayling fish and also trout, and game of all kinds inhabit this region, it being comparatively a wilderness yet, such as bears, wolves, deer and other wild beasts of the forest.

Schools and churches will compare favorably with any part of the State. At Grayling, the county seat, we have a high school with six teachers, and some of our graduates have gone direct to the University from here. One graduate from this school passed examination for West Point successfully, in competition with over forty others in this district, and schools in other parts of the county are excellent.

We have four churches at Grayling, and several others in other parts of the county, all prosperous and doing good work. The Michigan Central Railroad and its branches passes through the county north and south.

Wages paid for common labor $1.50 per day; skilled labor from $2 to $6 per day.

DELTA COUNTY.

Delta county was organized in 1861. It is bounded on the north and east by Schoolcraft, on the south by Green bay and Lake Michigan and on the west by

Menominee and Marquette. It has an area of 1,152 square miles and a population in 1890 of 15,330. Escanaba, a town of 6,808 inhabitants, situated on an arm of Green bay, is the county seat.

The country is generally level. There are areas of rolling land along the rivers, nine of which traverse the county from north to south. The soil on the rolling lands is a sandy loam, with clay subsoil and a limestone foundation; on the plains it is sandy, and on the marshes a vegetable loam with sandy subsoil. On the rolling lands the timber is principally beech, birch and maple, on the plains pine abounds, while in the swamps cedar and tamarack are found in large quantities. The principal crops are wheat, oats, all the grasses, potatoes, and garden vegetables of the hardier sorts. No fruit is grown, although apples might be successfully grown upon the clay soil. The cost of clearing varies. Swamps are the most expensive clearing, hardwood and pine lands costing less, with good wood markets at the towns and charcoal furnaces.

There were subject to entry in 1890, 64,064 acres of land. Unimproved lands near the settlements can be purchased at from $3 to $8 per acre, while improved farms are proportionately higher. "Stump lands" are held at from 50 cents to $2 per acre. A State road traverses the county from north to south, but is neglected and but little used. It passes through Escanaba, and connects Green bay with Marquette. Another extends from Days river to Manistique in Schoolcraft county.

Snow falls in November, and averages from three to four feet in depth. The ground freezes quite deep, and spring work cannot be begun before May 1. The schools are in a very creditable condition for a comparatively new county. Lumbering and fishing are the principal industries, although the charcoal business is extensively carried on along the line of the railway. Labor is not in good demand save in the lumber camps. Immigrants with limited means will find this county a good field for agricultural development. The Chicago & Northwestern Railroad passes through the county. Escanaba has been and is still the leading iron port in the land. It has a magnificent harbor, and it is claimed to be the largest ore shipping port in the world, and is destined to become one of the leading manufacturing and business centers in northwestern Michigan.

DICKINSON COUNTY.

Dickinson county was organized in 1891 from Iron, Marquette and Menominee. It has a population of about 16,000 and has an area of 491,917 acres. Iron Mountain is the county seat and had a population in 1891 of 8,559. The principal interests are mining and lumbering, some of the largest iron mines in the Menominee range being here, namely, the great Chapin, Pewabic, Ludington, Hamilton or Aragon, East and West Vulcan, and several others. The amount of iron ore produced by these mines from 1878 to December 31, 1892, was about 11,000,000 tons, which was shipped by rail to Escanaba and thence by lake to Cleveland and Ashtabula, Ohio. The lands generally are unimproved and heavily timbered, principally pine, hemlock, cedar, maple and birch, about three-fourths of which remains uncut. The soil is sandy loam and adapted to oats and vegetables of all kinds, particularly potatoes. The value of improved lands, about the sixteenth of the total, is $8 to $10 per acre, and the average value of unimproved lands is $2.50 per acre.

Lumber and shingles are manufactured at Norway, Sagold, Metropolitan, Foster City. About 100,000,000 feet board measure is cut annually.

The principal rivers are the Menominee, Michigamme and Sturgeon, not navigable on account of the numerous rapids and falls which afford abundance of water power, very little developed as yet. There is one pulp mill and one hydraulic power works which furnishes the power that operates the machinery of the Chapin mine, which is conveyed in iron pipes a distance of two and one-half miles. The principal markets are Chicago and Milwaukee.

The schools and school buildings are among the best in the State. At Iron Mountain the school building is of gray granite, costing $40,000. There are numerous churches, nearly all denominations having places of worship. There are three railroads, namely, the Chicago & Northwestern, Milwaukee & Northern, and the Escanaba, Iron Mountain & Western, the latter exclusively used for carrying ore.

Wages for woodsmen from $18 to $35 per month, common labor $1.40 to $1.60, skilled, $2.50 to $4.50 per day.

Small lakes and streams are numerous and abound in fish, principally speckled trout, black bass, pickerel, wall-eyed pike and perch. Deer are quite numerous, and by the strict enforcement of the new game law are increasing every year.

A Representative Mine.

EATON COUNTY.

Eaton county was organized in 1837. It is bounded on the north by Ionia and Clinton, on the east by Ingham, on the south by Jackson and Calhoun, and on the west by Barry. It has an area of 576 square miles, and had a population in 1800 of 32,094. Charlotte, a flourishing town of 3,867 inhabitants, is the county seat.

The surface of the county is generally rolling, with small prairies or plains in some parts. Grand river waters the four eastern townships, Battle creek and its tributaries the central and northwestern towns, and the Thornapple the northern, central and western towns. The first named streams furnish good water powers.

All varieties of soil may be found. The subsoil is generally clay. The township of Bellevue has a limestone subsoil. In the central parts of the county a gravelly subsoil is found in a few townships.

The timber is principally oak, beech, maple, elm, ash, hickory, walnut, whitewood and tamarack. The principal crops are wheat, oats, corn, potatoes and barley. Maple sugar is made in large quantities. Fruit does well, apples, grapes and berries of all descriptions being especially successful, while peaches are raised in small quantities. The cost of clearing ranges from $12 to $20 per acre. There are good wood markets in all of the villages.

There are no government or State lands of any value in the market. Scarcely any unimproved lands can be had, as such land is retained by the farmers for its timber. Improved farms are held at from $30 to $50 per acre. The roads of the county are all good.

Snow falls by December 1, the average depth during the season reaching fifteen inches, the ground freezing to the same depth. Farmers plow in April. The schools are good and rapidly improving. Olivet college, a Congregational institution at the town of the same name, is in a flourishing condition.

Agriculture is the principal industry. There is some lumbering and tie-cutting, also considerable lime burned at Bellevue. There is no special demand for labor, unless perchance in the summer season. The Chicago & Grand Trunk, Grand Rapids division of the Michigan Central and the Lansing branch of the Michigan Southern railroads cross the county in different directions, affording excellent market privileges.

Eaton county is a rich agricultural county, and most of its inhabitants are thrifty, well-to-do citizens.

EMMET COUNTY.

BY J. C. BONTECOU, PETOSKEY, MICH.

Emmet county was organized in 1853. It is bounded on the north by the Straits of Mackinac, on the east by Cheboygan, on the south by Charlevoix and Little Traverse bay, on the west by Lake Michigan. It has an area of 414 square miles, and had a population in 1890 of 8,756. Harbor Springs, a beautifully located town of 1,000 inhabitants, is the county seat. Petoskey, a town of 4,000 inhabitants, located across the bay from Harbor Springs, is the most important town in the county. The surface of the county might be termed rolling. There are some townships which are level, others are rolling, while certain portions of the county are very hilly. A large part of the county is well watered by creeks, spring brooks and lakes, while but a small portion is without water. Bear creek which flows into Little Traverse bay at Petoskey, has fine water powers for some distance back from its mouth, now fully utilized for manufacturing purposes. The soil is variable. In some localities will be found a patch of sandy or gravelly loam, with or without clay subsoil. In others a patch of clay loam, alternating with a patch of sandy loam or limestone sand with a sandy subsoil. As a rule the soil is very productive in all parts of the county. Sugar maple, beech, birch, hemlock, cedar, pine, elm, ash, and basswood timber is found in quantities throughout the county.

Wheat and all grain crops, with the exception of some varieties of corn, are grown successfully. Early corn does well, as does the late Dent variety. Grass in nearly all its varieties, is a productive crop. Potatoes and all root crops also yield bountifully.

Fruit growing is yet in its infancy, but a large acreage has been planted with apple, pear, plum, and cherry trees. All these fruits do finely, especially all varieties of the plum, which is here a perfect fruit, and gives a marvelous yield. Small fruits also do well, especially the raspberry and strawberry.

The timber is generally heavy, and the cost of clearing averages about $20 per acre. The villages afford a fair market for wood.

There are 4,000 acres of government and State land subject to sale or entry. Unimproved lands are held at from $5 to $20 per acre, while improved lands range from $15 to $50.

There are fine State roads in the county, and the townships are now well supplied with roads which are being greatly improved each year.

Snow falls by December 1, the average depth attained during the winter being about twenty inches. The winters are very steady. The ground does not freeze to any depth, and plowing can always be undertaken in April. The schools are in good condition and compare favorably with those in the older portions of the State. Excellent graded schools can be found at Petoskey and Harbor Springs.

There is very little pine in the county, but hardwood, hemlock and cedar lumbering is a heavy industry on Maple river, Carp river, Bear creek, Birch, Pickard and Crooked lakes, also along the line of the Grand Rapids & Indiana Railroad. Tanbark is also shipped in large quantities. Lime, lumber, handles, wood pulp, ties, posts, telegraph poles, woodenware and leather are shipped in large quantities by rail and by vessel. The Grand Rapids & Indiana Railroad crosses the county on its way to Mackinac, and a branch extends from Petoskey to Harbor Springs. The Chicago & West Michigan railroad now terminates at Petoskey but will eventually run to the Straits of Mackinac. It connects Emmet county with Charlevoix, Bellaire, Elk Rapids and Traverse City, besides giving through fast trains to Grand Rapids, Detroit and Chicago.

Little Traverse bay and the resorts along its banks, have become famous, owing to wonderful climatic advantages. Petoskey, Bay View, Wequetonsing, Harbor Springs and Harbor Point, are thronged every season with tourists in search of health or pleasure, and the Summer Assembly and Summer University at Bay View is now second alone to Chautauqua, both in attendance and the extent of its programs and curriculum.

GENESEE COUNTY.

Genesee county was organized in 1836. It is bounded on the north by Tuscola and Saginaw, on the east by Lapeer, on the south by Livingston and Oakland, and on the west by Shiawassee and Saginaw. It has an area of 648 square miles, and had, in 1890, a population of 39,430. Flint, a flourishing city of 9,803 inhabitants, is the county seat. The State institution for the Deaf and Dumb is located in the suburbs of this city.

The surface of the county is comparatively level, although a few townships are quite rolling. It is well watered by the Flint and Shiawassee rivers, the Thread and Swartz creeks, and by several smaller streams. Several fine water powers are found in different parts of the county. There are several inland lakes of considerable size, notably Long lake in Fenton township, which is famed for its beautiful shores, and has become during the last few years a pleasure resort of considerable prominence.

The soil of the southern townships is a sandy gravel, such as is usually found in oak openings, with a clay loam on the lower lands. The rest of the county has a clay loam with a clay subsoil in most localities. The timber remaining is mainly oak, beech, maple, elm, and basswood.

Genesee is emphatically a representative county when its grain producing qualities are taken into consideration. Corn, wheat, oats, barley, and in short any grain that can be grown in this latitude, do remarkably well with proper attention. Wheat in particular is regarded as a sure crop, and will average one year with another, 25 bushels to the acre. The cultivation of fruit has been well tested. Apples are grown and shipped in large quantities. Few peaches are raised, but grapes, cherries, and all sorts of berries grow to great perfection.

There are no government or State lands of any description in the market. Even the pine stump lands have been improved, and are held at from $15 to $25 per acre. Improved farms range from $30 to $100. The roads of the county are all good, the long-constructed State roads being no better than the ordinary township roads.

Snow falls in December, and sleighing often lasts two months. The ground freezes to an average depth of ten inches. Plowing usually begins by April 1.

The country and village schools are among the finest in the State. The high school at Flint is one of the few schools from which students are admitted to the University without further examination, and has a very large resident and non-resident attendance.

Lumbering, once the principal industry, is looked upon as a thing of the past, although some logs are now cut in different parts of the county, and considerable sawing is yet done. Agriculture and manufacturing are now the recognized industries. Among its many manufactories are to be noticed extensive wagon works, woolen and cotton mills, charcoal works, machine shops, foundries, flouring mills, shoe, cigar, pickle, and agricultural implement factories, all of which employ a large number of men. Labor is in fair demand on farms during the summer season; but there is usually an over supply of this commodity during the winter months.

The Flint & Pere Marquette, its Otter Lake division, the Detroit & Milwaukee, and the Chicago & Grand Trunk railroads furnish the outlets for the marketable productions of this county.

Genesee is rapidly becoming one of the wealthies counties in the State, and is receiving large accessions to its population annually from all points of the compass.

The following is from Hon. Josiah W. Begole, Ex-Governor of Michigan:

Flint Mich., May 3, 1893.

I am just in receipt of your circular asking me to give you the present history of Genesee county. In reply will say that I have carefully compared the old compilation of Genesee county with its present condition. Her present and past condition is and has been a flattering one. Large improvements have been made in most everything that pertains to Genesee county. Her cities, towns, and villages are all growing and prosperous. There are no more woods in our county except small patches that the most of our farmers have left for wood lots; all of our lands are improved. We have but few small lakes and no swamps. Nearly all is good land and that is the greatest source of our prosperity. We have three good saw-mills now running successfully, in Flint. The logs are mostly brought from the north part of the State. There is but very little rolling land in our county and good drainage everywhere. In addition to those mentioned in the old compilation we have four large and prosperous carriage and wagon factories in Flint, three of which I know turn out one thousand dollars worth of goods each and every day. I came to this town when it was an unbroken wilderness, in the summer of 1836, the year that both the State and county were organized, though the State was not received into the grand union of states until in the winter of 1837. I have the honor to be

Truly yours,
JOSIAH W. BEGOLE.

GLADWIN COUNTY.

BY EUGENE FOSTER, GLADWIN.

Gladwin county was organized in 1875. It is bounded on the north by Roscommon and Ogemaw, on the east by Bay, on the south by Midland, and on the west by Clare. It has an area of 504 square miles, and had a population in 1890 of 4,208. Gladwin, a village of about 100 inhabitants, is the county seat.

The eastern and southern portions of the county are level, while the northern and western parts are quite rolling. The county is well watered by the Tittabawassee, Molasses, Tobacco, and Cedar rivers and their smaller tributaries. There are a number of available water powers on the above streams. Good arable land is found throughout the entire county, although in the northwestern corner and in the eastern center of the county the soil is rather light. The timber is pine, hemlock, cedar, oak, ash, elm, beech, maple, basswood, ironwood, poplar, wild cherry, and butternut. All sorts of crops are raised successfully. The soil is especially well adapted to the raising of clover and timothy. Fruit growing is as yet in its infancy; all kinds of berries, however are found in abundance. The cost of clearing averages from $10 to $20 per acre, with a good market for wood.

There are no government lands in the market, but there were subject to entry January 1, 1893, 392 acres of State swamp, 775 acres of primary school, and some Flint & Pere Marquette railroad lands. Unimproved lands are held at from $5 to $10 per acre. There are large tracts of stump land that can be had at a low figure, and are said to be admirably adapted to farming. A State road runs from Midland through this county to Houghton lake, and thence to Grand Traverse. There is also a State road from Loomis to Gladwin, and one from Coleman to Gladwin. The other roads of the county are mainly new.

Snow falls by December 1 and may last until April 1. Every alternate winter less snow falls, and the ground freezes to some depth. Some winter potatoes will keep in the patch.

The schools are good, every locality supplied. Lumbering is the principal industry and labor is always in good demand in the camps, wages ranging from $20 to $25 per month with board. Lands are cheap and productive, society good, and the prospect of a rapid growth very favorable. A logging road has been built by the Flint & Pere Marquette Railroad company, extending from Coleman a short distance into Gladwin county. It will eventually reach Gladwin.

The county is rapidly developing and is destined to be one of the most prosperous counties in the State.

GOGEBIC COUNTY.

BY W. H. DOYLE, IRONWOOD.

Gogebic county was organized in 1887. It is the most northwesterly county in the State, and is bounded on the north by Lake Superior and Ontonagon county, on the east by Iron county, and on the west and south by the state of Wisconsin. Bessemer is the county seat. It has a population of 2,500. Ironwood is the principal city. Its population is over 10,000. The other principal settlements in the county are at Wakefield, Watersmeet and Marenisco. Previous to 1885 there was no settlement in the territory comprising the county, outside the few miners who were then engaged in exploring for iron ore, and whose efforts were crowned by the development of the largest iron mine in the world and a number of the largest in the country.

The surface of the county is rolling, several ranges of mineral bearing hills extending through it from east to west. The lowlands are easily reclaimable, and many of the swamps dry up as the timber is cut. There are numerous lakes and rivers in the county, many of which afford splendid opportunities for the development of water power, either for direct use or generating electrical energy. Although not as rich in pine as most counties in the upper peninsula, Gogebic is possessed of vast timber resources. Sugar and bird's-eye maple, birch, bass, ash, spruce, cedar, and hemlock exist in great abundance. The soil varies, but in many portions of the county it is a heavy loam with a clay subsoil.

The county is penetrated by three railroads; the Duluth, South Shore & Atlantic; the Milwaukee, Lake Shore & Western, and the Wisconsin Central, now under lease to and a part of the Northern Pacific system. The nearest lake port is Ashland, Wis., located about forty miles from Ironwood and forty-six miles from Bessemer. The railroad companies enjoy a very lucrative traffic in carrying the iron ore produced in the county to Ashland whence it is carried in ships to the furnaces at Milwaukee and Chicago, and to Cleveland for reshipment to Pittsburg and the other iron manufacturing points in Pennsylvania and Ohio.

The principal industries of the county are mining and lumbering, although manufacturing is receiving great encouragement and growing to be an industry of considerable importance. The greatest iron mine in the world, the Norrie, which has, during the past few years, received great attention from mining and iron men is located at Ironwood. There are also a number of other large iron mines at Ironwood, Bessemer and Wakefield, and excellent indications of the existence of ore at points in the vicinity of Watersmeet and Marenisco, and about twelve miles southeast of Lake Gogebic. There has been some exploring for silver in the vicinity of Wakefield and south of Bessemer. There is a large outcropping of galena near Marenisco, indications of the existence of tin and cobalt near Lake Gogebic, and numerous veins of copper bearing rock north of the iron range, but no systematic effort has ever been made to ascertain whether those minerals exist in paying quantities. There are also indications of the existence of an iron range in the southern part of the county. The Gogebic range extends through the county from the Montreal river on the west to Lake Gogebic, a distance of over thirty miles. Mining is conducted with considerable profit on nearly every forty acre tract along the range from the Montreal river to several miles east of Wakefield, a distance of about fifteen miles. The explorations further east give promise of developing into good mines. The county consequently offers excellent inducements to those who wish to explore. The owners of the land will extend mining privilege or "option" to any company offering to conduct exploratory operations, on their agreeing to pursue the same in good faith and energetically, and by paying a royalty on all ore mined. It was on agreement similar to this that nearly all the large mines in the county were explored and developed. A party of men desirous of speculating in a mining venture in a small way, can thus find plenty of opportunities in Gogebic county. Every 40-acre tract along the range may not turn out to be productive of ore in paying quantities, but where a few men organize a company or copartnership for the purpose they will find that five or ten thousand dollars will go a long way toward exploring a property. When it is considered that previous to the opening of the great mines here, all the provisions for the explorers had to be carried into the county on the backs of men, and that now the county is traversed by several railroads, it can be seen how economically exploratory operations can be conducted now in comparison to a few years ago. Still, the chances are that as many great mines will be developed in the future as in the past. The six mines located within the corporate limits of the city of Ironwood were assessed last year at over six million dollars or less than one-half their value. The development of such immense wealth in a few years is only an indication of the untold wealth that still remains undisturbed in the earth, awaiting the expenditure of capital for its revelation to the world.

Lake Gogebic in this county is a veritable nature's sanitarium. This lake is twelve miles distant and 900 feet above the waters of Lake Superior. It is fifteen miles long and one and one-half to three miles wide, and it is generally conceded to afford the best black bass fishing known anywhere. Brook trout are found in tributary streams, and at certain seasons of the year very large brook trout are caught in the open lake. Gogebic lake is a favorite resort for those suffering from hay fever or throat and lung troubles. The hotel and cottages furnish first class accommodations for 100 guests. At the lake is a fine fleet of boats and a steam yacht. The trout fishing near Watersmeet is also very fine. Both places are reached by the Milwaukee, Lake Shore & Western.

Timber lands are sold at from $5 to $12 per acre. Within a radius of one mile of the center of Ironwood land is valued at from $50 to $100 per acre. Within two or three miles of the mines it is held at about $25 per acre.

Ironwood and Bessemer, although young towns, are places of considerable activity. The business places in both cities are substantial brick and frame structures. Both cities have excellent systems of water-works, and electric light plants. The county buildings in Bessemer cost $50,000. The large mines in the vicinity of the place furnish employment for a great many men.

Among the more important objects of interest in Ironwood besides its great mines are the electric street railway, several saw mills, chair factory, and an arc lamp manufactory. Its system of water-works cost nearly $500,000, and it has an excellent paid fire department.

The assessed valuation of city property is about $7,000,000. The monthly pay roll of mining and other companies is over $250,000. It has seven school houses, thirteen churches, fifteen secret and benevolent societies, and three banks. The business houses are nearly all of brick and brown sandstone. The hotels are commodious and well patronized. Numerous visitors from the large cities patronize them during the summer months. A party of capitalists have given a bond of $50,000 to commence the erection of a large furnace before July 1. There are few cities in Michigan that can boast of more rapid progress or greater prosperity than Ironwood.

The accompanying table shows the amount of iron ore shipped from the mines of Gogebic county up to the close of 1892. The importance of the mining business can easily be seen from the fact that the average monthly pay roll for 1892 at the Norrie mine was $73,486.

30

Shipment of ore from Gogebic county.

Name of mine.	Tons.		Name of mine.	Tons.	
	1892.	Total.		1892.	Total.
Ashland, Ironwood	233,490	1,611,352	Jack Pot, Bessemer	3,960	7,338
Aurora, Ironwood	319,481	1,284,390	Imperial, Bessemer	8,840	36,768
Norrie, Ironwood	985,044	4,095,451	Lowell, Bessemer		58,068
Pabst, Ironwood	113,245	620,971	Ruby, Bessemer		86,525
Newport, Ironwood	165,962	610,029	Mikado, Wakefield	* 12,000	12,000
Davis, Ironwood	21,727	25,221	Comet, Wakefield	54,778	67,804
Colby and Tilden, Bessemer	304,240	1,549,680	Sparta, Wakefield	2,912	2,912
Eureka, Bessemer	10,685	48,336	Sunday Lake, Wakefield	56,046	157,463
Anvil, Bessemer	41,807	169,321	Brotherton, Wakefield	130,986	382,553
Palms, Bessemer	100,350	229,515	Iron Chief, Wakefield		12,300

* Amount produced but not shipped.

GRAND TRAVERSE COUNTY.

Grand Traverse county was organized in 1851. It is bounded on the north by Leelanaw and Traverse bay, on the east by Kalkaska, on the south by Wexford, and on the west by Benzie. It has an area of 612 square miles, and had a population in 1890 of 13,355. Traverse city, situated at the head of Grand Traverse bay, a town of 4,353 inhabitants, is the county seat. The Northern Asylum for the Insane is beautifully located near the city.

At least two-thirds of the county is quite level, while the remaining third is gently rolling, with a hilly tendency along the shores of the bay and inland lakes. Pine plains are quite extensive along the Boardman river, and cedar swamps, generally reclaimable, traversed by streams of running water, are found in nearly every township. There is good water power on the Boardman river which is utilized at Traverse City. Half a dozen or more smaller streams furnish power for local saw and grist mills.

The soil is principally a sandy loam. There are, however, some tracts of clay and clay loam. The soil of the table land and its declivities is boulder drift of great thickness, in some places being fifty feet in depth, having the same mineral characteristics as that of the surface, except as it is modified by the influence of vegetation and the elements. The timber is mainly sugar maple, beech, basswood, elm, hemlock, pine, and cedar. Wheat, corn, oats, potatoes, clover, timothy, and all varieties of roots do well in this county. Corn in particular does much better than would be expected in so high a latitude.

Grand Traverse is a great fruit county. Apples and grapes are raised on all but the swamp lands, but the more tender varieties of apples need the protection of the bay or the more elevated situations. Pears, peaches, plums and cherries, are very successful when proper attention is paid to the selection of the site. Thousands of bushels of huckleberries grow on the pine plains, while all other varieties of berries are perfectly at home, either in the field or garden. The famous Parmalee fruit farm on the peninsula is widely known for its great productiveness. As fine peaches and cherries as can be found in Michigan are grown on this farm, and, in fact, all over the peninsula. There is a great demand for the fruit of this county in the Chicago market. The cost of clearing will average $20 per acre, on the heaviest timbered land with a fair market on the bay shore.

There are 3,120 acres of land subject to sale or entry. Good unimproved lands, other than government or State, are held at from $5 to $8 per acre. "Stump lands" have not been in great demand, and can be bought at from fifty cents to $5 per acre, while improved farms bring from $15 to $60 per acre.

A State road runs from Traverse City to Elk Rapids, thence northward to Charlevoix and Petoskey. Another runs southeasterly to Houghton lake. The roads may be said to be in a fair condition for so new a county. Snow falls in November to an average depth of two and one-half feet. The ground usually freezes but little, often not at all. Plowing usually begins in April. The schools are quite numerous, and are very prosperous considering the newness of the county. In some districts the people have voted a tax upon themselves for school purposes greater than all other taxes combined. Lumbering is the principal industry, and labor is in good demand at fair prices. Agriculture and fruit-raising are advancing rapidly, and a speedy development of the resources of the county is near at hand.

There are a number of pleasure resorts along the bays. Traverse City, Elk Rapids, and Old Mission are very popular during the summer season. The Grand Rapids and Indiana railroad has a branch from Walton to Traverse City. The Chicago and West Michigan railroad traverses the county passing through Traverse City thence to Charlevoix. Grand Traverse has great shipping facilities. Steamers connect Traverse City with Chicago, Milwaukee, etc., and a shore line touches at all points of interest between Traverse City and Mackinac.

GRATIOT COUNTY.

Gratiot was organized in 1855. It is bounded on the north by Isabella and Midland, on the east by Saginaw, on the south by Clinton, and on the west by Montcalm. It has an area of 576 square miles, and has a population of 28,668. Ithaca, a town of 1,627 inhabitants, is the county seat. The eastern portion of the county is generally level while the western portion is more rolling.

It is watered by the Pine, Maple and Bad rivers, and a few smaller streams, with available water power on the Pine only. The soil is a rich sand and gravelly loam, mixed with a clay loam, generally on a clay subsoil. The prevailing varieties of timber are oak, ash, maple, basswood, and elm.

Wheat is the principal crop although corn, oats, potatoes, and grass find a soil admirably adapted to their growth. The apples, pears, and plums grown in this county are unusually fine. Peaches are not always a sure crop, though in localities very fine peaches have been raised in favorable seasons.

The cost of clearing averages $20 per acre. There is a market for wood in the villages along the railroad, stove wood bringing from $1 to $1.25 per cord, and four foot wood from $1 to $1.75. There is no government lands remaining unsold. There are 640 acres of land subject to sale or entry. There are unimproved lands in the market which can be had at from $8 to $15 per acre, according to their distance from the railroads. There are also large tracts of "stump lands" which are held at from $3 to $10 per acre. Wheat is generally successful on these lands. Improved farms range from $20 to $60 per acre, according to location. A State road runs from St. Johns in Clinton county, through Ithaca to St. Louis. Another one extends from Ovid, through the eastern part of the county to St. Charles, and still another runs through the western part, from Hubbardston to Mt. Pleasant. The highways generally are in a fair condition.

Snow falls in December, and averages two feet in depth. The ground generally freezes to a considerable depth. Plowing begins by April 1.

The public schools are in a prosperous condition. The country schools are quite numerous, and the graded schools of the villages are very fine. Lumbering in hard wood is engaged in somewhat extensively. Labor is in good demand on farms, in clearing lands, and in saw mills, etc.

The mineral springs at St. Louis have a world wide reputation and an extensive patronage at all seasons of the year. A fine sanitarium is connected with the mineral springs.

The D. L. & N. & S. R. R. traverses the county from east to west, and the T., A. A. & N. M. R. R., running northwest also passes through the county.

HOUGHTON COUNTY.

BY B. T. JUDKINS, HOUGHTON, MICH.

Houghton county is situated in almost the extreme northern portion of the upper peninsula of the State, the only county north of it being Keweenaw. It is bounded on the west and northwest by Lake Superior and on the east by Keweenaw bay. It had a population, in 1890, of 35,389.

Houghton, the county seat, is situated on the southerly shore of Portage lake, a narrow sheet of water which cuts Keweenaw Point, as it is called, in two, and by its canals, which are now owned by the general government, connects on the northwest with Lake Superior and on the southeast with Keweenaw bay forming direct water communication west with the head of Lake Superior and east also with Lake Superior and the remainder of the great chain of lakes. It is the terminus of the Houghton branch of the Duluth, South Shore & Atlantic railroad and is also the terminus of the Mineral Range railroad which communicates with the towns north of it. Here is situated the Michigan Mining School, an institution fostered by the State and becoming widely known as a seat of learning in its specialty, that of mine engineering and its several branches. Houghton county is noted as a particularly healthy locality; the air is dry and clear and although its winters are cold such is the dryness of the atmosphere that it is felt far less than in portions of the country farther south. In summer though the days are sometimes warm, the atmosphere is clear and the nights are always cool and invigorating. Its several principal towns, Houghton, Hancock, Calumet, Red Jacket and Lake Linden, all have complete water systems and good drainage, making the county particularly healthy. The business of the county is largely given up to that of mining and kindred industries. The copper range passes through it from a southwesterly to a northeasterly direction, and along the range are situated within its territory the Atlantic, Huron, Quincy, Franklin, Osceola, Tamarack, Calumet and Hecla, Tamarack Junior, Centennial, Wolverine and Kearsarge mines; making it more noted as a copper producing district than any other spot in the world. Indeed, the Tamarack, Quincy, and Calumet and Hecla mines are noted the world over.

Each year more and more attention is given to agriculture. The soil is of the best and all of the hardier crops, such as oats, wheat, potatoes, etc., do exceedingly well. Up to date very little attention has been given to wheat owing to the limited market, but as the yield is from 25 to 45 bushels per acre more wheat will be grown each year. The season is usually long enough to grow garden truck which matures very rapidly. Small fruits, particularly strawberries, yield very abundantly.

Although hundreds of acres of timber have been cut off there are still thousands of acres of as fine timber standing as are to be found anywhere in the world. It largely consists of pine, maple, Spruce, Hemlock, Birch, etc., much of it being easy of access.

With the extension of our manufacturing enterprises throughout the country Houghton county is bound to attract attention from those looking for a suitable locality to settle as its advantages are numerous, having as it does both rail and water communicaction, pure water, schools that are not to be excelled any where in the State, and a climate which enables a man to do a larger day's work than a locality situated farther south.

Houghton county is one of the wealthiest in the State, standing as it does third in point of valuation.

HILLSDALE COUNTY.

Hillsdale county was organized in 1835. It is bounded on the north by Jackson and Calhoun, on the east by Lenawee, on the south by Ohio, and on the west by Branch. It has an area of 594 square miles, and had a population, in 1890, of 30,660. Hillsdale, a fine town of 3,915 inhabitants, is the county seat. The general surface of the county is undulating, yet in no place is it so hilly as to interfere with easy cultivation. It is well watered, being the source of the following rivers: Raisin, St. Joseph, Little St. Joseph, Kalamazoo, Tiffin, and Grand, and will average two small lakes to each of the eighteen townships. There are many small water powers, but none sufficient for heavy manufacturing. The soil of the north half is a gravelly loam mixed with clay, with a gravel and clay subsoil. That of the south half is clay and clay loam, with clay subsoil. The timber is of the following varieties: Oak, hickory, burr oak, black walnut, ash, basswood, maple, beech, white wood, elm, cherry, and tamarack. The principal crops are wheat, corn, potatoes, and grass. All crops usually found in this latitude are successfully grown. Fruit growing has been well tested by a long experience. Apples, peaches, pears, and the smaller fruits seldom fail of fine crops. Shipping is confined principally to apples, although the drying industry has become a considerable one within the last few years. The cost of clearing will average $15 per acre, with excellent wood markets on every hand. No government or State lands of any description is in the market. But very little unimproved land can be had at any price. Improved farms range from $30 to $100 per acre.

The roads of the county are uniformly good. The seasons are of a good length. Snow falls from November 20 to December 15, to an average depth of a foot. When no snow falls, the ground freezes to the depth of a foot and a half. Plowing frequently begins by March 20. The schools all rank high. There are at least ten graded schools in the county. Hillsdale college at Hillsdale is one of the largest educational institutions in the State. Agriculture is the main industry. Cheese making is also an important enterprise. There is a good demand for labor on farms by the year, and particularly from early spring until after harvest. The Michigan Southern, its Lansing branch, the Fort Wayne & Jackson, and the Detroit, Hillsdale & Southwestern railroads cross the county in different directions. Few if any counties in the State surpass Hillsdale in privileges of markets, railroads, schools, churches, and all of the surroundings that make a locality a desirable residence.

HURON COUNTY.

BY FRANK W. HUBBARD.

The principal industries of the county of Huron are agriculture, and the manufacture of lumber, salt, grindstones, scythe stones, lime, cement, and staves and heading, and the mining of coal and quarrying stone. The agricultural products are wheat, rye, oats, barley, hay and clover seed, potatoes, carrots, turnips and mangels, and all kinds of orchard fruits particularly apples and plums, which thrive better and yield more abundantly than in any other county in the State. This county has an average yield of eighteen bushels of wheat to the acre, many fields where properly drained yielding from 30 to 45 bushels. There were shipped from this county last year over 80,000 barrels of apples, notwithstanding the fact that most of the orchards are young, having nearly all been destroyed by the fire of 1881. Plums are a certain crop and frequently yield 300 bushels per acre selling in our home markets at about $2.00 per bushel.

The county is bounded by water, navigable for large boats, on three sides, by Saginaw bay on the west and Lake Huron on the north and east, which results in three weeks later autumn and frosts than occur a hundred miles south of it. The ice in the lakes results in a later spring and accounts for the exceptionally fine fruit, as it delays the budding until after danger of frosts have passed. The land is not hilly but has a gradual slope from the center to the lakes being about 175 feet above the level of the lakes in the center, affording fine facilities for drainage with little artificial help.

Originally the timber was diversified, consisting of maple, beech, oak, elm, ash, hemlock, pine, and cedar. The eastern part of the county was swept over by the fire of 1881, leaving but little green timber, but there is still considerable in the western part. The pine has been principally cut though there is sufficient pine, hemlock, and cedar for home consumption. There are probably 50,000 acres of green timber in the county. There are about 150,000 acres of improved land in the county worth on an average about $30 per acre, and about 250,000 acres of unimproved land worth from $10 to $15 per acre according to location.

This county is not excelled in America as a grass county.. Two tons per acre is an average yield of hay. Timothy and clover appear to seed themselves as they grow abundantly wherever the fire has killed the timber. The soil is usually a clay loam. The burnt timber lands can be cleared for from $5 to $10 per acre and when cleared leave no stumps. Pine stumps in this clay soil burn out and leave no roots. The manufactures of the county are at present limited to salt, lumber, grindstones, scythe stones, staves and heading, lime and cement, though there is a fine opportunity for many other industries. Salt is manufactured at Caseville, Port Hope, and Sand Beech to the extent of about 50,000 barrels per annum. Of late years the lumber manufactured is limited to about ten or twelve million feet per year. There are two grindstone quarries a Grindstone City, employing about three hundred men, paying good wages. At Bayport the stone and lime quarries employ about one hundred men. At Sebewaing are two coal mines employing about one hundred and fifty men and producing about 600 tons of fine bituminous coal daily.

The streams of the county are from 25 to 30 miles long, rising near the center and, with a gradual fall of ten feet to the mile, empty into Saginaw Bay and Lake Huron. They are Cass river. Pinnebog river, Pigeon river, Willow creek, Bird creek and Sebewaing river. There is no water power of any consequence. The chief villages are Bad Axe, the county seat, Sebewaing and Sand Beach with about 1,200 population each. The county has a population of over 30,000. There are large fisheries at Port Austin and Sand Beech, but no large vessel interests. The markets are exceptionally good. With deep water around three sides of the county, connecting with all eastern lake ports, and four railroads intersecting every part of the county, freight rates are very reasonable. Bad Axe has two railroads and there are one hundred miles of railroad in the county.

There are over fifty churches in the county, so located as to afford all an opportunity to worship according to their creed, the churches being of nearly all denominations. There are 110 schools in the county and but few are so situated but what the schools are convenient for them.

The wages for farm labor run from one dollar to a dollar and a half per day, or from eighteen to twenty-five dollars per month, and board. Skilled labor commands from $2.50 to $5 per day. The great lakes abound with all kinds of fish. The game of the county consists of deer, bears, partridges, ducks and quail. The birds are particularly plentiful.

SAND BEACH VILLAGE.

BY A. H. BROWNE.

The village of Sand Beach, the most important town in Huron county, stands well in the lead of being classified among the cities of Michigan at no distant day. Nature has endowed it with all that is necessary to make it deserving of the flattering recognition it receives. Sand Beach is situated 120 miles from Detroit on the shore of Lake Huron. The government harbor of refuge, costing $2,000,000, lies at the foot of the town and is a haven for all shipping on the great lakes. The village slopes back from the town by a system of terraces, the town proper being located on an elevation that affords the finest natural drainage in the world. A number of industries have already sought this place and are dispensing to the world the necessities of life. Sand Beach is the terminus of that division of the F. & P. M. railroad which bears its name, and the water and railroad privileges provide it with the best shipping facilities of any town in Michigan. A fine system of water works offers excellent fire protection, as well as water for ordinary use. Its inducements to manufacturing industries are unsurpassed, a $10,000 bonus now awaiting some enterprising manufacturer. Within the last two years one of the finest mineral waters in the country has been discovered at this place, and its large bath house is daily visited by anxious patients who hesitate not in proclaiming the efficacy of the waters.

The resources of this thriving town are without equal, and its 1,500 inhabitants are enterprising and progressive. The climate of this part of Michigan is perfect, and the beauty of the town, coupled with this advantage, makes it a healthful resort, and hundreds of tourists find their way here in summer.

INGHAM COUNTY.

Ingham county was organized in 1838. It is bounded on the north by Clinton and Shiawassee, on the east by Livingston, on the south by Jackson, and on the west by Eaton. It has an area of 576 square miles, and had a population in 1890 of 37,666. Mason, a town of 1,875 inhabitants, is the county seat. Lansing, the capital of the State, a city of 18,000 inhabitants, is located in the northwestern part of the county. The State School for the Blind, the Industrial School for Boys, and the State Agricultural College, are also located in and about Lansing.

The surface of the country is gently rolling, just enough so to furnish fair drainage. It is watered mainly by the Cedar river, although the Grand enters the county on its western border and flows through Lansing township and city. There are good water powers at Lansing on the Grand and at Okemos on the Cedar rivers. The soil on the original oak openings is somewhat sandy, while on the timbered lands it is a clay or black loam, with clay subsoil. The prevailing varieties of timber are beech, maple, ash, oak, elm, basswood, and tamarack. Wheat is the staple crop, although the soil of this county is well adapted to grass, corn and oats. In fact all grains and vegetables do well, with the exception of barley. All fruits usually raised in this latitude are found in Ingham county. Large quantities of apples are annually shipped to the Chicago market.

The cost of clearing ranges from $10 to $20 per acre, with good wood markets in every direction. There are no government or State lands in the market, with the

SAND BEACH VILLAGE.

SAND BEACH HARBOR OF REFUGE.

COSTING $2,000,000.

exception of 80 acres of school land which was subject to entry 1890. The timbered or wood lands are held by the owners of improved farms for the timber, and are valued at from $10 to $25 per acre. There are two State roads which were built many years ago, and which are kept in good order. The ground freezes by Nov. 15, and remains frozen until April 1. Snow falls about December 1, but the sleighing is by no means continuous. Spring work generally commences by April 1. The schools are all good—those of the villages and larger towns particularly so. At Lansing there is a fine high school which would be a credit to any city in the land. The principal industries are agriculture and manufacturing. Lansing has of late become quite a manufacturing city. There are extensive agricultural implement and engine works at this place, while at Williamston and Webberville the manufacture of barrel heading, staves, etc., is extensively engaged in. Common labor is in fair demand, particularly during the warm seasons.

The Chicago & Grand Trunk Railroad, Detroit, Lansing & Northern, Jackson, Lansing & Saginaw, Lansing branch of the Michigan Southern, and the Grand Rapids branch of the Michigan Central, all traverse the county in different directions, placing every township in the county within easy reach of the best markets.

IONIA COUNTY.

BY E. J. WRIGHT, OF IONIA.

Ionia county was organized by the territorial legislature in 1831, is bounded north by Montcalm, east by Clinton, south by Eaton and Barry and west by Kent. It appreciates its friendly neighbors, but is as independent of the outside world as any community of equal size. Its lands are watered by many streams, and its undulating surface is richly productive. Its rivers furnish valuable water power at several points. The native fish of the Grand, Maple and Flat rivers and their tributaries, and of several small lakes, have been reinforced within the last five years by 1,500,000 wall-eyed pike, 500,000 brook trout, 20,000 eels and 1,000 carp, supplied by the State Fish Commissioner and planted by the Ionia County Fishing Club and others, and furnish rare sport and valuable food products.

No finer farms than those of Ionia county can be found in the State. Their value is attested by the many handsome farm residences and fine farm buildings. The price of farming lands range from $30 to $75 with buildings, and $25 to $40 without, and there are numerous highly cultivated farms that would bring $100 per acre if they were open to purchase. Wheat, corn, oats, barley, hay, potatoes, rutabagas, turnips, beets, and other cereals and roots yield abundant crops. The value of the fruit crop is large, and the many advantages of both soil and climate for fruit production are receiving constanaly increasing recognition. Apples, pears, grapes, plums and other fruits grow to a degree of perfection, and Ionia strawberries have no superiors and few equals. Ionia county cattle, horses, sheep and swine are notable among the exhibits at State and district fairs, and are in wide demand by breeders. The high grade wool is an important and valuable product. Though the land is principally cleared, there is considerable timber still standing, oak, maple and beech predominating. The pioneers of the county are largely from western New York. Sturdy men possessing enterprise, intelligence and knowledge of affairs, and women of many virtues. They early took a prominent part in the affairs of the territory, and with the growth and advancement of the State to which they contributed largely, they and their descendants and successors have received merited recognition. Those who are wise enough or sufficiently fortunate to cast their lot among the people of Ionia county find themselves in the midst of churches presided over by learned and eloquent pastors, schools that rank as the best in the State, and social advantages rivaling those of the much older eastern states. Among such a people commerce is well sustained. The stores of the county metropolis—Ionia—as well as of its sister city—Belding—and the numerous thriving villages about the county, are as well supplied as those of the larger cities. The thrift of the people is made evident by the strong banks to be found at Ionia, Portland and Belding as well as in smaller communities. The value of Ionia farms is attested by the recognized fact that these banks are always well supplied with farmer's money, which they loan with safely conservative liberality in aid of legitimate enterprises.

The handsome city of Ionia (population nearly 6,000), is the county seat. Several important and well established manufacturing establishments are located in this city, notably the D. L. & N. car shops, the wagon works, furniture, clothing and cigar factories, pottery and pickling works. A fine creamery gives added facilities for the disposition of an important farm product. The State House of Correction and the Asylum for Dangerous and Criminal Insane are located just outside the city limits. Ionia has good reason to be proud of its handsome Court House, one of the best in the State.

The infant city of Belding (population 3,000) was a commons less than a half a score of years ago. Silk manufacturing made it what it is, and today it not only has two of the most important silk factories in the country, but prosperous furniture, casket, fire extinguisher, basket and paper box factories, and is the manufacturing center of the county and the wonder of the State. There are good roads about the county and shipping facilities are ample and rates advantageous. The main line, the western division and the Stanton branch of the Detroit, Lansing & Northern Railroad and the Detroit, Grand Haven & Milwaukee Railroad, traverse the county, all but the first passing through the city of Ionia.

The advantages of settlement in Ionia county are numerous. Taxation is not burdensome, a two mill tax more than sufficing for all county purposes, while township taxes are proportionately light, and municipal taxes below the average. The county is free from debt and the superior system of schools has been established and maintained without incurring any indebtedness worth consideration. The municipal indebtedness reported in the last census was confined to three townships, $4,800; one village, $2,000; and the city of Ionia. $47,000, of which $30,000 is the bonded indebtedness incurred several years ago for a system of water-works worth several times the amount of the bonds.

Ionia is a county of beautiful homes, productive farms, excellent shipping facilities and superior educational and social advantages, and has within its borders enough prosperous communities engaged in manufactures and commerce to give to the farmer a valuable home market, and to both capital and labor remunerative employment.

IOSCO COUNTY.

Iosco county was organized in 1857. It is bounded on the north by Alcona, on the east by Lake Huron, on the south by Arenac (the new county formed from the north part of Bay), and on the west by Ogemaw. It has an area of 590 square miles. and had a population in 1890 of 15,224. Tawas City, a town of 1,544 inhabitants, is the county seat. The surface of the county is gently rolling, and is watered by the Au Sable, the Au Gres, the Tawas, and numerous creeks, inland lakes and spring brooks. Most of these streams afford a fair water power. There is considerable swamp land timbered with cedar or ash, nearly all of which is reclaimable. About one-tenth of the county is a sandy plain. On the uplands the soil is mostly a sandy loam with clay subsoil. There is very little stiff clay. On the lowlands the soil is entirely muck with clay or sand subsoil. On the plains the soil is very light, but is well adapted to grazing purposes. The timber is pine, hemlock, beech, maple, black and white ash, cedar, and some tamarack.

On the tillable lands, wheat, oats, rye, peas, beans, potatoes, etc., are grown very successfully. Rye and grass do well on the sand plains. Potatoes yield from 100 to 400, and onions from 400 to 600 bushels to the acre. All the hardier varieties of apples do well, and plums and cherries grow to great perfection, no trouble being experienced from insects. The home markets consume all the fruit that has yet been produced in this county.

It costs about $20 per acre to clear the timbered lands, with fair wood markets at the villages along the Tawas and Bay County railroad, hard wood averaging $2.50 per cord. There is 51,800 acres of land subject to sale or entry. Good unimproved lands, with all of the timber standing, excepting the pine, can be had at from $3 to $10 per acre. There are also thousands of acres of "burnt lands" of good quality of soil, on which all the timber has been destroyed. which are held at from $3 to $5 per acre. The "stump lands" from which white pine has been cut are good farming lands, and the prices range as above, while the stump lands from which the Norway pine alone has been cut are considered as second rate, and of no value for farming purposes. The Iosco and Ogemaw State road runs through the center of the county from east to west, and connects Tawas City with West Branch. The highways generally are new, but quite numerous, and the county is well opened up by them.

Snow falls by November 15, and attains an average depth of 12 inches. The ground seldom freezes more than eight inches, unless the snow fall is light. Plowing begins by April 15.

The public schools, particularly those along the shore, are in a good condition, great care being taken that a high standard shall be maintained.

Lumbering is the main industry. Ties, telegraph poles and posts are cut in large quantities. The manufacture of salt and plaster is also extensively engaged in. Labor is in good demand, and the demand will increase as the county develops. The Tawas and Bay County Railroad crosses the county, connecting Tawas with the Mackinac division of the Michigan Central Railroad. The Bay City and Alpena Railroad enters the southwest corner of the county and traverses the entire length of the county, passing out of the northeast corner. The county has forty miles of coast line and several good harbors. During the season of navigation there is a large amount of shipping to and from these shore towns, steamers from Bay city and Alpena arriving daily.

IRON COUNTY.

BY HON. C. T. ROBERTS, CRYSTAL FALLS, MICH.

Iron county is situated in the upper peninsula of Michigan and is nearly the geographical center of the great Michigan iron belt, being bounded on the north by Houghton and Baraga counties, on the east by Marquette and Dickinson counties, on the south by the state of Wisconsin, and on the west by Ontonagon and Gogebic counties. It was organized in the year 1885 from territory taken from the counties of Marquette and Menominee. Few counties in Michigan have been endowed with resources equal in number and volume to those of Iron county. Located at an altitude of 950 feet above the level of Lake Michigan, its lofty, picturesque hills and timber clad plateaus are free from the germs of disease and obnoxious gasses that render many equally beautiful sections of Michigan undesirable habitations. Gushing from the closets of its mineral wealth, sparkle forth many fountains of crystalline water laden with mineral properties of medicinal value.

Iron County Court House.

Iron county is the haven of the invalid, a veritable sanitarium. Underlying a goodly portion of this beautiful territory is nature's hidden wealth of ores and rocks, not a little of which man's diligence has brought to light and into the world of usefulness, developing their sources in a way that would afford support, to the people of the county were they suddenly deprived of the other diversified resources. From these inexhaustible reservoirs of metallic wealth were taken and shipped to the markets in 1892, 580,620 tons of iron ore. In this connection it must also be noted that the mineral lands of Iron county have been as yet only partially explored.

Ribbing the hills whose bosoms yield this wealth of ore are vast quantities of valuable stone granite of various hues and textures, all susceptible of the highest polish. Much of the territory of this county is yet clad in nature's garment of hard woods, sugar, bird's eye and curly maple; yellow birch, and hemlock, all of which are most available, both in point of price and transportation facilities, for the requirements of the manufacturer. A considerable amount

31

of pine is also standing in the northern portion of the county. Through these tracts of wooded land flows many streams, the Paint, Michigamme, Net, Deer, Iron, and Hemlock rivers being the larger; all of which afford ample water power facilities besides being liquid highways over which the product of the forest may be transported.

Nor is the soil of Iron county productive alone of mineral and timber wealth. Its fertile plateaus, when stripped of their natural robes of hard wood, yield rich crops of wheat, oats, potatoes, hay and garden vegetables, all of which find a ready market at good prices. No class of people are more thrifty and prosperous than Iron county's farmers. The present transportation facilities of this county are adequate for any demand, no matter how rapidly increasing, for many years to come. Two railroads, the Chicago & Northwestern and the Milwaukee & Northern, with their several branches, traverse its territory in all parts, with stations at accessible points. Its highways are numerous and well kept and a majority of its bridges are of iron.

As the retreat of the sportsman Iron county has few peers, its woods abound in game, deer, bear and wood fowl of various species; and every stream teems with speckled trout, while in some of its lakes whitefish and herring thrive, besides an abundance of fish of more common kind. The banks of the many beautiful lakes that thickly dot its rugged bosom are tempting camping grounds for the resorter, the sportsman and the health seeker.

The population of the county in 1890 was 4,432.

Crystal Falls, the county seat of Iron county, is a town of 2,500 inhabitants. It enjoys a most picturesque location and is absolutely free from the menace of disease. It is peopled by progressive inhabitants. It is a little city of metropolitan ideas, and has all modern equipments, such as electric light, water plant, etc. The high school of Crystal Falls has no superior in the State, and its many religious societies are in thrifty circumstances. Within Crystal Falls are represented nearly all the secret orders of this country, among which are several masonic orders, including a commandery of Knights Templar.

In these few paragraphs have been written only a few of the diversified resources, advantages and inducements which Iron county is extending to the manufacturer, the farmer, the capitalist, the sportsman and the health seeker. This volume might easily be devoted to the work which this page has attempted to accomplish without danger of repetition or exaggeration. All that present circumstances afford in addition, however, is the cordial commendation to all— *come and see.*

ISABELLA COUNTY.

BY HELEN E. C. BALMER.

Isabella county was organized in 1859 and is geographically the center of the lower peninsula of Michigan. Bounded on the north by Clare county, on the east by Midland, on the south by Gratiot and Montcalm and on the west by Mecosta. It has an area of 576 square miles and in 1890 a population of 18,784, being an increase of 6,625 over that of the census of 1880. The eastern and northeastern portions of the county are comparatively level. The remaining portions are rolling (affording excellent drainage), but not hilly.

The Chippewa, Salt river and many smaller streams flow through the county, and afford, together with the facilities for transportation, excellent advantages for fishing.

The soil is varied, but good, some parts being of black sandy loam, interspersed with yellow sand. The subsoil is generally of clay.

Of the different kinds of timber, in large quantities may be found maple, beech, pine, hemlock, oak, cedar, white and black ash, rock and salt elm.

The railroad facilities are good. The F. & P. M., the D. L. & N. and the F. & A. A. make good connections with all points and offer the best of accommodations for transportation.

The water is of excellent quality and in great abundance, there being no less than eleven flowing wells within a distance of eight miles.

The rapid current and fall of the Chippewa afford good opportunities for manufacturing, and its waters are now being utilized for that purpose.

31

Cost of land depends, as in all counties, upon location. Good farms can be bought for from $40 to $50 per acre, with easy terms of payment. There are about 150,000 acres of good wild land that can be made into as good farms as any in the county. These lands possess a first-class soil, and can be bought for prices ranging from three to five dollars per acre.

Wheat, corn, oats, hay and clover seed and all crops that can be grown in this latitude are to be found here. Fruits are also grown successfully. In fact Isabella county apples are obtaining a noted reputation.

Attractions to settlers are found in the opportunities for power for manufactories, unexcelled school advantages, namely, a school house in every school district, three graded schools with a high school placed upon the Normal list, the new Michigan Central Normal School, with Prof. Bellows at its head, the government Indian Industrial School and parochial school. Where can be greater attractions to the parents of those who are to be the men and women of the future?

All religious denominations are well represented, and churches are being built throughout the county, the city of Mt. Pleasant alone containing seven.

Saw mills, grist mills and factories furnish employment to many. Labor is always in good demand and well paid.

Isabella county contains the villages of Loomis, Dushville, Calkinsville, Isabella City, Blanchard and the thriving town of Shepherd, situated on the T. & A. A. Railroad, and the city of Mt. Pleasant with a population of over 3,000.

Postoffices are established throughout the county at convenient distances.

The people are mostly from the states of New York, Ohio and Indiana, with nearly every state in the union represented. They are hospitable, kind and intelligent, welcoming to their midst all who seek for a new home in the beautiful county of Isabella.

ISLE ROYAL COUNTY.

Isle Royal county was organized in 1875. The county comprises Isle Royal and the islands adjacent. It is located in the northwestern part of Lake Superior. It has an area of 252 square miles, and had a population in 1880 of 55 inhabitants. Minong, a lake port near the upper extremity of Isle Royal, is the county seat. The surface of the country is mountainous, with large-sized swamps at intervals. The land is so rocky that the soil is practically valueless. The timber is mainly a light, scrubby, bush maple, balsam, spruce and cedar. No crops or fruits have been raised on these islands. There is 21,868 acres of government and State land subject to sale or entry. The winters are six months in length, and snow falls to a depth of five feet.

What is pronounced by government engineers, and proved not only by scientific but by practical test, to be the best curbing and paving stone in the United States, superior to the Medina sandstone or any of the granites, exists in unlimited quantity on Siscowit point, Isle Royal. This stone can be laid down on the docks of any of the lake cities at a cost not much in excess of half the amount which is being paid for the paving material now being used in Chicago and other lake cities.

There are also good fishing grounds in among the islands. Steamers call at the lake ports quite frequently during the summer season.

The history of Isle Royal is somewhat traditional. It has been organized into a county, surveyed and laid off into townships. County organizations were never very prosperous or permanent. In fact its population was very transient. At some times it had none, then again fishermen and copper hunters would locate temporarily. The island does not seem to be a part of any territory. Its geological formation would indicate its origin from upheaval. Indications of copper deposits are very prominent and several attempts have been made to mine it, all of which were failures financially. What the future has in store for Isle Royal no one knows.

KALAMAZOO COUNTY, MICHIGAN.

BY FRANK LITTLE.

This is one of the best agricultural counties in the State. It is located midway between Detroit and Chicago on the line of the M. C. R. R., 140 miles by rail west from Detroit, and 139 miles east from Chicago. Kalamazoo county is bounded north by Allegan and Barry, east by Calhoun, south by St. Joseph and west by Van Buren. It comprises 16 townships, each six miles square, total area 576 square miles. Altitude above sea level 850 feet, above Lake Michigan 269 feet.

It was surveyed by U. S. government in 1829; organized in 1830, and offered for sale in 1831. By treaty stipulations the Indians vacated the county in 1833. First white settlement at Prairie Ronde in 1828. Present population estimated at 42,000, eight-tenths American.

The general surface of the county is undulating, somewhat broken along the margin of streams. General character of the soil alluvial with a stiff substratum of loam, gravel and clay in some portions. Mainly dry. About seventy-five per cent prairie and oak openings, balance heavy timbered bottoms and marsh. Native timber consists of all the varieties of oak, maple, beech, elm, hickory, black walnut, cherry and butternut. But a small portion comparatively of the original trees remain. Second growth forest trees are now maturing rapidly and will soon furnish a medium supply for timber and fuel.

Excellent transportation facilities in various directions are furnished by the Michigan Central, Grand Rapids & Indiana, Lake Shore & Michigan Southern, Chicago, Kalamazoo & Saginaw, Kalamazoo and South Haven, Michigan & Ohio, and the Grand Trunk lines.

Pure water, ample supply of good quality throughout the county secured by wells of moderate depth. The Kalamazoo river is the principal stream with a large number of tributaries, all well stocked with speckled trout. Inland lakes abound well supplied with edible fish, bass, pickerel, perch, sunfish and other varieties.

Gull Lake, in the northeastern part of the county, is a magnificent body of water nearly seven miles long, two miles wide and in places 100 feet deep. Twelve miles distant from the city of Kalamazoo. A very popular summer resort. Two steamers, sail and row boats. Excellent fishing.

Health conditions are of a high order. No climatic diseases. Cultivated and uncultivated lands vary in prices from twenty dollars to one hundred dollars per acre according to quality, character of improvements and location. No U. S., railroad or State lands for sale in the county. Soil productive, wheat, oats, corn, barley, beans, potatoes, hay, rye, apples, pears, grapes and small fruits are grown successfully. Much attention is paid to raising thoroughbred and high grade stock.

Estimated average annual product of the county. Two thousand nine hundred and ten farms averaging 110 acres each. Wheat, 1,000,000 bushels; corn, 1,700,000 bushels of ears; oats, 775,000 bushels; potatoes, 105,000 bushels; clover seed, 5,000 bushels; hay, 50,000 tons; wool, 410,000 pounds. Total stock on hand; horses, 10,800 head; cows, 8,500; sheep, 55,000; hogs, 15,000. Kalamazoo ranks second in the State for the largest number of acres in wheat.

Assessed valuation of real and personal property in 1892, $21,382,372. Real actual wealth of the county estimated to be upwards of 32,000,000 dollars.

Celery culture at Kalamazoo takes high rank as a special and important branch of agricultural industry, having grown to gigantic proportions. It is estimated that the celery gardens embrace 2,500 acres, furnishing employment to nearly 3,000 laborers, men, women and children, mostly Hollanders. Kalamazoo celery has attained a world wide reputation. It takes precedence in all the leading markets, being shipped in large quantities daily throughout the season. The annual product of celery from Kalamazoo is valued at 1,000,000 dollars. Kalamazoo, a beautiful, thriving inland city of more than 20,000 inhabitants is located near the geographical center of the county. Its broad, shady avenues, paved streets, parks, lawns, flower gardens, pure water, churches colleges, seminaries, schools, public library, electric lighting and railway, and neat comfortable residences all evince enterprise and elicit universal commendation.

Kalamazoo is noted for its varied and extensive manufactures. A large number of operatives of both sexes are employed. Estimated annual output 7,500,000 dollars. As an evidence of business activity and magnitude far excelling other cities in proportion to their population. Kalamazoo postoffice ranks third in the State. Its annual income $52,000. Value of building $80,000. The United States depository for southwestern Michigan.

This imperfect sketch briefly outlines the wonderful growth of an inland county of Michigan from a wilderness condition in 1830, but a little more than sixty years ago.

KALKASKA COUNTY.

BY A. A. BLEAZBY.

The principal industries are lumbering and farming. The lumbering interest is well established and quite general. The farming interests are now taking a larger development in our county, and so far our farmers have been very successful. The products of the farm are wheat, rye, oats, tubers generally, and for the last five years a good deal of dent corn has been raised. All grains grown in southern Michigan do well here. The face of the country is gently rolling, and the soils are sandy, or sand and gravel loam with a mixture of light clay. It is what is known as warm, quick soil. Those who have given their attention to fruits have succeeded beyond their expectations. They have raised successfully pears, cherries, plums, apples and all sorts of small berries. Originally the land stood one-third pine and two-thirds hardwood. The pine timber is very largely cut. The hardwood timber, except where a few farms have been cleared, remains an almost unbroken forest. The principal hard woods are maple, grey elm, rock elm, basswood, beech, and some cherry and white ash. The hardwood timber lands average in value about $10 per acre. To clear up the hardwood timber lands and fit the same for the plough, after the saw-logs have been taken off, costs about $15 per acre. The manufacturing so far has been along the line of the lumber and timber products, such as shingles, lath and flooring. We have institutions manufacturing all sorts of woodenware, such as pails, chopping trays, butter bowls and ladles, and almost everything that is made in those lines. So far, the manufacturing interests are centered in Kalkaska, the county seat, a town of 2,000 inhabitants, and in South Boardman, a town on the G. R. & I. railroad, of about 500 population. There are no navigable streams in the county, except as the Manistee river and the Boardman river are used for the running of saw logs. There is but little water power in the Manistee river, and that of the Boardman river is utilized at Kalkaska and South Boardman, but neither of these are developed to more than a small percentage of their capacities. The Rapid river, rising in the northeast portion of the county and running in a southwest direction to Torch river, is one continuous chain of water privileges. There are only two or three water powers developed in its entire length. There are no mineral interests in the county. The chief towns are Kalkaska, South Boardman, Leetsville, Westwood. The market for the products of the farm, so far, is largely a home market, as the lumber interests consume a great amount of hay and grain, thus giving to the farmer the benefit of the general market and freight added on all he has to sell. The only exception to this is the potato crop, which has developed very largely during the last three or four years, and in the raising of which the farmer has taken much interest. There is no crop here more certain or more profitable than the potato crop. Our schools are well developed for a young county, especially the one in Kalkaska village, which has seven departments presided over by competent teachers, and is the equal of the better class of graded schools throughout the State. Our church interests are represented by organizations of Congregational, Baptist, Methodist and Disciple, all of which seem to be prospering and are well supported. Our present railroad facilities are the G. R. & I. only. Wages for the common laborer are well maintained here, as the cheapest labor earns $1.25 per day. Woodsmen get from $1 to $1.50 per day and board. The mill and yard men average $1.75 to $2 per day, and the skilled laborer in our better class of mills earns from $3 to $5 per day. Farm labor generally brings from $15 to $20 per month and board. All our streams are homes of the trout and grayling. In no portion of the State are waters so richly stocked with these gamey fish. The hunter finds here what interests him, the partridge, pheasant, woodcock, deer, fox, and occasionally bears. The development of iron in this vicinity has made a market for all the rough grades of wood and timber. After the sawing timber has been removed, this wood cut four feet long and delivered to the kilns along the railroad brings $1.35 per cord, and this pays the farmer for what he desires to have done, namely, the clearing up of his farm. The farmer in this country has learned that his land will produce better, and seems to have greater staying qualities, when as much of the forest growth as possible can be removed from the land and not burned upon it, as was formerly done. The lands in this vicinity which are covered with pine are largely if not entirely a light sandy soil, and so far have not been put to any farming purposes. It is doubtful if at present there is any known way of making them profitable to the farmer.

KENT COUNTY.

Kent county, in the west central portion of the lower peninsula, consists of twenty-four surveyed townships in six tiers, and ranges west from 9 to 12 inclusive, each township having a civil organization of its own.

Beautiful Grand River drains a fertile valley traversing the county from east to west, the sides of which rise as they recede, and down which flow, over cascades, the spring waters of the Thornapple, the Flat and the Rogue rivers.

The whole county, somewhat level in the north but more rolling in the south, is dotted here and there with beautiful lakes abounding in fish, affording pleasure and recreation to the rural population, as well as to that of the neighboring cities and villages.

The soil, varying from a limy sand and gravel to the heaviest clay, is adapted to raising cereals and vegetables with great profit, while the choicest varieties of fruits of all kinds grow to a perfection attained only in western Michigan.

Very little timber lands, excepting that set aside by each farmer for his own use, remain and while there are yet many farms in the first stages of improvement, the county as a whole is well developed, and prices are from $25 to $50 per acre for those some distance from the county seat, and from $50 to $200 for those from one to four miles from its city limits, according to location and quality of soil.

The climate is comparatively temperate, rarely exceeding 85 degrees, with an average of about 68 in summer; or below zero, with an average of about 25 above in winter.

Grand Rapids, the metropolis of western Michigan, the second city in the State, containing 90,000 souls, is the capitol of the county. It is surrounded in the county by such villages as Sparta. Byron Center, Grandville, Rockford, Ada, Caledonia and Lowell, with many smaller ones more isolated, while the whole of western Midhigan contributes to its prosperity.

The county is traversed by railroads centering from all directions to the city, which ships its immense product to the world. Its furniture has no bounds, its land plaster and gypsum products no rivals.

The school system of the county and city is of the best, and the best is made of it.

In the city and villages, manufacturing, and in the country agriculture, horti culture and pomology are all extensive.

Grand river, preparations for which are made to deepen from Grand Repids to its mouth, a distance of forty miles, so as to be navigable for lake vessels.

Grand River already furnishes an immense water power, which the improvement will increase, by adding largely to its fall. Flat river, pouring into the Grand at Lowell, is now furnishing power to an electric plant, to distribute electricity for manufacturing and other purposes to the city of Grand Rapids, and the Thornapple, a few miles nearer the city, offers like opportunities.

Preliminary surveys and preparations have been made to deepen Grand river from Grand Rapids to its mouth so as to make it navigable for lake vessels. Virtually making the city a seaport. The importance of this work could hardly be overestimated.

It is claimed that Grand Rapids manufactures more furniture than any other city in the world, which taken with the immense amount of other productions the question of transportation or shipping is necessarily of vast importance.

KEWEENAW COUNTY.

Keweenaw county was organized in 1861. It is bounded on the north, east and west by Lake Superior and on the south by Houghton. It has an area of 300 square miles, and had in 1890 a population of 2,894. Eagle River, a village of 100 inhabitants, is the county seat. The county is traversed by two ranges of hills, known as the north and south range. On the slopes of these hills are heavy growths of timber, while between the ranges the land is swampy. It is subject, however, to drainage, and furnishes excellent pasturage. The county is watered by a number of small streams flowing from the hills to the lake, and some of them furnish small water powers. The timber is principally beech, maple, pine, spruce, balsam, tamarack, ash, cedar, and occasionally black oak. The soil is sand and gravel, and when first cultivated yields fair root crops, after which it will produce hay for a few seasons. Garden vegetables do well in the valleys, and potatoes yield bountifully. Strawberries of fine size and flavor are grown to a considerable extent. Fruits generally are not successfully cultivated. The wood cut finds ready sale among the miners or at the docks along the lake.

There are 76,380 acres of public land subject to sale or entry, and there are some unimproved lands, from which the pine alone has been cut, but their timber as yet is of little value, owing to their distance from the markets. There are good roads throughout the settled portions of the county. The seasons are well defined, there being fully six months of winter and six months of warm weather, with a very even temperature. The ground does not freeze in winter owing to the depth of snow. The schools in this county are said to be excellent. The principal industries are lumbering, the cutting of ties, posts and telegraph poles, fishing and mining. Labor is always in good demand, high wages being paid to the right sort of men.

There are no railroads as yet in the county, but the largest vessels call at several of the lake ports during the summer season, affording every opportunity for the commercial transactions of the county.

Keweenaw county is in the copper belt, and in the past quite an amount of copper was mined, but owing to cost of mining and low price of copper the work was abandoned. It is, however, not dead, but quietly resting, and great developments may yet be made there and some rich findings.

LAKE COUNTY.

Lake county was organized in 1871. It is bounded on the north by Manistee and Wexford, on the east by Osceola, on the south by Newaygo, and on the west by Mason. It has an area of about 576 square miles, and had a population in 1890 of 6,505. Baldwin is the county seat.

The surface of the county is level or gently rolling. There is some swamp land which is nearly all reclaimable; also large tracts of sandy land, most of which is tillable. The county is well watered with springs, spring streams and lakes. The headwaters of the Pere Marquette, Pine, Sauble and Manistee rivers are within the borders of the county. Excellent water power is found at a number of points. The soil on the sand plains is of red and yellow sand, with no subsoil. The prevailing soil on the beech and maple lands is generally of a loamy, gravelly nature with clay subsoil. The timber is pine, hemlock, beech, maple, rock elm, ash, cherry, oak, white cedar, basswood, birch, tamarack and spruce. Wheat, potatoes, corn, buckwheat, ruta bagas, millet, vines of all descriptions, beans, peas, rye, timothy and clover—in fact all crops peculiar to this latitude—are raised in Lake county. Apples, pears, plums, grapes, and the smaller fruits do well. Many young orchards are just beginning to bear. The cost of clearing averages $20 per acre on the heavily timbered lands, while on the plains the cost will average from $5 to $10. The wood produced finds a ready market at the railroad stations and at the charcoal kilns at Luther. The railroad companies buy all of the ties and posts which are offered. There is 4,891 acres of public lands for sale or entry. Unimproved lands are held at from $3 to $10 per acre, while improved farming lands range from $3 to $25 per acre, according to location and improvements. Hard wood is rapidly rising in value, as there is a great foreign demand. There are large tracts of "stump lands," also of "plains land," ranging in price from 50 cents to $5 per acre, which eventually will make good agricultural lands. There are no State roads, but the county roads are uniformly good for a new county.

Winter sets in by November 15. Snow falls to an average depth of two and one-half feet, the ground rarely ever freezing. Plowing begins in April.

The schools are comparatively few, but good, and every effort is being made to elevate their standard.

There are a considerable number of lumber and shingle mills in the county. There are also large charcoal and chemical works at Luther. Ties, posts and poles are gotten out in large quantities. Labor is always in good demand, particularly in the lumbering districts, wages averaging $23 per month with board. The Flint and Pere Marquette railroad traverses the county from east to west, and a branch of the Grand Rapids and Indiana runs from Milton Junction to Luther. There are several logging roads in the county of from four to ten miles in length. The lands held by the railroads are for sale on time, at prices within the reach of every one.

LAPEER COUNTY.

Lapeer county was organized in 1835. It is bounded on the north by Tuscola and Sanilac, on the east by Sanilac and St. Clair, on the south by Macomb and Oakland, and on the west by Genesee and Tuscola. It has an area of 666 square miles, and had, in 1890, a population of 29,213. Lapeer, a city of 2,753 inhabitants, is the county seat. The surface of the county is quite rolling, with very little swamp land. It is well watered by rivers and spring brooks. There is little available water power except for light work. The soil varies in the different townships from a sandy loam to a clay loam. The subsoil is invariably clay. The prevailing varieties of timber are, beech, maple, ash, hickory, elm and walnut.

The principal crops are winter wheat, corn, oats, potatoes, clover and timothy. Apples, pears, plums and grapes succeed well; peaches only in favorable localities, and in favorable seasons. The small fruits and berries grow in abundance, and good markets are found at the railroad stations for all the surplus fruit. There are no government or State lands of any value in the market.

There is considerable unimproved land, with the pine and oak cut off, which can be had at from $5 to $15 per acre. The soil is of good quality, well adapted to agriculture. The "stump lands" also have a good soil, and are rapidly being taken up. Improved farms range in price from $20 to $80 per acre.

There are three State roads running north and south; one from Imlay City to the forks of Cass river, one from Attica to Cass river, and one from Lapeer to Lexington, via North Branch. The county roads are generally in a good condition.

Snow falls in November but no sleighing is looked for before Christmas. The average depth is about a foot. When the fall of snow is light the ground freezes to the average depth of two feet. Spring plowing begins from the 20th of March to the first of April.

The schools and school buildings of Lapeer county are all good. Agriculture is the principal industry, though lumbering, charcoal burning, and the getting out of ties, posts, and telegraph poles, is carried on to a considerable extent.

Labor is in fair demand, particularly on farms during the summer season. Farm labor brings from $16 to $20 per month, with board.

The Chicago & Grand Trunk, the Detroit & Bay City, its branch to Five Lakes, the Almont branch of the Port Huron and Northwestern, and the Pontiac, Caseville and Port Austin railroads, enter the county at different points. The Otter lake extension of the Flint and Pere Marquette, and the Port Huron and Northwestern also touch the borders of the county, hence the farmer can find good markets in any direction, for anything he may have for sale.

The numerous railroad facilities found within the borders of this county offer special advantages to many kinds of manufacturing enterprises, and there is every prospect that Lapeer will have its full quota of factories at no distant date.

LEELANAU COUNTY.

BY WILLIAM HITCHCOCK, LELAND.

Leelanau county was organized in 1863. It is bounded on the north and west by Lake Michigan, on the east by Grand Traverse bay, and on the south by Benzie and Grand Traverse. It has an area of 360 square miles, and had a population in 1890 of 7,944. Leland, a growing village, is the county seat.

The entire county is a peninsula lying between Traverse bay and Lake Michigan. The surface of the country is quite rolling. There are two ridges lying in the same direction as the bay, and varying in altitude from a water level to 482 feet. Between these ridges are a few cedar swamps which are reclaimable at $2.50 per acre. Also about 4,000 acres of cedar swamp at head of Carp lake which after the timber is removed will make fine grass lands. There are a few sandy plains of no considerable extent.

The county is watered by Carp lake, Carp river and several smaller streams and lakes. There is a fine water power at the mouth of Carp river, there being a fall of about eight and one-half feet. Other water powers are found on the rapid streams in the interior of the county.

The soil is a dark sandy loam of remarkable uniformity, easily worked, with a gravelly subsoil. There are, however, patches of clay soil in every township. The timber is principally beech, maple, elm, ash, hemlock, birch, cedar and basswood. Wheat, rye and oats are the most successful of the grains. The quality of potatoes and nearly all garden vegetables cannot be surpassed. The entire county furnishes what are known as "Traverse bay" potatoes, which command an extra price in the Chicago market. The orchards are new, but quite extensive and considerable surplus fruit is raised. Peaches, pears, apples, plums, and cherries do well wherever proper attention is paid to their cultivation. The cost of clearing will average from $10 to $20 per acre. There are good wood markets at all points where the steamers land. There is 2,282 acres of land subject to sale or entry. There are plenty of good, unimproved hardwood lands which can be had at from $4 to $10 per acre. They are all within a few miles of water shipping points, and the southern portions of the county find an outlet via the Manistee & Northeastern railroad which now passes through the south tier of towns and a branch is now proposed to run from Lake Ann in Benzie county northwest to Glen Arbor. The "stump lands" are really of more value to the settler than the timbered lands, as they have been practically cleared, and the soil is of a superior character. They are held at from $5 to $10 per acre. There are two State roads, viz: the Northport and Newaygo road, running in a southerly direction through Sutton's Bay and New Mission to Traverse City, and the Northport, Leland and Frankfort road, leading southwestward to Manistee. The county is also well opened up by the local roads which are generally in a fair condition. Snow falls late in November to an average depth of one foot. The ground does not freeze to any depth, and spring work generally begins by April 1. The summer months are tempered by the lake breezes, and the climate is usually delightful from May to November.

The district and village schools are generally well attended and well kept. The principal industries of the county are hardwood lumbering, charcoal burning, the cutting of ties, posts, poles, hemlock bark, and agriculture.

Common labor is always in good demand at the mills and furnaces, wages ranging from $20 to $25 per month with board. Several large bays afford some of the finest harbors on the lakes. There are several important ports along the coast, where vessels to and from Chicago land for fuel, passengers and freight. Carp lake, an inland body of water 18 miles in length, is a great resort for sportsmen during the summer and fall seasons. The county is destined to become a great fruit district. In the spring of 1893, it is estimated, as many fruit trees were planted as were already growing and fully $200,000 worth of fruit was shipped from this county the previous year.

LENAWEE COUNTY.

BY NORMAN GEDDES, ADRIAN, MICH.

Lenawee county was organized in 1826. Is bounded north by Jackson and Washtenaw, east by Monroe, south by the State of Ohio, and on the west by Hillsdale. The northwestern portion is somewhat hilly, the central undulating and the eastern and southern portions level. It has almost every variety of soil, producing bountiful crops of wheat, corn, oats, barley, rye, potatoes, and in some localities most excellent celery. Nearly all the fruits, apples, pears, peaches and the small fruits peculiar to this latitude, are successfully raised. In dairy products, it takes high rank, having in successful operation from twenty to thirty cheese factories and creameries. Agriculturally, it is one of the richest counties in the country, and in the United States census of 1880 was given the first place among all the counties in the various states in the matter of agricultural products. It has very little swamp or waste land. About one-third of the county was what in its early settlement was called oak openings, and the residue heavily timbered with oak, black walnut, whitewood, maple, beech, basswood, hickory, ash, elm, sycamore, etc. It is well watered by running streams, the principal being the River Raisin and its branches, the Raisin rising in one of the small lakes of the county and emptying into Lake Erie at Monroe. In the northeastern part of the county are numerous small lakes, some covering only a few acres, while others are several miles in circumference, and so beautiful are they, and so healthful their locality, that some of them have become favorite summer resorts, with hotels and cottages, one having already some forty cottages upon its banks, mainly owned by residents of Adrian, Detroit, Toledo, Tecumseh and the farmers of the county. The price of farming lands varies

32

from $30 to $100 per acre, depending on proximity to or distance from the cities and villages and the character of the buildings and improvements. The county is traversed by three great lines of railroad, from east to west by the L. S. & M. S. and the C. J. & M., and from northeast to southwest by the Wabash Railway, in addition to which are the L. S. & M. S. from Adrian to Monroe and Detroit, the branch from Adrian to Jackson, the Dundee branch from Adrian to Trenton and Detroit and the Fayette branch from Adrian to Fayette, Ohio.

The well improved farms and farm houses to be seen on every hand plainly indicate that the farmers of this county are an exceptionally prosperous people. The excellence of the soil and its adaptability to mixed farming and fruit rais-ing, the healthfulness of the climate, its railroad facilities (no farm in the county being over six miles from a railroad station), the character, intelligence and high moral tone of its people, make this one of the most desirable counties for agri-culture or manufacture to be found in this or any other State.

Its largest town, Adrian, the county seat, one of the most beautiful of the many beautiful inland cities of the State, offers peculiar advantages for manu-facturing enterprises, competing railroads, facilities for shipping in all directions, and as a place of residence superior, in point of health, beauty and comfort, to any city of its size in the country. Its educational advantages are unsurpassed, its high school ranking among the best in the country, while Adrian College, one of the best in the State, supplements the high school by affording oppor-tunities for obtaining a thorough collegiate education at very moderate cost. The State Industrial Home for Girls is located here. Among its manufacturing establishments (some of them in their infancy), already employing in the aggre-gate nearly 2,000 men, may be mentioned the L. S. & M. S. car shops, the Gilli-land Electric Co., Adrian Furniture Manufacturing Co., Straw and Felt Goods Man-ufacturing Co., three large canning factories, Page Woven Wire Fence Co., Adrian Brick and Tile Machine Co., Kells & Sons' Brick Machine Works, three lumber yards and planing mills, the Washington Milling Co., the Hand Milling Co., electric light and gas works, the Church Manufacturing Co., Palmers Manu-facturing Co., and large numbers of smaller establishments.

The city of Hudson and the villages of Tecumseh, Blissfield, Clinton, Clayton, Morenci, Weston, Fairfield, Addison, Deerfield, Onsted, Ridgeway, Riga, Jaspar, Palmyra, Addison, Mason and Britton, are all delightful, and most of them pros-perous towns, affording convenient and excellent markets, shipping facilities, good schools, society and churches.

LIVINGSTON COUNTY.

Livingston county was organized in 1836. It has an area of 576 square miles and had a population in 1890 of 20,858. Howell, the county seat, had at the same time 2,387 inhabitants.

It is strictly an agricultural county. Her products embrace all the grains, grasses and vegetables of the temperate zone. Her soil is mainly sand, gravel or clay loam, well adapted to the growth of wheat, corn, oats, rye and grass, being high, rolling and well drained. Nearly all fruits are grown successfully, as the county is exceptionally free from early or late frosts. The timber is mainly hard wood, all the varieties of oak, beech, maple, hickory, elm and ash. Very little timber is left in the county except what is kept for home use. The lands are well improved and average value of farm land is $30 to $50 per acre. Unimproved being mostly woodland is as valuable as improved. We have little manufacturing, except flour for home use. Livingston has no large rivers, the Huron being the largest, which is not navigable, but furnishes water power along its whole length. No mines or minerals or quarries are as yet discovered. Our chief towns are Howell, population 3,000; Brighton, 1,200; Fowlerville, 1,500, whose chief industry is retail trade and mechanics of various trades. No vessel inter-ests, though she has a multitude of small inland lakes, which afford good sport for local fishing.

The county is crossed by three lines of railway, the D., L. & N., T. & A. A. and Grand Trunk, which give the farmers good markets with short hauls. The county is dotted with schools and churches. Farm wages range from $16 to $20 per month with board, and $25 to $30 without board. Skilled labor from $2 to $3 per day. Our lakes are stocked with all kinds of native fish, and our woodland with small game.

LUCE COUNTY

Organized by legislature in 1887. The territory comprising the county was taken largely from Chippewa county, with five townships from Mackinac. It has an area of 581,437 acres, and a population in 1890 of 2,455. The county is bounded on the north by Lake Superior, east by Chippewa county, south by Mackinac county, and west by Schoolcraft and Alger counties.

The farming lands are rich and productive and this county offers many inducements to the immigrant to settle here and procure free a home of eighty or one hundred and sixty acres of fine timbered and agricultural lands. The Tahquamenon river, with its several branches, wind through this county for over one hundred miles, not only furnishing excellent water privileges but drainage as well. The valleys along this river abound in great quantities of yellow birch and bird's-eye maple. These valuable woods are used largely for veneering purposes in the manufacture of furniture. Large tracts of pine still remain standing in the northern part of the county. This timber is the most valuable of any now remaining in the State. There remains 39,041 acres of public lands subject to sale or entry. In addition to the public lands, there are many thousands of acres of railroad lands for sale cheap and on long time. The county is organized into four townships, and already has hundreds of prosperous farmers, with good buildings and well worked farms. The roads are excellent for a new country, have been made so by the many large lumbering firms operating here. The schools are the very best; each township is organized on the unit system with but one board to establish and control district schools at convenient intervals.

Newberry, the county seat, is a thriving village beautifully laid out with broad avenues and streets, has a fine system of water works, electric lights and other modern improvements to be found in a live and hustling town. Located here is a large iron smelting furnace employing several hundred hands the year round. In connection with the furnace are a large number of charcoal burners, which makes a ready market for wood from the farmers. Large chemical works are operated here, the chief product of which is wood alcohol. These works also employ many men.

Adjoining the village is the great celery farm operated by the Newberry Celery Co., which also employs many hands. This celery has gained a widespread reputation for its rich, tender and brittle branches Large shipments are daily made as far west as Montana, south to Illinois, and east to Montreal, Toronto and Quebec. St. Paul, Minneapolis and Duluth are all prominent markets for Newberry celery. The soil in this vicinity is especially adapted for growing this excellent culinary plant. H. L. Harris, the secretary of the company, recently forwarded a quantity of this celery growing soil to the State Agricultural College, and Bulletin No. 99, of this institution, gives the following analysis:

Sand and silicates	24.56
Alumina	2.21
Oxide of iron	1.30
Lime	4.18
Magnesia	.75
Potash	.42
Soda	.40
Sulphuric acid	.67
Phosphoric acid	.46
Carbonic acid	1.10
Organic matter, containing 1.75 nitrogen	63.75
Water	7.31

There are many fine churches, excellent schools, a good newspaper, the News, numerous secret and benevolent societies, and other organizations to make social life pleasant in this village.

MACKINAC COUNTY.

BY P. D. BISSELL, ST. IGNACE.

Mackinac county was organized in 1818. It is bounded on the north by Chip-pewa and Luce, on the east by Chippewa and Lake Huron, on the south by Lakes Huron and Michigan, and on the west by Schoolcraft. It has an area of 953 square miles, and had a population in 1890 of 7,830. St. Ignace, a city of 3,000 inhabitants, located on the Straits of Mackinac at the southern extrem-ity of the county, is the county seat. It is at present the great distributing point for the eastern portion of the upper peninsula. One of the largest blast furnaces in the State, with a capacity of 60 tons of charcoal pig iron daily, and employing 100 men, is located here.

Another of the city's industries is the large lumbering concern of the J. A. Jamieson Lumber Company, a corporation with $75,000 capital stock, manufact-urers of lumber, car sills, etc. St. Ignace has two finely appointed and commo-dious hotels of the first class, which are thronged with tourists each summer, and a number of hotels of less size and pretensions. The city schools are graded according to the Michigan system, occupy two roomy ward buildings, and the high school, the latter a very handsome brick structure. There are Catho lic, Congregational, Methodist, Presbyterian, Episcopal, Baptist and Lutheran societies, the latter only lacking a church home. The city has a grand harbor, with 25 feet of water right up to her piers, and is already a large shipping-point and destined to rapidly increase in commercial importance. The system of docks, large as it is, will soon be too small for the increasing traffic center-ing at this point. The First National bank of this city, a prosperous banking house, reports for the past year an average of $100,000 of savings deposits, an increase of $25,000 over the year previous. This total is made up of small deposits and represents the savings of the wage earners. The commercial deposits aggregate as much more.

The city has the usual number of stores and business houses, many of them carrying very heavy stocks and jobbing to dealers in adjacent towns. Each year increases the tide of summer travel to St. Ignace, and to accommodate the tourists a project for the erection of a big summer hotel is well under way, and much of the capital stock is already subscribed.

Mackinac island, situated in the Straits of Mackinac, six miles from St. Ignace, near the junction of Lakes Huron and Michigan, and now a national park, is widely known as one of the most delightful summer resorts in the northwest. The historical associations attached to this beautiful island and its surround-ings are of great interest. This magnificent resort has abundant hotel accom-modations. No other port in Michigan has as many passenger steamers call-ing at its docks as has Mackinac in the tourist season, and very many of these steamers are great floating palaces. It is estimated that from 40,000 to 50,000 tourists visit Mackinac each season. Very many wealthy families of Chicago, Detroit and other cities have leased holdings of the government and have erected summer homes thereon. The chief points of interest are Arch Rock, Sugar Loaf Rock, Lover's Leap, Robinson's Folly, British Landing, Old Fort Holmes and Battle Field, the venerable Fort Mackinac, still occupied by U. S. troops, Pontiac's Lookout, etc. Mackinac island is the Newport of the great northwest.

The eastern portion of the county is an elevated plateau. Up the valleys of the Pine and Carp rivers there is considerable cedar swamp, all of which is considerably elevated above the level of the lake. Along the line of the Duluth, South Shore & Atlantic Railroad the land is generally level, with occasional cedar swamps, which are so high as to admit of excellent drainage. The large swamps of the Tahquamenon lie almost entirely north of this county, their southern border being nearly 250 feet above the lake level. The western por-tion of the county is more rolling, some of its hills rising 200 or 300 feet above Lake Michigan. There is, however, but little waste land, even the hilly portions being easily cultivated. Along the border of Lake Michigan there is a narrow strip of quite sandy land. The county is well watered by the Pine, Carp, Black, Mille Coquin and Milakoka rivers, and by the branches of the Tahquamenon and Manistique. There are also many fine inland lakes, the most notable of which is the Manistique groups, the banks of which are high, but slope grad-ually to the water's edge. There are a number of undeveloped water powers in.

this county, the one at the outlet of North Manistique lake having a current of four miles an hour, and is sufficiently large to furnish power for any number of mills.

The soil is generally clay, limestone, gravel and loam, with a subsoil of limestone. Here and there will be found a rich sandy loam of a chocolate color over a clay subsoil. The Manistique lake region having as its northern boundary the Duluth, South Shore & Atlantic Railroad, and Lake Michigan on the south, has in many places a rich vegetable mold on the surface, underneath which is found a layer of red clay, then white marl containing a large percentage of lime, and lastly a white clay resting on a limestone foundation. The timber is principally pine, cedar, white birch, poplar and tamarack, the last three varieties being found in large quantities along the streams. On the dryer lands are splendid tracts of birds-eye and curly maple, black and yellow birch, beech, basswood, etc.

The agricultural lands of this county cannot be excelled in richness of soil or in producing qualities. Wheat, barley, oats, buckwheat, hay, potatoes, turnips, etc., all grow in great abundance and of the finest quality. The vegetables are especially productive and attain an enormous size. Peas could be raised for southern markets with great profit, as they are about three weeks later than southern peas. As soon as the beaver dams are destroyed which are now scattered over the so-called swamp lands, the drainage will be perfect and there will be left some of the best grass land in the country. Near St. Ignace tobacco is raised to a limited extent. On Mackinac island fine plums have been raised for years. On the main land any number of blue plums, which were doubtless planted by the early French settlers, are found growing in a wild state. Strawberries, cranberries, etc., grow to great perfection. Young orchards set out six and eight years ago now bear fruit in gratifying quantities. There are a dozen thrifty apple orchards in St. Ignace. Siberian crabs, pears, green gage and egg plums and cherry trees not only endure the winter well, but thrive and bear fruit seemingly as well as in lower latitudes.

The cost of clearing averages $20 per acre on the heavier timbered lands, while on the "burnt lands" it will not exceed $5 or $10. Good wood markets can be found along the line of the railroad, particularly at the furnaces in St. Ignace and Newberry. The roads of the county are very good indeed. Snow falls by December 1 to an average depth of two feet, the ground never freezing. The winters are steady, and the atmosphere is much drier than in southern Michigan. Plowing begins in April, and although the season is comparatively short, the growth of crops is much quicker than in lower latitudes, the lime in the soil giving it great vigor.

Lumbering, the cutting of ties, posts, poles, etc., charcoal burning and agriculture are the main industries, employing a large number of men at wages ranging from $1.50 to $1.75 per day. The Duluth, South Shore & Atlantic Railroad traverses the county from southeast to northwest, and an extension from the vicinity of Newberry to the Sault connects St. Ignace with the Soo. The St. Paul, Minneapolis & Sault Ste. Marie Railroad crosses the county east and west, starting into life the thriving towns of Gilchrist, Naubinway, Gould City and Corinne. These roads have opened up a vast amount of hitherto undeveloped territory, which is soon to become the home of the farmer, the merchant and the manufacturer.

MACOMB COUNTY.

BY ROBERT T. ELDRIDGE, MT. CLEMENS.

Macomb county was organized in 1818, and primarily included all the land now embraced in the counties of St. Clair, Lapeer, Macomb, Oakland, Livingston, the larger part of Shiawassee, Ingham. Genesee, Sanilac and small portions of Huron, Tuscola and Saginaw. It was the third county in the State to be organized. It has been repeatedly reduced until the present county has an area of 440 square miles, with a population, in 1890, of 31,813. It is bounded on the north by Lapeer and St. Clair counties, east by St. Clair county and Lake St. Clair, south by Wayne and west by Oakland. Mt. Clemens, its metropolis and county seat, is a flourishing city of about 5,000 population, in which are situated the famous mineral springs, whose waters are renowned and attract thousands annually from all parts of the country. The waters are especially effective in the treatment of rheumatism, skin and blood diseases and nervous affections. Five large bath houses and many hotel and boarding houses stand as evidences of the wonderful success of the waters. The leading manufactories in the city are of lumber, sash, blinds, etc., agricultural implements, including threshers, staves and heading, and ship building. Quite an amount is invested in the vessel interests on the great lakes by the people of the city, as well as of New Baltimore.

The northern and western portions of the county are quite rolling, with considerable cobblestone, while the remainder of the county is level or only slightly undulating. The Clinton river, with its numerous branches and feeders, furnish excellent drainage to the larger part of the county, and good water power at Utica and other points. The low swampy lands of the southern portions have been drained largely and now furnish the most productive farms of the county, so that now the only waste lands are the marshes at the outlet of the streams along the shore of Lake St. Clair. The soil of the northwestern portion of the county is a gravelly loam, while that of the south and east portions is gravel and sand with clay and clay loam subsoil. The timber, once abounding, is now nearly all cleared off. The resources of the county are almost entirely agricultural, wheat, oats and hay being the chief products. Some fine cattle are being bred in the county, and the improvement in the grade of the stock in general has been marked. Apples, pears, plums, and small fruits are raised successfully in nearly all parts of the county.

Improved lands range in price from $30 to $100 per acre, and the lands along the southern line command even higher prices, being purchased as prospective suburban residence property for Detroiters. The Grand Trunk, its Ridgway & Pontiac branch, and the Detroit & Bay City branch of the Michigan Central are the railroads of the county. There is projected a railroad up the lake shore from Detroit to Port Huron. The Clinton river is navigable for small vessels as far up as Mt. Clemens.

The press is represented in the county by the Press and Monitor at Mt. Clemens, the Hydrant and Observer at Romeo, the Review at Richmond, the Sentinel at Utica, the Graphic at Armada, and the Watchman at Warren.

The schools of the county are very good, there being 10 graded schools in the county and 113 school districts with houses and fair equipments. The high schools at Mt. Clemens, Utica and Romeo are on the list of schools whose graduates are admitted to the University without examination.

The early settlements of the French along Lake St. Clair and the Clinton, and of the Moravians at Frederick, the struggles of the early English settlers, the enterprises at Bellvidere and Liverpool, of the Kalamazoo and Clinton canal, and the like, furnish an inviting and rich field for the work of the loial historian or of the story writer.

MANISTEE COUNTY.

Manistee county was organized in 1855. It is bounded on the north by Benzie, on the east by Wexford, on the south by Mason and Lake, and on the west by Lake Michigan. It has an area of 349,214 acres and had a population, in 1890, of 24,230. Manistee, a city of 12,812 inhabitants located on Lake Michigan, is the county seat.

The surface of the county is greatly diversified, that portion lying south of the Manistee river being comparatively level, while the portion lying north of that river is quite rolling. The two northern tiers of towns are very hilly in some parts, although easy of cultivation. The county is well watered, both by streams, and by lakes and ponds. The Manistee, a large navigable stream, crosses the county from east to west. This river has three large tributaries on the south, and one on the north, viz: Bear creek which in turn has a number of small tributaries, and extends diagonally across the country to the northeast. There is some water power but it is not available at present, owing to the fact that the streams are so jammed with logs. There are some sand plains in the southern part of the county, also swamps here and there which are easily reclaimed. The soil is generally a sandy or gravelly loam, mixed with more or less clay. Some tracts along the shore have a pure clay soil hundreds of feet in depth. The southern tier of towns are quite sandy, yet the soil is quite productive. Pine and oak timber predominate in the southern part of the county, white beech, maple, elm, and ash of the finest quality abound in the northern portions. Nearly every crop known in Michigan grows successfully in this county; late corn is the only exception. Wheat averages from 15 to 18 bushels to the acre. Apples, pears, peaches, grapes, and plums do remark-ably well. Berries of all sorts are indigenous and grow abundantly on every hand. On the light soil of the southern tiers of townships strawberries, rasp-berries, blackberries, etc., grow to great perfection.

On the heavily timbered lands in the north part of the county the cost of clearing would be considerable, but in every instance the wood and timber would pay for the clearing. There are good wood piers all along Lake Michigan, at Burnham, Pierpont, Arcadia, Bear Lake, Portage and Manistee. The Milwaukee market consumes a great deal of wood shipped from this county. There is 9,418 acres of public lands subject to sale or entry.

There are plenty of good unimproved lands near the markets which can be had at from $5 to $20 per acre. There are also large tracts of stump land which can be bought at from $1 to $10 per acre. The soil on these lands is light but produces good crops of vegetables, fruits, etc. Two State roads traverse the county from south to north, one keeping near the lake shore, the other extending from Manistee to Bear lake, and thence north across the county. The local highways are generally in a fair condition.

The climate is equable, and free from the extremes of heat and cold. The mercury seldom goes below zero in winter or above 80° in summer. Considerable snow falls, and the ground seldom freezes. Plowing begins by the middle of April.

The county is well supplied with schools of a high grade. The public schools of Manistee are favorably known and well patronized by northwestern Michigan. The principal interests are lumbering, agriculture, the manufacture of salt, shingles, ties, posts and telegraph poles. There are about 40 lumber and shingle mills at Manistee. Labor is in good demand at remunerative prices. Skilled labor in particular is well paid. The Flint & Pere Marquette railroad has a branch from Buttars Junction in Mason county to Manistee. The Chicago & West Michigan and the Grand Rapids & Indiana Railroads will eventually have branches to that city. A local road extends from Pierpont to Bear Lake.

The county is settling rapidly and offers every opportunity to settlers, whether farmers, mechanics or laborers. Lands are cheap, the soil is productive, the privileges of schools and society are unsurpassed, and a large immigration to this section may be looked for during the next few years.

MANITOU COUNTY.

Manitou county was organized in 1855. It comprises a number of islands lying in the northeastern part of Lake Michigan. Big Beaver, Garden and Hog islands form the northern, and the north and south Manitous the southern boundaries of the county, while the north and south Fox islands lie midway between these groups. The county has an area of 180 square miles, and had a population in 1890 of 800. Big Beaver island is the largest of the group, and is divided into three townships, viz: Chandler, Peaine and Galilee. St. James at the northern extremity of this island is the county seat. The surface of the county is rolling, and is well watered. There are a few easily reclaimed swamps and small areas of sand plains. The soil is generally quite productive. The timber is principally beech, maple, birch and hemlock. Wheat, oats, rye and potatoes are the staple crops. The seasons are too short and cool for corn. Apples do well, and other fruits, when properly tested, will no doubt show encouraging results. Berries grow in a wild state and yield bountifully. It costs about $12 per acre to clear and fence land. Hardwood brings from $2 to $2.50 per cord, and softwood about half as much. There is 4,990 acres subject to sale or entry. Good unimproved lands can be obtained at from $2.50 to $3 per acre. There are no State roads, but plenty of good local roads over the islands.

Snow falls by Oct. 1, and attains an average depth of three feet, the ground seldom freezing. Plowing begins by the 20th of April in favorable seasons. The schools are few, but are in a good condition. The principal industries are agricult-ure, fishing and boat making. More fish are shipped from these islands than from any other point on the lake. There is but little demand for labor. During the season for navigation, communication is had with Petoskey, Harbor Springs and other shore towns by means of fishing boats and tugs. Large steamers also call at St. James weekly, connecting the islands with Mackinaw and Petoskey.

The harbor at St. James is one of the best, if not the best on Lake Michigan, with an entrance about 80 rods wide and a perfectly land-locked harbor inside, all formed by nature, it is the city of refuge for vessels caught in storms.

A society of Mormons once located here, but after a short, uncomfortable existence was driven out, and the chief elder. Strang. murdered. At one time a considerable amount of boat building was carried on and no better opening for a boat-yard for ship building is anywhere found.

MARQUETTE COUNTY.

BY GEO. A. NEWETT, OF ISHPEMING.

Marquette county was organized in 1851. Its boundaries are Lake Superior and Baraga upon the north, Schoolcraft and Delta upon the east, Delta, Menominee and Dickinson upon the south, and Dickinson, Iron and Baraga upon the west. Marquette City, located upon the shore of Lake Superior, is the county seat. In the northern portion the county is mountainous, rugged hills being covered with timber native to the region, where there are numerous lakes abounding in food fish, and where a natural paradise can be had by those seeking rest from the sultry sun of places farther south and of less altitude. In the central portion of the county occur the mines which provide the chief support of this district. The mines of iron ore are numerous, the deposits wonderfully large and of rare purity. Since their opening the total tonnage sent out to the markets of the county have amounted to 37,761,828 long tons. It is pertinent to add that they show better in large bodies of ore at this time than at any previous one in their history. Besides the mines of Iron ore there are those of gold and silver, galena, and quarries of brownstone, marole and talc. The northern and central portions of the county are timbered with white pine, Norway pine, hemlock, cedar, spruce, tamarack, maple, and white yellow and black birch, and many mills are employed in reducing them to mercantile proportions. The railroads traversing the county are the Duluth, South Shore & Atlantic, the Chicago & Northwestern, the Chicago, Milwaukee & St. Paul, and the Huron Bay. Large tracts suitable for farming purposes are found in the lands in the central region of the county. Apples, cherries, currants, raspberries, huckleberries, strawberries, etc., thrive to a remarkable degree. Hay is a profitable crop, oats and barley do well, while roots, such as turnips, beets, carrots, parsnips, etc., grow to perfection.

Potatoes are a sure crop, and are of the finest quality and size. The grasses are wonderfully nutricious, and vegetables of all kinds native to the district are wonderfully developed. Ishpeming is the largest city in the county, containing a population of 11,194; Marquette comes next with 8,987, and Negaunee third with 6,053. The schools of the county compare favorably with the best in the country, and no portion of the State is more liberal in providing facilities for the education of its children.

There are rare advantages for the conducting of various factories for the manufacture of wooden ware, and a fine field for furnaces and mills for the conversion of the iron ore to manufactured forms. Marquette county has an area of 1,071,426 acres, being the largest county in the State and tenth in point of wealth. There are 91,546 acres of public lands subject to sale or entry.

BY R. A. PARKER, OF MARQUETTE.

Marquette county consists of approximately 1,071,426 acres, of which 100,000 acres have been cut. There are about 10,000 acres under cultivation, and such land is worth about $25 per acre. Timber land has an average of $10 per acre. The woods found consist of pine, spruce, hemlock, cedar, tamarack, elm, ash, and hard and soft bird's-eye maple and curly maple. The soil is usually sandy sometimes clayey and loamy, the general country consists of low, rolling hills. The saw mill industry has $628,000 invested in plants. There is one blast furnace in operation using charcoal, having two stacks, one stack producing fifty and the other seventy-five tons pig iron daily. There are about 50,000 horse power in its streams. Of this amount only 600 is utilized, this being done by the city of Marquette for its electric light and to operate a flour mill. Mining is the principal industry of the county. During the past year the mines of this county shipped 2,674,233 tons of iron ore, and since the first shipments of ore were made has sent away 37,921,968 tons.

The railroads of the county are the Trunk system of the Canadian Pacific, by its line of the Duluth, South Shore & Atlantic (traversing the south shore of Lake Superior), the Chicago & Northwestern, and Chicago, Milwaukee & St. Paul. In addition the plans and estimates have been made for a road to operate between Ishpeming and Marquette, a distance of fifteen miles to caray ore. It will afford Marquette an additional outlet for its products and give access by two roads to the markets of the west. There is one stone quarry operating near the city of Marquette that has been shipping its celebrated "rain drop" and brown stone for thirty years. North and west of Ishpeming are hills of serpentine. It polishes beautifully and is an industry that will attract capital.

The chief cities are Ishpeming, population 1890 census, 11,197; Marquette, 9,093; Negaunee, 6,078; total population in the three cities, 26,368. In the county the census showed that there were 39,527 inhabitants, being a gain of over eight thousand in six years and over fourteen thousand in ten years.

The fishing catch at the port of Marquette amounted to 177,000 in 1891. There is about $26,000 invested in the business. The catch consists mainly of whitefish and lake trout.

The vessel interests or tonnage of the port showed in 1890, 1,540 arrivals of vessels; the tonnage amounted to 3,077,566 tons, an average of 1,061 tons. The imports were 178,036 tons.

The school statistics of the county are as follows:

	No. of children.	Value of property.	No. of teachers.
Marquette	2,868	$100,000	30
Ishpeming	3,203	81,000	25
Negaunee	1,926	45,000	20
Michigamme	393	5,000	6
Republic	811	16,000	13
Champion	872	12,000	30
Scattered in ten townships	1,841	25,125	32
Totals	11,924	$284,125	146

The average wages of labor, both common and skilled, is high, the former being $1.00 per day, and miners receiving $2.20 per day; carpenters, $2.25; masons, $3.50; stonecutters, $4.

The game consists of rabbit, partridges, deer and bear. Wolves, otter, beaver, mink, muskrats and other fur-bearing animals are trapped. Speckled brook trout are plentiful in the streams, and Lake Superior affords fishing grounds for them second to no place in the United States.

MASON COUNTY.

Mason county was organized in 1855. It is bounded on the north by Manistee, on the east by Lake, on the south by Oceana, and on the west by Lake Michigan. It has an area of 504 square miles, and had, in 1890, a population of 16,385. Ludington, a city of 7,517 inhabitants, located on Lake Michigan, is the county seat.

The surface of the county is rolling. It is well watered, three streams running east and west through the county, viz: the Grand Sable, the Little Sable, and the Marquette. The southern portion of the county is drained by the Pentwater river, flowing into Lake Michigan in the northeast corner of Oceana county. There is considerable swamp land, nearly all of which is reclaimable and which will ultimately prove among the best lands in the county. The eastern tier of towns is quite sandy, but there are but few sand plains, properly so called. The soil in one-half of the county is a sandy loam, in one-quarter sand, and in the remaining quarter clay. The subsoil varies from hard clay to sand thirty feet in depth. The timber is principally beech and maple, ash, basswood, hemlock, some pine and the other varieties usually found in northern Michigan. The main crops are wheat, oats, potatoes, and all kinds of vegetables. Some years wheat will average 20 to 25 bushels per acre. Fruit raising has been thoroughly tested, and peaches, pears, plums and apples grow to great perfection. The Chicago and Milwaukee markets consume all of the surplus fruit.

The cost of clearing will average from $20 to $25 per acre. There are good wood markets at all of the railroad towns, hardwood bringing from $2.50 to $3.50 per cord, and softwood from $1.25 to $1.50. There are 2,780 acres of public lands subject to sale or entry. Good unimproved lands can be had at from $6 to $25 per acre. These lands are all accessible to market and their nearness to Pentwater, Ludington and Manistee will cause a brisk demand for everything the settler may have to offer for sale. The "stump lands" are held at merely nominal prices. The soil is fair, and eventually they will develop into fine agricultural districts. There are two State roads running through the county, one running from Ludington due east, and the other from Manistee in a southerly direction. The local highways are improving each year. Snow falls early in December, having an average depth during the season of two feet, the ground seldom freezing. Spring work commences as soon as the snow leaves, usually by April 15.

The schools of the county are in a good condition, and are multiplying rapidly. The principal industries are farming, lumbering, and the getting out of poles, ties, posts, and hemlock bark. Labor is in good demand, $20 to $30 per month being the average prices paid common labor. The Flint & Pere Marquette, its Manistee branch, and the Chicago & West Michigan railroads afford excellent outlets for the products of the county. Ludington is a shipping point of considerable prominence, and during the season for navigation is regularly visited by the largest boats on the lakes.

MECOSTA COUNTY.

BY S. G. WEBSTER, BIG RAPIDS.

Located in the middle division of the lower peninsula, was organized in 1859. It is bounded on the north by Osceola, east by Isabella, south by Montcalm, and on the west by Newaygo county. It has an area of 576 square miles and a population in 1890 of 19,647. The surface of the county is slightly rolling and the soil rich and productive of all kinds of crops. The timber is largely beech and sugar maple, elm, ash, oak, and cherry, with much valuable cedar along the banks of streams and around its many beautiful inland lakes.

Mecosta is already supplied with railroads, and others now proposed and surveyed will doubtless be built in the course of a few years. The Grand Rapids & Indiana runs north and south through the county, the Chicago & West Michigan, also the Detroit, Lansing & Northern traverse the county from the west and east with the terminus of each at Big Rapids, the county seat. The county is watered by the Muskegon, Chippewa and Little Muskegon rivers and their tributaries. Nearly every farm has its spring or spring brook. There are also from thirty to fifty lakes of clear, cold water, surrounded as a rule by high banks. The lakes abound in fish, principally bass and pickerel, while the brooks swarm with speckled trout which thrive in these waters, and are kept stocked from the State fish hatchery located at Paris in this county. All the rivers and small creeks have as yet many undeveloped water power sites. The county may well boast of its abundant supply of pure water and the health of its inhabitants. There is no government land in the market. Good unimproved lands, well timbered with beech, maple, etc., near a railroad, can be had at from $5 to $12.50 per acre, while much of the "stump lands" with a heavy clay subsoil, which make fine productive farms, can be purchased at from $1 to $5 per acre, thereby offering inducements to those with small means to secure cheap but valuable farms. Single crops of potatoes have been raised on a few acres of these lands and sold for sufficient to pay the purchase price of the entire farm. The main productions are corn, oats, wheat, potatoes and grass. Hay is a sure and profitable crop. Timothy and the finer grasses, particularly red clover, which grows luxuriantly, being the favorite varieties. All find a ready and easy market at remunerative prices. Experience has demonstrated that all kinds of fruits can be raised in abundance, not only apples, but plums, pears, cherries, grapes, etc., have proved a great success, being very fine in appearance and quality, while the trees are vigorous and thrifty, growing rapidly they come into bearing early. Those who have been experimenting with peaches are convinced that this locality is in the great peach belt of Michigan, and the slope of the hill sides are being set out largely to peaches, and soon the county will take rank as one of the first fruit growing counties in Michigan, the southern peninsula of which is destined to be the garden fruit belt of the world.

Big Rapids, the county seat, as a manufacturing city, is growing in prosperity and popularity and has a water power second to none. The Muskegon river with a sixteen-foot fall and two dams within the city limits, furnishes power sufficient to drive the wheels of almost an unlimited number of factories, which with its railroad facilities and special inducements offered by the business men of the city for new enterprises, afford great opportunities to those seeking new locations.

The city contains a fine modern court house erected at an expense of $40,000 and a jail costing $15,000, two iron bridges costing $18,000 and $22,000 respectively.

The educational advantages are the pride of the county and city. Big Rapids is noted for its schools. A central building, erected at a cost of $20,000, and three ward buildings at $5,000 to $8,000 each. The Ferris Industrial College, a new commodious structure costing $20,000, although of only a few years' existence, has already secured a national reputation, and with its attendance of several hundred students from the different states of the Union, has already earned its title of being one of the best liberal educational schools in the country.

MENOMINEE COUNTY.

Menominee county was organized in 1863. It contains an area of 667,153 acres, and in 1890 had a population of 33,639, an increase in ten years of 21,652. Menominee city in 1890 had a population of 10,630 and is the county seat. Located at the extreme southern point of the county, at the mouth of the Menominee river on Green bay, it occupies a place in front rank of lumber producing cities, in fact is claimed to be the first. With excellent shipping facilities, both by rail and water, the advantages of the locality for manufacturing are excellent.

The surface of the county is rolling with some swamp which is reclaimable by drainage. It is nicely drained by the Menominee, Sturgeon, Cedar rivers, and numerous creeks and small streams. The soil is somewhat sandy with clay subsoil, quite productive and easily tilled. Heretofore the land has been valued in proportion to its timber, but the greatest value is not in the timber. It is true that the wealth in timber can soonest be reached, and is generally held by persons who care but little for the fate of the land after they have made their fortunes by stripping the timber off. However this cannot be prevented. This is not a case of killing the goose that laid the golden egg, for after the land is denuded of its productive grand forests it is yet good, and when cultivated intelligently with skilled hands, rich harvests will be gathered, and Menominee instead of being a city of transient interests will count its permanent manufacturing industries, its prosperous surrounding farms and its permanent and reliable citizenship.

Of its entire area 44,189 acres are in farms, 604,116 acres uncultivated and 18,848 acres held by the State and general government and subject to entry or sale. Not one-tenth part of the land is farmed. This looks like an opening for persons wanting cheap farms and we know of no reason why the investment would not be good. With good land, good markets, healthy climate, cheap homes, with plenty of wood for fuel, what is the matter of Menominee county?

MIDLAND COUNTY.

Midland county was organized in 1855. It is bounded on the north by Gladwin, on the east by Bay, on the south by Gratiot and Saginaw, and on the west by Isabella. It has an area of 504 square miles. and had in 1890 a population of 10,657. Midland, a city of 2,277 inhabitants, is the county seat. The surface of the county is slightly rolling, excepting the extreme southern portion, where it is quite level. It is well watered by the Tittabawassee. Chippewa, Pine, Salt and Tobacco rivers, and the small streams tributary to them. There is plenty of available water power throughout the county. There are no swamps of any size, and no sand plains. The soil of the southern portion of the county is mostly clay; that of the northern part is a clay loam, while the western and eastern portions have a sandy loam. A clay subsoil underlies the entire county. The timber is mostly beech, maple, ash, oak, birch, elm, pine and hemlock. The principal crops are wheat, oats, corn, barley, roots of all kinds, and especially hay. Every fruit that has been tried has grown successfully. Apples, plums and other small fruits have invariably done well. There can be no doubt but that fruit will be one of the staples of Midland county. The cost of clearing will average from $10 to $12 per acre. There is a good demand for wood at the salt blocks and bromine works in Midland City. Hardwood, eighteen inches in length, brings $1.50 per cord; softwood averages $1.25.

There is no government land in the market. One thousand and twenty-eight acres of land subject to sale or entry.

Good unimproved lands are plentiful. They can be obtained within a few miles of the settlements at from $5 to $12 per acre. The "stump lands" of this county have a good soil, and wherever cultivated have produced good crops. They are held at from $4 to $8 per acre. Improved farms range in price from $20 to $60 per acre, according to their location. There are two State roads leading from Midland City, one running in a southerly direction to St. Louis, in Gratiot county, and the other running west and north to Houghton Lake, in Roscommon county.

Snow falls by December 1, to an average depth of one foot. Spring work commences in May. The winters are generally steadier in this latitude than in the southern part of the State. The schools of the county are numerous and excellent. At Midland City there is a $20,000 school building, and every effort is made to have the standard compare favorably with that of any city in the State.

Agriculture, lumbering, the manufacture of salt and bromine, charcoal burning, and the cutting of ties, posts and telegraph poles, are the principal industries of the county. The is a good demand for common and skilled labor. The Flint & Pere Marquette Railroad crosses the county from southeast to northwest. There are several logging roads in the northern part of the county and a road between Midland and Bay City.

MISSAUKEE COUNTY.

BY A. G. SMITH, LAKE CITY.

Missaukee county was organized in 1871. It is bounded on the north by Kalkaska, on the east by Roscommon, on the south by Osceola and Clare, and on the west by Wexford. It has an area of 576 square miles, and had a population in 1890 of 5,048. Lake City, the county seat, is a wide-awake village and had 663 population in 1890. Beautifully located on the east shore of Musk-rat lake, the place is built with good substantial buildings, has four saw mills and one planing mill, two banks, two weekly newspapers, and is a thriving town in every sense. It is the present terminus of the Missaukee branch of the G. R. & I. R. R.

Ten miles south of Lake City is located the thriving village of Mc Bain, lately incorporated. The principal industries of the place are several hardwood manufactories. It is located on the T. A. A. & N. M. R. R.

Five miles west of Mc Bain, on the same railroad, is the village of Lucas, also fast coming into prominence on account of its hardwood manufactories.

The surface of the county is gently rolling, and is well watered by the Clam and Muskegon rivers, and by small lakes and spring brooks of clear, cold water. There is good water power to be found, particularly on the Clam river. The soil varies from a sand and sandy loam to a clay loam, with a clay subsoil. The timber on the hardwood lands is principally sugar maple, beech, elm, basswood and hemlock. There are also belts of valuable pine scattered through various portions of the county. The successful crops are wheat, oats, hay, barley, potatoes, corn, and in fact all root crops. The early kinds of corn do well. Apples and plums are grown successfully. All varieties of berries also grow in great abundance. Peaches, however, are not to be relied on.

The cost of clearing hardwood land will average $12 to $15 per acre. The logs are in good demand at the local mills, and at the roll ways along the streams, and large quantities are shipped to Grand Rapids to be manufactured into furniture, and wood brings a fair price in the several villages in the county.

There are 7,555 acres of government and State land for sale or entry in this county, also some G. R. & I. R. R. land, which can be bought at prices ranging from $1 to $7 per acre. These invariably have a good soil and will develop into good agricultural districts. The stump lands, some of which are very desirable, are also quite numerous, and can be had at from $1 to $5 per acre. There are five State roads running through the county, viz.: one north and south through the center of the county, one east and west from Lake City to Cadillac, one from Falmouth to Cadillac, another east and west through the north part of the county, and still another north and south along the Muskegon river. The townships of this county are well opened by section line roads. Snow falls by the last of November, the average depth of the season reaching 20 inches. The ground does not usually freeze, save in places where the wind blows away the snow. Potatoes are frequently left in the ground all winter. Plowing begins by the last of April.

The people of Missaukee county have always shown a lively interest in education, and the district schools, as well as the graded schools in the villages, are in a thriving condition. Usually the school buildings are of good quality, some of them fine brick structures.

Lumbering has been the principal industry in the past, but agricultural interests are now making rapid advancement, and already there are a large number of as finely improved farms as are found anywhere. Common labor is always in good demand, wages ranging from $20 to $35 per month, and there are fine markets for everything that can be raised.

It is expected that the G. R. & I. Railroad company will extend their line to Moorestown in the northeastern part of the county in the near future and connect with a projected line of road through Grayling to Alpena.

The sand on the bank of Musk-rat lake at Lake City has been tested and found to be a fine quality of glass sand. Some fine samples of glass are are on exhibition here made from a shipment of sand sent away as a test. It is thought that further experiments will prove that the sand will make plate glass. It is expected that a glass factory will be built here in the near future.

MONROE COUNTY.

BY W. H. BOYD, MONROE.

Monroe county was organized in 1817, and has fifteen townships, including the city of Monroe, which has four wards. The county is bounded on the north by Washtenaw and Wayne, on the east by Lake Erie, on the south by Ohio, and on the west by Lenawee county. It has an area of 504 square miles, and a population in 1890 of 32,247. Monroe city has 5,246 inhabitants and is the county seat with a fine court house and jail, also fine churches and school buildings. The county house and farm are among the best in the State. The county is well watered the river Raisin running through the county from west to east, with numerous branches; also the Huron on the north, with several creeks running into Lake Erie; also artesian wells in many parts of the county. There are several villages of size: Dundee, Petersburg, Carleton, Milan and Ida, all growing places. The eastern portion is level, especially along the lake, where the soil is clay loam and very rich and productive. The western portion is higher and more sandy, especially the southwestern, and easy to work, and for some products equally valuable.

The timber is composed of all kinds, except pine, hemlock and trees of that class. Oak of all kinds, with hickory, maple and ash, are the most abundant. Raisin river, with its branches, Macon, Saline and others, afford abundant water power, especially at Monroe, Dundee, Petersburg and other points on the line of the river. All kinds of grain are largely grown in all the towns and the eastern portion produces hay in abundance and is sold in the Monroe, Toledo and Detroit markets. Stock is raised in all parts of the county, and our markets are well supplied with the choicest beef, mutton and pork, large quantities of each both alive and slaughtered being shipped on the railroads east, the Monroe market for dressed hogs being one of the best in the State. There are extensive fisheries near Monroe, where fish are caught in abundance and sold fresh and frozen, which supply the home markets and are shipped to the interior of the State. Fruits of all kinds are largely grown. The export of grapes and all small fruits is large and of very fine quality, and command the highest price in the markets of Detroit, Toledo and Chicago, and are very profitable to the producers. Monroe contains three of the most extensive nurseries in the western States, and ships trees of all kinds to almost all the western states in large quantities, the soil being well adapted to that business. The highways of the county are uniformly good except in the eastern portion where the clay lands abound; they are bad in the rainy season. The winter seasons vary, though not more so than in other counties in the State and are not subject to high winds or cyclones. Monroe city has communication with Lake Erie by vessel and steamboat, and large quantities of lumber and telegraph poles are brought into the harbor to be sold and distributed over the State. The Western Union Telegraph company have the largest depot at Monroe for poles in the country, from which they supply their lines. There are four large paper mills, which with other manufactories, give employment to labor. Limestone abounds on the line of the river Raisin, and extensive quarries have been and are still being operated both for lime and building stone, which are shipped to Detroit and other places, besides supplies for home demand. There are no government lands in the county. Farm lands sell for prices according to their situation and improvements, the best from $40 to $100 per acre, and others not so good from $20 to $30. There is not now a more healthy county in the State, as there are no stagnant marshes or pools and the streams are rapid and clear water. Extensive county ditches have been built in all parts of the county so as to drain all the wet lands into the rivers and streams, and farmers are using tile extensively on their farms. Clay is abundant, and brick and tile are cheap.

As for transportation, no county in the State is more favorably situated. The Lake Shore & Michigan Southern, Michigan Central, Flint & Pere Marquette, Wabash, Toledo & Ann Arbor railroads traverse the county, with another road extension from Detroit to Toledo being now projected. These, with the lake, make transportation of all kinds very easy and cheap, the railroads only charging two cents per mile and boats, twenty-five cents to Toledo from Monroe.

For manufacturing the facilities are not surpassed in any portion of the State. This is one of the oldest counties of the State and had much to do with its early history.

MONTCALM COUNTY.

BY EDWARD A. RUNDELL, EDMORE, MICH.

Montcalm county was organized in 1850. It is bounded on the north by Isabella and Mecosta, on the east by Gratiot, on the south by Ionia, and on the west by Kent and Newaygo. It has an area of 720 square miles, and had a population in 1890 of 32,637. Stanton, a town of 1,352 inhabitants, is the county seat.

The surface of the country is generally rolling. It is watered by Flat river in the western part of the county, and by Pine river in the northeastern portion, also by a number of creeks and small lakes scattered throughout the entire county. There are water powers on every stream in the county. There are a number of swamps which are all reclaimable. The soil of the northern and western townships is of a sandy loam, very productive, while that of the eastern and southern townships is a fine loam, very productive. The subsoil is clay throughout. The principal varieties of timber are pine, oak, beech, maple and ash. Wheat, oats, corn, potatoes and grass all do well. Wheat has averaged 20 bushels to the acre for several years. All sorts of vegetables are remarkably successful. Fruit of all kinds is grown with favorable results; peaches, however, are not a sure crop. Apples are shipped in large quantities to the western market.

Some very large flour mills are located in the county, principally at Greenville, Edmore and Howard City.

The soil of Montcalm is peculiarly adapted for the production of potatoes, and the county has been justly noted for this particular product. During the year 1891, 602,914 bushels were shipped out of the county, and in the year 1892 this amount was largely increased. In 1892 the price ranged from fifty to sixty cents per bushel. The acreage planted to potatoes in 1893 far exceeds that of any previous year. The railroad companies have built large potato store houses at the principal points, viz.: Greenville, Edmore, Stanton, Lakeview, Sheridan, Howard City, Six Lakes, and McBrides. These store rooms are built to guard against the most severe cold weather and will store several hundred thousand bushels of potatoes.

The cost of clearing will average $15 per acre, with excellent wood markets in every direction, hardwood, stove length, bringing from $1.25 to $1.50 per cord, and soft, wood about 85 cents. No government lands remain unsold, and but little State land. Desirable unimproved lands can be had at an average price of $10 per acre, while the "stump lands" range from $1 to $5. These lands often prove to be good wheat lands. There is a State road from Greenville to Big Rapids, one running north from Ionia to Houghton lake, and two running east and west through the county. Snow falls by December 1, its average depth during the season being fifteen inches, the ground not freezing to any great depth. Plowing usually begins by April 20.

The schools and churches are both numerous and excellent. Agriculture, lumbering and the manufacture of coal, posts, ties, telegraph poles, furniture, refrigerators, barrels, hoops and agricultural implements are the principal industries. Labor is always in good demand at prices ranging from $20 to $25 per month with board. The Detroit, Lansing & Northern, its Big Rapids branch, and the Saginaw Valley & St. Louis, the Grand Rapids and the Toledo, Saginaw & Muskegon railroads cross the county, affording excellent market facilities to every township, north, south, east and west. No better inducements can be offered to the settler with small means than that offered by this county. Land is cheap, the soil good, society, churches and schools first class, and the development and permanent prosperity of the county assured.

MONTMORENCY COUNTY.

Montmorency county was organized in 1881. It is bounded on the north by Cheboygan and Presque Isle, on the east by Alpena, on the south by Oscoda, and on the west by Otsego. It has an area of 576 square miles, and had a population in 1890 of 1,487. Hillman is the county seat. The eastern part of the county is very level, the central portion is rolling, and the western portion is rolling and somewhat inclined to be hilly. It is watered by the Thunder bay river, which runs through the center of the county from west to east, and is intersected by small streams from the north and south. There are a number of valuable water powers. About one-fourth of the county is swamp land, all of which is reclaimable; another quarter of the county consists principally of sand plains with a good clay subsoil in some places. The soil in the eastern part of the county is mainly a red clay; that of the central portion varies from a light sand to a heavy red clay, while that of the western portion is a clay and sandy loam. The two upper ranges of towns have a fair soil, of which at least two-thirds is suitable for agriculture; this is also true of the southwestern townships. The region is timbered with beech and maple, with hemlock interspersed and some scattering pine. One or two townships contain large tracts of "burnt land," which have been nearly cleared by fire, and which have an excellent clay soil There are many improved farms in town 31, range 4, on which reapers are now in use. It is the most thickly settled township in the county, and formerly had the county seat. The southern portion of the county is chiefly composed of yellow sand plains. Spruce and Norway pine prevail on these plains, also white pine along the headwaters of the Thunder bay river. With proper attention any crop peculiar to the latitude can be successfully grown in most portions of this county. Vegetables, roots, hay, wheat and corn do well, except in unusually cold seasons. Fruit growing has been tested, to a limited extent, with fair results. The cost of clearing the timbered land averages $20 per acre.

There are 37,759 acres of land subject to sale or entry. The unimproved State swamp lands are easily drained, and make valuable farms. The county also contains large tracts of "stump lands," with fair soil, which can be bought at prices ranging from $1 50 to $3 per acre. The Agricultural college and school lands are well adapted to farming purposes. A State road runs east and west through the county, connecting Hillman with the village of Atlanta. The local highways are as yet very new and are in great need of improvement.

Snow falls by the middle of November to an average depth of ten inches, the ground not freezing to any depth. Plowing begins by May 1, or as soon as the snow melts.

The public schools are few, but every effort is made to have the standard as nigh as that of the adjoining counties, where schools are more plentiful.

There are about sixty million feet of pine cut annually in this county. Large quantities of posts, ties and poles are gotten out, which employs all of the labor that is available, at wages ranging from $26 to $30 per month with board. The taxes average about $5 per 40 acres, and are chiefly local.

MUSKEGON COUNTY.

Muskegon county was an offspring from Ottawa. 1859. It is located on Lake Michigan, between Ottawa and Oceana counties. In 1890 it had a population of 40,013, composed of a good class of people, largely from New York and Ohio. A great many Swedes and Hollanders, most of whom are honest, sober, industrious and reliable, settled here; also many Germans and good people of other nationalities.

Some of the best and leading citizens are Americans by adoption, and love their adopted country.

The county covers an area of 321,403 acres of various kinds of land, a large portion of which is sandy, but when properly tilled produces great results. Sandy soil is not so good for cereal crops and hay as clay land, but for fruit and vegetables it is more reliable than clay. Potatoes produced on this soil, while not so large, are superior in quality. Rarely is a diseased potato found in sandy soil. The largest cabbage we have any knowledge of was raised near Muskegon city, weighing over 67 pounds net.

The sandy soil of West Michigan requires fertilizing, but to fertilize and properly cultivate is like putting money in a bank (in fact it can be recovered sooner than from some banks).

Potatoes, sweet corn, melons, strawberries, and all other kinds of berries, cabbage, celery, and flowers, all such things, grow to perfection.

This county was formally a dense forest of pine, hemlock, birch, maple, ash, elm, etc. The pine and hemlock were cut, leaving large amounts of the other kinds. The beech and maple is held for fuel, and the supply is nearly inexhaustible.

The prevailing winds are from the west, and come pure off Lake Michigan, making it a remarkably healthy locality. Hay fever patients who have suffered for twenty-five years, have spent summers in Muskegon county, on the margin of the lake, without a symptom of the disease. At an early day there was some ague, but since the country was opened up and drained, as is the case generally over the State, it disappeared.

The county is well watered by numerous streams and lakes, which are plentifully stocked with fish. There are some bear, deer and other game, while ducks and feathered game are plenty.

Muskegon, the county seat, is located on Muskegon lake, an arm of Lake Michigan, five miles long and over one mile wide, covering about 5,000 acres, with a harbor capable of sheltering from storm all the vessels on the great lakes at one time. The population of the city is about 27,000. Until recently, it was said to be the greatest lumber producing city in the world. Within the last four or five years, this industry has dropped off to some extent, and the manufacturing is taking a more solid form. No city can be permanently prosperous upon a lumber producing basis only; mills are built, makeshifts of houses thrown together, the land skimmed of its wealth, then mills and men flit away leaving nothing but stump land, worthless shanties, and high equalization of value to pay taxes on. An exclusive saw mill industry is no benefit to any county. The aim of the Muskegon people has been to place manufacturing on a solid basis, and success is crowning their efforts. Shipping accommodations at Muskegon will attract manufacturing. While rates are exceedingly low, the time between Muskegon and Chicago and Milwaukee is, in a business point of view, exactly nothing. Shipments at the close of business from Muskegon reach Chicago the next morning before business begins, and so with travel. Business men can take a day in Chicago and be away from business at home only a day, leaving Muskegon in the evening and arriving at Chicago the next morning at about six o'clock, leaving Chicago at night and arriving home in early morning, all at a small cost.

The city is abreast with the times in modern conveniences. Water is pumped from Lake Michigan, and the supply is not liable to be exhausted. Electric lights and cars, churches, schools, hotels, railroads, a new court house, one of the best in the State, about completed, all first class. Muskegon has many public spirited citizens, who do not stand on the order of their going, but go promptly; business is their watchword, fair dealing their motto, enterprise the spirit, success the aim, and to "get there" the incentive. Knowing the transient character of the saw mill business, they aim to solidify manufacturing to permanent works with skilled labor and a permanent citizenship, with permanent homes and interests. If enterprise with opportunity will succeed (and it generally does) Muskegon will get to the king row.

There are several thriving villages, among which are Whitehall, Montague, Ravenna, Fruitport, Sullivan, etc. A five cents outlay and fifteen minutes time will carry citizens to Lake Michigan Park, where the pure air and water of Lake Michigan can be enjoyed to a full extent; but that is not all, 25 cents will pay the round trip to Hackley Assembly ground, "the gem of the Chautauquas." In short, there are resorts in all directions, very fine but cheap. Visitors generally report Muskegon a good place to summer, and after one visit almost invariably return the next season.

NEWAYGO COUNTY.

BY THAD WATERS, FREEMONT, MICH.

Newaygo county was organized in 1851. It is bounded on the north by Lake, on the east by Mecosta and Montcalm, on the south by Muskegon and Kent, and on the west by Muskegon and Oceana. The name is an Indian one and means "Here we rest." There are a number of thriving villages in the county, the principal of which are Newaygo, the county seat, Freemont, Hesperia, White Cloud and Grant. The village of Newaygo has, without exception the best water power in the lower peninsula. It is a manufacturing town. Freemont is situated in a very fertile farming country, and is also extensively engaged in manufactures. Vast forests of pine timber a few years ago covered this county, but the pine is now harvested and the lands are being rapidly improved. There are 1,779 acres of government and State land for sale or entry in this county. All pine stump lands underlaid with a clay subsoil are the best wheat and orchard lands in the State. Grant, Garfield, Sherman, Lincoln and Denver have large bodies of such land. The township of Goodwell is nearly all such land. They can be bought at from $3 to $5 per acre, and the stumps pulled and put into fences at from 75 cents to $1 per rod. When once cleared these lands are far superior to prairie lands for wheat, apples and peaches. Apples and peaches are destined to be the crop of this county in the near future. Thousands of peach trees have been set in the last year and are beginning to yield a bountiful harvest. The economical way of setting fruit, apples every four rods and peaches' one rod apart between has not been practiced much as yet. The peach is a short lived tree and set with apples in the manner indicated, leaves when old and worthless, an apple orchard just coming fully into fruiting. Those who rush by the State of Michigan for big red apples do not know what they are doing. Over 15,000 bushels were shipped from Freemont alone in the fall of 1892. Two railroads traverse the county north and south and one east and west. The county is well watered with innumerable spring brooks, all stocked with speckled trout, which flow into the Muskegon, White and Pere Marquette rivers. The water in these streams is as clear, cold and pure as heaven can make it, and no miasmatic taint sends the stranger who pitches his tabernacle on their shady banks to the drug store for quinine to relieve his shakes. Thousands of acres of blackberries furnish us with this luscious fruit, to be had only for the picking. Thousands of bushels are picked every year and yet probably not one-half are saved. No better schools can be found in Michigan than those found in Newaygo county, and the school system of Michigan is equal to any in the world. The patriotism, hospitality and push-aheadativeness of the people of this county are not excelled, and we say to all who wish to make a comfortable home and become active business citizens: "Newaygo"—here we rest!

OAKLAND COUNTY.

Oakland county was organized in 1820. It is bounded on the north by Genesee and Lapeer, on the east by Macomb, on the south by Washtenaw and Wayne, and on the west by Livingston and Genesee. It has an area of 900 square miles, and had a population in 1890 of 41,245. Pontiac, a town of 6,200 inhabitants, is the county seat. Near this town is located the Eastern Asylum for the Insane, a magnificent structure, which accommodates a large number of patients. At Orchard Lake, near Pontiac, is also a fine military school, which enjoys a large patronage. The surface of the county is generally rolling, though not hilly. The highest land of that section of country lying between Lake Michigan, Lake St. Clair, Saginaw Bay and Detroit river is found in this county, it being from 400 to 600 feet above the Detroit river. Four important rivers rise near the center of the county, flowing in entirely different directions, viz.: the Shiawassee, the Huron, the Clinton, and the Rouge. The county is well watered also by numerous smaller streams and inland lakes, there being no less than 100 of these small lakes within the border of the county. There is some swampy land along the border of the lakes, nearly all of which is reclaimable. A number of available waters are found along the larger streams, many of which are in use.

34

The soil is a mixture of sand, clay and loam; this combination prevailing in every township in the county. The subsoil is uniformly clay. The eastern portion of the county was originally timbered with beech, maple, basswood, oak, ash, elm, etc., while the northern portion was timbered chiefly with oak. But little timber now remains, and this is carefully husbanded for domestic use.

Wheat is the staple, though large crops of corn, oats, barley, rye, buckwheat, potatoes, and all garden vegetables are annually harvested. Apples, pears, peaches and grapes are profitably cultivated. The Canada Red, Baldwin and Greening apples, the Bartlett pear, the Crawford peaches (early and late varieties), and the Concord grapes have a large sale in Detroit, Toledo and Chicago markets. As stated above, timbered lands are scarce, hence, hardwood brings from $3 to $4 per cord, and soft wood about a dollar less. There are no government, State or railroad lands for sale in this county. Improved farms are the only available lands, at prices ranging from $50 to $100 per acre. The highways of the county are unexceptionally good. The two great wagon roads, viz.: the Saginaw turnpike, and the Grand River turnpike (both leading to Detroit), are extensively traveled.

About seven months constitute an ordinary season for productive farm labor. Little snow falls prior to January 1. It generally averages from 6 to 12 inches in depth. The ground usually freezes to a moderate depth, depending entirely on the fall of snow. A gravelly open soil in an exposed situation will sometimes freeze to a depth of three feet. Spring work begins usually by April 1st.

The schools are very numerous and sustain a fine reputation. Agriculture is the principal industry, and creates a constant demand for farm labor during the summer season, wages usually ranging from $15 to $24 per month with board. A large peat bed was discovered a few years since, not far from Highland, on the line of the Flint & Pere Marquette railroad, which yields a considerable amount of this peculiar fuel. The Detroit, Grand Haven & Milwaukee, the Detroit & Bay City, the Flint & Pere Marquette and a branch of the Grand Trunk Railroad place every section of land throughout the county within easy reach of market facilities.

OCEANA COUNTY.

BY FRED J. RUSSELL, HART, MICH.

Oceana county was organized in 1855. It is bounded on the north by Mason county, on the east by Newaygo, on the south by Muskegon and on the west by Lake Michigan.

It has an area of 540 square miles, and had a population in 1890 of 15,698. The principal villages are Hart, Shelby and Pentwater. Hart the county seat has a population of 1,200, and is a thrifty, enterprising village, with excellent schools, churches, two banks and first class hotel accommodations.

The extreme eastern portion of the county is comparatively level for several miles near the lake shore, the land is gently undulating, while the eastern portion is still more rolling, and some parts to a person accustomed to a flat country might be called hilly.

The entire county is beautifully watered by springs and spring brooks the finest in the world, joining each other on their way to Lake Michigan, and forming the north and south branches of the Pentwater river in the northern portion, and the north and south branches of the White river in the southern portion, together with many island lakes and other small streams wending their way to the great lake single handed and alone. Good well water is abundant, and the streams abound in speckled trout, and the lakes are well stocked with fish. The soil is a sandy loam, with a large amount of lime gravel, with a black vegetable mold, with clay subsoil in the central and eastern portion, running to lighter soil in the western.

The timber is principally sugar maple, elm, basswood and beech, unsurpassed for size and beauty.

Every crop that is peculiar to Michigan is grown successfully in this county, and especially is this true of fruits and vegetables. The potatoes of Oceana county are the standard of excellence, and are surpassed by none. They have a national reputation in potato markets; that crop responds to the labor of the farmer so that he is often surprised at his success, 250 to 300 bushels per acre is not an uncommon yield, with an occasional crop of 400 to 500 bushels per acre. Wheat, corn, oats, timothy and clover are raised with success.

Apples, pears and cherries and small fruits are grown to great perfection throughout the entire county. Oceana county seems to be the home of the plum, the perfection in which it is grown in this county is not surpassed in any county, either in or out of Michigan, and it is not uncommon for the plum growers in this county to receive a net income from their plums of $200 to $350 per acre annually for a series of years. The peculiar location of this county extending westerly into Lake Michigan, so that that great body of open water tempers and warms the northwest, west and southwest winds thereby extracting the sting which the great northwest is so apt to furnish, rendering the winter weather mild and peculiarly fitting for a fruit county, and especially is this necessary to raise the peach successfully. Peach trees have not heretofore been killed in this county by freezing, the rolling lands furnish an ideal location for this beautiful fruit. None of the diseases peculiar to the peach, and which have so devastated the older peach belts in this and other states have been discovered here. The crops of peaches in this county have been annual for a long series of years, and the trees that are in full bearing, and are being planted are numbered by hundreds of thousands until the hills and high table lands are being set to peaches, and the lower lands to plums. The growing of peaches is claimed to be still more profitable than that of plums, and a ready market is furnished in Chicago, Milwaukee, and the great west and northwest for all fruits grown here. In the great markets these fruits are advertised as Oceana county fruits. Good fruit land can be furnished uncultivated for $10 to $20 per acre. With a good demand for the timber products, the value of fruit farms with bearing orchard depends entirely upon the quantity and age of trees. There is much unimproved land in this county which can be purchased at reasonable prices, that is well adapted for either general farming or fruit growing, or both. Large quantities of maple ugar and syrup are made annually.

The Chicago & West Michigan Railway extends from the south through the county, terminating at Hart and Pentwater. The Mason & Oceana Railroad from Ludington enters the northeast part of the county, terminating at Walkerville. The highways are in very good condition for a new county, and they are especially free from mud, compared to those in most timbered lands.

The winters are milder than in other parts of the State, away from the lake shore, for the reasons given. There are 1,320 acres of government and State land subject to sale or entry in this county.

There is usually sufficient snow for good sleighing, the ground rarely freezing, and active work on the farm commences about the first of April.

The schools and churches are good and well attended. The principal industries are agriculture, fruit raising and lumbering of hardwood. There are manufactories for working hardwood at Hart, Pentwater and Shelby. Pentwater has a good harbor, and is a well known lake port and enjoys a large shipping trade.

The health of the entire county is good and the residents are possessed of thrift and enterprise rarely found, being settled with people from New York and Ohio largely.

OGEMAW COUNTY.

Ogemaw county was organized in 1875. It is bounded on the north by Oscoda, on the east by Iosco, on the south by Gladwin and Arenac, and on the west by Roscommon. It has an area of 576 square miles, and in 1890 had a population of 5,583. West Branch, a town of 1,700 inhabitants, is the county seat.

The surface of the county is undulating, and is well watered by the Rifle river and its many branches; also by numerous springs and spring brooks. There are occasional swamps with cedar, tamarack, black ash, white maple, and other similar timber.

These swamps are generally reclaimable, and it is believed will make good meadow lands. The southwestern part of the county contains a large tract of hardwood (beech and maple with hemlock and pine interspersed) growing in a good clay soil. North of this lies a ridge of white and Norway pine. The rest of the county to its eastern border is occupied by a series of ridges and valleys having a north and south tendency, and located in the following order, commencing in the west: 1st, the plains of yellow sand; 2d, ridges and valleys with much Norway and white pine, and considerable gravelly soil of fine quality; 3d, a hardwood ridge with a good clay soil; 4th, in the extreme eastern part of the county commence what are known as the Tawas plains, which extend far into Iosco. These plains have a soil of yellow sand. The prevailing timber is jack or spruce pine, which makes a good fuel, and can be used for fencing. They have been burned over often, the fires burning down into the land itself, the soil apparently rendered combustible by the drippings of pitch from the pines. They are without a regular subsoil, but still retain moisture. Lakes are scattered through the plains, and surface springs are also found. There are many homesteaders farming on these plains, who raise good crops of clover and rye, excellent vegetables, also corn and wheat in favorable seasons. Fertilizers are used to a considerable extent, and what this soil will do under continued cultivation is yet to be tested. There is considerable maple timber in the county, the soft maple growing in the sand, while in the clay lands the hard sugar maple flourishes and predominates over the beech. On the clay lands vegetables and rye are good crops, as are hay and clover. Corn and wheat also do well in favorable seasons. The capacity of the county for fruits has not yet been thoroughly tested, and the later frosts are now considered a serious obstacle to successful fruit raising. Berries, however, grow in abundance.

The cost of clearing averages $20 per acre on the heavy timbered lands and from $1 to $5 on the plains. There are, as yet, no wood markets of any consequence. There are 5,214 acres subject to sale or entry, also some railroad lands. There are plenty of unimproved lands within a few miles of the county seat which can be had at prices ranging from $2.50 to $10 per acre. These lands have a soil of clay loam, and make the best of farms. When located in remote parts of the county the price varies from $3 to $6 per acre. There are large tracts of stump land which are rapidly coming into the market. The Manistee and Tawas State road runs east and west through the county. There is also a State road running north and south which passes about a mile east of the county seat, Snow falls early in November to an average depth of 20 inches. Spring work begins early in April.

There are about thirty schools in the county, all of which have more than six months' school each year. Lumbering is as yet the principal industry. Ties, posts and telegraph poles are gotten out in large quantities. Labor is in good demand, wages ranging from $1 to $1.50 per day. In the lumber woods wages range from $20 to $30 per month with board. The Mackinac division of the Michigan Central and the Tawas & Bay County railroads are the only ones traversing the county at present. The Michigan Central Railroad company has surveyed a line 25 miles in length, extending in a northeasterly direction from Beaver lake. This line will, eventually, reach Alpena. There is also a projected extension of the Toledo, Ann Arbor & Northern from North Bradley, on the Flint & Pere Marquette railroad, to Alpena, which will cross the county.

ONTONAGON COUNTY.

Ontonagon county is situated in the northwestern part of the upper peninsula, and borders on Lake Superior. In area it is one of the largest counties in the State, containing over thirty-seven surveyed townships of land. The principal industries of the county are lumbering in the interior and fishing on the coast. Formerly copper mining was extensively carried on, but at the present prices of copper none of the mines can be worked at a profit except by tributers. The Minnesota and National copper mines are located at Rockland this county. These mines were formerly noted for their large masses or native copper found in their depths. One such mass taken from the former mine weighed over five hundred tons and is the largest single mass of copper ever discovered. It took nearly two years to cut this huge boulder of copper and hoist it to the surface. At the present price of copper mass mining is no longer profitable and the scene of great copper mining has been transferred to Houghton county, where the stamp veins being more uniform in their formation can be mined at a profit.

A large portion of the county is covered with pine and hardwood forests, and lumbering may be said to be the chief industry. The soil along the line of the Mineral Range mountains which traverse the county from northeast to southwest is very rich and productive. Many of the miners along the range have lately turned their attention to farming. Oats, barley, potatoes, and all kinds of garden vegetables are grown in great abundance, the yield of oats to the acre often exceeding sixty bushels. Apples, plums, and small berries are also raised with profit.

For many years, during the summer season, fishing for whitefish and Lake Superior trout has been extensively carried on at Ontonagon, the county seat. The latter place has an elegant brick court house and jail, good school houses, several stores, and a population of about 1,800. It is situated on Lake Superior at the mouth of the Ontonagon river. The Methodist, Catholic, Presbyterian and Episcopal are the leading churches, each one owning a church edifice of fair proportions, and having a fair sized congregation. The Milwaukee & Northern Railroad connects Ontonagon by a direct line with Milwaukee and Chicago, and the mouth of the Ontonagon river furnishes a good harbor for all vessels navigating the great lakes

The residents of Ontonagon, Rockland and Greenland, known as the old part of the county, are noted for their hospitality and genial old fashioned social ways.

The greater portion of the county, especially in the southern part, is covered with vast forests of pine and hard maple. Lumbering is extensively carried on in the pineries. The Diamond Match Co. operates two large saw mills at Ontonagon. Several other smaller mills are located at Ewen, on the Duluth, South Shore & Atlantic Railroad in the southern part, which is the second place in population and enterprise in the county. It is situated in the heart of the pineries, and although but four years old is already known as a hustling town. It has water works, a fire department, good hotels and churches, and what is of more importance, a progressive people. A prosperous future is assured for Ewen as well as for the adjacent lumbering towns of Trout Creek, Interior and Matchwood.

Improved hardwood lands are worth $10 an acre. Pine lands are worth from $3 to $7 per thousand feet stumpage, depending on the quality. The county will be made conspicuous at the World's Columbian Exposition for its huge exhibit load of pine logs, containing 36,055 feet of timber, in fifty-five logs, loaded and hauled by the Nester estate at Ewen, Ontonagon county, in February, 1893.

Ontonagon county is a good place for settlers looking for cheap homes. Several thousand acres of good hardwood land adjacent to railroads are yet subject to homestead entry, but are fast being taken up by enterprising settlers who are rapidly turning the wilderness into beautiful farms. Wood brings from $3 to $4 per cord in the towns and more than pays for the clearing of the land.

OSCEOLA COUNTY.

BY C. E. DERMONT, EVART, MICH.

Osceola county was organized in 1869; is located in the northwestern half of the lower peninsula; a line drawn north and south equi distant from Saginaw bay on the east and Lake Michigan on the west forms its eastern boundary line.

It is seventy-six miles west from Saginaw, and sixty-nine miles north of Grand Rapids; is in the same latitude as Portland, Maine, and not so far north as Ogdensburg, New York.

It has an area of 576 square miles, and a population, in 1890, of 14,630.

The surface of the county is greatly diversified, the larger portion of the county, however, being comparatively level. The northwestern portion is quite hilly. An extensive belt of pine barrens is found on the line of the Flint and Pere Marquette Railroad, east and west of Evart, with a generally level surface. Back of this the land is more desirable, beech and maple lands predominating, with occasional white cedar swamps, which make fine grass lands when reclaimed. The county is well watered by the Muskegon river and its tributaries; also by a large number of spring brooks. A sandy loam predominates, but all kinds of soil, varying from a light sand to a heavy clay, are found in nearly every township. The subsoil is generally clay. The principal varieties of timber are maple, rock-elm, black and white ash, beech, and basswood. There are, however, belts of pine, hemlock, and some birch in most townships. All nothern crops grow to perfection. That the soil of Osceola county is well adapted to growng wheat is made evident by the fact that wheat has been known to yield forty bushels to the acre, although the average yield is much less. Corn, buckwheat, potatoes, peas, etc., do well. Apples are a successful crop. Plums, pears, cherries, and berries, particularly whortleberries, yield abundantly. Peaches, however, are not to be depended on.

Only 576 acres of public lands remain subject to sale or entry. Plenty of good unimproved lands can be had at prices ranging from $4 to $10 per acre. The stump lands are also plentiful, and are to be had at from $3.50 to $10.00 per acre. The highways are constructed on section lines, and are as good as the average highways throughout the State. The seasons are possibly a fortnight later than in the counties further south. Snow falls to a considerable depth, the ground seldom freezing.

The schools are plentiful and good, there being sixty-eight school districts in the county. Lumbering, the cutting of ties, posts, and poles, river driving, tan-bark peeling, the manufacture of shingles, and agriculture, are the principal industries. The

Flint & Pere Marquette, the Grand Rapids & Indiana, and its Luther branch, and Toledo, Ann Arbor and North Michigan, traversing the county on all sides, east, west, north and south, affording good and convenient facilities to both settlers and shippers.

Among the principal towns and villages is Reed City, in the southwestern part of the county, at the junction of the Flint & Pere Marquette and Grand Rapids & Indiana railroads. It is an incorporated village, having a population of 1,776. Contains a number of manufacturing industries, a National bank, many fine stores, churches, and an opera house, and is surrounded by a fine farming community.

Evart, the second village in size and importance, is also incorporated and is located in the southern central part of the county, fourteen miles east of Reed City, on the Flint & Pere Marquette Railroad, where this road crosses the Muskegon river. It is a very thriving village with a population of 1,270 in 1890. It contains two saw mills, planing mill, shook factory, stave and heading mill, flour mill, a good bank, churches, many fine stores, and the finest plant for supplying the village with spring water in the State; mains are laid in all the principal streets, affording most excellent fire protection. The water works plant was erected by the village, at a cost of $10,000, and is paid for. Evart is also the home of the Champion Tool and Handle Works, the largest manufacturers of all kinds of tools used in lumbering operations in the United States. Their goods are sold all over this country, and large bills are exported. It is also the rendezvous for trout fishers, there being no less than seven spring creeks in this vicinity, that are noted for the number and size of the trout; many thousands are taken from the waters of these streams every season, affording both sport and recreation to the many who annually make a pilgrimage to this lovely little town. Graduates from its public schools are eligible for admission to the State University and the State Normal School.

Marion, located in Marion township, in the northeastern corner of the county, is a lively town of recent growth, on the Toledo, Ann Arbor & North Michigan Railroad. It has a splendid flour mill, run by water power, and a couple of saw mills, also does a good business in tan-bark, ties. cedar posts and shingles. It is a growing place, with a population of about six hundred.

Other towns of importance are LeRoy, population 450, Ashton, population 400, Tustin, population 300, on the Grand Rapids & Indiana Railroad, in the western part of the county, and Sears, on the Flint & Pere Marquette. in the southeastern part of the county. All have some local industry devoted to working up the products of the forest. Hersey, the county seat, is a quiet place of 328 population, on the F. & P. M. Railroad, in the southwestern part of the county.

No county in the State has better water. Not a township in the county but is well watered with spring creeks, and in this connection the settlers attention is called to the important fact that these streams are alive with brook trout, affording to any who choose to seek them, the sport and profit of a good catch at any time during the season, for the trout streams in this State are rigidly protected by the game and fish laws. There are over thirty fine spring lakes in the county abounding in pike, perch, pickerel, bass of all kinds, and sun fish. Partridge are plenty, also red squirrels; quail are increasing, though the people of the county have been very chary of shooting any, wishing to get them well and prolifically located before hunting them, as they do the partridge.

On the whole, Osceola county offers to intending purchasers and settlers splendid opportunities. There are, at this writing. 103,057 acres of land under cultivation; the assessed valuation of the county is $4,000,000; there is but 5,204 acres subject to sale or entry. The pine stump lands are being rapidly taken up and converted to grazing, for which purpose they have proven of considerable value. There is some poor land in the county, known as "the plains;" originally it had a large growth of Norway and pine, which was long since cut and marketed; these lands are of a flinty, sandy soil, requiring extraordinary rain fall to moisten, and as yet no fertilizer has been discovered that will make them productive, hence all efforts in this direction have proved futile. The northern half of the county possesses some of the most desirable sites and locations for the herding and grazing of sheep that could be desired. The prices at which these lands are held is very reasonable, and as they have been burnt over to some extent the cost of putting them in shape for stock purposes is very small. Root crops of all kinds grow here in a most abundant and prolific manner.

Osceola county is one of the banner counties of the northern half of the lower peninsula, and cordially invites settlers to its boundaries, having good lands, good markets, low taxes, and a healthy, conservative and growing population.

OSCODA COUNTY.

Oscoda county was organized in 1881. It is bounded on the north by Montmorency, on the east by Alcona, on the south by Ogemaw, and on the west by Crawford. It has an area of 365,299 acres, and had a population in 1890 of 1,904. Mio is the county seat.

About one-third of the county is hard timbered land, with an undulatory surface. Another third is covered over more or less thickly with pine timber, and the remaining third is a comparatively level plain covered with a growth of small timber, generally of the spruce pine variety. The soil is of a heavy clay variety on the heavier timbered lands, and of a sandy and gravelly nature on the pine lands and plains. The subsoil varies from a clay to coarse gravel. The county is well watered by the Au Sable, a large and rapid stream, which traverses in its windings about forty miles of territory before it leaves the county. There are also numerous smaller streams, some of them in the northern part forming the head waters of the Thunder bay river. As indicated above the timber on the heavier lands is principally beech, maple, oak, ash and basswood. On the pine lands it is Norway and white pine and cedar, while on the plains it is small oak, spruce pine, etc. The range of crops is quite varied. Root crops do remarkably well. Wheat is successful, even on the plain. Clover is also uniformly successful where the land has been worked for two or three years. The timbered portions are well adapted to grass. Potatoes are raised in large quantities for the many lumbering camps in this and adjoining counties. On the plains rye and buckwheat are sure to succeed as first crops, and field peas, sown broadcast, would probably do well preparatory to putting in winter wheat. After the first plowing a greater range of scope is admissable. Fruit growing is in its infancy in this county, yet there are many young orchards which are growing rapidly and do not winter kill.

The lightly timbered lands can be cleared at from $1 to $4 per acre, while the expense on the heavier timbered lands will average from $10 to $15.

There is 61,307 acres of public lands for sale or entry in the county.

Unimproved lands range in price from fifty cents to $5 per acre, according to the amount of timber and location. The "stump lands," which were originally timbered only in part with pine, prove to be excellent for farming purposes, and are held at the same price as unimproved lands. There is a State road along the Au Sable river, running east and west. The local roads are easily built and are smooth and passable at all times of the year. The winters are a little longer, and fall and spring somewhat shorter than farther south. Snow falls early, from six inches to two feet in depth.

Schools, churches, roads and general improvements are as good as could be expected and progressing.

OTSEGO COUNTY.

Otsego county was organized in 1875. It is bounded on the north by Charlevoix and Cheboygan, on the east by Montmorency, on the south by Crawford, and on the west by Antrim and Charlevoix. It has an area of 540 square miles, and had a population in 1890 of 4,270. Gaylord is the county seat. It is pleasantly located near the center of the county, and has an elevation of 800 feet above Lake Huron. In fact this county is the highest in the lower peninsula and its climatic advantages are unexcelled.

The surface is generally level, the north half more rolling, particularly a belt running northwest and southeast, just north of the center of the county. This belt has some nicely improved farms, yet is rather hilly. Several of the larger streams of the State have their headwaters in this county, viz., the Au Sable, the Manistee and the Cheboygan. Small streams and inland lakes are quite numerous. There are some cedar swamps in the northwestern towns which are all reclaimable. There are also some sand plains in the southeastern and northeastern portions of the county which it is thought, will make good farming lands. There are several available water powers on the larger streams. The soil is generally sand and gravelly loam with a heavy subsoil in some places. The timber is maple, elm, basswood and hemlock, and about one-fourth of the county contains some pine. Winter and spring wheat, potatoes and root crops of all kinds are raised successfully. Owing to the frosts corn is not a certain crop. Peas, oats and rye are staple crops. Grass and clover also do well. The orchards are as yet young, but the prospects are very flattering for a successful fruit country.

The plains cost $5 per acre to clear, while the timbered lands average $20. There are good markets for wood along the railroad. There are 11,723 acres of land subject to sale or entry. Large tracts of beech and maple land, unimproved, can be had at prices ranging from $4 to $10 per acre. These lands are in good demand. The "stump lands" are also numerous and cheap. They have not been extensively cultivated, but as far as tested produce well. A State road running east and west between Lake Michigan and Lake Huron, passes through the center of the county.

OTTAWA COUNTY.

Ottawa county was organized in 1837. It is bounded on the north by Muskegon, on the east by Kent. on the south by Allegan and on the west by Lake Michigan. It has an area of 510 square miles, and had a population in 1890 of 35,358. There about 10,000 Hollanders, located principally in the southern part of the county, where they have a prosperious colony. Grand Haven, a city of 5.023 inhabitants, situated at the mouth of Grand river, is the county seat. Holland City had a population in 1890 of 3,945.

Much of the surface of the county is level; the balance is gently rolling, and all susceptible to drainage. The Grand river flows through the county from east and west. It is navigable for small vessels as far up as Grand Rapids. The county is also watered by the Bass, Black and Pigeon rivers, Crockery, Deer, Sand and other creeks, and by Black, Pigeon and Spring lakes. There is a large stretch of swamp or wet prairie, which is all reclaimable, and has a rich soil, raising fine grass. The entire county by proper and inexpensive cultivation, could be made arable and adapted to grazing. There are no water powers, owing to the level character of the land. The soil is principally of a sandy nature with a subsoil of gravel. There is some loam with a clay subsoil in different sections throughout the county.

The timber is oak, beech, maple and pine. Corn, wheat and all cereals, root crops and garden vegetables flourish in the warm quick soil, while the fruits cannot be excelled. This county lies in the celebrated fruit belt of western Michigan, and peaches, pears, apples, plums, cherries, currants and grapes grow in great abundance. and are shipped to the Chicago and Milwaukee markets, where there is a great demand for Michigan fruit.

The cost of clearing averages from $12 to $15 per acre. Wood finds a ready sale throughout the county, hardwood bringing from $4 to $5 per cord, and softwood from $2 to $2.50. There is no government land in the market, with the exception of one 80-acre tract. There are 440 acres of land subject to sale or entry. The stump lands of the county are receiving considerable attention, and no doubt will develop into good fruit and farming lands. They are held at prices within the reach of all. Improved farms range in price from $30 to $100 per acre. Good wagon roads bring all parts of the county into easy communication with the markets. The lake winds moderate both extremes of temperature. The average temperature for the month of January, during the last ten years, was 26° Fahr., while the average temperature for June was 62.7°.

The schools of the county are very prosperous. At Holland is located Hope college, an institution extensively patronized by local and non-resident Hollanders. Agriculture is the principal industry. One of the largest flouring mills in the State is located at Holland. Large machine shops and engine works are located at Ferrysburg. Labor is in fair demand, both on farms and among the lumbering and manufacturing industries. wages ranging from $1 to $1.25 per day for common labor. Skilled labor commands proportionately higher wages. The Chicago & West Michigan, its Grand Rapids branch, and the Detroit, Grand Haven & Milwaukee railroads traverse the county. The lake ports also afford excellent shipping facilities, and enjoy an extensive commerce.

Grand Haven for many years was a very large lumber point. Several extensive saw mills were located there, all of which have removed, having exhausted the supply of logs. It is, however, claimed that other manufactories are locating and the city is becoming a manufacturing point of importance. The charcoal furnace at Fruitport has produced a large amount of pig iron of a very superior quality. Ship building has for a long time been an important business at Grand Haven, and the sands in the bluffs may sometime be utilized in the manufacture of glass and stone. The excellent shipping facilities will be a great inducement to manufacturers.

PRESQUE ISLE COUNTY.

BY W. A. FRENCH.

The principal industries of this county consists of lumbering pine and cedar, also farming. Fully 65,000,000 feet is annually lumbered from this county. There yet remains of uncut pine 250,000,000 feet. There are 150,000 cedar ties marketed annually and as much more each of pine posts, and there are yet remaining large quantities. The hemlock timber is practically untouced and runs up in the hundred millions. This applies to hardwood consisting of red oak, maple, hard birch, beech, elm and basswood, in which the county is well supplied. All products are shipped by water (Lake Huron), there being no railroads in this county. Mineral has been found in limited quantities.

For agricultural purposes this county stands high for the following products and cannot be surpassed: Hay, two and one-half to three tons to the acre; peas, thirty to forty-five bushels to the acre; potatoes (no bugs) 300 to 400 bushels to the acre, in fact all roots are of the best growth and also flavor, the soil is peculiarly adapted for the cultivation of roots. Wheat is another grain that this soil excels in. It grows very plump and full and in nearly every case is over weight.

Considerable limestone is to be found in the county. The soil is a very nice clay loam. No navigable rivers in this county. The principal rivers for lumbering are the Ocqueoc river, Swan river and other small streams. Rogers City is the county seat and chief city of the county. population 1,000, industries milling. There is considerable fishing along the lake fronting this county, but it is carried on by Cheboygan and Alpena fishermen, as we have no railroads for shipping. The game consists of partridges in great quantities. Deer and bear (black) are found in limited quantities. Wages command $1.50 to $1.65, skilled $2.50 to $4. Improved land $25 per acre, unimproved $1.50 to $5 per acre. Schools are fairly distributed throughout the county. Farm labor $22 per month. Fruit cultivated is limited, but the soil and climate is perfect for apples and plums. No worms ever trouble them and they have an excellent flavor. Wild fruit, huckleberries and red raspberries are abundant, also blackberries.

ROSCOMMON COUNTY.

Roscommon county was organized in 1875. It is bounded on the north by Crawford, on the east by Ogemaw, on the south by Gladwin and Clair, on the west by Missaukee. It has an area of 576 square miles and had a population in 1890 of 2,033. Roscommon, an enterprising town of 511 inhabitants, located in in the northern part of the county, is the county seat.

The surface of the county is for the most part level, interspersed with ridges. It is well watered by the south branch of the Au Sable and the headwaters of the Muskegon rivers, also by Houghton, Higgins and other lakes. There is considerable swamp land in the county, nearly all of which, when reclaimed, would make admirable meadow lands or cranberay marshes. The altitude of the county is such that there are streams flowing both east and west, and the fall is such as to make plenty of available water power on several of the larger streams. There is considerable land known as "sand plains," some of which is already taken up by homesteaders. The soil is a sandy loam on the high lands, with a fair percentage of clay. There is generally a sandy subsoil on the lower lands near the marshes and streams.

The timber is principally white, Norway and spruce pine, with occasional belts of beech, maple, oak, cedar, tamarack, spruce and balsam. Potatoes have thus far been the most successful crop on the heavier timbered lands, although the earlier and hardier varieties of corn can be as successfully produced as in any part of the state. But little attention has been paid to the raising of the cereals, owing to the lack of milling facilities, but wherever tests have been made, the results have been uniformly good. Wheat, oats, rye buckwheat, and millet have yielded very satisfactory crops. It has been suggested that the experiment of planting amber cane be tried on the lighter soils, as this cane has been grown very successfully on light soils in other parts of the State.

There are a number of young orchards with flattering prospects of future success. The hardier varieties of apples should always be chosen in setting out trees. Berries grow in great abundance.

The cost of clearing varies from $5 to $15, according to the kind of timber on the lands. There are good local markets for wood along the line of railroad, hardwood bringing $1.50 per cord stove length, and softwood from 75 cents to $1. There are 77,857 acres of land subject to sale or entry. There are large tracts of "stump land," which have a good soil, and make very desirable farms, and can be had at prices ranging from $1 to $2.50 per acre. There is a State road running from Roscommon, via Houghton lake, to Midland, also a complete system of local roads which, owing to the sandy nature of the soil, are always in a good condition. Snow falls by Nov. 1, to an average depth of sixteen inches, the ground freezing but little. Plowing begins from the first to the middle of May.

The schools are as yet few, but compare favorably with those of the surrounding counties. Lumbering is, and will be for years, the principal industry. Wood, ties, posts and telegraph poles are gotten out in vast quantities, employing a large number of men, wages ranging from $20 to $30 per month with board. The Mackinac division of the Michigan Central Railroad passes through the county, affording excellent market facilities. There are also one or two logging roads in the southern part of the county. Higgins Lake is a delightful summer resort and is visited every season by a large number of hay fever and asthmatic patients, who generally find speedy relief.

SAGINAW COUNTY.

BY SAMUEL G. HIGGINS, SAGINAW, E. S.

The Saginaw Valley is one of the richest agricultural regions of the State, possessing an alluvial soil, very productive, adapted to the growth of wheat, corn, oats, rye, barley, peas, potatoes, hay, and, in short, all farm crops, fruits and vegetables. Saginaw county lies in the center of the Saginaw Valley and occupies 588 square miles, or 376,320 acres. Of this area 275,508 acres are in farms, 174,209 acres being improved, and 102,-209 acres unimproved. The Cass, Flint, Shiawassee and Tittabawassee rivers unite near the center of the county, just above the city of Saginaw, the county seat and from the Saginaw river, which flows north eighteen miles to Saginaw bay, an arm of Lake Huron, the whole county is well watered, springs and flowing wells being abundant. Beech, maple, oak, ash and other timbers are plentiful. Great improvements have been made in drainage, as roads have been opened up and the lands cleared. A system of Macadamized roads is being planned, which will be of great benefit to the whole county. Excellent unimproved farming lands, well located and on good roads can be purchased for $5 to $15 per acre, on long time and reasonable interest. Improved farms near the city are worth $50 to $100 per acre, and even higher.

In 1891 the yield of wheat in Saginaw county was 519,632 bushels, an average of 19.32 bushels per acre. The corn crop was 1,133,560 bushels, 72 bushels per acre. The oat crop was 1,189,597 bushels, 41 bushels per acre. The land is especially well adapted to dairy farming, the cheese product for 1892 being over 8,000 pounds.

The population of Saginaw county, according to the United States census of 1890, was 82,273, an increase of 40 per cent over the census of 1880.

The Saginaw Valley has long been known as the most important lumber manufacturing center in the country, and this fact has given rise to the erroneous impression that the land was unsuitable for farming purposes. But a very large portion of the territory is hardwood land, and many of the best farms in Saginaw county were originally pine forests. Saginaw county is one of the largest salt producing districts in the United States, the brine being pumped from a depth of about 700 feet and evaporated by means of the exhaust steam from the engines of the various factories. Chemical works are in contemplation to manufacture from the brine many articles of great commercial value, soda ash for making glass and soap, caustic soda for making wood pulp paper, etc.

The city of Saginaw is a large manufacturing city of 60,000 population, which gives the farmers an excellent market for their produce. Eleven lines of railroad radiate from Saginaw, reaching all parts of the country. In the early days Saginaw bore the reputation of having an unhealthful climate. The large areas of uncultivated and undrained land naturally produced malaria, but with the settlement and drainage of the lands these conditions have long since changed, and this is one of the most healthful sections in the United States. The summers are delightful, the nights being cool and refreshing even during the midsummer season. The autumns are the perfection of fine weather, continuing often until near Christmas before snowfall commences. Then follows a steady winter with plenty of snow, giving good sleighing until March. Farming operations commence about the middle of April. Tornadoes and violent wind-storms, blizzards and hail storms, such as often sweep with such terrible force over certain sections of the country, are unknown in the Saginaw Valley. There are usually no strong winds in winter, especially in the coldest weather. The great lakes, surrounding on every side, have a marked influence in moderating the climate, cooling the extreme heat of summer, and tempering the cold winds of winter. The air is fresh and invigorating, imparting health and energy to the people, in this respect being much superior to more southerly locations.

The extensive coal beds recently discovered, underlying nearly the whole county, will greatly increase the growth of manufactures. This is the nearest coal to the rich Bessemer iron ores of the upper peninsula of Michigan, and it is expected that large iron industries will soon be located in Saginaw. The manufactures of Saginaw include lumber, lath, shingles, salt, boxes, brick, cigars, brooms, dress braids, carriages, cash carriers, crackers, confectionery, dust separators, files, flour, feed, harness, lumber tools, hoops, staves, heading, leather, lime, graphite, furniture, stone, marble, railway gates, woodenware, rules, fertilizers, roofing, saws, soap, potash, wire goods, awnings, baskets, shade rollers, seed cleaners, washboards, pulleys, boiler works, machine shops, railroad shops, etc. There is no better location in the country for planing mills, sash, door and blind factories, and other industries using timber and lumber, as the supply of raw materials is very large. The lumber mills draw great quantities of logs from the Georgian bay region, across Lake Huron. Over 300,000,000 feet of pine saw logs are being rafted from that district to the Saginaw river this year. The hardwood in the territory north and west of Saginaw, suitable for the manufacture of furniture, carriages, etc., is practically as yet untouched. This is most excellent farming land, and the timber taken off in clearing will pay a large portion of the purchase price of the land. The combination of excellent farming land with good markets close at hand makes this country very desirable for the farmer.

SANILAC COUNTY.

Sanilac county was organized in 1848. It is bounded on the north by Huron, on the east by Lake Huron, on the south by St. Clair and Lapeer, and on the west by Tuscola and Lapeer. It has an area of 900 square miles, and had a population in 1890 of 32,589. Sanilac Center, formerly Sandusky, a thriving village of 400 inhabitants, is the county seat.

Along the extreme eastern and western boundaries, and also through the central portions of the county the surface is comparatively level; between these lines are ridges gradually breaking into short hills which form the water-shed of the county. The general appearance might be decided as undulatory. Through the center of the county extends the so-called "great swamp," which is rapidly being drained and cultivated, proving itself among the most fertile and productive land in the State. The county is watered by the Black and Cass rivers, Elk creek and numerous smaller streams, many of the latter flowing into Lake Huron. There are desirable water powers on Black river and some of the creeks. The soil along the lake shore varies from sand to clay, but is nowhere unproductive. On the ridges it is generally clay, with occasional patches of lighter soil. The subsoil is generally clay. The timber is mainly beech, maple, pine, hemlock, birch and oak, with ash and cedar on the low lands. Wheat, barley and oats are the staple crops. Corn and beans are also successfully cultivated. Potatoes and garden vegetables are also raised in abundance throughout the entire county. The reclaimed swamp lands are especially valuable as meadow lands, and the business of cutting and shipping hay has become extensive and profitable. In the older townships fruit raising is already an important industry. Young orchards present a thrifty appearance in the newer townships, and the future of this county as a fruit growing region is well assured.

The cost of clearing land has been greatly reduced by the great fires of 1881, the present cost averaging from $6 to $15 per acre. Good wood markets are found along the line of the Port Huron and Northwestern Railroad. Hardwood brings from $2 to $3 per cord, and softwood from 75 cents to $1. There are 507 acres of land subject to sale or entry. Government lands are no longer in the market.

Plenty of good unimproved agricultural lands are to be had at prices ranging from $5 to $15 per acre. They are near market, have a good soil, and are rapidly increasing in value. There are also large tracts of "stump lands" which have enough timber on them for domestic use, and can be had at correspondingly low prices. Some of the best farms in the county have been made out of these lands. Improved farms range in price from $20 to $50 per acre, according to the location.

The Forestville and Tuscola, Sanilac and Tuscola, Lexington and Lapeer, lake shore north and south road, and Lexington and Minden State roads thoroughly open up the county. The first snow falls in December, the depth varying with the season. Oftentimes there are five or six weeks of good sleighing. Plowing usually begins in April.

School districts are organized in every township: The school buildings are generally comfortabe, and the schools themselves exceptionally good. Agriculture is the principal industry, although considerable lumbering is still done. Large quantities of posts, ties and telegraph poles are gotten out every season, creating a steady demand for labor at wages ranging from $20 to $26 per month with board. The Port Huron & Northwestern Railroad extends through the county in two divisions; the Sand Beach division running from south to north into Huron county, at a distance of from six to twelve miles from the lake shore, and the Saginaw division running in a northwesterly direction from Port Huron, and passing through the southwest portion of the county, touching at Marlette. Lexington, on the Lake shore, twelve miles north of Port Huron, is the largest town in the county. It has a fine flouring mill, a woolen mill, foundry, two planing mills, and a large interior trade. It is visited regularly by several lines of steamers during the season for navigation.

SCHOOLCRAFT.

BY D. W. THOMPSON.

The principal manufacturing industries is in pine, cedar and hardwood lumber, of which the output is approximately valued at $10,000,000 annually, and the value of the plants for the manufacture of the same $1,000,000. Iron output 36,000 tons annually, value of furnaces, etc., $150,000 to $300,000 including charcoal kilns; $250,000 is annually paid for wood for charcoal. Lime kilns ship 30,000 barrels of lime each season. Agricultural interests are comparatively small, although there is perhaps 5,000 acres under cultivation, and enough potatoes and turnips raised for local consumption, and perhaps half the hay that is used is grown here. Oats and wheat but little grown, as there are no flouring mills in this county. The small fruits grow in abundance, and apples, pears and plums do well. The soil is a sandy loam with subsoil of clay in places. Country slightly rolling, drained by the Manistique, Taquamanon and Sturgeon rivers with their numerous branches. The country is dotted with many lakes, in which is found fine fishing, bass, perch, pickeral, etc., and the streams are full of trout and other fish. There is upward of 700,000 acres of unimproved lands, more than half of which is well timbered. Game, such as bear, wolves, deer, partridge and smaller game is plentiful, while on the lakes and streams are to be found many ducks. Streams are only navigable for logs at present.

Improved lands are valued at about $30 per acre, and unimproved lands from fifty cents to $50. There are no cities in the county, and but one incorporated village, Manistique, the county seat, which has a population of 5,000, is at the mouth of the Manistique river, where nearly all the industries of the county are located. A. Booth has a fishery here employing about $300,000 capital, and the vessel interests of the county are about $500,000. There are two railroads besides several private logging railroads. Besides the county seat there are several hamlets with from 300 to a 1,000 inhabitants each, viz.: Cooks, Thompson, South Manistique, Whitedale and Seney. We have good schools and eight or ten churches. Farm labor is $20 per month, common labor $1.50 to $2 per day and skilled labor $2.25 to $8. Cost of clearing timber lands $20 per acre. Kiln wood, four foot, $1.50 per cord, for household use $2.75, but little used; eighteen inch wood, $1.50. No stumping has been done.

SHIAWASSEE COUNTY.

BY A. L. BAIRD, CORUNNA, MICH.

Shiawassee county was organized in 1837. It is bounded on the north by Saginaw, on the east by Genesee, on the south by Livingston and Ingham, and on the west by Clinton county. It has an area of 530 square miles and had a population in 1890 of 30,950. Corunna, a city of 1,500 inhabitants, is the county seat.

The northern half of the county is comparatively level, while the southern half is more rolling. In the southern portion are also a number of sandy plains, commonly called oak openings, and numerous marshes, some of which are quite extensive and which have outlets in the Lookingglass and Shiawassee rivers. The northern part of the county has several thousand acres of tamarack swamp and open marsh, which are drained by the Shiawassee, Maple and Bad rivers. These swamps are nearly all reclaimable and are being ditched quite extensively. The principal water powers are on the Shiawassee river, at Byron, Knagg's Bridge, Shiawasseetown, Corunna and West Haven. The general character of the soil in the southern part of the county is sandy and gravelly, while in the northern portions it is of a clay and clay loam mixed with gravel. The subsoil is generally clay. The timber is oak, beech, maple, basswood and elm. The Detroit, Grand Haven & Milwaukee, the Jackson, Lansing & Saginaw, the Chicago & Grand Trunk, the Toledo, Ann Arbor & North Michigan, and the Cincinnati, Saginaw & Mackinaw railroads traverse the county, affording excellent market facilities.

The county is well supplied with both hard and soft water, making it one of the most beautiful, productive and healthiest counties in the State. The staple crops are wheat, corn, oats, potatoes, beans, and vegetables of all descriptions. As a wheat producing county, it stands in the first rank. Apples are the principal fruit crop, although pears, plums, the smaller fruits and berries are raised in abundance, and are shipped in large quantities to the Detroit, Chicago and Saginaw markets.

Improved farms range in price from $30 to $100 per acre, with a low percentage on the market. Unimproved lands are generally held for the timber and are worth from $20 to $100 per acre.

A large coal mine is in active operation near Corunna, producing about 100 tons of coal daily. The coal tract is estimated to cover hundreds of acres.

The schools of this county are all in first-class condition. The public schools of Corunna and Owosso attract a large non-resident attendance. Agriculture is the principal industry, though large manufacturing establishments have been erected in Owosso during the past few years, including furniture, mattress, carriage, shook, handle and Toledo, Ann Arbor & North Michigan car shops, and burial case factories. On account of its railroad facilities, Durand, Vernon, Corunna and Owosso all furnish excellent inducements to manufacturers. Owosso had a population of 6,564 in 1890.

ST. CLAIR COUNTY.

St. Clair county was organized in 1821. It is bounded on the north by Sanilac, on the east by Lake Huron and St. Clair river, on the south by Macomb and Lake St. Clair, and on the west by Lapeer and Macomb. It has an area of 720 square miles, and had a population in 1890 of 52,105. Port Huron, a city of 13,543 inhabitants, situated at the head of St. Clair river, is the county seat.

The surface of this county is generally level, although there are portions of several townships which are quite rolling. There is considerable swamp land scattered over the county, nearly all of which is reclaimable. There is also considerable sandy land along the lake shore. The county is well watered by the Black, Belle, and Pine rivers, also by Smith and Mill creeks, and numerous smaller streams. Owing to the level character of the land there is but little water power to be found. The general character of the soil is a clay loam with a clay subsoil. The only exceptions are found in the townships of Fort Gratiot, Clyde, Kimball, and Port Huron, where much of the soil is sandy. A clay subsoil underlies the sand, except in some portions of Fort Gratiot township, where the sand is very deep. The timber is maple, beech, oak, elm, and some scattering pine. Hay is the staple crop, although wheat and other cerials are raised successfully. The lighter soil is especially adapted to vegetables, which are raised in great quantities for the Port Huron market. Apples, plums, cherries, and some varieties of grapes are grown in this county with success. Thousands of bushels of apples are shipped every year to Lake Superior ports.

Clearing costs from $5 to $15 per acre, according to the density of the timber. There are no public land for sale or entry in the county. There are plenty of unimproved agricultural lands near the railroads, which can be had at prices ranging from $10 to $25 per acre. There is also considerable stump land, with the very best of soil, to be had at moderate prices. The Port Huron and Detroit, the Romeo and St. Clair, and the Port Huron and Lexington State roads run through the county in different directions. The local roads are constructed on section lines, and as a rule are kept in a fair condition. Snow falls in December and disappears by the last of February. Plowing begins in April, or as soon as the frost is out of the ground.

The schools of the county have improved rapidly during the past few years. The public schools of Port Huron are especially deserving of mention, as they sustain a high reputation, not only at home, but all through the "Thumb" peninsula, and even Canada. Agriculture, lumbering, charcoal burning, the manufacture of staves, etc., and fishing are the principal industries. One of the richest salt beds in the United States has recently been discovered at Marine City. These enterprises create a steady demand for common labor at wages ranging from $15 to $22 per month with board. The Chicago & Grand Trunk, the Detroit branch of the Grand Trunk, the Port Huron & Northwestern, its Lake Shore branch, its Almont division, and a branch of the Canada Southern Railroad traverses the county. The Grand Trunk Railroad has the finest tunnel in the world connecting its lines between east and west at Port Huron. (See description and illustrations.) Port Huron is very favorably situated as to its shipping advantages, and no doubt will become a great manufacturing center. It is already the seat of a flourishing commerce, and its docks and harbors are lined with vessels of every description from the opening to the close of navigation. At Marine City are located ship yards where some of the largest of lake vessels are constructed, while at the city of St. Clair are the celebrated Oakland mineral springs, which are visited annually by thousands of people, and which have the best of hotel and bathing facilities. St. Clair as a county is admirably adapted to grazing, and already attention has been directed to the subject of stock-raising, which will eventually prove one of the most important enterprises of the county.

ST. JOSEPH COUNTY.

BY LEVI T. HULL, CONSTANTINE, MICH.

St. Joseph county lies mainly in the valley of the St. Joseph river, a noble stream, which traverses the county from the northeast corner to its southwest corner. Nine of its sixteen townships border upon it. The other streams in the county, affording sufficient volume of water for water power to drive manufacturing machinery, are, Pigeon river, Fawn river, Hog creek, Big and Little Swan creeks, Nottawa creek, Bear creek, Portage river, Little Portage, the Rocky and Mill creeks. All of these have been improved and the power utilized. The St. Joseph river is dammed at Three Rivers and Constantine, and affords a large amount of cheap power. These streams, through nearly all their length in the county, flow over gravelly beds, between high banks, and at their highest flood do little or no damage by covering adjacent lands. No purer or more sparkling water is to be found in the streams of any section of the United States. There are three large prairies in the county: Nottawa, Sturgis and White Pigeon. The greater proportion of the balance of the county is undulating, gravelly or sandy loam, broken in a few townships by hilly or rolling land of similar quality. The land is all productive. Originally there was a large amount of excellent timber in the county, consisting of burr, white, red and yellow oak, maple, beech, ash, elm, hickory, whitewood, butternut, cherry and blackwalnut, but it has been mostly removed. Wheat, corn, rye, oats, beans, hay, potatoes and essential oils are the chief productions, and large quantities are annually shipped. The farmers who have given attention to raising good horses, cattle, sheep and swine have usually found the industry profitable. The essential oil of peppermint has long been a staple product with many farmers. Of late years spearmint, wormwood and tansey oils have been raised, but not to such an extent as peppermint. Until within a few years, the peppermint was all raised on the uplands, but it is now mostly raised on low lands and reclaimed marshes, the yield being more than double that formerly obtained from high lands.

There are no unoccupied lands in the county. Farm lands are worth from $20 to $100 per acre, according to quality, location and improvements. The public roads are generally good.

The county is traversed by two east and west railroads, and by three north and south railroads. Every township in the county, except two, has a railroad station in it, and those townships have railroad stations within a mile of their line. All parts of the county are convenient to market. Excellent schools are sustained throughout the county. Great interest is taken in educational matters. In all the villages are elegant and commodious school buildings.

There are a number of fine inland lakes, which have become places of pleasant summer resort for the people of the villages.

The county borders on Indiana, is the third county east from Lake Michigan, has an area of 504 square miles, and in 1890 had a population of 25,356. Centreville is the county seat—population, 775.

TUSCOLA COUNTY.

BY JOHN H. BURGESS, VASSAR, MICH.

Tuscola county was organized in the year 1850. It embraces the following townships: 10, 11, 12, 13 and 14 north of range 7, 8, 9, 10 and 11 east, and fractional township 15 north of range 8 east. The county is bounded on the north by Saginaw bay and a portion of Huron county, on the east by Sanilac county, on the south by Genesee and Lapeer counties, on the west by Saginaw and Bay counties. The land in townships in range 7, and towns 13, 14 and fractional 15 north of range 8 east are quite level, though having sufficient decent towards the Saginaw bay to give fine drainage to a large part of it, in fact to a large proportion of the county.

Its principal stream is the Cass river, which runs through the county from the northwest to the southwest dividing the county into nearly equal parts, thus affording good drainage and available water power along its entire course.

The soil is rich and in great variety, with clay loam surface and a stronger clay subsoil, and here and there drifts or patches of sandy loam or sand and gravel. The eastern portion of the county is more rolling with more gravel and less clay. Its timber consists of beech, hard and soft maple, white and black ash, elm, oak, basswood, hickory, hemlock and cedar.

There are five State roads in the county and these, with the local highways, are kept in good condition. The Detroit & Bay City division of the Michigan Central Railroad, with its Caro and East Saginaw branches, the Flint & Pere Marquette and its Watertown extension, the East Saginaw, Tuscola & Huron, the Pontiac, Oxford & Northern railroads traverse the county.

Lands can be had at prices ranging from $5 to $10 for "stump" lands. Good unimproved agricultural lands range in prices from $10 to $20 per acre.

A good supply of pure water is found in all parts of the county. In many localities flowing wells are obtained by drilling, The county is generally healthy.

Tuscola county can boast of soils that produce in abundance all the staple grains and root crops, such as are suitable to this latitude. Fruits, such as apples, pears, plums, cherries, and in some localities in the county, peaches do well. Small fruits yield in abundance and find a ready sale in the markets of the Saginaw valley, Detroit and Port Huron.

There are a number of flourishing villages in the county, among which is Caro, the county seat. It is located near the center of the county. Its push and enterprise are proverbial. It boasts of electric lights and water works. It is also the terminus of the Caro branch of the Michigan Central Railroad. Vassar is the metropolitan village of the county. Its location makes it, so to speak, the gateway of traffic and travel to and from the county. At this point the Michigan Central crosses the Flint & Pere Marquette Railroad, forming a junction for traffic to Detroit, Bay City, Saginaw, Port Huron, also the Caro branch of the Michigan Central Railroad. Vassar justly prides itself on the fact of having pure drinking water from flowing artesian wells, as supplied by its water works. It has modern electric lights, several manufactories, and is the central market of the county. Mayville is a growing village of the county, situated in a splendid agricultural district, it keeps pace with the movement "forward." Millington, Cass City, Unionville, Fair Grove, and a number of other towns and villages, are all steadily pushing to the front.

With splendid transportation facilities, good highways, fine agricultural lands, with a soil that yields bountifully in the grains and root crops, as well as fruits, with good markets, accessible at all seasons of the year, backed up with a good climate, partially free from "cyclones" and heavy paralyzing storms, pure water, thriving village and farming regions, first class schools, and thoroughgoing enterprise among its inhabitants, Tuscola county offers to the seekers after homes, to the manufacturers in search of openings, inducements not to be overlooked. In 1890 the population was 32,508.

WAYNE COUNTY.

BY A. A. BOUTELL.

Wayne county was organized in 1796, nine years before the territory of Michigan was established, and but a few weeks after the surrender of the garrison at Detroit by the British. It was named after Gen. Anthony Wayne, at that time the most popular man in the northwest, owing to his great victory over the savages.

This county was at first large, comprising a considerable part of Ohio, Indiana and Illinois, as well as the whole of the State of Michigan. At present it occupies a very important position near the southeast corner of the state and contains about 666 square miles.

The land formerly somewhat low and swampy, has been nearly all reclaimed, so that some of the best farming land in the state is now in this county, the market gardens in and about Detroit being wonderfully productive. The large and increasing demand for fruit and vegetables at Detroit makes farming very profitable, and dairymen thrive with the good pasturage afforded, and the ready sale of milk and butter.

But the most profitable thing for farmers has been the great increase in the value of their land, especially within a radius of seven or eight miles of the city of Detroit.

While the city of Detroit comprises only twenty-nine square miles within its corporate limits, yet its suburbs extend over many additional square miles of territory.

From Grosse Pointe six miles above the city limits on the north, to Wyandotte eight miles below the city on the south, out Woodward avenue from the center of the city north to the county line, and west ten miles to Dearborn, the land is either already platted or held and sold as acerage for future platting into lots.

The farmers through all this extent of territory have been greatly benefited by the rise in values and many of them are enabled to retire with a competence for their old age from the sale of small farms.

This suburban territory will continue to extend and widen as electric roads and rapid transit make it possible to reach points ten or even twenty miles from the city hall in a few minutes, and the very rapid increase in the population of the city makes homes in the suburbs in great demand.

Wayne county is bounded on the east by Lake St. Clair and the Detroit river. This river flows majestically through a wide and deep channel, its water, pure and limpid, floats on its ample bosom more vessels and a greater tonnage than any other river in the world. The facilities for transportation of products and passengers during the season of navigation are unexcelled and the low freight rates and cheap fares on vessels plying up and down this beautiful river at all hours of the day and night, are appreciated and enjoyed by many.

The railroad facilities are also good. Detroit, the entrepot, as well as metropolis of the state and county, is an important station on three of the most prominent trans-continental lines, the Michigan Central, Grand Trunk and Canadian Pacific, while the Wabash and Lake Shore & Michigan Southern tap the great west and southwest, and the Detroit, Lansing & Northern, the Detroit, Grand Haven & Milwaukee, the Flint & Pere Marquette, and the Detroit & Bay City make direct connection with the various portions of the State.

The climate of Wayne county is healthy and salubrious, and its water supply pure and inexhaustible. The supply for Detroit is obtained from Detroit river, fed by the great lakes above, and is acknowledged to be the best obtained by any large city in the world, while good water is supplied by wells through the farming districts.

The city has a well developed sewage system, and is thoroughly drained. The farming lands are also well drained, with broad, deep ditches, emptying into the Detroit river on the east, into Connor's creek in the northern portion, River Rouge in the central and Huron river in the southern. Farming lands outside the radius affected by the proximity of Detroit, can be purchased for from $40 to $100 per acre, and, on account of the nearness of excellent markets and the continued increase of values as suburban lines of electric cars penetrate farther and farther into the interior of the county, affords opportunity for solid investments. While the soil of Wayne county is particularly adapted to the raising of hay and grazing, yet all kinds of cereals are grown with profit and advantage. It is computed that 10,208 horses are kept in the city of Detroit and the large amount of manure produced is carted out upon the lands in the vicinity, which, with the great number of dairy farms, adds richness to the soil and increases its great productiveness. Farmers in Wayne county are not unlike those in other of the older settled counties, always ready to move on, and land can always be bought to advantage with almost absolute security of profit. Wayne county enjoys unequaled facilities for manufacturing. Its geographical position is unexcelled. Situated midway on the chain of great inland lakes, and with a frontage on the westerly side of the entire length of Detroit river or strait, its manufactured products can be carried cheaply to all parts of this immense territory. The raw material also, iron and copper ore from Michigan's great mines in the upper peninsula, lumber from the vast forests of Michigan and Ontario, are freighted here by immense boats at a very low price, and coal is brought up from Ohio and Pennsylvania as return cargoes, at a nominal rate. The great railroad systems furnish rapid and economical transportation for manufactured goods to all parts of the United States and Canada. The manufacturing interests of Detroit alone are very large and constantly growing. We have here the largest seed house in the world, the largest stove foundries in the world, the greatest freight and passenger car factories in the world, the largest manufacturing chemists in the world, while its tobacco factories, electrical supplies, etc., etc. compete with the world in extent of product and excellence.

The secretary of the Detroit Real Estate Board, from a personal canvass, which is reliable, states: "The seven hundred manufacturing institutions canvassed employ in the aggregate 32,750 males and 8,000 female operatives, or a total of 40,750. To this army of employés is paid each month $1,541,700, or the enormous sum of $18,500,000 annually. The product in 1891 amounted to $36,500,000 and the invested capital to $52,500,000."

Outside of Detroit manufacturing is also extensively carried on in this county. This is particularly true of Delray, the River Rouge district, and Wyandotte on the south. Added two very favorable locations on both rail and water routes, cheap taxation, cheap water and fuel, there are many inducements offered by owners of vacant lands. The thriving villages of Plymouth, Northville, Wayne, Dearborn, Norris and Romulus, in the interior of the county, are competing for manufacturing plants and many are already established, producing finished work of great excellence. Any account of Wayne county would be incomplete without some reference to the beautiful islands in the Detroit river, which are comprised within its limits. The largest of these are Grosse Isle in the south and Belle Isle in the north.

Grosse Isle is beautifully situated on the American side of the main channel of the Detroit river, and is about seven and one-half miles in extreme length, with an average breadth of one and one-half miles, and contains about ten square miles or 6,400 acres. The river below the island is some four miles wide, opening out into Lake Erie six miles away. The cooling breezes of lake and river, together with its arable soil and the vernal shade of the native trees, make this an ideal spot for summer homes. Many of the substantial men of Detroit spend their summers here.

Belle Isle, just above Detroit and extending northward to Lake St. Clair, is a little over two miles long and contains 673.98 acres. The entire island, with the exception of about six acres in the northeast corner, which belongs to the United States and is set apart for the light house which guards the entrance to the main channel of the Detroit river, is owned by the city of Detroit, making one of the most beautiful parks in the world. The island is flat and but little above the surface of the river. Most of it is shaded by native trees, and the plan of ornamentation adopted by the park board, with the advice and assistance of one of our most eminent landscape engineers, has been to utilize these trees to the utmost extent, quite large portions of the island being left in its natural state, with carriage roads, canals and foot paths cut

36

through The low lying grounds and marshes have been reclaimed by cutting out inland lakes connected by canals to the river, above, below and on either side. Splendid roads have been built, and suitable buildings, while acres of flowers are kept blooming every year The island is connected with the main land by an iron bridge about five-eights of a mile long, and numerous palatial boats make frequent trips from various points of the city during the warm weather As many as 50,000 people have visited this island park in a single day.

DETROIT.

The above meagre sketch of Wayne county has only mentioned the city of Detroit incidentally, but any compilation of Michigan and Its Resources should have some particular account of its metropolis. Those who may contemplate a change from homes in foreign climes, or from the more thickly populated states in the east, will do well to investigate the inducements offered by Michigan for their future home. And if they enter this great State in furtherance of their quest, they will quite naturally do so through the portal at Detroit. If first impressions of a new country are worth anything, then their first sight of Detroit from its noble river, their rides through broad streets to palatial hotels, the appearance of its mammoth stores whose windows show samples of the wealth of goods within, must make this impression favorable. A few days spent in a careful survey of the city will increase these impressions. First take a ride from the center of the city over the splendidly equipped electric roads which traverse broad avenues fringed with the elegant homes of its solid citizens, embowered in umbrageous trees and with well kept lawns, to the termini in either direction. Then walk or ride through street after street of comfortable homes of merchants, artisans and mechanics. Even laborers here own their own little homes, which, as a rule, are trimly kept, while fruit, vines, and flowers abound Detroit has been well called the "city of homes," and very few cities in this or any other land, according to their population, have so many houses occupied by their owners. You can take a seat in a comfortable electric car, and for ten cents ride in a northerly direction, near the river banks, to the picturesquely beautiful village of Grosse Pointe Farms, upon the placid shores of Lake St. Clair. Here magnificent summer cottages on wide extended lawns, shelter, during the summer months, Detroit's most substantial citizens.

Boat houses dot the lake front and palatial steam yachts make daily trips to the city. For the same sum, ten cents, you can be whirled by electricity along the river banks to Wyandotte, twenty miles to the south. Or take the Woodward avenue line and ride out to Highland Park and Senator Palmer's famous Log Cabin farm, to the north.

For ten cents you can make the round trip from the city to Belle Isle Park above, to Des-chree-shos-ka below, or ride for half a day on boats fitted with every convenience for safety and comfort. During the warm days of summer tired men and women and countless children are revived, benefited and made strong and healthy by these cheap water excursions. For fifty cents you can take the round trip by boat up the river, across Lake St. Clair to the Flats, the American Venice, and there at hotel or private club, partake of an elegant fish supper for fifty cents more, and ride home again by moonlight. For one dollar this trip can be extended to Port Huron at the foot of Lake Huron, sixty miles away.

Boats also ply daily down the river to way ports, to Toledo, Sandusky and the famous islands of Put-in-Bay. Every night large and beautiful boats leave for Cleveland, and four times each week up the river to Mackinaw Island and the summer resorts to the north.

In the city itself, if inclined to read, you can visit our large and commodious public library building with its 108,720 volumes of excellently selected works, treating on all subjects.

Detroit is also gaining a reputation as a convention city. And those who visit the city on these occasions never fail to carry away pleasant recollections of their cordial welcome and handsome treatment, and of the countless attractions of the beautiful city of the straits. Those who live in the malarial districts of the south, after once tasting the delights of a summer at Detroit, always come again and bring their friends.

Detroit is an old city, having been first visited by the French in 1610, two years after the founding of Quebec. The first fort was built here in 1701. It has always had the reputation of being a solid but conservative city, and has never been affected by booms or very seriously by depressions. While progress has been slow yet is has always been sure, with no steps backward. Its favorable location has made for it a large and substantial city in spite of its conservatism, and now its progress is marked by the enterprise of its younger men. New buildings and new enterprises are rapidly succeeding each other, and a few years more will transform its business streets with new and modern buildings. Among the new buildings now under way are the new postoffice, occupying an entire square upon Fort street and Lafayette avenue, the Masonic Temple, the Home Savings building, the Union Trust building, and the Chamber of Commerce building. The two latter are to be modern in every respect, twelve or thirteen stories high, made of structural steel, fire proof and with every known convenience for their hundreds of tenents.

The city government is well administered, with a most energetic mayor at its head, and commercial matters are looked after by several important exchanges. The Board of Trade was organized in 1856. It is a strong organization, capable of handling the immense cereal products of the State, which here find their natural market.

The Merchants and Manufacturers' Exchange was founded in 1878 and has done efficient work ever since. Its information and collection departments are of very great assistance to its members. The Detroit Real Estate Board was more recently organized. Its members are mostly young men and a great impetus has been given to real estate matters since it was organized. Equitable arrangements are made among themselves for dividing commissions on listed property and anything savoring of sharp practices are severely frowned upon. The Detroit Builders' Exchange was also recently formed and has done good work in regulating building operations. The Detroit Clearing House has supervision of the clearances of the seventeen State and eight national banks in Detroit, whose combined capital amounts to $8,300,000 with a surplus and undivided profits of $2,927,414, and total deposits of $58,387,225.

The Detroit Chamber of Commerce was organized in 1891 and has a membership of nearly seven hundred of the city's best and most progressive business and professional men. It includes in its membership the larger number of those in the other exchanges and its new building, a cut of which is given elsewhere, is expected to become the home of the other exchanges, so that all can unite in developing the interests of the city.

Its object, as set forth in its by-laws, reads: "It shall have for its object the advancement of the public interests of the city of Detroit, the development of all legitimate enterprises tending to increase its prosperity, the uniting of the energies and influence of its citizens upon all subjects affecting the welfare of the city, the improvement of facilities for transportation, the diffusion of information concerning the manufactures, trade and business of the city and the State, the cultivation of friendly relations and the promotion of equitable principles among the business men of Detroit and vicinity."

To sum up, Detroit and Wayne county afford many opportunities for the investment of money and enterprise. Farmers, merchants mechanics, manufacturers and capitalists can here find comfortable homes and unexcelled chances for the profitable investment of money. Any inquiries directed to the secretary of The Detroit Chamber of Commerce will have prompt attention.

WEXFORD COUNTY.

Wexford county was organized in the year 1869. The population at present is estimated at 13,000. The surface of the county is diversified, varying from gently rolling to hilly ranges entending east and west through the center of the county. This range is the divide between the Manistee river on the north and the basin of the Clam lakes and Clam river on the south. It is decidedly an agricultural county, the soil is very productive when properly cultivated. The prevailing soil is a sandy loam, although a rich clay soil is found in many places. All of the cereal products are grown successfully. Potatoes are one of the principal crops and attain to a great degree of perfection, command good prices, and are largely shipped to the southern markets and to the east and west. Six hundred thousand bushels of potatoes were shipped from this county last season by one Cadillac dealer. Wexford county is also gaining a reputation as a fruit growing county. Apples, pears and plums are grown to perfection. Peaches are grown in favorable localities, while berries and small fruits are grown in abundance. Wexford county was awarded first premium on fruit exhibits at the West Michigan Fair in 1892.

The hardwood timber is a great source of wealth to the county and affords rare opportunity for the investment of capital in its manufacture. The quality of its hardwood is excelled nowhere and its quantity is immense. There is a good system of schools, and good school houses sufficient for all requirements. There is also a good system of roads.

Not the least attractive are the numerous streams of pure spring water which abound in speckled trout. The climate is one of the most healthful in the world. The spring season and plowing commence from the 10th to the 15th of April.

Two lines of railroad extend through the county, the Grand Rapids & Indiana, running north and south, T., A. A. & N. M. Railroad running northwest by southeast, afford excellent shipping facilities for the large amount of timber, cedar posts, and telegraph poles produced in the county, and also for shipping farm products which are produced largely in excess of home demand. Thriving towns are building on these lines.

The city of Cadillac, located on the east shore of Little Clam lake, at the crossing of the T., A. A. & N. M. and G. R. & I. railroads, was founded in 1870 and has now a population of 6,000. Little Clam lake is a beautiful sheet of pure water three miles long by one wide, is well stocked with pike, pickerel and perch, and affords excellent fishing. Its waters are traversed by pleasure steamers and it is destined to become a famous pleasure resort. For a new city in a new country Cadillac is excelled nowhere and the energy and enterprise of the people is unbounded. Manton, the second town in the county, on the line of the G. R. & I. railroad, is a village of about 800 inhabitants. It is a flourishing town and a lively shipping point for the products of the county. Boon, Harriette and Sherman are thriving villages on the line of the T. A. A. & N. M. R. R. Great inducements are offered to settlers. There is an increasing demand for hardwood timber of which Wexford county has an abundant supply of the best quality, the proceeds of which will defray all expenses of clearing the wild lands ready for the plow. No county offers greater inducements to the energetic man with small means to make a home. On January 1, 1893, there were 17,700 acres of government and State land subject to sale or entry in the county, but the amount is constantly being reduced.

THE PENINSULAR STATE.

SUMMARY.

Population 1890, 2,003,889. Increase over 1880, twenty-eight per cent.

Tax value in 1892 _____ $1,130,000,000
Square miles, as per United States survey_____ 58,915
Acres in farms as per Farm Statistics of 1893 _____ 12,720,619
Acres improved in farms _____ 8,328,189
Acres unimproved in farm_____ 4,392,430
Total acres not in farms_____ 24,254,741

MICHIGAN STANDS

First in Lumber Products.—$68,141,189 by 1890 census; one-fifth total domestic product; increase over 1880, $15,691,261.

First in Iron Ore.—$15,800,524 by 1890 census; more than one-third total product, and one-half its value. Product for 1892, 7,267,874 tons; increase over 1890 census of 1,411,609 tons.

Second in Copper.—In 1891, 54,685 tons. The United States produces one-half the world's copper, and Michigan one-third that of the United States.

First in Charcoal Iron.—$3,982,278, by 1890 census, of $11,985,103 total domestic product.

First in Salt.—Nearly one-half in amount and value; $2,302,579 in 1890; 3,927,671 barrels in 1890; 3,812,054 barrels in 1892.

First in Gypsum.—Almost half the total domestic product—131,767 tons in 1890; New York next with 52,208 tons.

First in Yield of Wheat per Acre.—18½ bushels in 1891, and in the front rank of wheat states; 27,900,148 bushels in 1891.

First in Value of Farm Crops Generally, per Acre.—Leading Ohio, Indiana, Illinois and all the great northwest. For ten years, ending 1890, Michigan led all these states, not only in yield per acre of wheat, but also in the value product per acre of wheat, corn, oats, barley, buckwheat and hay crops.

First in Hardwood Forests.—Quality, quantity and nearness to consuming centers, and in hardwood manufactures.

First in Furniture.—One hundred and seventy-eight factories in sixty cities, capital $9,855,000. Grand Rapids, forty-five factories, $5,000,000 capital and 5,000 hands. Detroit, twenty factories, capital $750,000.

First in Fruit.—Apples, peaches, plums, pears, etc.

First in Peppermint Oil.—More than all the rest of the State combined. Product for 1892, 88,000 pounds, value $176,000 at still. In 1890–1 the United States exported 45,321 pounds of oil, valued at $2.66 per pound; while Japan (only other surplus producer) exported same year 39,149 pounds, valued at eighty-five cents per pound.

Third in Value of Sheep and Wood.—Only Ohio and California leading her. Michigan, $8,552,679; California, $9,559,475; Ohio, $13,900,263. Michigan 1891 wool clip, 11,732,395 pounds—average per fleece, six and one-third pounds. Total domestic product, by 1890 census, 258,757,101 pounds.

First in Extent of Coast Line.—Lakes Superior, Michigan, Huron, St. Clair, Erie, over 2,000 miles coast.

First in Lake Commerce, and Second in Vessel Tonnage of all kinds.—Center of commerce of great lakes. Tonnage on these lakes in 1891, 1,063,063; vessels, 2,015; value, $75,590,950. Total ton mileage on lakes in 1890 was 25 per cent of total United States railway ton mileage. Freight tonnage passing Sault canal in 1890, 8,454,434, 1,064,341 more than Suez Canal; through Detroit river, 21,684,000 tons, about same as London and Liverpool combined, or our entire Atlantic coast foreign trade tonnage. Steamers, 1,237; sail, 927; unrigged, 771; steel 89; iron, 39; wood, 2,817. "About one-quarter the tonnage of our entire merchant marine is on the northern lakes, and the large steam tonnage on the great lakes (1.000 tons and upward) exceeds the total similar tonnage of all the rest of the country by 131,093 tons."—*U. S. Statistician Dodge.* Michigan leads in this commerce, and her vessel tonnage is surpassed only by New York, the great ocean carrier. Vessel tonnage for year ending June 30, 1892: Michigan, 390,920; Massachusetts, 389,942; Pennsylvania, 353,057; Maine, 352,574; California, 316,872; Ohio, 315,849; Maryland, 143,536; New York, 1,339,937; total for United States, 4,764,961. Since 1886 Michigan's tonnage has increased 164,529, and New York's 121,824 tons.—*Statistics U. S. Bureau of Navigation.*

First in Ship Building.—Total tonnage built in 1890: northern lakes, 108,526; whole sea-board, 160,091; western rivers, 16,506; grand total, 294,123. Of this 108,526 lake tonnage, Michigan yards at Bay City, Detroit and Grand Haven built 45,733 tons, 65 vessels, including two 4,000 tons steel steamers for the ocean trade. "The steam tonnage built on great lakes in 1890 was 40 per cent greater than that of the entire sea-board; lakes, 86,023 tons; entire sea-board, 61,137 tons."—*Statistician Dodge.*

First in Inland Commercial Fisheries.—Catch in 1892 valued at $1,058,028 in first hands. Michigan fish-freezing industry alone employed 4,000 hands.

First in its State University.—Science, literature, law, medicine, with its 2,800 students. And not second in its common, high, normal, and mining schools and Agricultural College.

First in Summer Resorts.—Brook trout, grayling, black bass and other stream and lake fishing.

State Benevolent Institutions.—School for Blind, Lansing; Deaf Mutes, Flint; State Public School, Coldwater; Soldiers' Home, Grand Rapids; Industrial Home for Girls, Adrian; Industrial School for Boys, Lansing; Asylums for Insane, Kalamazoo, Pontiac and Traverse City; Asylum for Dangerous and Criminal Insane, Ionia; Home for Feeble Minded, (not located).

Railway Mileage—Seven thousand three hundred and five increase of 3,482 miles over 1880, or 91 per cent; in 1870, 1739; in 1860 only 770 miles.

Street Railways.—Three hundred and twenty-six miles in twenty-five cities; 216 electric, 90 horse, 20 steam.